Lecture Notes in Computer Science   7633

Commenced Publication in 1973
Founding and Former Series Editors:
Gerhard Goos, Juris Hartmanis, and Jan van Leeuwen

Shi-Min Hu   Ralph R. Martin (Eds.)

Computational Visual Media

First International Conference, CVM 2012
Beijing, China, November 8-10, 2012
Proceedings

 Springer

Volume Editors

Shi-Min Hu
Tsinghua University, Department of Computer Science and Technology
Tsinghua Yuan, Beijing 100084, China
E-mail: shimin@tsinghua.edu.cn

Ralph R. Martin
Cardiff University, School of Computer Science and Informatics
5 The Parade, Roath, Cardiff CF24 3AA, UK
E-mail: ralph@cs.cf.ac.uk

ISSN 0302-9743   e-ISSN 1611-3349
ISBN 978-3-642-34262-2   e-ISBN 978-3-642-34263-9
DOI 10.1007/978-3-642-34263-9
Springer Heidelberg Dordrecht London New York

Library of Congress Control Number: 2012949182

CR Subject Classification (1998): I.4, I.5, I.2, H.3, I.2.10, H.4

LNCS Sublibrary: SL 6 – Image Processing, Computer Vision, Pattern Recognition,
and Graphics

Typesetting: Camera-ready by author, data conversion by Scientific Publishing Services, Chennai, India

Printed on acid-free paper

Springer is part of Springer Science+Business Media (www.springer.com)

Preface

With the rapid development of multiple technologies, from the Internet to mobile phones and cameras, visual data are now widely available in huge amounts, and great variety, bringing significant opportunities for novel processing of visual information as well as for commercial applications.

The Computational Visual Media Conference 2012 (CVM 2012) was the first in a new conference series, providing a major international forum for exchanging novel research ideas and significant practical results both underpinning and applying visual media. The primary rationale for this new conference series is to bring together cross-disciplinary research which amalgamates aspects of computer graphics, computer vision, machine learning, image processing, video processing, visualization, and geometric computing. Original research topics in this area consider, inter alia, the classification, composition, retrieval, synthesis, and understanding of visual media.

Although CVM 2012 was a new conference, it attracted broad attention from researchers worldwide. A total of 81 submissions were made, of which 33 full papers were accepted. The conference took place during November 8–10, 2012, in Tsinghua University, Beijing, China, and was co-sponsored by ACM SIGGRAPH, the China Computer Federation and Tsinghua University.

We are grateful to all the authors, Program Committee members, and paper reviewers for their contributions, as well as to those individuals who helped to organize the conference.

Special thanks are given to the 973 Program of China (2011CB302200) and the National Natural Science Foundation of China (61120106007) for their support.

Shi-Min Hu
Ralph R. Martin

Organization

Honorary Conference Chair

Jia-Guang Sun   NSFC and Tsinghua University, China

Conference Chairs

Nadia Thalmann   University of Geneva, Switzerland
Hongbin Zha   Peking University, China

Program Co-chairs

Shi-Min Hu   Tsinghua University, China
Ralph Martin   Cardiff University, UK

Local Organizing Chair

Kun Xu   Tsinghua University, China

Program Committee

Marc Alexa	Technische Universität Berlin, Germany
Hujun Bao	Zhejiang Uinversity, China
Bruno Lévy	LORIA/INRIA Lorraine, France
Jinxiang Chai	Texas A&M University, USA
Baoquan Chen	Shenzhen Institute of Advanced Technology, China
Robin Bing-Yu Chen	Taiwan University
Daniel Cohen-Or	Tel Aviv University, Israel
Thomas Ertl	University of Stuttgart, Germany
Sebti Foufou	University of Burgundy, France
Hongbo Fu	City University of Hong Kong
Xianfeng Gu	Stony Brook University, USA
Xiaohu Guo	University of Texas at Dallas, USA
Peter Hall	University of Bath, UK
Jiwu Huang	Sun Yat-sen University, China
Tao Ju	Washington University at St. Louis, USA
Leif Kobbelt	RWTH Aachen University, Germany
Myung-Soo Kim	Seoul National University, South Korea

Young Kim	Ewha Womans University, South Korea
Yu-kun Lai	Cardiff University, UK
Seungyong Lee	Pohang University of Science and Technology, South Korea
Dani Lischinski	The Hebrew University Jerusalem, Israel
Yuncai Liu	Shanghai Jiaotong University, China
Dinesh Manocha	University of N. Carolina, USA
Nelson Max	UC Davis, USA
Makoto Okabe	The University of Electro-Communications, Japan
Valerio Pascucci	University of Utah, USA
Holly Rushmeier	Yale University, USA
Hans Peter Seidel	Max Planck Institute for Computer Science, Germany
Ariel Shamir	Interdisciplinary Center of Israel
Hiromasa Suzuki	Tokyo University, Japan
Zhuowen Tu	University of California, Los Angeles, USA
Wang Rui	University of Massachusetts, USA
Wenping Wang	The University of Hong Kong
Tien-Tsin Wong	Chinese University of Hong Kong
Yizhou Yu	The University of Hong Kong; University of Illinois at Urbana-Champaign, USA
Jianmin Zheng	Nanyang Technological University, Singapore
Kun Zhou	Zhejiang Unversity, China

Table of Contents

Section 1: Image Processing I

Section 2: Image Processing II

Section 3: Geometry Processing

Section 4: Saliency

Section 5: Recognition, Perception and Learning

Section 6: Shape Analysis

Section 7: Media Retrieval

Section 8: Capture, Rendering and Visualization

Identifying Shifted Double JPEG Compression Artifacts for Non-intrusive Digital Image Forensics

Zhenhua Qu[1,3], Weiqi Luo[2,*], and Jiwu Huang[1]

[1] School of Information Science and Technology, Sun Yat-Sen University, Guangzhou, China
[2] School of Software, Sun Yat-Sen University, Guangzhou, China
[3] Guangdong Research Institute of China Telecom, Guangzhou, China
qzhua3@gmail.com, weiqi.luo@yahoo.com, isshjw@mail.sysu.edu.cn

Abstract. Non-intrusive digital image forensics (NIDIF) aims at authenticating the validity of digital images utilizing their intrinsic characteristics when the active forensic methods, such as digital watermarking or digital signatures, fail or are not present. The NIDIF for lossy JPEG compressed images are of special importance due to its pervasively use in many applications. Recently, researchers showed that certain types of tampering manipulations can be revealed when JPEG re-compress artifacts (JRCA) is found in a suspicious JPEG image. Up to now, most existing works mainly focus on the detection of doubly JPEG compressed images without block shifting. However, they cannot identify another JRCA – the shifted double JPEG (SD-JPEG) compression artifacts which are commonly present in composite JPEG images. In this paper, the SD-JPEG artifacts are modeled as a noisy 2-D convolutive mixing model. A symmetry verification based method and a first digit histogram based remedy method are proposed to form an integral identification framework. It can reliably detect the SD-JPEG artifacts when a critical state is not reached. The experimental results have shown the effectiveness of the proposed framework.

1 Introduction

Digital images have been pervasively used as evidences in many applications. Their credibility has become increasingly important yet also challenging to establish for the abusive use of modern digital image editing software, such as Photoshop and GIMP. Digital signature and digital watermarking are the typically used techniques to ensure the image content trustworthy. These methods need additional processing at the time of data creation, such as signature generation and watermarking embedding, for facilitating tampering detection at a later time. In many forensic cases, however, the provider himself is the fraudster. Image inspectors cannot depend on these active methods since the side information for detection is not available, for instance, most images on the Web. The demands from practical use, therefore, have urged the researchers to reconsider the image authentication problem from a different perspective.

Recently, many non-intrusive digital image forensics (NIDIF) methods have been proposed by researchers. In NIDIF, the image provider is untrusted and the authentication is performed on the inspector side solely based on the image data. By analyzing the

---

* Corresponding author.

S.-M. Hu and R.R. Martin (Eds.): CVM 2012, LNCS 7633, pp. 1–8, 2012.

disturbance or violation of some intrinsic characteristics of original images, the NIDIF can detect tampered or fake digital image content in many forms. Many characteristics have been used for the purpose of image forensics, for example, lighting consistency [7], color filter array (CFA) interpolation [1], fixed pattern noise(FPN) [4], and camera response function (CRF) [11]. However, due to the intricate mathematical nature of these problems, each method works under some preconditions and there is currently no universal solution for all tampering conditions.

JPEG re-compression artifacts (JRCA), one kind of such characteristics can be utilized to detect tampering in JPEG images. When tapering a JPEG image, we have to decode it into spatial domain, and then modify some regions within the image, and finally re-compress it as a JPEG file. So once JRCAs were found in a JPEG image, the image is highly suspected to be modified and is untrustworthy. Currently, researches have focused on addressing the so-called *Double JPEG Compression Problem*, which entails identifying images that suffered from lossy JPEG compression twice without block shifting. Lukáš et al. [9] use neural network to estimate the primitive quantization table coefficients. Popescu et al. [12] utilized the periodical artifacts of the re-quantized blockwise discrete cosine transform (BDCT) coefficient histograms. Fu et al. [5] contributed a generalized Benford's Law model of the BDCT coefficients. He et al. [6] use the artifact to identify JPEG image splicing. However, when the fraudster simply shift or crop the JPEG image with several rows or columns before recompression, all the mentioned methods would fail. In this paper, therefore, we will focus on the detection of JPEG recompressed images with block shifting.

This work is originated from our previous studies [10,13]. In this paper, we analyze the SD-JPEG problem, and then proposed an identification framework. We found that the SD-JPEG problem can be modeled as a noisy 2-D convolutive mixing model (CMM) and the solution has a blind source separation (BSS) essence. However, it cannot be well handled with conventional BSS methods, such as independent component analysis (ICA), since the noisy here is often too strong. By utilizing a cyclosymmetry property of the independent value maps (IVM) of ordinary JPEG (Ord-JPEG, i.e. compressed only once) images , we managed to overcome this problem. But it also results a few undetectable conditions (UDC). They need to be further treated with a remedy scheme. With the shifted distance(s-dist), obtained as a by-product of this identification framework, one can also reveal some image manipulation histories, such as cropping, copy-paste or both, of a suspicious JPEG. The effectiveness of this method is evidenced with extensive experimental results.

2   Modeling the SD-JPEG Compression

Illustrated in Fig. 1, the SD-JPEG compression process generates an SD-JPEG image in three steps: 1) Decompress an Ord-JPEG into the spatial domain; 2) Crop/shift the resulting image with Δx columns and or Δy rows; 3) Re-compress it into a JPEG file.

It can be formulated as a 2-D CMM as follows:

$$\widehat{\mathbf{S}}_{m,n} = \sum_{i=0}^{1} \sum_{j=0}^{1} \mathbf{A}_{\Delta y,i} \mathbf{S}_{m-i,n-j} \mathbf{A}_{\Delta x,j}^{T} + \widehat{\mathbf{E}}_{m,n} \tag{1}$$

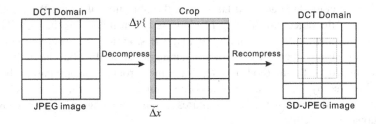

Fig. 1. Gernerating an SD-JPEG image with s-dist=$(\Delta x, \Delta y)$

where $\mathbf{S}_{m,n}$ and $\widehat{\mathbf{S}}_{m,n}$ are the input and output $M \times M$ BDCT coefficient blocks respectively. $\widehat{\mathbf{E}}_{m,n}$ is the quantization noise of the secondary JPEG compression.

$$\{\mathbf{A}_{\Delta x,0}, \mathbf{A}_{\Delta x,1}, \mathbf{A}_{\Delta y,0}, \mathbf{A}_{\Delta y,1}\}$$

are called a set of mixing matrices determined by the s-dist $(\Delta x, \Delta y)$ and the BDCT transform matrix. In practice, the multiplications of these matrices are done implicitly by the JPEG compression. Equation (1) indicates that an output block $\widehat{\mathbf{S}}_{m,n}$ is a linear mixture of four input blocks $\{\mathbf{S}_{m,n}, \mathbf{S}_{m,n+1}, \mathbf{S}_{m+1,n}, \mathbf{S}_{m+1,n+1}\}$ overlapped by it. Then the identification of SD-JPEG image can be defined as

Definition 1 (SD-JPEG). *A JPEG image is identified as SD-JPEG if and only if its s-dist is not* $(0,0)$

As to identify SD-JPEG, one needs to reveal the s-dist or more specifically de-mix the mixture by estimating its mixing matrices. This is the essence of BSS.

3 A Framework for Identifying SD-JPEG Images

The proposed identification framework includes two complementary methods. Firstly, a questionable JPEG image is examined with an ICA-based identification method. If the image is identified as SD-JPEG, the identification process is over and one can further estimate the s-dist to identify the type of image editing. Otherwise, the image is treated with a first digit histogram based method to check out if the s-dist is in one of the three non-trivial UDCs.

3.1 ICA-Based Identification Method

In our previous work [13], we proposed an ICA-based identification method which is able to detect SD-JPEG in most conditions. It works by firstly generating an IVM from the BDCT coefficients of the image, and then calculating a RAVM (relative asymmetric value map) from the IVM's cyclosymmetricity , and finally 13 discriminative features are extracted from the RAVM to train an SVM classifier to automate the identification process. For details of this method please refer to [13].

The above method [13] adopted kurtosis as the objection function. We found that the selection of the objection function is a key issue that influences the identification accuracy of our method. As the fourth order statistics, kurtosis is sensitive to out lies, and thus is not a robust measure of the non-Gaussianity of the distribution. In this work, we further improved the method by adopting a more robust entropy-based objective function. Inspired by the famous InfoMax algorithm [2], we use the entropy objective function here as to more distinctively captures the sparse histogram. The entropy of a BDCT subband s is defined as:

$$J(\mathbf{s}) = \sum_i h(i) \log h(i) \tag{2}$$

where $h(i)$ is the i-th bin of the hitogram of BDCT coefficients. Here the discrete entropy is used to approximately calculate the continuous entropy.

We calculate the IVM with this new objective function, and keep the other steps the same as before. With some intrinsic characteristics of natural images, we can prove that the cyclosymmetry property of IVM will hold as well. Due to page limitation, the detailed derivations will not be presented in this paper. This new implementation can significantly improve the performance of the ICA-based method, and the experimental results are given in section 4.

For the same reason, the formulas used for estimating the s-dist would usually work better than the method [13]. By comparing the s-dist estimated from the image regions that correspond to a foreground object under suspicion and its background respectively, we can identify at least three major types of image manipulation methods. For example, if the foreground and the background have the same s-dist other than $(0, 0)$, the image can be generally judged as a "cropping" manipulation, otherwise, when the two s-dists are inconsistent, a "splicing" manipulation is detected. In particular, the condition in which either of the two inconsistent s-dists is not $(0, 0)$ cannot be well handled by most of existing methods.

3.2   Handling the Undetectable Conditions

There are a totally four UDCs as indicated by their s-dist, that is $(0, 0), (0, 4), (4, 0)$ and $(4, 4)$. Because if an Ord-JPEG image is re-compressed with one of these special s-dists, the cyclosymmetry of the IVM will not be violated. It will be identified as Ord-JPEG in the symmetry verification scheme and need special treatments here. The UDCs can be classified into two types. Firstly, when the s-dist is $(0, 0)$, this refers to double JPEG mentioned in Section 1. It can be identified by several existing methods [5,12]. Thus, it is a trivial UDC and will not be discussed here. The other three conditions are non-trivial cases. Each of them occurs with a probability of $1/64 = 1.56\%$ if the shifting was performed randomly. However, they demand more effects than the detectable s-dists. Here we proposed a learning-based approach to detect SD-JPEG in the non-trivial undetectable conditions. By training a classifier with the histograms of Ord-JPEG and SD-JPEG images, we can use the classifier for judgment. However, doing this will result a very high dimension feature set by concatenating the all 63 AC BDCT coefficient histograms each with approximately 200 bins which is also computationally intractable with many modern classifiers.

To bring down the feature dimension while maintaining its discriminative power, we adopt a learning-based approach with the FDH [8] derived from the famous *First Digit Law* or "Benford's Law" [5]. It simply counts the coefficients with their first digits to form a histogram with only nine bins. It has been shown that for a wide variety of "ordinary" distributions, e.g., the exponential family, the resulting FDH can be fitted with a generalized function [5]. On the contrary, an "abnormal" distribution with multiple plumbs resulting by SD-JPEG, will cause irregular rises and falls in the FDH.

For a given JPEG image, we try every UDC s-dist to de-mix it. With each of the de-mixed AC components, we obtain one FDH. And then these 63 FDHs are concatenated as one feature vector that is fed to a classifier. Non-linear regression based statistical classifiers, such as the RBF kernel SVM [3] used here, can implicitly fitted these histograms to a generalized function. In addition, a binary judgment can be given by adaptively weighting these fitting errors. The benefit of this method is that one does not need to have any explicit knowledge of the distribution of the SD-JPEG BDCT coefficients.

4   Experimental Results

In our experiments, the test image database [10] includes 1000 uncompressed TIFF images taken by a Panasonic DMZ-FZ30 digital camera with indoor and outdoor scenes. The performance in detectable and undetectable conditions is evaluated separately with the two methods mentioned in Section 3.1 and Section 3.2. The image sizes are ranging from 640×480 to 600×1200, and $QF_1, QF_2 \in [60, 65, ..., 95]$. A pair of Ord-JPEG and SD-JPEG is generated from each image with strict consistency in their image contents. In the experiments, the primary quality factor QF_1 and and s-dist are chosen with uniform distributions. The SVM classifier is trained with half of them and tested with the other half. This process is repeated 5 times to obtain the average results.

Figure 2(a) shows the performance of detectable conditions with the symmetry verification scheme. Figure 2 (b–d) shows the classification accuracy for three UDCs. It is observed that for those images with a fixed size, the identification performance of SD-JPEG is mainly depended on the three parameters: the s-dist $(\Delta x, \Delta y)$, the primary quality factor QF_1, and the secondary quality factor QF_2. And the detection accuracy will become better with increasing image sizes.

A fraudster will always prefer to "wipe out" the artifacts caused by the primary compression so as not to raise any suspicion. Intuitively, there should be a critical state for QF_2. For example, if the secondary compression is weaker than the primary one, say $QF_2 > QF_1$, more traces will be preserved and it will be fully detectable. In contrast, because the secondary compression is stronger than the former one, it might have completely removed the traces of the first compression and make the re-compressed image unidentifiable in any sense. Therefore, when a QF_1 is specified, we are greatly concerned about whether there exist some QF_2, in which the re-compressed image will be identified as an Ord-JPEG image.

Figure 3 shows how the classification performance would vary with different combination of QF_1 and QF_2 both for detectable and undetectable condition. It is evident that there is a "cliff" where the performances begin to deteriorate quickly. This figure also shows, however, that the critical state is *NOT* at $QF_1 = QF_2$. For example, in Fig. 3(a),

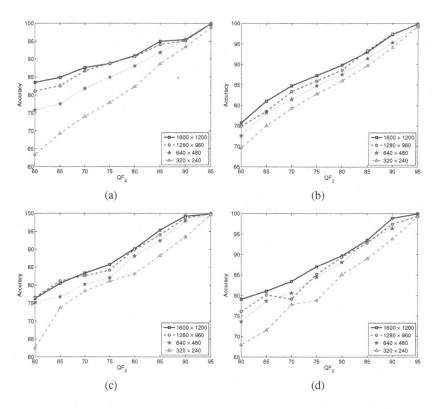

Fig. 2. The classification performance in detectable and three non-trivial UDCs. (a) symmetric verification method (b–d) FDH method with three UDCs $(4, 0)$, $(0, 4)$, $(4, 4)$.

when $QF_2 = 60$ the performance does not begin to deteriorate until $QF_1 = 75$. In addition, this bias will be smaller with a larger QF_2. A similar condition is also observed in Fig. 3(b). This indicates that an SD-JPEG image is still identifiable even if the secondary compression is slightly stronger than the primary one.

We also measured the goodness of the estimation of s-dist. It is measured by the *average shifted distance error* (ASDE).

$$ASDE = mean\left(\sqrt{(\hat{x} - \Delta x)^2 + (\hat{y} - \Delta y)^2}\right) \tag{3}$$

where $(\hat{x}, \hat{y})$ and $(\Delta x, \Delta y)$ are the estimated and ground truth s-dist, respectively. Table 1(a) and Table 1(b) show the ASDE of the condition when $QF_1 \leq QF_2$ and $QF_1 > QF_2$ respectively. As shown, when $QF_1 \leq QF_2$ nearly all the s-dists are correctly estimated. This suggests that the s-dist can be revealed without error when the critical state is not reached. However, when $QF_1 > QF_2$, and there would be estimation errors. The estimation errors are relatively large in the location near the four UDCs.

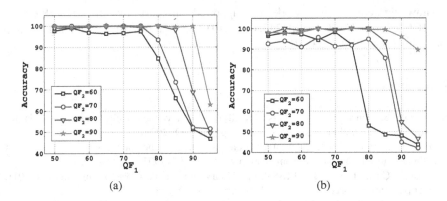

(a)   (b)

Fig. 3. The classification accuracy curves decline suddenly with the increase of QF_1 at a specified QF_2. (a) ICA-based method for detectable condition. (b) FDH-based method for the UDC with s-dist$=(0,4)$.

Table 1. (a)The ASDE of $QF_1 \in [50 \ldots 80]$ and $QF_2 = 75$. (b)The ASDE of $QF_1 \in [80 \ldots 95]$ and $QF_2 = 75$.

(a)

Δy \ Δx	0	1	2	3	4	5	6	7
0	NA	0.00	0.00	0.03	NA	0.01	0.00	0.00
1	0.00	0.00	0.00	0.00	0.00	0.00	0.00	0.00
2	0.00	0.00	0.00	0.00	0.00	0.00	0.00	0.00
3	0.00	0.00	0.00	0.00	0.00	0.00	0.00	0.00
4	NA	0.00	0.00	0.00	NA	0.00	0.00	0.00
5	0.00	0.00	0.00	0.00	0.00	0.00	0.00	0.00
6	0.00	0.00	0.00	0.00	0.00	0.00	0.00	0.00
7	0.00	0.00	0.00	0.00	0.00	0.00	0.00	0.00

(b)

Δy \ Δx	0	1	2	3	4	5	6	7
0	NA	1.63	2.00	2.52	NA	1.85	1.45	1.50
1	1.42	1.16	1.43	1.93	2.01	1.52	1.17	0.91
2	1.60	1.48	1.50	2.08	1.91	1.51	1.34	1.06
3	2.55	1.70	1.90	2.24	2.82	1.77	1.75	1.74
4	NA	2.34	2.41	2.92	NA	2.50	2.22	2.24
5	2.70	2.04	2.02	2.33	2.88	2.21	1.97	1.64
6	1.90	1.54	1.57	2.50	2.22	1.61	1.38	1.24
7	1.50	1.18	1.37	2.09	1.94	1.56	1.18	0.87

5   Conclusion

In this paper, we proposed a method to identify the shifted and re-compressed JPEG image blocks. We extend our previous work [13] in two aspects. Firstly, an entropy-based function is used to more distinctively capture the abnormal BDCT coefficient histograms of SD-JPEG image. Secondly, an FDH based method is provided as a remedy for the three non-trivial UDCs that were undetectable in our previous approach.

One limitation of the proposed method is that the exhaustive search scheme can only deal with pixel-wise shifting. However in some image editing software, the shifting can be conducted in sub-pixel level which would result in a continuous space for searching the de-mixing matrices. Based on the same reason, rotated or scaled JPEG re-compression is also not detectable here. It would be interesting but challenging to determine whether there exist continuous optimization based methods that can learn these parameters without the restriction of limit number of s-dist. These topics will be addressed in future works.

Acknowledgment. This work is supported in part by the 973 Program (2011CB302204), NSFC (61003243, 61272191), and the funding of Zhujiang Science and technology (2011J2200091).

References

1. Bayram, S., Sencar, H., Memon, N.: Identifying digital cameras using cfa interpolation. In: Advances in Digital Forensics II, vol. 222, pp. 289–299 (2006)
2. Bell, J.A., Sejnowski, T.J.: An information-maximization approach to blind separation and blind deconvolution. Neural Computation 7, 1129–1159 (1995)
3. Chang, C.C., Lin, C.J.: LIBSVM:a library for support vector machines (2001), http://www.csie.ntu.edu.tw/~cjlin/libsvm
4. Chen, M., Fridrich, J., Lukáš, J., Goljan, M.: Imaging Sensor Noise as Digital X-Ray for Revealing Forgeries. In: Furon, T., Cayre, F., Doërr, G., Bas, P. (eds.) IH 2007. LNCS, vol. 4567, pp. 342–358. Springer, Heidelberg (2008)
5. Fu, D.D., Shi, Y.Q., Su, W.: A generalized benford's law for jpeg coefficients and its applications in image forensics - art. no. 65051l. In: Security, Steganography, and Watermarking of Multimedia Contents IX, vol. 6505, p. L5051 (2007)
6. He, J., Lin, Z., Wang, L., Tang, X.: Detecting Doctored JPEG Images Via DCT Coefficient Analysis. In: Leonardis, A., Bischof, H., Pinz, A. (eds.) ECCV 2006, Part III. LNCS, vol. 3953, pp. 423–435. Springer, Heidelberg (2006)
7. Johnson, M.K., Farid, H.: Exposing digital forgeries in complex lighting environments. IEEE Trans. Inf. Forensics Security 2(3), 450–461 (2007)
8. Li, B., Shi, Y.Q., Huang, J.W.: Detecting doubly compressed jpeg images by using mode based first digit features. In: IEEE Workshop on Multimedia Signal Processing, pp. 730–735 (2008)
9. Lukas, J., Fridrich, J.: Estimation of primary quantization matrix in double compressed jpeg images. In: Proc. of DFRWS, Cleveland, OH, USA (2003)
10. Luo, W., Qu, Z., Huang, J., Qiu, G.: A novel method for detecting cropped and recompressed image block. In: IEEE Int. Conf. on Acoustics Speech and Signal Processing, April 15-20, vol. 2, pp. II-217–II-220 (2007)
11. Ng, T.T., Chang, S.F., Tsui, M.P.: Using geometry invariants for camera response function estimation. In: IEEE Computer Society Conf. on Computer Vision and Pattern Recognition, June 17-22, pp. 1–8 (2007)
12. Popescu, A.: Statistical Tools for Digital Image Forensics. Ph.D. thesis, Department of Computer Science,Dartmouth College (2005)
13. Qu, Z., Luo, W., Huang, J.: A convolutive mixing model for shifted double jpeg compression with application to passive image authentication. In: IEEE Int. Conf. on Acoustics Speech and Signal Processing, March 31-April 4, pp. 1661–1664 (2008)

A Novel Customized Recompression Framework for Massive Internet Images

Shouhong Ding[1], Feiyue Huang[2], Zhifeng Xie[1], Yongjian Wu[2], and Lizhuang Ma[1,*]

[1] Department of Computer Science and Engineering, Shanghai Jiao Tong University,
Dongchuan Road 800, Shanghai, China, 200240
[2] Tencent Research, Gumei Road 1528, Shanghai, China, 200233
ma-lz@cs.sjtu.edu.cn

Abstract. Recently, device storage capacity and transmission bandwidth requirements are facing a heavy burden on account of massive internet images. Generally, to improve user experience and save costs as much as possible, a lot of internet applications always focus on how to achieve the appropriate image recompression. In this paper, we propose a novel framework to efficiently customize image recompression according to a variety of applications. And our new framework has been successfully applied to many commercial applications, such as web portals, e-commerce, online game and so on.

Keywords: Massive Internet Images, Image Recompression, Image Quality Assessment.

1 Introduction

Along with the development of network and multimedia techniques, more and more information on internet is demonstrated and propagated in the form of picture. The rapid growth number of images and their increasing quality make a heavy burden on the device storage capacity and transmission bandwidth requirements. Therefore, it's very important to sufficiently reduce the file size of images and meanwhile efficiently achieve the recompression customization for different applications. For decades, a lot of methods have been effectively proposed for image compression, which can reduce the file size of images without severely affecting their quality, such as JPEG standard [1], JPEG2000 standard [2], and other techniques [3,4]. Most of images on internet belong to JPEG image format due to its higher compression quality and efficiency. Therefore, we can mainly focus on how to recompress the massive JPEG images in order to further reduce their file size. On the other hand, image recompression also aims to preserve their perceptual quality using image quality assessment (IQA), which can accurately evaluate the quality performance of image compression. We can employ objective assessment to automatically evaluate recompression results and also organize subjective evaluation to verify and adjust recompression settings.

In this paper, we present a novel framework that can not only sufficiently reduce the file size without perceptual quality loss but also efficiently customize image recompression for different applications based on massive internet images. Moreover, we have

---

* Corresponding author.

S.-M. Hu and R.R. Martin (Eds.): CVM 2012, LNCS 7633, pp. 9–16, 2012.

applied our new framework to many commercial applications such as web portals, e-commerce, online game and so on. After a brief review of related work in the next section, we elaborate our novel recompression framework and its six main components in Section 3 and Section 4. Then, several representative applications are introduced in Section 5.Finally, the conclusion and discussion about this paper are given in Section 6.

2 Related Work

Image Compression. For still image compression, the Joint Photographic Experts Group (JPEG) [1] standard has been established by ISO (International Standards Organization) and IEC (International Electro-Technical Commission). Recently, many techniques have been introduced into the context of image compression. Based on image inpainting techniques, [5] proposed an image compression framework towards visual quality rather than pixel-wise fidelity. Machine learning based approaches [4,6] have been proposed to do lossy image compression. These approaches learn a model from a few representative pixels and predicts color on the rest of the pixels.

Image Quality Assessment. Image quality assessment(IQA) plays a fundamental role in the design and evaluation of imaging and image processing systems, such as those for compression, enhancement, restoration, etc. Subjective evaluations are considered to be the most reliable way to assess image quality. A significant effort has been done in the field of subjective image quality assessment [7,8]. There are also standards on subjective evaluation of image quality [9,10]. Although subjective evaluations are reliable to assess image quality, in practice they are usually too cumbersome, time-consuming, expensive; most importantly they cannot be incorporated into automatic systems that adjust themselves in real-time based on the feedback of output quality.

The interest in objective image quality assessment has been growing at an accelerated pace over the past decade [11,12].The goal of research in objective IQA is to develop quantitative measures that can automatically predict the quality of images or videos in a perceptually consistent manner. We focus on the full-reference IQA in this paper. Zhou Wang et al. in [13] reviewed advantages and disadvantages of MSE and reviewed emerging alternative signal fidelity measures. One recently proposed approach to image fidelity measurement, which may also prove highly effective for measuring the fidelity of other signals, is the SSIM index [11]. If the type of distortions are known, then the design of full-reference IQA is quite straightforward. Based on the artifacts that will introduced by JPEG image coder, Tamar Shoham et al. in [14] proposed a perceptual image quality measure called BBCQ (Block-based Coding Quality) which is composed of three components.

3 Overview

Figure 1 provides an overview of our framework. First of all, we estimate the source compression level of an input image, and initialize its target compression level. Secondly, we combine those two compression levels to compute a re-coding matrix and

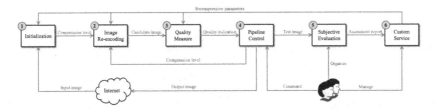

Fig. 1. Our new framework can be described for customized image recompression, which includes six main components: initialization, image re-coding, quality measure, pipeline control, subjective evaluation, and custom service

generate a new compression result. Thirdly, we measure the perceptual similarity between the input image and the new result using BBCQ. Fourthly, its output can be controlled into three available pipelines: (a) update the target compression level; (b) return the final recompression result; (c) change into the subjective evaluation. Fifthly, guided by each different application, we organize the corresponding subjective evaluation and obtain its assessment report. At last, based on the report, we customize the whole recompression for each application by setting up a series of appropriate parameters.

4 Customized Recompression

In this section, we describe our new framework for customized recompression in detail, which includes six main components: initialization, image re-coding, quality measure, pipeline control, subjective evaluation, and custom service.

Initialization. For reducing the iteration number and improving the efficiency of recompression, we focus on how to initialize an appropriate target compression level according to a customized application. Given a series of its default parameters, we first analyze the relationship between the compress level and the BBCQ's similarity score. As shown in Figure 2, we observe more than 5,000 internet images and construct a perceptual similarity prior, i.e., the Quality-Score distribution of one image can be fitted by a partial Gaussian Distribution Function, which is defined as:

$$Q(s) = \frac{k}{\sqrt{2\pi}\sigma} \exp\{-\frac{(s-\mu)^2}{2\sigma^2}\}, \tag{1}$$

where s is the BBCQ's similarity score; $Q(s)$ is the compression quality factor, also known as Q factor in the Independent JPEG Group (IJG) [15]; μ and σ is the mean and standard deviation of the Quality-Score distribution, μ is fixed to 1.0; k is a scaling factor. If two pairs of Quality-Score are provided, we can subsequently compute σ and k, which are unknown in Equation 1. According to an important observation: when s is 1.0, $Q(s)$ approximates to the source compression level of input image, we can efficiently avoid one of those two pairs by estimating its compression quality from the source image. Given the quantization matrix of the source image M_s and the baseline matrix M_b, $Q(1)$ can be estimated as:

$$Q(1) \approx \min_q \sum_i \frac{|M_q(i) - M_s(i)|}{M_b(i)}, \tag{2}$$

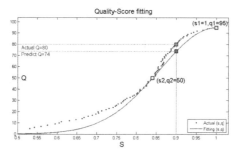

Fig. 2. Quality-Score fitting. The Quality-Score distribution of one image can be fitted by a partial Gaussian Distribution Function; after two pairs of Quality-Score ($s1 = 1.0, q1 = 95$) and ($s2 = 0.8406, q2 = 50$) are initialized, we can predict the target compression level $q = Q(0.9) = 74$ by using Equation 1; based on the quality score threshold $s_t = 0.9$ and the initialized compression level $q = 74$, we can continuously update the target compression level until its optimal level $q^* = 80$.

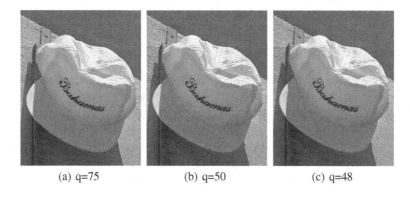

(a) q=75   (b) q=50   (c) q=48

Fig. 3. Nonmonotonicity of the IJG quality rating scale. (a) is a JPEG image with quality level equals to 75; we recompress (a) to quality level 50, and obtain (b); (b) has considerable visual grainy artifacts. However, recompress (a) to quality 48, the grainy artifacts will disappear. Comparing with (b), (c) is perceptually much closer to (a).

where q is the compression quality and M_q is its quantization matrix based on M_b. Moreover, given $Q = 50$, we can compute another pair $(s_2, Q(s_2) = 50)$ by BBCQ. After obtaining two pairs of Quality-Score, we can produce the corresponding target compression levels for the different applications. As shown in Figure 2, after two pairs of Quality-Score $(1.0, 95)$ and $(0.8406, 50)$ are initialized, we can predict the target compression level $q = Q(0.9) = 74$ by using Gaussian Function.

Image Re-coding. Many experiments have shown that the IJG quality rating scale is not perceptually monotone[16]. An example is shown in Figure 3. This nonmonotonicity in the IJG quality rating scale can bring bad effects to our system, since part of our framework such as initialization, and pipeline control require a monotonicity between quality and perceptual score. H. H. Bauschke et al. [16] report a novel heuristic for

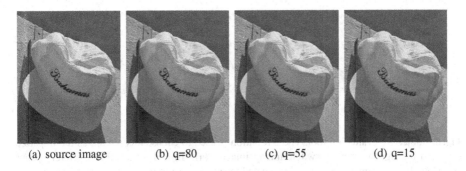

(a) source image   (b) q=80   (c) q=55   (d) q=15

Fig. 4. JPEG images with different compression level

requantizing JPEG images by incorporating the Laplacian distribution of the AC discrete cosine transform (DCT) coefficients with an analysis of the error introduced by requantization. Here, we modify the Quantization matrix QM using heuristic algorithm proposed in [16]. Denote QM_o and QM_q to be the quantization matrix of the input image and the target quantization matrix, respectively. We want to modify QM_q based on QM_o to obtain a new quantization matrix QM_n which is closed to QM_q in order to requantize the input image. Denote the corresponding element of QM_o, QM_q and QM_n by mo_{ij}, mq_{ij} and mn_{ij}. The new mn_{ij} is constructed as follows: First compute $k = \lfloor mq_{ij}/mo_{ij} \rfloor$. Then define

$$mn_{ij} = \begin{cases} mo_{ij} & if \quad k = 0; \\ k \cdot mo_{ij} & if \quad k > 0. \end{cases} \tag{3}$$

Using Equation 3, we obtain a new quantization matrix QM_{qn} and compress the input image with this quantization matrix.

Quality Measure. For a new recompression image, we further measure its recompression quality by a block-based coding quality method (BBCQ), which can evaluate the degradation in image quality compared to the original image [14]. As shown in Figure 4, we compress the original image Figure 4(a) into different compression levels Figure 4(b), Figure 4(c), Figure 4(d) with quality 80, 55, 15 and their corresponding BBCQ's scores 0.8986, 0.8479, 0.6677. Obviously, when compressing the original image with a lower quality, the compressed image will has more visual grainy artifacts, and the coding block grid is more visible.

Pipeline Control. After obtaining the recompression result and its quality score, we can control them into three available pipelines according to the different requirements, which aim to update the target compression level, return the final recompression result or change into the subjective evaluation.

(a) Update the Target Compression Level: As shown in Figure 2, given a quality score threshold s_t, we can initialize a target compression level $Q(s_t)$. We next recode the source image with the compression level $q = Q(s_t)$, compute its BBCQ's score $S(q)$ and compare it with the threshold. If $S(q) > s_t$, update the target compression

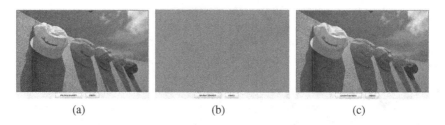

(a)   (b)   (c)

Fig. 5. Subjective evaluation tool. The left button is used to choose this picture as the impaired one; and the right is used to switch among images. (a), (b) and (c) are three different pages corresponding to source image, gray image and the recompressed image. The gray image is used to eliminate human vision residuals.

level $q = q - w$, and repeat the above operations until $S(q) < s_t$; If $S(q) < s_t$, update the target compression level $q = q + w$, and repeat the above operations until $S(q) > s_t$. Finally, we can assume a local linear relationship and find out the optimal target compression level q^*. Based on q^* we can get our final recompression result.

(b) Change into the Subjective Evaluation: Here, we collect the recompression results and organize the subjective evaluation in order to fix a series of appropriate recompression parameters, which can guarantee the recompression quality and meanwhile meet the bandwidth and storage requirements of different applications.

Subjective Evaluation. In order to evaluate the performance of our recompression system and guide each different application to reach its own compression level, we perform standardized subjective image quality assessment based on [9,10].In our framework for perceptually lossless compression, assessing thresholds of different application is required. Forced-Choice Double-Stimulus (FCDS) method [9] which was specifically designed for assessing thresholds of visibility is suitable for this task. In our framework, the testing were performed using identical Microsoft Windows workstations. As shown in Figure 5, a web-based interface showing the image to be compared and a Java button applet for choosing the impaired one was used. On the other hand, subjective assessment methods, such as Double Stimulus Impairment Scale (DSIS) [10], can be used to evaluate the perceptual quality of images by computing the mean opinion scores (MOS) from human ratings. In our framework of high compression levels we take this subjective evaluation to evaluate the perceptual quality of the output images. In our testing, observers are asked to rank the quality of the recompressed image using a standard 5 step impairment scale, as shown below: 5 - imperceptible, 4 - perceptible, but not annoying, 3 - slightly annoying, 2 - annoying, 1 - very annoying.

Custom Service. On basis of the subjective evaluation, we can provide the appropriate custom service for each different application. First of all, for a new application, we try to find a similar application from a database in which a lot of operational applications are recorded completely. Secondly, we extract a series of parameters from the similar application info to initialize the whole recompression. Thirdly, after image recompression, we achieve the subject evaluation to verify the effectiveness of recompression parameters. Fourthly, according to the assessment report, we iteratively adjust the parameters

Table 1. Framework performance of offline service for perceptually lossless compression on three applications

Applications	Total images number	Running time (s)	Average running time(s)	Original total file size	Total file size after compression	Compression ratio(%)
Yixun e-commerce	305988	16527.04	0.054	13.67 GB	7.24 GB	47.067
Huyu online game	207428	16410.02	0.079	9.54 GB	7.40 GB	22.420
Tencent AdCenter	2752	245.12	0.089	142.26 MB	111.93 MB	21.319

until the assessment report can meet the application requirements. Finally, we finish the custom service for the application and write its info into the database.

5 Representative Applications

The customized recompression framework introduced in the previous section can be used to effectively reduce the file size of images for a wide variety of applications. In fact, we have applied our customized recompression framework to a number of applications, such as web portals, e-commerce, and online game. Table 1 shows the performance of our customized recompression framework for perceptually lossless compression on three typical applications. The second row of table 1 shows that the compression ratio of our framework applying to Yixun e-commerce is up to 47.067%. However, the compression ratios in the third row and the fourth row are not that high as the compression ratio in the second row. This is mainly because that the input images of these two applications have already been highly compressed. Both average running time are less than 0.1 second that indicates the efficiency of our framework.

6 Conclusion and Discussion

In this paper, a novel customized recompression framework for massive internet images was proposed. Using a prior knowledge on compression level and perceptual quality score, the efficiency of our framework are guaranteed by predicting a exact initial compression level for our iterative recompression. Application based subjective evaluations effectively customize the most appropriate recompression for each different applications by finding a trade-off between image file size and image perceptual quality.

Moreover, our framework only takes JPEG images as inputs, but there are still many PNG, BMP, or GIF pictures on the Internet. In the future, we plan to further generalize our framework so that it can handle more images with different image formats.

Acknowledgments. We would like to thank the anonymous reviewers for their valuable comments. This work is supported by a joint project of Tencent research and Shanghai Jiao Tong University. This work is also partially funded by the National Basic Research Project of China (No. 2011CB302203), and the National Natural Science Foundation of China (No. 61073089 and No. 61133009).

References

1. Pennebaker, W.B., Mitchell, J.L.: JPEG - Still Image Data Compression Standards. Van Nostrand Reinhold (1993)
2. Rabbani, M., Joshi, R.: An overview of the jpeg 2000 still image compression standard. Signal Processing: Image Communication 17(1), 3–48 (2002)
3. Do, M.N., Vetterli, M.: The contourlet transform: an efficient directional multiresolution image representation. IEEE Transactions on Image Processing 14(12), 2091–2106 (2005)
4. He, X., Ji, M., Bao, H.: A unified active and semi-supervised learning framework for image compression. In: IEEE Conference on Computer Vision and Pattern Recognition, CVPR 2009, pp. 65–72 (June 2009)
5. Liu, D., Sun, X., Wu, F., Li, S., Zhang, Y.-Q.: Image compression with edge-based inpainting. IEEE Transactions on Circuits and Systems for Video Technology 17(10), 1273–1287 (2007)
6. Cheng, L., Vishwanathan, S.V.N.: Learning to compress images and videos. In: Proceedings of the 24th International Conference on Machine Learning, ICML 2007, pp. 161–168. ACM, New York (2007)
7. Hamberg, R., de Ridder, H.: Continuous assessment of time-varying image quality. In: Rogowitz, B.E., Pappas, T.N. (eds.) Society of Photo-Optical Instrumentation Engineers (SPIE) Conference Series, vol. 3016, pp. 248–259 (June 1997)
8. de Ridder, H.: Psychophysical evaluation of image quality: from judgment to impression. In: Rogowitz, B.E., Pappas, T.N. (eds.) Society of Photo-Optical Instrumentation Engineers (SPIE) Conference Series, vol. 3299, pp. 252–263 (July 1998)
9. ITU-R BT.1082-1 Report. Studies towards the unification of picture assessment methodologies (1990)
10. ITU-R BT.500-11 Recommendation. Methodology for the subjective assessment of the quality of television pictures (2003)
11. Wang, Z., Bovik, A.C., Sheikh, H.R., Simoncelli, E.P.: Image quality assessment: from error visibility to structural similarity. IEEE Transactions on Image Processing 13(4), 600–612 (2004)
12. Liu, Y.-J., Luo, X., Xuan, Y.-M., Chen, W.-F., Fu, X.-L.: Image retargeting quality assessment. Computer Graphics Forum 30(2), 583–592 (2011)
13. Wang, Z., Bovik, A.C.: Mean squared error: Love it or leave it? a new look at signal fidelity measures. IEEE Signal Processing Magazine 26(1), 98–117 (2009)
14. Shoham, T., Gill, D., Carmel, S.: A novel perceptual image quality measure for block based image compression. In: Society of Photo-Optical Instrumentation Engineers (SPIE) Conference Series, vol. 7867 (January 2011)
15. Various Documents. Independent jpeg group, http://www.ijg.org
16. Bauschke, H.H., Hamilton, C.H., Macklem, M.S., McMichael, J.S., Swart, N.R.: Recompression of jpeg images by requantization. IEEE Transactions on Image Processing 12(7), 843–849 (2003)

Decomposition Equation of Basis Images with Consideration of Global Illumination

Xueying Qin[1,2], Rui Zhang[1], Lili Lin[1], Fan Zhong[1,*], Guanyu Xing[3], and Qunsheng Peng[3]

[1] School of Computer Science and Technology, Shandong University, P.R. China
[2] Shandong Provincial Key Laboratory of Network Based Intelligent Computing, P.R. China
[3] State Key Laboratory of CAD&CG, Zhejiang University, P.R. China
zhongfan@sdu.edu.cn
http://vr.sdu.edu.cn/

Abstract. In augmented reality, it is required to sense the changing of the light condition for achieving illumination consistency. In this paper, we build up the decomposition equation of basis images of static scenes for this purpose. It is proved that the basis images are invariants of the scene, which is the global illumination effects of a distributed light source with unit power, and it is unnecessary to assume that the reflectance of appearance of objects in scenes is ideal diffuse. Our method can also be applied in image understanding and compressing.

Keywords: basis image decomposition, illumination invariants, global illumination.

1 Introduction

In Augmented Reality, many application requires to achieve photo-realistic effects when integrating virtual objects into a real scene. However, due to the complexity and diversity of dynamic changing illumination such as outdoor scenes, it is still a challenge to sense the changing of the light condition.

The appearance of a scene is decided by its geometry, reflectance, texture as well as light source, and should obey the rules of global illumination model [1]. Therefore, illumination plays an important role in images, and it is also desired to analyze illumination component from images in many other applications, especially the invariants. In computer vision or pattern recognition, the illumination effects often become interferer of image understanding, thus it is strongly desired to be removed or decreased. For compression of surveillance image sequences, the illumination may be the most important component with variation in a time-lapse image set, and therefore is desired to separate the invariance components. In all these areas, Augmented Reality has special requests on the understanding of light environments, such as online real-time, and high precision.

---

* Corresponding author.

S.-M. Hu and R.R. Martin (Eds.): CVM 2012, LNCS 7633, pp. 17–24, 2012.

For a photo image, its lighting condition may be very complex, such as outdoor scenes. The basis image decomposition then plays an important role to estimate light condition changes. Aiming for Augmented Reality application in outdoor scenes, Liu et al. [2] proposed first a light parameter estimation method for outdoor scenes without any knowledge about geometry and reflectance, in which the concept of basis images of the sunlight and skylight is proposed and resolved by a linear decomposition model from images with different weather condition but the same sun position. However, the reflectance of the objects are supposed to be diffuse, and the distribution of the light source is uniform. Although the concept has been proposed, it is not properly explained and resolved.

Image decomposition is an important topic for image understanding. For image decomposition in early stage, intrinsic images are separated from single images [3,4], or multiple images [5,6]. Recently, data collection and surveillance of webcams raised the problems to decompose the image set of outdoor scenes captured in a whole day into different factors of shading [7,8], in which [8] is for fine day only, and [8] for variety of weather, with the limitation of only the diffuse material in the scenes. For sensing the light parameters, basis images are fundamental since we need invariants of a scene about illumination.

The global illumination model of outdoor scenes is quite simple [9]. The dominate light in landscapes is the sunlight and the skylight, and the skylight is distributed on the sky dome. However, since both the sunlight and skylight are far away from the scenes, the light condition are considered all the same in the scene. We do not consider any other man-made light sources.

In this paper, aiming for Augmented Reality, we build up a decomposition equation of basis images with consideration of global illumination, which are the illumination invariants of a static scene. This equation has no limitations on object reflectance, and also does not require the distribution of the light source to be uniform.

2   Previous Model

The global illumination of any scenes could be modeled by Kajiya's rendering equation [1]. The pixel values of an obtained image are those radiance transferred to image RGB level by CCD of a camera [10], which are investable up to scale. Therefore, the following process is performed in radiance space.

The rendering equation states that the images we viewed are from either emission of the direct light source, or reflection of light sources and inter-reflection of all scenes. There are different formula of this equation, and we use the following:

$$L(x,\omega,\lambda,t) = E(x,\omega,\lambda,t) + \int_{\Omega} \rho(x,\omega',\omega,\lambda)S(x,\omega')L(x,\omega',\lambda,t)cos\theta(x,\omega')d\omega',$$
(1)

where x is an observed point, λ denotes the wavelength of the light, t is time, ω and ω' are reflection and incident ray direction, respectively, $E(x,\omega,\lambda,t)$ is the emission light intensity, Ω is the sphere or hemi-sphere of the incident light, and $\rho(x,\omega',\omega)$ is the BRDF at point x from direction ω' to ω, and $S(x,\omega')$ is occlusion function, $L(x, \omega', \lambda, t)$ is the incident light at x from direction ω', $\theta(x, \omega')$ is angle between the incident light and the normal at point x. This equation expresses multiple inter-reflection among surfaces through BRDF, which means that the light arrived at the camera may be reflected arbitrary times in the scenes.

Liu et al. [2] once proposed a decomposition model of basis images, by ignoring the inter-reflection among objects, and assuming the sky light is uniformly distributed with linear HDR function, they get a linear decomposition equation as follows:

$$\mathbf{I} = \mathbf{E} \cdot \mathbf{C} \tag{2}$$

where $\mathbf{I}$ stand for the input images captured by a fixed camera, $\mathbf{E}$ stands for the sunlight and the skylight radiance, and $\mathbf{C}$ is the images of the direct lighting without inter-reflectance and defined as following:

$$\begin{aligned} C_{sun}(x, \lambda, t) = \int_{\Omega_{sun}} \rho(x, \omega', \omega, \lambda) S(x, \omega', \omega) cos\theta(x, \omega') d\omega' \\ C_{sky}(x, \lambda, t) = \int_{\Omega_{sky}} \rho(x, \omega', \omega, \lambda) S(x, \omega', \omega) cos\theta(x, \omega') d\omega', \end{aligned} \tag{3}$$

where ω is removed as a parameter in C_{sun} and C_{sky} due to fixed camera and geometry in the scene. This model is unsuitable for the cases of inter-reflection and non-diffuse surface. In this paper, we derive the decomposition model from another aspect.

3   Linear Decomposition Model

3.1   Global Illumination Model with Inter-Reflection

We consider only the landscape scenes without emission of any man-made light. Based on the rendering equation, we have $E(x) = 0$ for all pixels of object surface. A global illumination model should include all layers of inter-reflectance of light in the scene. We will show that the linearity is kept for the global illumination model if the radiance distribution of an area light source is up to scale.

The rendering equation express the inter-reflection with a recursive light transfer. An equivalent expression is to classify the collect rays according to layers of the inter-reflectance. The first layer of illumination is from the direct light source, and then those illuminated surfaces become light sources of the second layer of inter-reflection, and so on. The inter-reflectance is infinitely processed. Therefore, it is accumulated via infinite inter-reflectance:

$$L(x, \omega, \lambda, t) = \sum_{k=0}^{\infty} L^{(k)}(x, \omega, \lambda, t) \tag{4}$$

where k denote the order of the inter-reflection of light, $L_{sun}(x, \omega, \lambda, t)$ and $L_{sky}(x, \omega, \lambda, t)$ consist of all orders of the inter-reflection of light source, respectively. More in detail, according to rendering equation we have for each layer of inter-reflection:

$$L^{(0)}(x, \omega, \lambda, t) = E(x, \omega, \lambda, t)$$
$$\cdots\cdots$$
$$L^{(k+1)}(x, \omega, \lambda, t) = \int_{\Omega} \rho(x, \omega', \omega, \lambda) S(x, \omega') L^{(k)}(x, \omega', \lambda, t) cos\theta(x, \omega', \omega) d\omega'. \tag{5}$$

From these equations, we can derive the linear property of decomposition equation.

3.2   Linearity of Global Illumination

The input images are captured at a fixed viewpoint of an outdoor scene. For the moment, we assume that the scene is static, the reflectance of scene points is not limited to Lambertian, and the irradiance of any scene point is entirely due to natural light.

We assume that all the geometry terms, including geometry model of the scene, the camera position and orientation, the distribution of all the light source, are determined. If the distribution of the light source is constant, and we only tune the scale, that is:

$$E'(x, \omega, \lambda, t) = \alpha(\lambda)E(x, \omega, \lambda, t) \tag{6}$$

We use inductive method to prove the radiance of any layer (for $k = 0, 1, \ldots$) of inter-reflection will be multiple by $\alpha(\lambda)$. For $k = 0$, we can obtain from Eq. 5 that:

$$L'^{(0)}(x, \omega, \lambda, t) = \alpha(\lambda)E(x, \omega, \lambda, t) = \alpha(\lambda)L^{(0)}(x, \omega, \lambda, t) \tag{7}$$

Suppose that it is true for k:

$$L'^{(k)}(x, \omega, \lambda, t) = \alpha(\lambda)L^{(k)}(x, \omega, \lambda, t) \tag{8}$$

Due to linearity of Eq. 5 on radiance of light source, we can get from Eqs. 4, 5, and 8:

$$
\begin{aligned}
L'^{(k+1)}(x, \omega, \lambda, t) &= \int_\Omega \rho(x, \omega', \omega, \lambda)S(x, \omega')L'^{(k)}(x, \omega', \lambda, t)cos\theta(x, \omega', \omega)d\omega' \\
&= \int_\Omega \rho(x, \omega', \omega, \lambda)S(x, \omega')\alpha(\lambda)L^{(k)}(x, \omega', \lambda, t)cos\theta(x, \omega', \omega)d\omega' \\
&= \alpha(\lambda)L^{(k+1)}(x, \omega', \lambda, t)
\end{aligned}
\tag{9}
$$

Therefore, we can have:

$$
\begin{aligned}
L'(x, \omega, \lambda, t) &= \sum_{k=0}^{\infty} L'^{(k)}(x, \omega, \lambda, t) \\
&= \alpha(\lambda)\sum_{k=0}^{\infty} L(k)(x, \omega, \lambda, t) \\
&= \alpha(\lambda)L(x, \omega, \lambda, t)
\end{aligned}
\tag{10}
$$

The above equation show that: if the light distribution keeps constant and only the radiance scale is tuned, then the illuminated scene is also tuned by the same scale.

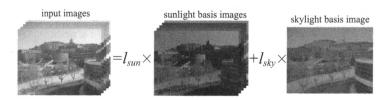

Fig. 1. The image decomposition model

3.3   Decomposition Equation of Basis Images

A natural scene is reasonable to be separated into two part according to light sources: one is lit by the sunlight, and another is lit by the skylight.

It is also reasonable to suppose that the distribution of the skylight source keeps unchanged all day long, and the scaled sunlight distribution only depends on the position of the sun, or time. We define the normalized radiance distribution of the sunlight and skylight along direction ω at time t, respectively, as:

$$
\begin{aligned}
\check{E}_{sun}(x,\omega,\lambda,t) &= E_{sun}(x,\omega,\lambda,t)/\int_\Omega E_{sun}(x,\omega,\lambda,t)d\omega \\
\check{E}_{sky}(x,\omega,\lambda,t) &= E_{sky}(x,\omega,\lambda,t)/\int_\Omega E_{sky}(x,\omega,\lambda,t)d\omega
\end{aligned}
\tag{11}
$$

It is easy to prove that $\check{E}_{sun}(x,t)$ and $\check{E}_{sky}(x,t)$ are with unit radiant exitance:

$$
\begin{aligned}
\int_\Omega \check{E}_{sun}(x,\omega,\lambda,t)d\omega &= 1 \\
\int_\Omega \check{E}_{sky}(x,\omega,\lambda,t)d\omega &= 1
\end{aligned}
\tag{12}
$$

With these normalized lighting environment, we denote the global illumination radiance of the scene as $\check{L}_{sun}(x,\omega,\lambda,t)$ and $\check{L}_{sky}(x,\omega,\lambda,t)$. The viewing direction of basis images is decided by photometry, therefore the incident direction ω is fixed, and we can denote the basis images as:

$$
\begin{aligned}
B_{sun}(x,\lambda,t) &= \check{L}_{sun}(x,\omega,\lambda,t) \\
B_{sky}(x,\lambda,t) &= \check{L}_{sky}(x,\omega,\lambda,t)
\end{aligned}
\tag{13}
$$

When the radiance of the sunlight and skylight changes, they only tune the scale, respectively. Any daylight light condition can be represented by a linear combination of the sunlight and skylight distribution:

$$
E(x,\omega,\lambda,t) = l_{sun}(\lambda,t)\check{E}_{sun}(x,\omega,\lambda,t) + l_{sky}(\lambda,t)\check{E}_{sky}(x,\omega,\lambda,t)
\tag{14}
$$

Due to linearity of the illumination effects of the sunlight and skylight, we define basis images of the sunlight and skylight as the global illuminated results of scenes by the sunlight and skylight with unit radiant exitance of light source. Therefore, the sampling images can be rewritten as the superimposing of the illumination results of the sunlight and skylight:

$$
L(x,\lambda,t) = l_{sun}(\lambda,t)B_{sun}(x,\lambda,t) + l_{sky}(\lambda,t)B_{sky}(x,\lambda,t)
\tag{15}
$$

in which $l_{sun}(\lambda,t)$ is the measure of sunlight radiance coefficients arriving at time t, $l_{sky}(\lambda,t)$ is the measure of the radiance coefficients of the skylight at t, $B_{sun}(x,\lambda,t)$ and $B_{sky}(x,\lambda,t)$ are respectively defined as the global illuminated results of scenes by the sunlight and skylight with unit radiant exitance. Our decomposition model is described as Fig. 1.

From Eq. 15, any view of a scene is a linear combination of basis images, and the coefficients are a kind of measurement of intensity of the light sources. However, for photogrammetry, we can only recover the intensity up to scale. The exposure and aperture of the camera are unnecessary to be considered in our decomposition model. We use a linear corresponding function of HDR, and we can rewrite Eq.15 to a linear equation of decomposition as the following:

$$\mu \mathbf{I} = \ell \cdot \mathbf{B} \tag{16}$$

where $\mathbf{I}$ is a tensor that consists of the sampling images, ℓ is the tensor of vectors of the light coefficients, and $\mathbf{B}$ is a tensor that consists of the basis image vectors, μ is a coefficient for photometry, which is calibrated when virtual objects are inserted. Since ℓ is up to scale, we ignore μ and absorb it into ℓ in the following.

4   Decomposing Basis Images from a Sequence of Images

Our input images are captured at a fixed viewpoint of an outdoor static scene, based on which basis images can be obtained by minimizing a quadratic energy function. We optimize the following equation for decomposing the basis images:

$$\arg\min_{B_{sun}(x,\lambda,t),B_{sky}(x,\lambda)} \sum_{x,\lambda,t} (I(x,\lambda,t) - l_{sun}(\lambda,t)B_{sun}(x,\lambda,t) - l_{sky}(\lambda,t)B_{sky}(x,\lambda))^2 \tag{17}$$

The optimization of the above function is very unstable, and $l_{sun}(\lambda,t)$ and $l_{sky}(\lambda,t)$ are also unknown. We start from the shadowed areas of the sunlight that are detected by k-means clustering. With the mean image serving as the initialization of the skylight basis image, we can resolve the $l_{sky}(\lambda,t)$ and the skylight basis image from Eq.17. After that the sunlight intensity and basis images can be computed easily, the result is then used to update the shadow function. The above procedures can be iterated to progressively refine the results. In the whole process the sky region is excluded from the computation through a mask image, which is easy to be produced because both the camera and the scene are static.

5   Experiment Results

In our experiments, we use a series of outdoor scene images captured every 5 seconds per frame at a fixed viewpoint by Cannon SX110, and the original resolution is 1600×1200, and then is resized to 640×480. The algorithm is implemented on a computer with a Core E7500 2.93GHz CPU, and 3.21GB of RAM. The running time is about 200 seconds for 1080 images totally.

In Fig. 2, the first row is the source image taken in our campus, the second row is the reconstruct images of our algorithm, and the third row is the error images of the two images above. From the error images we can see, the reconstructed error of most pixels is below 5 gray level obviously, and the pixels with error more than 15 gray level are mostly dynamic objects, like the people or the car on the road. From another aspect, we can use the error images to detect the dynamic objects. The RMS error of each RGB channel of all the three scenes we examined is within 3.3 grey levels, from which we can see that the results of our theory is correct.

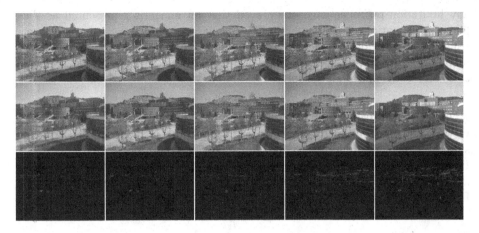

Fig. 2. The top row shows the 10, 256, 436, 726 and 1069 frame from the original sequence, the middle row is the reconstruction of our model. The third row is the absolute error marked by different colors standing for different error ranges, where the black areas stand for the pixels whose absolute error is below 5 pixels, similarly, blue areas stand for the error range of 5 to 10 pixels, green areas stand for the error range of 10 to 15 pixels, and the red areas stand for the range of other else.

(a)   (b)

Fig. 3. (a) The sunlight basis image containing the effect of the mirror reflection; (b) the amplification figure of the red rectangle of (a)

The advantage of our algorithm is that we do not have any limitation on the reflectance. We can deal with the mirror reflection. Fig. 3 shows the mirror effect in the sunlight basis image. On the road, we can see the clearly reflection projection effect of the green mirror of the building.

6   Conclusion

In this paper, we have proposed a decomposition equation with consideration of global illumination of static outdoor scenes. As the main light source of outdoor scenes is sunlight and skylight, by using the global illumination model without any limitation on reflectance, we proved that an image is represented as the linear combination of the sunlight basis image and the skylight basis image, which are invariants of the scene that is illuminated by the sunlight and skylight with unit energy, respectively. Experimental results demonstrate the effectiveness and correctness of our algorithm.

Acknowledgments. The authors gratefully acknowledge the anonymous reviewers for their comments to help us to improve our paper. This work is supported by 973 program of China (No.2009CB320802), NSF of China (No. U1035004, No.61173070), Natural Science Fund for Distinguished Young Scholars of Shandong Province (No.JQ200920), and Chinese Postdoctoral Science Foundation (No.2012M511509).

References

1. Kajiya, J.: The rendering equation. In: SIGGRAPH 1986 Proceedings of the 13th Annual Conference on Computer Graphics and Interactive Techniques, vol. 20(4) (1986)
2. Liu, Y., Qin, X., Xu, S., Nakamae, E., Peng, Q.: Light source estimation of outdoor scenes for mixed reality. The Visual Computer: International Journal of Computer Graphics 25(5-7), 637–646 (2009)
3. Barrow, H., Tenenbaum, J.: Recovering intrinsic scene characteristics fromimages. In: Computer Vision Systems (1978)
4. Matsushita, Y., Lin, S., Kang, S.B., Shum, H.-Y.: Estimating Intrinsic Images from Image Sequences with Biased Illumination. In: Pajdla, T., Matas, J(G.) (eds.) ECCV 2004, Part II. LNCS, vol. 3022, pp. 274–286. Springer, Heidelberg (2004)
5. Kimmel, R., Elad, M., Shaked, D., Keshet, R., Sobel, I.: A variational framework for retinex. International Journal of Computer Vision, 7–23 (2003)
6. Tappen, M., Freeman, W., Adelson, E.: Recovering intrinsic images from a single image. In: Advances in Neural Information Processing Systems 15. MIT Press (2002)
7. Sunkavalli, K., Matusik, W., Pfister, H., Rusinkiewicz, S.: Factored time-lapse video. In: Proc. of SIGGRAPH, vol. 26(3), pp. 101–111 (2007)
8. Sunkavalli, K., Romeiro, F., Matusik, W., Zickler, T., Pfister, H.: What do color changes reveal about an outdoor scene? In: IEEE International Conference on Computer Vision and Pattern Recognition, pp. 1–8 (2008)
9. Tadamura, K., Nakamae, E., Kaneda, K., Baba, M., Yamashita, H., Nishita, T.: Modeling of Skylight and Rendering of Outdoor Scenes. Comput. Graph. Forum 12(3), 189–200 (1993)
10. Debevec, P., Malik, J.: Recovering high dynamic range radiance maps from photographs. In: Proc. of SIGGRAPH, pp. 369–378 (1997)

Intrinsic Image Decomposition with Local Smooth Assumption and Global Color Assumption

Zhongqiang Wang and Li Zhu*

Xi'an Jiaotong University
zhuli@mail.xjtu.edu.cn

Abstract. Intrinsic images, which describe independent characteristics of scenes, are very useful in many different fields. But it is difficult to get them because the problem is extremely ill-posed. Smooth assumption is widely used in many methods, but pixels in plain areas and in edge areas are not well distinguished. We improve this assumption by adding a weight to every pixel in the image so that the smoothness is measured accordingly. There are always large error in dark areas in previous methods due to the enlarged inaccuracy there. We proposed a global assumption to solve this problem. The results show that the performance is greatly improved by using our method.

Keywords: intrinsic image, smooth assumption, color line assumption.

1 Introduction

Every single image is a combination of many characteristics. In order to get independent characteristics of images, the concept of *Intrinsic images* is introduced in [1]. Every image can be decomposed into a reflectance image and an illumination image. Reflectance image shows the original color of the objects in the scene while illumination shows the lighting condition and how the surfaces reflect light.

By using intrinsic images, interplay between different characteristics can be perfectly avoided. Therefore, works which suffer from this interplay benefit a lot. Reflectance image can be used in re-coloring, re-texturing[2], and segmentation. Illumination image can be used in re-lighting[2], inter-reflection acquisition[3] and so on.

However, intrinsic image decomposition is severely ill-posed because two images are required while only one image is given. Denote the input image as $\mathcal{I}$ and reflectance image as $\mathcal{R}$ and illumination image as $\mathcal{L}$. Then the relation of the three images is:

$$\mathcal{I} = \mathcal{R} \cdot \mathcal{L} \qquad (1)$$

Here, $\mathcal{I} \in \mathbb{R}^3$ and $\mathcal{R} \in \mathbb{R}^3$ and $\mathcal{L} \in \mathbb{R}$.

In this paper, two assumptions are used. The first assumption is the smoothness of the illumination and reflectance. The smooth assumption is used in many previous methods but the probability of smoothness of each pixel is not introduced. We introduce weights into this assumption. The second assumption is a global assumption based on global color distribution and over-segmentation. In previous methods, error in dark area is usually larger than that in light area. We proposed an assumption based on color line[4] to solve this problem. Over-segmentation is used to handle the few outliers.

---

* Corresponding author.

S.-M. Hu and R.R. Martin (Eds.): CVM 2012, LNCS 7633, pp. 25–32, 2012.
© Springer-Verlag Berlin Heidelberg 2012

2 Related Works

[5] and [6] estimate intrinsic images from a fixed-viewpoint image sequence captured under changing illumination. [7] extends [5] so that Internet images with similar viewpoint can be used to get reflectance for colorization. Methods using machine learning such as [8] train a model of reflectance and illumination edges from a training set to classify the edges of input images.

Some methods introduce one or more assumptions as priors for every input image. [9], [10] and [11] used a local assumption that reflectance is piece-wise constant while illumination is smooth. Another local assumption is that pixels having same(similar) chromaticity have the same(similar) reflectance locally. Methods using this assumption include [10], [12] and [13].

Global clues are also important to get high quality intrinsic images. [10] assume the global sparsity of reflectance color. [12] assume areas with same texture of chromaticity have same reflectance.[11] over-segment the input image and assume similar reflectance within every single segmentation.

Recently, some method, such as [2] and [13], introduced user interaction as prior and get better results. [14] uses a method very different from most other methods. It retains intrinsic images by retrieving the 3-D structure of the 2-D image. [15] designs an ingenuous approach to get a dataset of intrinsic images of 16 objects and they are widely used in many methods. We also use this dataset.

3 Our Approach

3.1 Overview

Our method mainly consists of two parts. The first part is an improvement of the assumption of the smoothness of illumination image and reflectance image. We add a weight to every pixel according to their gradient in the input image to control the probability of smoothness of every pixel distinguishingly. The second part tackle with the problem of hight inaccuracy of dark area. This problem is not taken into consideration in previous methods. We use an assumption based on the observation that pixels with the same color locate on the same color line[4]. Outliers are handled using over-segmentation. The two assumptions are local and global assumption respectively and we use them together to get impressive result.

In our approach, the images is processed in log domain. Denoting by I, R, L the logarithms of $\mathcal{I}, \mathcal{R}, \mathcal{L}$, Equation(1) turns into:

$$I = R + L \qquad (2)$$

3.2 Local Assumption of Weighted Smoothness

Smooth assumption can be implemented by minimizing the following energy term:

$$E_{Ls}(L) = \sum_{p \in I} \sum_{q \in N(p)} ||L(p) - L(q)|| \qquad (3)$$

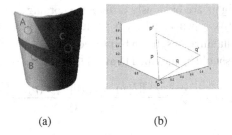

(a)   (b)

Fig. 1. Weight is influenced by edge and intensity

$N(p)$ denotes the four neighbours of pixel p.

Reflectance image has a similar property. For example, in Figure 1,reflectance gradients of points in area A are smooth. But in area B, gradients of points near the edge are not smooth. [9] constrains reflectance smoothness the same as illumination:

$$E_{Rs}(R) = \sum_{p\in I} \sum_{q\in N(p)} ||R(p) - R(q)|| \tag{4}$$

But the difference between edge and plain areas is not revealed in Equation(4).

[11] identify the edges by a method proposed by [15] and a different action is taken in edge areas. However, edges are identified in the first place so that any error in this step will lead to larger errors in following steps.

We consider improving this assumption by introducing weight into Equation(4). Weights of points in area A should be big to ensure the smoothness, while weights of points in area B should be small. We take the same action on illumination. A big weight in reflectance implies a small weight in illumination and vice versa.

Assume p and q are adjacent points, then $||L(p) - L(q)||$ is the illumination gradient and $||R(p) - R(q)||$ is the reflectance gradient. If $||I(p) - I(q)||$ is small, it is highly probable that the reflectance will be smooth. So a big weight is given to point p. On the contrary, if $||I(p) - I(q)||$ is big, weight of point p should be small. The weights of illumination are given contrary to reflectance weights. Then Equation(3) and Equation(4) are improved into:

$$E_{Ls}(L) = \sum_{p\in I} \sum_{q\in N(p)} c_1 * ||I(p) - I(q)|| \cdot ||L(p) - L(q)|| \tag{5}$$

$$E_{Rs}(R) = \sum_{p\in I} \sum_{q\in N(p)} c_2 * (maxw - ||I(p) - I(q)||) \cdot ||R(p) - R(q)|| \tag{6}$$

$maxw$ denotes $max_{i\in I, j\in N(p)}||I(i) - I(j)||$ to ensure the weights of reflectance are greater than 0. c_1 and c_2 are parameters to "stretch" the weight to a wide range.

However, the intensities of the same points in lightness and in darkness are different, so the weights of the same point will be different according to the equations above because the weight is determined by I. For example, in Figure 1(a), points near edge

B and edge C should have same weight of smoothness because they are the same edge actually, but the weights are obviously different according to Equation(5) and Equation(6). In Figure 1(b), a pair of adjacent points are drawn in the color RGB space under two different illuminations. It can be proved that $\frac{||I(p)-I(q)||}{||I(p)||} = \frac{||I(p')-I(q')||}{||I(p')||}$. So the equations above should be modified to avoid the influence of lighting condition.

$$E_{Ls}(L) = \sum_{p,q} \frac{c_1 \cdot ||I(p) - I(q)|| \cdot ||L(p) - L(q)||}{||I(p)||} \qquad (7)$$

$$E_{Rs}(R) = \sum_{p,q} \frac{c_2 \cdot (maxw - ||I(p) - I(q)||) \cdot ||R(p) - R(q)||}{||I(p)||} \qquad (8)$$

The assumption of weighted smoothness of illumination and reflectance can be used either independently or together with other assumptions, but it is recommended to use it with the global assumption we will propose in section 3.3.

3.3   Global Assumption Based on Color Line and Over-Segmentation

The chromaticity $C(p)$ of a pixel p is defined as follow:

$$C(p) = \frac{I(p)}{||I(p)||} \qquad (9)$$

Ideally, the three channels of color in original image and in reflectance image should be proportional. This is determined by Equation(1) and is used as hard constrain of most previous methods. However, as discovered in [4], this is not absolute due to inaccuracy or some other reasons. Usually, the difference is small and can't cause large error, but it can be seen from Equation(10) that, in the dark area of the image, small errors are enlarged because of a division to a small intensity value.

Inspired by [4], we use the color line found in I to constrain pixels in the image and allow pixels of dark area not follow Equation(2) strictly. In the first step, we use the method proposed in [4] to find color lines of the input image. Then, all points in the image are classified to the nearest color line. If the distances from a point to all found color lines are larger than a threshold, then we mark this point to be unclassified. The pixels belong to the same color line are considered to have the same color. That means, their reflectance values are close and the illuminations of every two points are proportional with the distance to the origin(not (0,0,0) but the origin determined by the color line we have just found). These are constrained by minimizing:

$$E_{Rl}(R) = \sum_{l} \sum_{p \in l} \sum_{q \in l} ||R(p) - R(q)|| \qquad (10)$$

$$E_{Ll}(L) = \sum_{l} \sum_{p \in l} \sum_{q \in l} ||L(p) - L(q) - (D(p) - D(q))|| \qquad (11)$$

where l denote every color line we found in the first step and $D(p)$ denotes the distance between p and the new origin. The new origin is the first intersection point of the line and three coordinate plane. As the number of pixels in an image is too large, it costs too much time calculating every two pixels. In fact, every two pixels are proportional means that all pixels are proportional, so we can calculate one pixel with all other pixels only. But in order to increase robustness, we use a set of pixels that appear frequently(i.e., have a high density in the RGB space) in the original image. The equations turn to be:

$$E_{Rl}(R) = \sum_{l} \sum_{p \in l} \sum_{q \in S(l)} ||R(p) - R(q)|| \tag{12}$$

$$E_{Ll}(L) = \sum_{l} \sum_{p \in l} \sum_{q \in S(l)} ||L(p) - L(q) - (D(p) - D(q))|| \tag{13}$$

where $S(l)$ denotes the small set of pixels which appear in input image frequently on color line l.

There may be some points which are classified to a line that is different from all surrounding points due to inaccuracy or anti-aliasing. To remove these outliers, we perform over-segmentation on the input image. Every segmentation is assigned to the color line which most pixels in this segmentation belong to.

Finally, Equation(2) is true in most bright area, but in dark areas, that equation may not be obeyed strictly. So we allow a little bias in those area. We use the energy term below:

$$E_{bias}(L, R) = \sum_{p \in I} w(p) \cdot ||L(p) + R(p) - I(p)|| \tag{14}$$

$w(p)$ is the weight controlling the error range. It can be designed diversely but we found the following simple function is sufficient in practice:

$$w(p) = \begin{cases} 0.001 & ||I(p)|| < th \\ 1 & otherwise \end{cases} \tag{15}$$

th is the threshold determining the dark area.

The final energy function we want to minimize is:

$$E(L, R) = w_1 \cdot E_{Ls}(L) + w_2 \cdot E_{Rs}(R) + w_3 \cdot E_{Ll}(L) + w_4 \cdot E_{Rl}(R) + E_{bias}(L, R) \tag{16}$$

w_1 to w_4 are weights controlling the importance of the four constrains respectively.

4   Result

We run our algorithm on the dataset of [15] so that the result can be compared with ground truth and other methods which also use this dataset. Figure 2 shows some images we used.

Figure 3 shows two results only using the weighted smoothness assumption. We can see that this assumption works well on images without large cast shadow. But because this assumption is flexible, it can easily combined with other assumptions to get better result which will be shown later.

Fig. 2. Original images

Fig. 3. Results with only weighted smoothness assumption

In Figure 4, we show that we solved the problem of high inaccuracy in dark area. In original image(Figure 4(a)), there is inaccuracy in dark area already, but it is so small that we can't identify it. However, it can be obviously seen that the dark area(right side) is different from light area(left part) in chromaticity image(Figure 4(b)) because it is enlarged by Equation(10). Previous methods such as [10] do not take this problem into consideration, so the dark area of their results(Figure 4(c)) is still hight inaccurate. Figure 4(d) is our result in which Equation(2) is constrained absolutely, so it has the similar problem with Figure 4(c). Figure 4(e) is our final result. We can see that the problem in dark area is perfectly solved.

Some results of Figure 2 are shown in Figure 5, and the parameters of them are shown in Table 1.

Since our algorithm bases on color lines, better result of color lines usually leads to better intrinsic images. In our experiments, all color lines are extracted automatically and they are good enough to get good intrinsic images. But it is possible that good color lines can't be extracted in complex images. In these cases, user can get color lines manually by assign arbitrary pixel to a color line.

Table 1. Parameters of results in Figure 5

image	w_1	w_2	w_3	w_4	c_1	c_2
cup	10	0.08	0.8	10	2	2
phone	1	0.008	8	5	5	5
sun	10	0.08	8	10	5	2

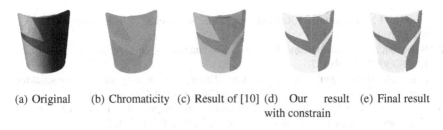

(a) Original   (b) Chromaticity (c) Result of [10] (d) Our   result (e) Final result
                                                     with constrain

Fig. 4. Solving the problem of inaccuracy in dark area

Fig. 5. Results

5   Conclusion

In this paper, we proposed a method to decompose an image into illumination and reflectance intrinsic images. First, our method improved the local assumption that illumination is smooth and reflectance is piecewise smooth by adding weights for every pixel. This improvement can be used in previous methods to replace their own smooth assumption to enhancing their performance. Moreover, we developed an global assumption according the observation that pixels of the similar reflectance in the input image appear on a same color line in the RGB space[4]. This assumption solved the problem that in dark area, the reflectance often deviate ground truth obviously, which are not considered in previous methods. The two assumptions are combined together to produce impressive results which show the effectiveness of out method.

References

1. Barrow, H., Tenenbaum, J.: Recovering intrinsic scene characteristics from images. Computer Vision Systems 1
2. Bousseau, A., Paris, S., Durand, F.: User-assisted intrinsic images. ACM Trans. Graph. 28(5), 130:1–130:10 (2009) 1, 2
3. Carroll, R., Ramamoorthi, R., Agrawala, M.: Illumination decomposition for material recoloring with consistent interreflections. In: SIGGRAPH 2011 (August 2011) 1
4. Omer, I., Werman, M.: Color lines: Image specific color representation. In: IEEE Conference on Computer Vision and Pattern Recognition, CVPR (2004) 1, 2, 4, 7
5. Weiss, Y.: Deriving intrinsic images from image sequences. In: ICCV, pp. 68–75 (2001) 2
6. Matsushita, Y., Lin, S., Kang, S.B., Shum, H.-Y.: Estimating Intrinsic Images from Image Sequences with Biased Illumination. In: Pajdla, T., Matas, J(G.) (eds.) ECCV 2004, Part II. LNCS, vol. 3022, pp. 274–286. Springer, Heidelberg (2004) 2
7. Liu, X., Wan, L., Qu, Y., Wong, T.-T., Lin, S., Leung, C.-S., Heng, P.-A.: Intrinsic colorization. ACM Transactions on Graphics (SIGGRAPH Asia 2008 Issue) 27(5), 152:1–152:9 (2008) 2
8. Bell, M., Freeman, W.T., Bell, M., Freeman, W.T.: Learning local evidence for shading and reflection. In: Proceedings of the IEEE International Conference on Computer Vision (2001) 2
9. Kimmel, R., Elad, M., Shaked, D., Keshet, R., Sobel, I.: A variational framework for retinex. International Journal of Computer Vision (2003) 2, 3
10. Shen, L., Yeo, C.: Intrinsic images decomposition using a local and global sparse representation of reflectance. In: CVPR, pp. 697–704. IEEE (2011) 2, 6, 7
11. Gehler, P.V., Rother, C., Kiefel, M., Zhang, L., Scholkopf, B.: Recovering intrinsic images with a global sparsity prior on reflectance. In: NIPS, pp. 765–773 (2011) 2, 3
12. Shen, L., Tan, P., Lin, S.: Intrinsic image decomposition with non-local texture cues. In: CVPR. IEEE Computer Society (2008) 2
13. Shen, J., Yang, X., Jia, Y., Li, X.: Intrinsic images using optimization. In: CVPR, pp. 3481–3487. IEEE (2011) 2
14. Sinha, P., Adelson, E.: Recovering reflectance and illumination in a world of painted polyhedra. In: Proc. 4th Int. Conf. on Comp. Vis., pp. 156–163 (1993) 2
15. Grosse, R., Johnson, M.K., Adelson, E.H., Freeman, W.T.: Ground-truth dataset and baseline evaluations for intrinsic image algorithms. In: International Conference on Computer Vision, pp. 2335–2342 (2009) 2, 3, 5

A Game-Theoretical Approach to Image Segmentation

Jing Li, Gang Zeng, Rui Gan, Hongbin Zha, and Long Wang

Key Laboratory of Machine Perception
Peking University, Beijing, 100871, China
{jing.lee,raygan,longwang}@pku.edu.cn,
g.zeng@ieee.org, zha@cis.pku.edu.cn

Abstract. This paper describes a novel algorithm for image segmentation within the framework of evolutionary game theory. Beyond the pairwise model, our objective function enables exploration on larger patches by introducing clique probability, and enforcing pixels within clique be assigned the same label. By combining the Public Goods Game, our algorithm can efficiently solve the multi-label segmentation problem. Experiments on challenging datasets demonstrate that our algorithm outperforms the state-of-art. We believe that this algorithm can be extended to many other labeling problems.

Keywords: segmentation, evolutionary game theory, Public Goods Game.

1 Introduction

In recent years, with the emergence of discrete optimization, many low-level computer vision problems, i.e., segmentation, are solved via energy minimization algorithms, such as graph cuts [1, 2], allowing us to perform approximate inference on graphical models, e.g., by maximizing a posterior probability on Markov Random Fields. Within this framework, one usually seeks the labeling L that minimizes the energy

$$E(L) = \sum_{p \in P} D_p(L_p) + \lambda \sum_{(p,q) \in N} V_{p,q}(L_p, L_q) \qquad (1)$$

Here, D_p measures individual label-preference of pixel p, and $V_{p,q}$ encourage spatial coherence by penalizing discontinuities between neighboring pixel pairs p and q. λ is a parameter controls strength of smoothness. Yet, the assumption that the energy is represented in terms of unary and pairwise potentials severely restricts the representational power of the model, as it is too local to capture rich statistics of natural scenes. More recently, solving energies with higher-order cliques [3–12] has received lots of attention. Although many methods have been proposed, the energy forms are simple and are within the framework of the pairwise model, which is far behind the need of effectively describing the underlying problem. Here we provide a new method to solve higher-order energy in the perspective of evolutionary game theory. Consider a m-label problem, with each pixel j in clique C be assigned a label $L_j \in \{1, ..., m\}$. Assume L^C represents label of clique C, we then define $p_k^C = p(L^C = L_k)$ the probability that clique C is assigned label L_k. More specifically, suppose the total number of pixels in

S.-M. Hu and R.R. Martin (Eds.): CVM 2012, LNCS 7633, pp. 33–42, 2012.

C is N, the number that pixels being labeled L_k is $p_k^C \cdot N$. In fact, our objective is to enforce pixels within each clique to take the same label, which is achieved by maximizing the total clique probability.

The Public Goods Game (PGG) [13] is a widely-used model describing an N-person game, which provide us a natural link between the higher-order clique with the group. In a typical PGG, up to N players can choose either to cooperate or defect. Cooperators each invest a certain amount c into the public good, whereas defectors do not contribute. The total contribution is then multiplied by an enhancement factor r and then equally distributed to all the players. Hence, each defector would get net benefit rkc/N providing k out of N players choose to cooperate, while that for cooperators should be reduced by the cost of contribution c. Simple reasoning tells us that an individual defecting ends up getting a higher payoff than cooperating in any given mixed group. However, each player gets the possibly maximal payoff had all players cooperated. The best choice for individual and that for the group conflicts with each other, giving rise to the dilemma. Previous work found that the underlying network topology can promote cooperation [14–16]. One rationale behind this phenomenon is that cooperators form clusters on graphs [17], thus they can easily spread their strategies to the surround, promoting and sustaining cooperation in the entire population. This explanation provides a new view to the task of image segmentation, where labels of pixels and strategies of players are connected, and each of the segmented part would correspond to one cluster of cooperators in a non-cooperative game.

A complete game includes the following four aspects, namely players, strategies, payoff function, and strategy updating rule. Generally speaking, players would choose the strategy that can maximize their own payoff. Simulation of a typical evolutionary procedure base on spatial PGG goes like this. For simplicity, we consider a population of size $h \times w$ on a regular lattice (Monte Carlo neighborhood), with each node locates an individual, and links represent possible interacting relationships. In spatial settings, each focal individual together with her direct neighbors defines a group and play one PGG. Initially, half proportion of the population is randomly assigned to be cooperators and the remaining defectors. Whenever playing PGG, an individual would participate in her own group, as well as each of the neighboring groups. The accumulated payoff for each player decides which strategy to choose in the next round following common practice that, individuals obtaining higher payoff are more likely to disseminate their strategies. The evolutionary process goes for a finite number of times until the fraction of cooperation in the population maintains stable.

Contributions of this paper includes:

- We propose a novel objective function to the problem of multi-label segmentation, which contains a higher-order clique term that is able to enforce pixels within each clique to take the same label.
- The proposed objective function can be solved via PGG with high efficiency .

The remainder of this paper is arranged as follows. Sec. 2 describes related work. And Sec. 3 presents details of the PGG-based segmentation algorithm. Experimental results and analysis are shown in Sec. 4. And concluding remarks are drawn in the end.

2   Related Work

Diversity has intensively studied on how to promote cooperation in PGG. Santos et al. [13] explored diversity by considering the limited resource one possesses. Wang et al. [18] studied diverse contribution in finite populations, and [19, 20], from another perspective, studied evolutionary dynamics on diverse distribution. However, Watts [21] argued that population structure is often more complex than a single graph can describe. Following this, Ohtsuki et al. [22] experimented the idea of two different graphs that players play games according to interaction graph, while the strategy updating is prescribed by replacement graph. More recently, Li et al. [23] proposed a selective investment scheme where the investment graph is dynamically changed. Our approach is more related to [23]. However, instead of imposing spatial selective investment, we here adopt selective investment among different graphs. Specifically, we propose to solve the an m-label segmentation problem via games played on m identical networks, with each pixel in the image denotes a player, and one player would simultaneously play m independent classical PGGs on each of the graphs. We define one graph a layer, so player i assigned label L_i would cooperate on the corresponding layer; she would also defect on all the other layers. Consequently, player i gets m payoffs at one time step, no matter what strategy she takes. When update, player i becomes cooperator on the layer with the highest payoff. In our model, diverse investment is also considered by combining color differences, which encourages segmentation boundaries be consistent with image edges.

3   PGG-Based Segmentation

We are now introducing the proposed PGG-based segmentation method. To make our approach clearer, we would first simplify the model without diverse distribution, which is in accordance with the traditional game of fair distribution. For an m-label segmentation problem, the input of our algorithm includes the image to be segmented, as well as m labeling preferences. The output is labeling of the input image.

Consider a population of constant size $h \times w$ locates on a 2D grid in the image coordinate. A regular graph with average degree $n \times n$ is employed to characterize the population structure. We define n the clique size. Thus the direct neighbors of player i consist of individuals locating on a $n \times n$ patch centered at i, with each $n \times n$ patch denotes a clique, or a group in the language of game theory. In this scenario, we would design m parallel games played on m separate layers, with each layer consisting the same population and spatial structure. Initially, each player on layer l is randomly assigned a strategy of whether cooperate or defect, where cooperation on layer l means the player is assigned label l. Whenever playing the game, player i would invest a certain amount to her direct neighbors, including herself, if she cooperates; otherwise for a free-rider of investing none.

In a classical PGG, each group benefits $(r-1)kc$, where k is the number of cooperators. One group would benefit more with more players cooperate (e.g. increasing k) for a fixed enhancement factor r. In our model, we define $q_{i,l}$ as the probability that clique C_i, which is centered at player i, of being labeled l. When $q_{i,l} = 1$, all players cooperate on layer l; and none for the case of $q_{i,l} = 0$. It is obvious that, in order to enforce pixels within C_i to take the same label, $q_{i,l}$ is expected to approach either 1 or 0. On the other hand, $q_{i,l} \to 1$ means more cooperators are involved, resulting in higher payoff for each clique. In this perspective, our objective can be expressed as maximization of the total group payoff

$$\max_L U = \sum_{C_i} \sum_{L_i} \varphi_{C_i}^{L_i} \tag{2}$$

Here U is the payoff of all players, and L is strategy distribution within the population. $\varphi_{C_i}^{L_i}$ is payoff of group C_i on layer L_i that

$$\varphi_{C_i}^{L_i} = (r - 1) \cdot q_{i,L_i} \sum_{j \in C_i} w_{j,i,L_i} \tag{3}$$

The amount w_{j,i,L_i} that cooperator j invests to neighbor i on layer L_i depends on the corresponding labeling preferences p_{j,L_i} from the input, as well as color difference to the investee, denoted as

$$w_{j,i,L_i} = p_{j,L_i}(\theta + e^{-\eta \|im_i - im_j\|_2}) \tag{4}$$

where im_i is color value of pixel i. The parameter η controls strength of intensity changes, and θ weights between individual label preference and the smoothness. This equation is analogous to the unary and smoothness term in pair-wise energy in graph cuts. And we could deduce that, after evolution, cooperators would form clusters around the corresponding salient regions with similar color.

In a non-cooperative game, players would make decisions independently to maximize their own payoff. So total group payoff in Eqn. 2 can in turn be approximated by maximizing the total accumulate payoff of each player i that

$$\max_L U = \sum_i \sum_{j \in c_i} \left\{ \frac{r \sum\limits_{k \in c_j, L_k = L_i} w_{k,j,L_k}}{N} - w_{i,j,L_i} \right\} \tag{5}$$

$L_k = L_i$ means player k cooperates on layer L_i in i's group. N is the group size. The significance behind this equation is that, the accumulate payoff for player i is derived from all her neighboring groups centered at $j \in C_i$, deducting her investment w_{i,j,L_i} to group j. On the right side of Eqn. 5, the first term is a clique term describing how the neighboring groups influence the focal player, and the second term is an unary term showing labeling preference of player i. Note that smoothness control is also included in our formulation described in Eqn. 4.

Eqn. 5 can be solved by maximizing the payoff of each player. We define payoff of player i being labeled l as

$$\pi_i^l = \max_l \sum_{j \in c_i} \left\{ \frac{r \sum\limits_{k \in c_j, L_k = l} w_{k,j,l}}{n} - w_{i,j,l} \right\} \tag{6}$$

This equation is used in the evolutionary process, where player i would choose to cooperate on the layer with the highest payoff.

In a more complex situation where distributing diversity is considered, the amount that group j allocates to player i is inverse proportional to the color difference between the corresponding pixels. In this way, players locating at salient regions with similar color are expected to get higher payoffs, and penalty is adopted on strong image edges. Thus, the payoff of player i is calculated as

$$\pi_i^l = \max_l \sum \{ \sum_{j \in c_i \quad k \in c_j, L_k = l} r \cdot s_{i,j} \cdot w_{k,j,l} - w_{i,j,l} \} \tag{7}$$

where

$$s_{i,j} = \frac{e^{-\eta|im_j - im_i|}}{\sum_{k \in c_j} e^{-\eta|im_j - im_k|}} \tag{8}$$

The color constraint on distribution is similar to that of diverse investment scheme. However, difference is that the investment represents individual behavior whereas distribution acts as group behavior. In experiment, we find that stronger color constraint on investment did better on locating segmentation boundaries at image edges. Note that when $\eta = 0$, this formulation degenerates to Eqn. 6 of fair distribution.

To optimize $\max_L U = \sum_i \pi_i^{L_i}$, the evolution goes like this. At each time step, players play the game on each of the m layers and get separate payoffs. When strategy update, player i learns to cooperate on layer k if the payoff is higher than that of the other layers. This new strategy is then used in the next round of the game. Eqn. 9 shows the updating rule of player i on layer l

$$S_i^l(t+1) = \begin{cases} C & \pi_i^l(t) > \pi_i^k(t), \forall k \neq l \\ D & otherwise \end{cases} \tag{9}$$

where $\pi_i^l(t)$ denotes the accumulate payoff at time step t, and $S_i^l(t+1)$ the strategy of player i on layer l in the next round. C, D are strategies of whether cooperate or defect. Finally, player i with strategy C is assigned label l. In the language of game theory, payoff denotes fitness of the strategy, thus, it is reasonable for strategies with higher payoff to survive. This procedure is repeated until the evolutionary stable state is reached. In our case, evolutionary stable state is defined that the proportion that players change their strategies below a threshold.

To better interpret our method, we show the metaphor in Tab. 1 revealing the connection between the classical energy function and our PGG-based objective function. In general, the underlying graph in the energy is a 4-neighbor regular lattice. The unary term provides information of label-preference of each pixel, and the binary term penalizes neighboring pixels of taking different labels. The clique term in the energy encourages pixels within clique take the same label. After optimization, each pixel is assigned a label under global minimum. On the contrary, for a PGG-based objective function, players play the game on a graph. In this paper, we consider a regular graph of average degree $n \times n$. Note that an energy minimization algorithm, i.e., graph cuts, can also optimize the function under such high-clustered graph. However, the spatial and

Table 1. Metaphor between pairwise energy and our PGG-based objective function

	PGG-based objective function	Energy function
Nodes	Players	Pixels
Edges	Direct neighbors	Direct neighbors
Label	Strategies	Pixel labels
Higher order	N-person PGG	Clique term
Objective	Maximum payoff	Minimum energy

temporal consumption is inconceivable, especially for images with high resolution. In our PGG-based method, each player plays with her $n \times n$ direct neighbors, including herself, so information of both label-preference and smoothness constraint is explored within a wider scope, which is superior compared with the 4-neighbor restrictions. As evolution on PGG explores how the strategy evolves, similarly, we are now studying how the labeling evolves during segmentation. So at evolutionary stable state, the strategy set is equal to the labeling set, which is obtained via maximize the total payoff. In fact, in our formulation, the higher order clique is not limited to a neighborhood of size $n \times n$. Because player i in group C_i would benefit not only from her direct $n \times n$ neighbors, but also from other neighboring groups centered at $j \in c_i$. So theoretically, player i can at most explore information in her $2n \times 2n$ neighborhood.

4   Experimental Results and Discussion

To test our algorithm, we implement it on the Berkeley Segmentation Dataset [24], where slight human interactions are needed. We also apply our proposed algorithm on urban scenes using Leuven dataset [25] and the Google Street View dataset [26]. In the

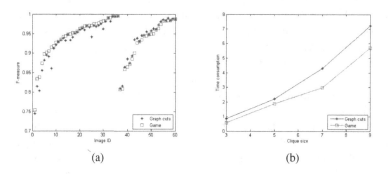

(a)   (b)

Fig. 1. (a) F-measure for each image. The red square shows performance of our method, and blue star for graph cuts with optimal $\lambda = 0.5$. (b) Time consumption versus increasing clique size. The red square shows performance of our method, and blue star for graph cuts.

latter case, we aim at segmenting the scene from geometric inconsistency base on vertical assumption. The labeling preference can be obtained using temporal projections from the simplified 3D model, and regions that defy the vertical assumption would result in strong color inconsistency. We also extend this work to 3-label segmentation, by introducing a reflective model. We tolerant a narrow band to distinguish reflective inconsistency from geometric inconsistency, based on the observation that geometric inconsistency can be eliminated when the accurate geometry is reached. Thus, for the 3-label case, we design to segment the scene from the background, geometric inconsistent objects under Lambertian assumption, and the reflective surfaces. Because of the limitation of color inconsistency on temporal projections, in our experiments, the dynamic regions and objects out of the narrow band are also considered to belong to reflective inconsistency category.

4.1 Quantitative Evaluation

For a quantitative evaluation of the proposed method, we use the Berkeley Segmentation Dataset [24] of up to 60 images, where human segmentation are used as ground truth. In graph cuts based segmentation, the parameter λ has great effect on the final results. So it may spend a significant amount of time for the user to search for the best segmentation with the most suitable parameter. In our experiment, we tested different λ and choose the one with the optimal performance (e.g. the highest average F-measure). Fig. 1(a) shows F-measure of each image, suggesting that our algorithm outperforms graph cuts over about $2/3$ of these images. And we would gain 0.28% of F-measure on average compared with graph cuts. Fig. 2 shows some of the segmentation results.

Fig. 2. Experimental results from the Berkeley Segmentation Dataset. Each colum displays one scene. The first row is the input image with user label, where red denotes foreground pixels and blue. The second row is the segmentation results using graph cuts, and our results are shown in the third row.

Table 2. Computational complexity

Image ID	GC, 3×3	PGG, 11×11	PGG (3-label), 11×11
Leuven 0300	43.492s	35.318s	41.235s
Leuven 1856	43.489s	57.991s	21.371s
Pittsburgh 09858	115.222s	121.384s	115.799s
Pittsburgh 13335	120.053s	84.177s	167.716s

Fig. 3. Experimental results. The first and second rows are from Leuven data set of images #0300 and #1856. The remaining rows are from Pittsburgh data set of images #09858 and #13335. The first column is the rectified input image. The following columns are results using graph cuts, PGG-based 2-label segmentation and PGG-based 3-label segmentation. The red regions are the segmented objects with geometric inconsistency, and the blue areas denotes reflective inconsistent regions.

All the experiments are done under clique size of 5. While graph cuts is superior on segmenting thin structures, we argue that our method can also achieve similar results if we set a smaller clique size. Experimentally, larger clique sizes would help smooth the segmentation result, while smaller ones may sensitive to noise. So the role of clique size is somehow similar to the smoothness control parameter λ in pair-wise energy.

For computational efficiency, Fig. 1(b) shows the average time (on both building the underlying graph and processing of the core algorithm) for different methods with increasing clique sizes. All of our experiments ran on an Intel(R) Core(TM)2 Duo CPU, with $3GB$ available RAM. And on average, our method is faster than graph cuts, while the acceleration is slower when clique size grows.

4.2 Extension on Urban Scenes

Fig. 3 shows our segmentation results on urban scenes. Compared with graph cuts, the PGG-based segmentation result is more like a segmentation from human drawing that the segmenting boundary is smoother and is more natural. Resolution of the input images are 288×360 for Leuven data set and 905×640 for Pittsburgh data set. Tab. 2 shows computational time of our method using 11×11 clique compared with graph cuts of 3×3 clique. While graph cuts can also be implemented using larger cliques, the temporal and spatial consumption is significant that a common machine cannot handle. From Tab. 2, our computing time on 11×11 clique is comparable to 3×3 clique of graph cuts.

5   Conclusion

In this paper we proposed a novel algorithm to segment the image within the framework of evolutionary game theory. Our optimization method can efficiently solve energies with higher order clique to the problem of multi-label segmentation via PGG. Given an image and the corresponding segmentation cues, our algorithm is able to do the segmentation efficiently. We tested our approach on several challenging scenes. Both quantitative and qualitative experiments show that our algorithm outperforms the state-of-art. And we believe this method is generic and can be used to solve many other labeling problems.

Acknowledgments. This work was supported by 973 Program (2011CB302202, 2012CB821203), NSFC (61005037, 90920304, 61020106005, 10972002).

References

1. Boykov, Y., Veksler, O., Zabih, R.: Fast approximate energy minimization via graph cuts. PAMI 23(11), 1222–1239 (2001) 1
2. Kolmogorov, V., Zabin, R.: What energy functions can be minimized via graph cuts? PAMI 26(2), 147–159 (2004) 1
3. Kohli, P., Kumar, M., Torr, P.: P3 & beyond: Solving energies with higher order cliques. In: CVPR, pp. 1–8. IEEE (2007) 1

4. Kohli, P., Ladicky, L., Torr, P.: Graph cuts for minimizing robust higher order potentials. In: CVPR (2008) 1

5. Kohli, P., Ladicky, L., Torr, P.: Robust higher order potentials for enforcing label consistency. IJCV 82(3), 302–324 (2009) 1

6. Rother, C., Kohli, P., Feng, W., Jia, J.: Minimizing sparse higher order energy functions of discrete variables. In: CVPR, pp. 1382–1389. IEEE (2009) 1

7. Tarlow, D., Givoni, I., Zemel, R.: Hopmap: Efficient message passing with high order potentials. In: AISTATS (2010) 1

8. Lan, X., Roth, S., Huttenlocher, D.P., Black, M.J.: Efficient Belief Propagation with Learned Higher-Order Markov Random Fields. In: Leonardis, A., Bischof, H., Pinz, A. (eds.) ECCV 2006, Part II. LNCS, vol. 3952, pp. 269–282. Springer, Heidelberg (2006) 1

9. Komodakis, N., Paragios, N.: Beyond pairwise energies: Efficient optimization for higher-order mrfs. In: CVPR, pp. 2985–2992. IEEE (2009) 1

10. Ladicky, L., Russell, C., Kohli, P., Torr, P.: Associative hierarchical crfs for object class image segmentation. In: ICCV, pp. 739–746. IEEE (2009) 1

11. Bleyer, M., Rother, C., Kohli, P.: Surface stereo with soft segmentation. In: CVPR, pp. 1570–1577. IEEE (2010) 1

12. Bleyer, M., Rother, C., Kohli, P., Scharstein, D., Sinha, S.: Object stereo - joint stereo matching and object segmentation. In: CVPR, pp. 3081–3088. IEEE (2011) 1

13. Santos, F., Santos, M., Pacheco, J.: Social diversity promotes the emergence of cooperation in public goods games. Nature 454(7201), 213–216 (2008) 2, 3

14. Lieberman, E., Hauert, C., Nowak, M.: Evolutionary dynamics on graphs. Nature 433, 312–316 (2005) 2

15. Santos, F., Pacheco, J.: Scale-free networks provide a unifying framework for the emergence of cooperation. PRL 95, 98104 (2005) 2

16. Santos, F., Pacheco, J., Lenaerts, T.: Evolutionary dynamics of social dilemmas in structured heterogeneous populations. PNAS 103, 3490 (2006) 2

17. Rong, Z., Yang, H., Wang, W.: Feedback reciprocity mechanism promotes the cooperation of highly clustered scale-free networks. PRE 82, 047101 (2010) 2

18. Wang, J., Wu, B., Chen, X., Wang, L.: Evolutionary dynamics of public goods games with diverse contributions in finite populations. PRE 81(5), 056103 (2010) 3

19. Zhong, L., Chen, B., Huang, C.: Networking effects on public goods game with unequal allocation. In: ICNC, vol. 1, pp. 217–221. IEEE (2008) 3

20. Peng, D., Yang, H., Wang, W., Chen, G., Wang, B.: Promotion of cooperation induced by nonuniform payoff allocation in spatial public goods game. EPJ B 73(3), 455–459 (2010) 3

21. Watts, D.: A twenty-first century science. Nature 445(7127), 489–489 (2007) 3

22. Ohtsuki, H., Nowak, M., Pacheco, J.: Breaking the symmetry between interaction and replacement in evolutionary dynamics on graphs. PRL 98(10), 108106 (2007) 3

23. Li, J., Wu, T., Zeng, G., Wang, L.: Selective investment promotes cooperation in public goods game. Physica A (2012) 3

24. Alpert, S., Galun, M., Basri, R., Brandt, A.: Image segmentation by probabilistic bottom-up aggregation and cue integration. In: CVPR (June 2007) 6, 7

25. Leibe, B., Cornelis, N., Cornelis, K., Van Gool, L.: Dynamic 3d scene analysis from a moving vehicle. In: CVPR, pp. 1–8. IEEE (2007) 6

26. Google street view, https://maps.google.com/ 6

Clothed and Naked Human Shapes Estimation from a Single Image

Yu Guo, Xiaowu Chen*, Bin Zhou, and Qinping Zhao

State Key Laboratory of Virtual Reality Technology and Systems
School of Computer Science and Engineering, Beihang University, Beijing, P.R. China
{guoyu,chen,zhoubin,zhaoqp}@vrlab.buaa.edu.cn

Abstract. This paper presents a novel method to simultaneously estimate the clothed and naked 3D shapes of a person. The method needs only a single photograph of a person wearing clothing. Firstly, we learn a deformable model of human clothed body shapes from a database. Then, given an input image, the deformable model is initialized with a few user-specified 2D joints and contours of the person. And the correspondence between 3D shape and 2D contours is established automatically. Finally, we optimize the parameters of the deformable model in an iterative way, and then obtain the clothed and naked 3D shapes of the person simultaneously. The experimental results on real images demonstrate the effectiveness of our method.

Keywords: human shape, deformable model, shape-from-contours.

1 Introduction

We address the problem of estimating a person's detailed 3D shape from a single image of that person wearing clothing. In this case, both the clothed and naked human shapes can serve the task of computer graphics and vision. However, most existing techniques on human shape estimation rely on multi-view images, and are insufficient and difficult to constrain a 3D body shape from a single image. Although some methods study the problem of estimating detailed body shape from a single image, they are not meant to deal with clothing, but mainly naked or minimally dressed humans.

Therefore, a practical method must recover a representation spanning variation in subject shape, pose and clothing. So we exploit a parametric deformable 3D shape model. This work is based on the SCAPE model, characterizing human body shape using a low-dimensional shape subspace learned from range scans of humans. The parameters of SCAPE can be directly estimated from contours but has been restricted to people wearing tight-fitting clothing. In the case of the clothed person, the exploited model must be sensitive to clothing which obscures the naked human shape.

Hence, beyond previous work we construct a database spanning variation of 70 poses[2], 111 subjects (56 men and 55 women)[9] and 7 kinds of clothes. The

---

* Corresponding author.

S.-M. Hu and R.R. Martin (Eds.): CVM 2012, LNCS 7633, pp. 43–50, 2012.
© Springer-Verlag Berlin Heidelberg 2012

exploited model is learned from this database, derived by the non-rigid surface deformation, and consists of various low-dimension parameters.

Central to our method is a learned human shape model. Given an input image and the user-specified clothing type, the parameters of the model are initialized and optimized with a few given 2D joints and contours of the person. Then the clothed and naked 3D shapes of the person can be obtained simultaneously.

In summary, the main contributions of our proposed method include: simultaneously estimating the clothed and naked 3D shapes of a person from a single image, and learning a deformable clothed human shape model consisted of low-dimension parameters.

2   Related Work

Pose from Monocular Images. Several researchers explore various data-driven methods[6] to reduce the pose ambiguity, and these methods work well only for a small amount of training data. Recently, Wei and Chai[13] combine the user's inputs with the prior embedded in millions of pre-recorded human poses, which enables a naive user to pose a 3D full-body character quickly and easily. We follow this method to initialize the pose estimation for our method.

3D Deformable Human Body Models. Human-specific models[1,2,9,8,5] are strong prior in many methods, and can be used to estimate body shapes from images or videos[11,7,4,8,5,3]. Among most human body models, variations in body shape and pose are explained by parameters. Then new shapes or poses can be generated with specific parameters. The well-know SCAPE model[2] encodes these two variation in uncorrelated parameters. We extend this method to clothing-related variation for fitting the contours of clothed people.

Body Shape from Images. Guan et al.[7] present the first solution to estimate pose and body shape from a single image. Kraevoy et al.[10] present a shape-from-contour method for general 3D shapes by fitting a given template to the contours in an iterative way. These two solutions both focus on naked or minimally clothed people.

Chen et al.[5] infer the detailed 3D shape from a single contour using a probabilistic generative model. They model the pose variation and shape variation from 3D meshes in an unsupervised way. Meanwhile, Leonid et al.[11] predict body shape and pose by training a mixture of experts model which directly maps the parameters of SCAPE model to contours. In both methods, the estimated shapes don't fit the contours well with inaccurate poses. Bălan and Black[4] estimate the detailed 3D body shape of clothed people with multi-view images, combining constraints among pose to recover the body shape under clothing.

3   Overview

We present a clothed human shape model to fit the contours of the target person, and simultaneously estimate both clothed and naked human shapes from a single

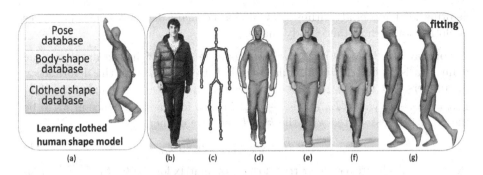

Fig. 1. Pipeline of our method. We first learn a deformable clothed human model from three kinds of 3D shape database in (a). Given an input image (b), initial pose (c) and contours (d) of the target person are estimated in semi-automatic way. We use the deformable model to fit the contours and get a pair of 3D human shapes (e)(f)(g) of the target person. (e) and (f) are the clothed and naked human shapes, respectively. (g) is another view of (e) and (f).

image with moderate amount of user inputs. The Pipeline of our method is given in Figure 1. Our method includes a learning phase and a fitting phase: in the learning phase, we extend the SCAPE method[2] and learn a deformable clothed human model from three types of 3D body database. The model is derived by the non-rigid surface deformation, and consists of 3 kinds of control parameters, including pose, body shape and clothes type. In the fitting phase, we estimate the optimal parameters and generate a clothed shape which matches the contours well. Meanwhile, a naked shape is created with only the pose and body shape parameters.

4   Learning the Deformable Model

We extend the SCAPE[2] and learn a deformable clothed human body model from three types of 3D shape database. Following the same phase of SCAPE, our method learns the non-rigid pose-dependent and body-shape-dependent deformation parameters. Then, we learn the clothing-related parameters for different kinds of clothes. The learned model can be deformed in pose, body shape and clothing type with corresponding control parameters: θ, β and γ.

Training Database. The training data for SCAPE includes a pose database containing 70 poses of one person, and a body shape database containing 111 people in a similar pose. A canonical standing pose is chosen to be the template mesh T, and all other meshes are brought into full correspondence with the template mesh using a mesh registration technique[2].

Furthermore, we expand the original training data with clothed human shape database. For each type of clothes, we select a pair of high-quality human models $\{P_{naked}, P_{clothed}\}$ as reference from POSER. Each mesh M_{naked} in the body shape database is aligned with P_{naked} and deformed to $M_{clothed}$ using the deformation transfer algorithm[12]. Our clothed shape database contains 7 types of clothes for each instance body shape.

Deformation Processing. Given an instance mesh M in the database, the main idea is to deform the template mesh T to M and learn the deformation parameters. Let $v_{k,1}$, $v_{k,2}$, $v_{k,3}$ be the vertices of the $k-th$ triangle face of T, $E_{k,j} = v_{k,j} - v_{k,1}$, and $\widetilde{E}_{k,j} = \widetilde{v}_{k,j} - \widetilde{v}_{k,1}, j = 2, 3$ for the $k-th$ face in M, $\mathbf{b}$ be the body part associated with the $k-th$ face, we define:

$$\widetilde{E}_{k,j} = R_b * C_k * S_k * Q_k * E_{k,j} \tag{1}$$

where C_k, S_k, Q_k are $3*3$ liner transformation matrix for the $k-th$ triangle, representing clothing-related deformation, body-shape-dependent deformation and pose-dependent deformation separately. R_b is the $3*3$ rotation matrix of the body part $\mathbf{b}$. We learn Q_k and S_k and extract associated parameters $\{\alpha, U, \mu\}$ for pose-dependent deformation function $\mathbb{Q}_\alpha(\theta)$ and body-shape-dependent deformation function $\mathbb{S}_{U,\mu}(\beta)$ using the same techniques as Anguelov et al. did. We refer the readers to[2] for further details.

Clothing-Related Deformation Learning. We learn a set of coefficients for each type of clothes in the database. Given an instance mesh M with clothes type γ, we extract the clothing-related deformation C by solving:

$$\underset{C}{argmin} \sum_{k=1}^{N_k} \sum_{j=2}^{3} \left\| R_k C_k S_k Q_k E_{k,j} - \widetilde{E}_{k,j} \right\|^2 \tag{2}$$

where $E_{k,j}$ are edges of the template mesh, and $\widetilde{E}_{k,j}$ are the corresponding edges of the instance mesh M. The body-shape deformation S is already obtained since M has a corresponding naked shape in the shape database. Meanwhile, the absolute rotation matrix of the template and the T-pose are also known values, which determine Q and R. Therefore, this problem can be solved by using a straightforward least-squares optimization.

To simplify the fitting phase, we assume that the clothing deformation is only related with body shape for specific clothes type γ. To predict the transformation matrices C_k as a function of (β, γ), we learn a regression function $\mathbb{C}_{\eta,\mu}^k(\beta, \gamma)$ for each triangle. The regression coefficients are learned by solving:

$$\eta_k^* = \underset{\eta_k}{argmin} \sum_{i=1}^{N} \left\| \eta_k \beta^i + \phi_k - \overline{C_k^i} \right\| \tag{3}$$

where C_k^i is the $k-th$ clothing-related transformation matrix of the $i-th$ instance mesh in the clothed shape database, $\overline{C_k^i}$ is the vector form of C_k^i, β_k is a $9 * length(\beta)$ vector, β^i is the body shape parameters of the corresponding mesh in the body shape database, ϕ_k is mean value of the vector $\overline{C_k^i}$ over the N instances mesh with γ. Given a new β, C_k can be predicted as the matrix form of $\eta_k \beta + \phi_k$.

So far, given a set of parameters (θ, β, γ), we can create a 3D clothed shape mesh efficiently.

5   Model Fitting

Given an input image of a subject wearing clothing, a pair of 3D human shapes $\{M_{clothed}, M_{naked}\}$ can be estimated for the subject by model fitting. We get the initial parameters $(\theta, \beta, \gamma)^0$ of the deformable model semi-automatically: a 3D initial pose θ^0 is recovered with the state-of-the-art IK algorithm[13], β^0 is set to the mean body shape, and the clothes type is chosen by the user. We follow the foreground segmentation of[7], and perform pose fitting and body-shape fitting iteratively to get the optimal parameters $(\theta, \beta)^*$ automatically. Finally, we generate a pair of estimated models $\{M_{clothed}, M_{naked}\}$ for further deformation.

5.1   Pose Fitting

Given the parameters $(\theta, \beta, \gamma)^i$, we generate a clothed 3D human shape M and update θ^i while fixing other parameters. The updating strategy includes two steps. Firstly, the optimal correspondence set $\{(c_p, v_p)|p = 1...Np\}$ between the image contours and the vertexes of M are determined, where c_p is a 2D point on the contours, and v_p is a 3D vertex of M. We follow the HMM base matching algorithm of[10], and use distance, normal vector and continuity as matching cues. However, we restrict that v_p should be a visible "edge vertex" which has at least one invisible neighbour vertex. Secondly, we update the pose parameters $R(\theta)$ to encourage a small distance between c_p and v_p. To avoid non-liner rotation operations, we use the standard approximation $R^{i+1} \approx (I + \widehat{t})R^i$, where $\widehat{t}$ is the skew matrix of twist t with small values.

Since we know the matrices R, C, S and Q, vertexes V of the target mesh are linearly dependent with twist t, and we can find the optimal t^* efficiently by solving:

$$\underset{t}{argmin} \sum_{p=1}^{N_p} \|c_p - F(v_p)\|^2 + w_t \|t\|^2$$

$$s.t. \ V^* = \underset{V}{argmin} \sum \left\|(I + \widehat{t})RCSQE_{k,j} - \widetilde{E}_{k,j}\right\|^2$$

(4)

where $F(\cdot)$ projects the 3D vertexes onto a 2D image point in a weak projection model, the term $\sum_{p=1}^{N_p} \|c_p - F(v_p)\|^2$ encourages a small distances between the corresponding points, the term $\|t\|^2$ penalizes large change of limb rotation, and $w_t = 1$ in all our experiments. Then we update $R^{i+1} = t_m R^i$, where t_m is the matrix form of t, and update pose-dependent matrices Q with R^{i+1}.

5.2   Shape Fitting

We keep (θ, γ) unchanged and update the shape parameters β. We follow the same matching step in pose fitting processing to get a new correspondence set and optimizing β by solving:

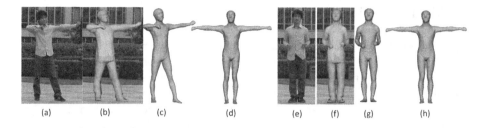

Fig. 2. Our fitting method is robust for various poses. (a)(e) Input image. (b)(f) Clothed shapes overlay. (c)(g) Estimated naked shapes. (d)(h) Naked shapes in T pose. Note the estimated body shapes are coincident with each other.

$$argmin_{\beta} \sum_{p=1}^{N_p} \|c_p - F(v_p)\|^2 + w_\beta \|\beta\|^2 \tag{5}$$

$$s.t. \quad V^* = argmin_{V} \sum \left\| R\mathbb{C}(\beta,\gamma)\mathbb{S}(\beta)QE_{k,j} - \widetilde{E}_{k,j} \right\|^2$$

where $w_\beta = 0.01$, $\mathbb{C}(\beta,\gamma)$ and $\mathbb{S}(\beta)$ are regression functions learned in previous section. We drop out the term $\mathbb{C}(\beta,\gamma)$ in the first iteration to get a good initial guess for β, thus vertexes V are linearly dependent on β and the problem can be solved efficiently. Then we run the optimization with the Levenberg-Marquardt algorithm. The optimization converges quickly due to a good initial guess.

We repeat the pose fitting step and shape fitting step until the residual error is smaller than a fixed threshold. Typically the fitting phase converges in several iterations.

6   Experimental Results

In this section the performance of our method have been evaluated in a number of experiments. We use the proposed method to estimate clothed and naked shapes for each input image, which come from the internet and hand-held cameras. All the experiments are done on a 3.0 GHz Intel Core 2 Duo with 2 GB RAM. Typical initialization step needs about 5 minutes for a user to click joint positions and assist the segmentation. The optimization step takes about 1 minute for each input image.

The difference between contours of heavily clothed subject and the real body shape presents challenges for body shape estimation. Our method benefits a lot from the clothing template and gives a pair of reasonable estimated models (as shown in Figure 1).

Figure 2 shows that our method is robust to different poses. Given two input images of the same person in different poses, we estimate two pairs of models separately. The naked shapes are placed in T pose for comparison and we rescale them to match the actual height of the subject. We find that the estimated naked shapes are coincident with each other. The mean distance of corresponding vertexes is 0.67 cm, and the arm span difference is 0.93 cm.

In Figure 3, we present an application to change clothes of the estimated subject. The pair of body shapes are estimated from the input monocular image at first, then we simply change the clothing-related parameters while fixing the parameters of body shape and pose. New models are created for each kind of clothes while the original pose and body shape are kept. All the models also can be used for animation.

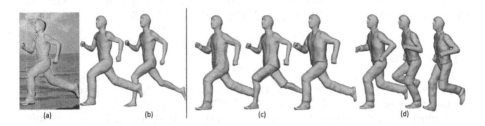

Fig. 3. Changing clothes and animation. (a) Input image with clothed shape overlay. (b) Clothed and naked shapes. (c) Redressed shapes of the subject. (d) Redressed shapes in new poses.

Figure 4 presents the results estimated from a monocular image with our method and straightforward SCAPE model. Note how well our estimated clothed shape matchs the target person, and the straightforward result is much fatter than the desired body shape for the clothing reason.

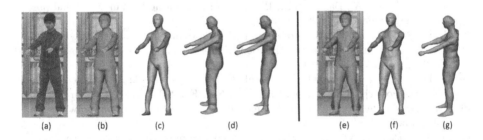

Fig. 4. Comparison with straightforward solution using SCAPE model. (a) Input image. (b) Input image overlaid by the our estimated clothed shape. (c) Estimated naked body shape. (d) Another view of clothed shape and naked shape. (e) Input image overlaid by the SCAPE model in (f). (g) Another view of (f).

7   Conclusions and Future Work

We present a novel method to simultaneously estimate 3D clothed and naked human shapes from a single image. The key of our method is to learn the clothing-related deformation for variation of body shapes. A characteristic of our method is that the estimated clothed shape matches the subject very well, even for a heavily dressed subject. Our experiments show that the method can estimate both the clothed and naked human shapes of dressed subject, and is robust to pose difference. In future work, we aim to extend our method to video, which promises to impose a set of new challenges.

Acknowledgements. This work was partially supported by NSFC (60933006), 863 Program(2012AA 011504 & 2012AA02A606), and ITER (2012GB102008).

References

1. Allen, B., Curless, B., Popović, Z.: The space of human body shapes: reconstruction and parameterization from range scans. In: SIGGRAPH, pp. 587–594 (2003)
2. Anguelov, D., Srinivasan, P., Koller, D., Thrun, S., Rodgers, J., Davis, J.: Scape: shape completion and animation of people. ACM TOG 24(3), 408–416 (2005)
3. Balan, A.O., Sigal, L., Black, M.J., Davis, J.E., Haussecker, H.W.: Detailed human shape and pose from images. In: CVPR (2007)
4. Bălan, A.O., Black, M.J.: The Naked Truth: Estimating Body Shape Under Clothing. In: Forsyth, D., Torr, P., Zisserman, A. (eds.) ECCV 2008, Part II. LNCS, vol. 5303, pp. 15–29. Springer, Heidelberg (2008)
5. Chen, Y., Kim, T.-K., Cipolla, R.: Inferring 3D Shapes and Deformations from Single Views. In: Daniilidis, K., Maragos, P., Paragios, N. (eds.) ECCV 2010, Part III. LNCS, vol. 6313, pp. 300–313. Springer, Heidelberg (2010)
6. Grochow, K., Martin, S.L., Hertzmann, A., Popović, Z.: Style-based inverse kinematics. In: SIGGRAPH, pp. 522–531 (2004)
7. Guan, P., Weiss, A., Bălan, A.O., Black, M.J.: Estimating human shape and pose from a single image. In: ICCV (2009)
8. Hasler, N., Ackermann, H., Rosenhahn, B., Thormählen, T., Seidel, H.-P.: Multilinear pose and body shape estimation of dressed subjects from image sets. In: CVPR, pp. 1823–1830 (2010)
9. Hasler, N., Stoll, C., Sunkel, M., Rosenhahn, B., Seidel, H.-P.: A statistical model of human pose and body shape. In: CGF (Proc. EG 2008), vol. 2 (March 2009)
10. Kraevoy, V., Sheffer, A., van de Panne, M.: Modeling from contour drawings. In: SBIM, pp. 37–44 (2009)
11. Sigal, L., Balan, A.O., Black, M.J.: Combined discriminative and generative articulated pose and non-rigid shape estimation. In: NIPS (2007)
12. Sumner, R.W., Popović, J.: Deformation transfer for triangle meshes. ACM TOG 23(3), 399–405 (2004)
13. Wei, X., Chai, J.: Intuitive interactive human-character posing with millions of example poses. IEEE Comput. Graph. Appl. 31(4), 78–88 (2011)

Image Colorization with an Affective Word

Xiaohui Wang, Jia Jia, Hanyu Liao, and Lianhong Cai

Key Laboratory of Pervasive Computing, Ministry of Education
Tsinghua National Laboratory for Information Science and Technology (TNList)
Department of Computer Science and Technology, Tsinghua University
wangxh09@mails.tsinghua.edu.cn,
{jjia,clh-dcs}@tsinghua.edu.cn, liaoliao1992@gmail.com

Abstract. An important role of image color is the conveyer of emotions (through color themes). The colorization is less useful with an undesired color theme, even semantically correct, which has been rarely considered previously. In this paper, we propose a complete system for the image colorization with an affective word. We only need users to assist object segmentation along with text labels and give an affective word. First, the text labels along with other object characters are jointly used to filter the internet images to give each object a set of semantically correct reference images. Second, we select a set of color themes according to the affective word based on art theories. With these themes, a generic algorithm is adopted to select the best reference for each object. Finally, we propose a hybrid texture synthesis approach to colorize each object. Our experiments show that the results of our system have both the correct semantics and the desired emotions.

Keywords: Image colorization, affective word, color theme.

1 Introduction

Color can enhance the rich expressive force of an image. A wonderful colorization not only gives a grayscale image good visual sense, but also endows it with much richer semantic meaning. The interaction based colorization method need users to manually specify scribbles and their colors [1]. To reduce this manual labor, some works focus on example based colorization which uses an existing color image for colorization [2–5]. However, these methods need a reliable reference image with both the similar contents and the same style for transfer. Sometimes choosing such a reference image is not an easy task. To avoid this problem, Chia et al. introduced a nice system to semantically colorize an image recently [6]. Using a semantic label, it automatically selects the most suitable references from the Internet. This approach provides a more friendly interface for non-experienced users, as it does not need to manually choose a proper reference.

The image color is the main conveyer of emotions through the color themes (templates of colors), which is convinced by various psychological studies [7–9]. Images with the same contents and the different color themes may have totally different emotions. So a proper colorization can also give the images much richer emotions. And the colorization with an undesired color theme is less useful, even if it is semantically correct. However, all the above methods do not consider the emotional aspect of colorization. Although semantically correct results may be produced by utilizing the internet

S.-M. Hu and R.R. Martin (Eds.): CVM 2012, LNCS 7633, pp. 51–58, 2012.

images [6], these results could not be affective enough, especially when the user wants a precise control on the target emotion. Semantic and richly affective colorization results can much better express the artistic conception and greatly improve the visual quality.

In this paper, we propose a novel framework to affectively colorize a grayscale image with consideration of the semantics at the same time. As far as we know, it is the first colorization system which considers both the semantics and the affective aspect. The input is a grayscale image and an affective word. Based on the art theories, we adopt the *image-scale* space to build the relation between affective words and color themes. For each object in the input image, a set of the internet images is downloaded and filtered. We propose a selection method based on the generic algorithm to efficiently select the semantically suitable reference images which also meets the desired emotion. We also offer a patch match based approach for the object level colorization.

2   Related Work

We have reviewed the work related to our colorization framework, which includes the colorization and the color composition in art theories.

2.1   Colorization

Colorization methods can be divided into interaction based methods and example based methods. Interaction based methods need users to give some colored scribbles on the grayscale image, and colors are automatically propagated to the remain pixels based on local similarities to complete the colorization process [1]. Since the users need considerable interactions, it is hard for non-professionals to select proper colors and draw approximate scribbles. Example based colorization methods usually do not require user interactions. Using some color images, these methods automatically colorize a given grayscale image [10, 2]. Recent methods borrow the ideas from machine learning to predict the correspondences between the reference color image and the input grayscale image [5, 4]. All these methods require users to find reference images with similar contents and appropriate appearance, which is usually a difficult task.

With the rapid development of the Internet, data driven processing is attracting more attentions than before. To find the suitable reference images, Chia et al. [6] proposed to filter the internet images, which shared the similar framework as Sketch2Photo [11]. This method is a nice supplementary for the example based colorization, and can also be used as a preprocessing step of these methods. However, it ignores the emotional appearance aspect when filtering, which is the main consideration in this paper.

2.2   Color Composition in the Art Theories

Color composition is the color distribution of an image and the key element for the artistic feeling [7]. Artists often use a set of colors called a *color theme* to represent the color composition. The most commonly used color themes are 3-color themes and 5-color themes, which are templates of three and five colors respectively. The rational study of color themes is a hot field in computer vision and graphics recently. Daniel

Cohen-Or et al. applied the existing aesthetical color harmony models to harmonize images [12]. P. O'Donovan et al. studied the color compatibility of 5-color themes from large datasets [13]. However, the emotional aspect of color themes is often ignored.

Kobayashi systematicly studied the relationship between color themes and emotions based on the psychophysical investigations [8, 9], which has already been successfully used in graphic design. In [8], it maps 1,170 3-color themes to 180 affective words, such as romantic, elegant, etc. Furthermore, the relation between 490 5-color themes and 180 affective words is built in [9]. An affective space called *image-scale* is used in [8, 9] to quantitatively describe the emotions. The space has two dimensions including *warm-cool* and *hard-soft*. Fig.1 illustrates a few examples of color themes and the corresponding affective words in this space.

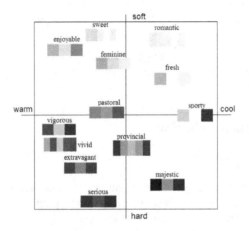

Fig. 1. Examples of color themes and the corresponding affective words in the *image-scale* space

3 Overview

The overall pipeline of our system is illustrated in Fig.2. The input is a grayscale image and an affective word which is used to express the emotion, such as romantic, intense, serious, etc. (a). The grayscale image is first semi-automatically segmented into objects by a graphcut based segmentation technique [14]. The user labels each object with a text label by which we download and filter a set of images from the Internet, and each object is given a set of candidate references (b). According to the affective word, a set of color themes are selected from a database built using on-line communities by means of the *image-scale* space (c). To select the best reference for each object, we design a hybrid energy function to balance various requirements mainly including the similarity between the references and the input objects as well as the conformity of the references with the candidate color themes. And a generic algorithm is adopted to optimize the energy (d). Finally, we use a patch match based approach (a hybrid texture synthesize) for object-level colorization to get the final result (e).

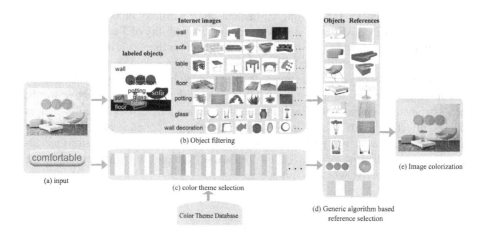

Fig. 2. Pipeline

4   Reference Image Selection

4.1   Object Filtering

To start our framework, we rely on a semi-automatic approach to segment the input grayscale image into multiple objects. The user roughly gives strokes to specify the objects, and a graphcut based segmentation [14, 15] is used to finally segment the image. To fully utilize the internet images, each object is manually labeled by a semantic text.

We first download a large set of pictures (about 500-1000) from the Internet such as Google Image Search and Flickr for each label. The salient region is automatically extracted from each downloaded image by applying the method called global contrast based salient region detection [16]. Then as same as the contour consistency filtering in [11], we select the images whose salient regions are similar to the outer contour of the grayscale image object with shape context descriptors [17]. In addition, we allow for the shape deformation. The shape context matching cost and the affine registration are summed up to get the overall score. This score is used to rank the extracted salient regions, and the top $50 - 100$ objects are retained for further reference image selection (Section 4.3).

4.2   Color Theme Selection

Color Theme Database Construction. We construct a color theme database with 400,000 color themes. Each color theme t_i is labeled with an affective vector $a_i = (wc_i, hs_i)$ in the image-scale space, where wc_i and hs_i are the values of the warm-cool axis and the hard-soft axis respectively. For details on the affective word-color theme relationship modeling, readers can refer to our recent work [18].

For each input affective word, it is first automatically labeled with an affective vector. If the word is in the set of the 180 words [8], it has the affective vector. If not, we calculate the semantic similarities between it and the 180 words by the HowNet knowledge system [19], which is a bilingual general knowledge database describing the relations between concepts and attributes. The affective vector of the word is the weighted average value of M ($M = 5$) most similar words. N_T ($N_T = 100$ in our experiments) candidate color themes nearest to the affective vector are selected.

4.3   Generic Algorithm Based Reference Image Selection

Even with the above rough filtering, choosing the appropriate reference images is still a difficult problem. Generic algorithm is adopted to select the most approximate reference image for each object. Here we call a set of all these object-reference correspondences a solution. Formally, the problem can be formalized as follows: There is a set of objects $O = \{o_1, o_2, ...o_n\}$, and each object o_i has a set of candidate reference images $R_i = \{r_{i,1}, r_{i,2}, ..., r_{i,t_i}\}$. In order to achieve an optimized solution $f : o_i \rightarrow R_i, i = 1, 2, ...n$, we design a comprehensive energy G measuring the suitability of the solution, and the goal is to calculate $argmin_f G(f)$.

The energy function considers the consistency with both the original input grayscale image and the given emotion. To formalize the energy, we rewrite it as

$$G(s) = G_s(s) + G_a(s) \tag{1}$$

where $G_s(s) = \sum_i E_s(o_i, r_i)$, $s = \{r_1, r_2, ..., r_n\}$ is a solution. E_s is an energy measuring the suitability of a single object-reference pair, and $G_a(s)$ measures the affective suitability of a solution.

$$E_s = \theta_1 E_{ss} + \theta_2 E_{sh} + \theta_3 E_{sc} \tag{2}$$

where E_{ss} is the shape context matching cost which is calculated in the object filtering (Section 4.1). E_{sh} is the histogram matching cost which is defined as the distance between the two histograms. E_{sc} measures the consistency between the color theme extracted from the reference image and the candidate color themes (refer to Equation 3). θ_1, θ_2 and θ_3 are used to balance the above factors. In our experiments, θ_2, θ_3 are usually set to 1. If the object is semantic sensitive (eg. orange, horse, etc.), θ_1 can be set to 1. On the other hand, for the objects such as sofa/furniture which are semantic insensitive, θ_1 can be set smaller, e.g. $[0.1, 0.2]$.

$G_a(s)$ is the affective suitability measurement which is the consistency between the color theme of the solution and the candidates, and is defined as

$$G_a(s) = \mathscr{D} \min_{i=1}^{M} D(theme_o, theme_i) \tag{3}$$

where $\mathscr{D}$ is a constant to normalize G_a to $[0, 1]$. $theme_i = \{c_1^i, c_2^i, ..., c_m^i\}$ is one of the M candidate themes where c_j^is are colors in the HSV color space and $theme_o$ is the theme extracted from the colorized image using K-means. $D(\cdot, \cdot)$ is the distance between two themes, which is defined as

$$D(theme_1, theme_2) = \min_{p \in P} \sum_{i=1}^{m} d(c_{p(i)}^1, c_i^2) \qquad (4)$$

where P is the set of permutations of $1, 2, \dots m$ and $d(\cdot, \cdot)$ is the Euclidean distance.

5 Object Colorization

We use a patch match based colorization method. In order to better understand our method, we first introduce some basic concepts. The example based colorization is essentially a correspondence finding problem. That is, given a grayscale image A and its reference color image B, our task is to find a function $U : A \rightarrow B$, and then each pixel in A can take the corresponding color in B. For convenience, here we use the term "image" to refer to previous "object". Though an "object" has an irregular shape rather than a rectangle, the coloring step shares nearly the same operation flow.

Our colorization can be considered as a process of grayscale guided texture synthesis, and can also be thought of as a hybrid of image correspondence finding and classical texture synthesis. To measure the quality of a colorization, we conceptually minimize the following energy function:

$$E = \sum_{i \in A} (e_1(i, U(i)) + e_2(i, U(i))) \qquad (5)$$

where i is the pixel iterating over image A. e_1 measures the consistency of two local patches with centers i and $U(i)$ respectively, noting that B needs to be grayed for the gray comparison. This term is mainly used in the image correspondence finding algorithms. While the first term considers the grayscale correspondence, the second term e_2 measures the quality of the synthesized colors which is also the main energy term in texture synthesis.

As in [20], we simply use a randomized initialization. For each point i in image A, we randomly select a point u_i in image B, that is $U(i) = u_i$.

The optimization of E is essentially a labeling problem, which is NP-hard. Here we use an iterative process similar to PatchMatch [20], which is also commonly used in the texture synthesis algorithms. In each iteration, we consider to update each point i in image A in the scan-line order. We consider the correspondence set S from point i, point i's neighbors and points chosen randomly and select the one with the minimal error:

$$U(i) = \min_{u \in S} e_1(i, u) + \alpha e_2(i, u) \qquad (6)$$

Note that we increase the energy term e_2 gradually, as it is not reliable in the first few iterations. In our experiments, we use 6 iterations and let α be $0, 0, 0, 0.15, 0.2, 0.2$ respectively.

6 Experiments

We have implemented our system on a machine with two quad-core 2.26GHZ CPUs. We apply 10 iterations in the generic algorithm based reference selection, and the algorithm terminates within 1 minute. The colorization step takes less than half a minute

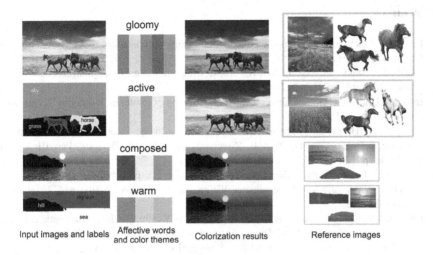

| Input images and labels | Affective words and color themes | Colorization results | Reference images |

Fig. 3. Colorization results

for a 1024×768 image. We also manually setup a small knowledge base indicating some objects which do not have common shapes, such as the floor, the sky, etc. They are usually used as backgrounds. We do not extract the salient regions from them and use the full images as references.

We have validated the system with various input examples. Fig. 3 shows the main results. The first column shows the input grayscale images as well as the segmentations and the corresponding labels. We achieve two different colorization results through optionally giving two affective words. The second column gives the words and the corresponding color themes. The third column demonstrates the colorization results and the last column shows the selected references. The colorization results well conform to the given affective words. And they are generally semantic as the selected objects usually belong to the same class.

7   Conclusions

We have proposed a novel system of the image colorization with an affective word. Using a generic algorithm, it unifies both the affective requirement and the semantics. It gives users a convenient and flexible interface to perfectly colorize a grayscale image. Experiments also convinced the effectiveness of our system.

Acknowledgments. This work is supported by the National Basic Research Program (973 Program) of China2011CB302201, and National Natural, and Science Foundation of China (60931160443). This work is also funded by Tsinghua National Laboratory for Information Science and TechnologyTNListCross-discipline Foundation.

References

1. Levin, A., Lischinski, D., Weiss, Y.: Colorization using optimization. ACM Transactions on Graphics 23, 689 (2004)
2. Welsh, T., Ashikhmin, M., Mueller, K.: Transferring color to greyscale images. ACM Transactions on Graphics 21(3), 277–280 (2002)
3. Ironi, R., Cohen-Or, D., Lischinski, D.: Colorization by example. In: Rendering Techniques, pp. 201–210 (2005)
4. Charpiat, G., Hofmann, M., Schölkopf, B.: Automatic Image Colorization Via Multimodal Predictions. In: Forsyth, D., Torr, P., Zisserman, A. (eds.) ECCV 2008, Part III. LNCS, vol. 5304, pp. 126–139. Springer, Heidelberg (2008)
5. Tai, Y.W., Jia, J., Tang, C.K.: Local color transfer via probabilistic segmentation by expectation-maximization. In: Computer Vision and Pattern Recognition, vol. 1, pp. 747–754. IEEE (2005)
6. Chia, A.Y.S., Zhuo, S., Gupta, R.K., Tai, Y.W., Cho, S.Y., Tan, P., Lin, S.: Semantic colorization with internet images. ACM Transactions on Graphics 30(6), 156:1–156:8 (2011)
7. Arnheim, R.: Art and visual perception: A psychology of the creative eye. University of California Press (1954)
8. Kobayashi, S.: Color image scale. Kosdansha International (1991)
9. Kobayashi, S.: Art of Color Combinations. Kosdansha International (1995)
10. Reinhard, E., Adhikhmin, M., Gooch, B., Shirley, P.: Color transfer between images. IEEE Computer Graphics and Applications 21(5), 34–41 (2001)
11. Chen, T., Cheng, M.M., Tan, P., Shamir, A., Hu, S.M.: Sketch2photo: internet image montage. ACM Transactions on Graphics 28(5), 124:1–124:10 (2009)
12. Cohen-Or, D., Sorkine, O., Gal, R., Leyvand, T., Xu, Y.Q.: Color harmonization. ACM Transactions on Graphics 25(3), 624–630 (2006)
13. O'Donovan, P., Agarwala, A., Hertzmann, A.: Color compatibility from large datasets. ACM Transactions on Graphics 30(4), 63:1–63:12 (2011)
14. Rother, C., Kolmogorov, V., Blake, A.: "GrabCut": interactive foreground extraction using iterated graph cuts. ACM Transactions on Graphics 23(3), 309–314 (2004)
15. Cheng, M.M., Zhang, F.L., Mitra, N.J., Huang, X., Hu, S.M.: Repfinder: finding approximately repeated scene elements for image editing. ACM Transactions on Graphics 29, 83:1–83:8 (2010)
16. Cheng, M.M., Zhang, G.X., Mitra, N.J., Huang, X., Hu, S.M.: Global contrast based salient region detection. In: IEEE Conference on Computer Vision and Pattern Recognition, pp. 409–416. IEEE (June 2011)
17. Belongie, S., Malik, J., Puzicha, J.: Shape matching and object recognition using shape contexts. IEEE Transactions on Pattern Analysis and Machine Intelligence 24(4), 509–522 (2002)
18. Wang, X.H., Jia, J., Cai, L.H.: Affective image adjustment with a single word. To apper in The Visual Computer
19. Dong, Z., Dong, Q.: HowNet and the Computation of Meaning. World Scientific (2006)
20. Barnes, C., Shechtman, E., Finkelstein, A., Goldman, D.B.: Patchmatch: a randomized correspondence algorithm for structural image editing. ACM Transactions on Graphics 28(3), 24:1–24:11 (2009)

Semantic Image Clustering
Using Object Relation Network

Na Chen and Viktor K. Prasanna

University of Southern California

Abstract. This paper presents a novel method to organize a collection of images into a hierarchy of clusters based on image semantics. Given a group of raw images with no metadata as input, our method describes the semantics of each image with a *bag-of-semantics* model (*i.e.*, a set of meaningful descriptors), which is derived from the image's Object Relation Network [5] - an expressive graph model representing rich semantics for image objects and their relations. We adopt the class hierarchies in a guide ontology as different levels of lenses to view the bag-of-semantics models. Image clusters are automatically extracted by grouping images with the same bag-of-semantics viewed through a certain lens. With a series of coarse-to-fine lenses, images are clustered in a top-down hierarchical manner. In addition, given that users can have different perspectives regarding how images should be clustered, our method allows each user to control the clustering process while browsing, and thus dynamically adjusts the clustering result according to the user's preferences.

1   Introduction

Image clustering is an important tool in processing large collections of images. The goal of image clustering is to organize a large set of images into clusters, such that images within the same cluster have similar meaning. Image clustering provides high-level summarization of large image collections, and thus has many useful applications. For example, clustered web image search results and image repositories are more convenient for users to browse. In addition, the efficiency of image search in large image database can be significantly improved by retrieving clustered image groups rather than individual images.

Many research efforts tackle the complicated problem of image clustering by solving three subproblems. Given a collection of images, first, a set of features are extracted from each image as its description. The features can be low-level visual features (*e.g.*, [17,7,13]), web context features (*e.g.*, [3,11,18]), or region-based features such as the well-known bag-of-words model [15,2,12]. Second, a clustering algorithm (*e.g.*, k-means, NCut, kNN) is applied based on certain distance measurements defined in the feature space, to split the image collection into multiple clusters. Finally, each cluster is labeled with either a text description or a representative image.

Although the previous research succeeds in many applications, we notice two major limitations. First, current visual feature based clustering methods usually

S.-M. Hu and R.R. Martin (Eds.): CVM 2012, LNCS 7633, pp. 59–66, 2012.

use local features that do not have semantic meanings. Thus, given two images, there is no significant correspondence between their semantic distance and their visual feature distance. These methods risk grouping images with different semantics into the same cluster, which is unsatisfactory from the perspective of human users. Although supervised machine learning approaches can be introduced to reduce the gap between local visual features and image semantics, they may fail when dealing with specific semantics. *E.g.*, they can hardly tell the semantic difference between the ball-playing scenes in Figure 1 left column.

The second limitation of the current image clustering methods is that they usually act as a black box to users, who has no control of the clustering performance. However, we observe that different users can have very different purposes of clustering. *E.g.*, a user focused on ball types wants to group the top two images in Figure 1 together since both of them contain a *soccer ball*, while a user targets at person types wants to group the bottom two images together as they are both about *athletes*. Thus, users should have control of the image clustering process.

We present a novel image clustering method to address the above two issues. Our approach is based on Object Relation Network (ORN) [5], a graph model representing informative and consistent semantics for objects and their relations in an image (*e.g.*, Figure 1 middle column). Given an ORN automatically generated for each image, we propose an image feature model named *bag-of-semantics*, which contains a set of semantic descriptors for the image based on its ORN (*e.g.*, Figure 1 right column). Since the ORN is derived from a *guide ontology*, the class hierarchies in the guide ontology can serve as different levels of lenses to view the bag-of-semantics model. In particular, a lens consists of a set of ontology classes that can be distinguished under it. For example, viewed from a coarse lens involving only *Person* and *Ball* nodes, the bag-of-semantics models for all three images in Figure 1 become the same set {*Person, Ball*}. In contrast, viewed through a finer lens involving *Basketball* and *Soccer ball*, the semantic difference in ball types between the bottom image and the other two images can be easily identified. Therefore, we cluster images by grouping images with the same bag-of-semantics viewed through a certain lens. We achieve hierarchical image clustering by going top-down through the class hierarchies in the guide ontology (and thus a series of coarse-to-fine lenses). In addition, user preferences in clustering can be captured by choosing different lenses at certain levels (*e.g.*, splitting *Person* into subclasses and splitting *Ball* into subclasses lead to different clustering results for images in Figure 1). Finally, each image cluster is labeled with its bag-of-semantics under the corresponding lens.

Given that our method is built on some prior work, we state our original contributions as follows:

1. We propose a bag-of-semantics model to describe images for the image clustering problem. The model explicitly reveals the semantics of an image. Thus, our clustering algorithm is guaranteed to group semantically-similar images into the same cluster.

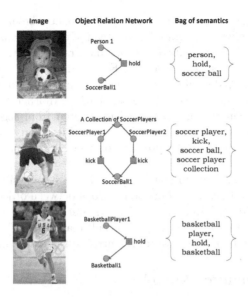

Fig. 1. Images and their bag-of-semantics descriptions automatically generated from our system. ORNs are shown in the middle as intermediate results.

2. We present a top-down hierarchical image clustering algorithm by viewing the bag-of-semantics model through levels of lenses with different semantic granularities, based on the class hierarchies in the guide ontology.
3. We are the first to enable user control in the image clustering problem. We provide a mechanism for users to browse through the image collection and make intuitive adjustment to the clustering results.

2   Related Work

Pioneer image clustering research [17,7,13] extracts low level visual features from input images, and applies different clustering algorithms based on these visual features. These algorithms include distance based clustering [17], Ncut [7], locality preserving clustering [19], and agglomerative clustering [13]. In particular, trees are suggested to be a natural organization of clusters [7]. But in these pioneer efforts, there is no correspondence between the cluster tree and the structure of image semantics.

For web images, textual context is believed to be a useful addition to the visual features. Co-clustering approaches are introduced to integrate visual features and multiple context features such as surrounding text [3,11], links [3,18], and attributes of various data objects [18]. In addition, Jing et al. [14] identify semantic clusters related to a given query, and assign the result images to the clusters. These methods work well for specific web applications, but lose generality and accuracy when dealing with images with limited or irrelevant web context.

In computer vision, *image categorization* targets at labeling images with one of a number of predefined categories [6]. Instead of directly using low level visual features (*e.g.*, colors and textures), intermediate representations are frequently introduced to capture image semantics. For example, the well-known bag-of-words model [15,2,12] describes an image as a bag of visual codewords and provides various measurements of image similarity. Another popular intermediate representation consists of image regions created from segmentation. With this representation, the image categorization problem can be formulated as a multiple-instance learning (MIL) problem by viewing an image as a bag of instances [6,1,16].

Although these image categorization methods share some similarities with our approach, we are the first to exploit the relations between objects in images. By exploring the relations between image objects, our bag-of-semantics model can express concrete semantics such as "basketball player" and "soccer player". In addition, we are the first to enable user control in the clustering process.

3   Bag-of-Semantics Model

We model an image as a collection of semantic descriptors for both static image objects and the binary relations between them. In particular, we adopt Object Relation Network (ORN) [5] to capture image semantics. ORN is a graphical model that links objects in an image through meaningful relations (Figure 1 middle column). Guided and constrained by a *guide ontology*, ORN represents the most probable meaning of the objects and their relations, by assigning each graph node to the most probable class in the guide ontology. Therefore, an image can be described by the ontology class assignments in the ORN, *e.g.*, Figure 1 right column. This image description model captures the semantics of both objects and their relations, and thus we call it *bag-of-semantics*.

This hierarchical structure of the semantic descriptors is very useful in our image clustering method, because it can describe an image with semantics from very general level to very specific level. Clustering is achieved by grouping images with the same semantics under certain semantic granularity. In the next section, we formally define *lenses* to control the semantic granularity and present our hierarchical image clustering algorithm based on the bag-of-semantics model.

4   Image Clustering

4.1   Lenses

Lenses characterize the semantic granularity for the bag-of-semantics model. We define a lens as a set of ontology classes $L \subseteq G$, where G is the node set of the guide ontology. Viewed through a lens L, a semantic descriptor s is regarded as its closest ancestor in L, denoted as s_L.

Intuitively, L determines the ontology classes that can be distinguished by the lens. The coarsest lens contains only three general classes, *i.e.*, *Object, O-O Relation*, and *Object Collection*. With this lens, every semantic descriptor is mapped to one of the general classes. Little difference can be found between the descriptors. On the contrary, under a fine lens containing many specific semantic concepts such as *Basketball* and *Soccer Ball*, the corresponding semantic descriptors (*e.g.*, the balls in Figure 1) are expressed with specific concepts and distinguished accordingly.

4.2   Image Clustering with Lenses

Viewed through a lens L, the bag-of-semantics $S(I)$ of an image I are expressed as set $S_L(I) = \{s_L | s \in S(I)\}$. Two images with the same bag-of-semantics expression $S_L(I) = S_L(J)$ are indistinguishable under the lens L. We thus group images with the same bag-of-semantics expression under a certain lens into the same cluster.

At first glance, this clustering algorithm may produce as many as $2^{|L|}$ clusters since $S_L(I) \subseteq L$ and there are $2^{|L|}$ possible subsets of L. However, since ORNs are created following the semantic constraints in the guide ontology, many of L's subsets do not have feasible ORNs, and thus the image clusters corresponding to these subsets are empty.

4.3   Hierarchical Clustering

We propose a top-down hierarchical image clustering algorithm by going through a series of coarse-to-fine lenses. We start with the coarsest lens containing only the general classes and cluster images accordingly. With more specific semantic concepts added to the lens, we divide each cluster into sub clusters according to the refined lens. In particular, we take advantage of the class hierarchies of the guide ontology $\mathbb{G}$. In each lens refinement step, we adopt a *split* operator to a class node f in L that has not been split. The split operator adds f's child class nodes in $\mathbb{G}$ to L, and divides the image clusters according to the refined lens. The hierarchical image clustering algorithm stops when there are sufficient number of clusters.

The pseudo code of the automatic hierarchical image clustering algorithm is shown in Algorithm 1.

4.4   User Control in Image Clustering

Since the bag-of-semantics model carries rich semantics of images, user preferences can be captured by choosing different coarse-to-fine paths for the lens. We design a user control mechanism that allows each user to modify the sequence of class nodes to be *split*. Figure 2 shows an example of a clustering process controlled by a user who is interested in various relations.

In our implementation, the image clustering system first applies the automatic clustering algorithm (Algorithm 1) to generate an initial cluster hierarchy for the user to browse through. In each lens refinement step, the user has the option to participate and choose a class node he thinks to be the most important. Our

---

Algorithm 1: Hierarchical Image Clustering

Input: Image collection $\mathbb{I}$ with bags-of-semantics $S(\mathbb{I}) = \{S(I)|I \in \mathbb{I}\}$, guide
ontology $\mathbb{G}$
Output: Image clusters $\mathbb{C} = \{C_i\}$
Initialization: $L, F \leftarrow \{\text{visible general classes}\}$
$\mathbb{C} \leftarrow$ clusters of $\mathbb{I}$ generated using L
while $F \neq \varnothing$ *and* $|\mathbb{C}| < \delta$ **do**
    find $f \in F$ with the smallest depth in $\mathbb{G}$
    find f's visible child node set $Child_v(f)$ in $\mathbb{G}$
    $F \leftarrow F \bigcup Child_v(f) \setminus \{f\}$
    if $Child_v(f) \neq \varnothing$ **then**
        $L \leftarrow L \bigcup Child_v(f)$
        foreach $C_i \in \mathbb{C}$ **do**
            divide C_i into sub clusters using L
            replace C_i in $\mathbb{C}$ with its sub clusters

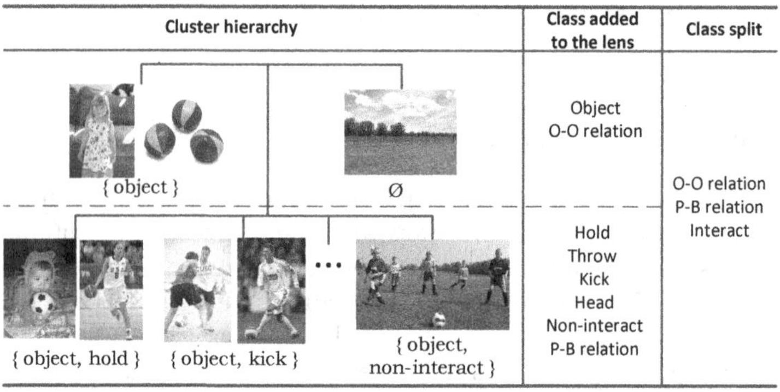

Fig. 2. Different choices of lens result in different cluster hierarchies. Lenses are chosen to cluster images according to relation types and person types in (A) and (B) respectively.

system splits the specified node, finds clusters based on the refined lens, then applies Algorithm 1 to update the subsequent cluster hierarchy that is used for further browsing. Finally, each image cluster is labeled with its bag-of-semantics under the corresponding lens.

5   Experimental Results

The dataset used in our experiment contains over 28,000 images from VOC2011 [9] and ImageNet [8]. We randomly choose 2,000 images for the training process of ORN generation. Our guide ontology contains class hierarchies and constraints for 6 generic object classes (*Person, Bicycle, Motorbike, Horse, Chair, Ball*) and their relation classes. We adopt the detectors in [10] to perform object detection.

{ cyclist, ride, bicycle }

{ person, ride, horse }

{ motorcyclist, ride, motorbike }

{ basketball player, throw, basketball }

{ soccer player, head, soccer ball }

Fig. 3. Several "good" clustering results obtained by using very fine lenses, *i.e.*splitting subclasses of *Person* class and all the relation classes. Each row includes example images and the label of a cluster.

Figure 3 illustrates several "good" results produced by our automatic clustering algorithm, obtained by splitting subclasses of *Person* class and all the relation classes. These result clusters demonstrate that our clustering algorithm has successfully classified semantically-similar images into the same cluster, even though the visual features of some images are quite different from each other.

More results and discussions are available in [4].

6   Conclusion

We presented a hierarchical image clustering method that groups semantically similar images into the same cluster. We proposed a bag-of-semantics model to describe the semantic features of images. Viewed through a series of coarse-to-fine lenses, images with the same bag-of-semantics under a certain lens are clustered in a top-down hierarchical manner. Our method allows each user to control the clustering process while browsing, and dynamically adjusts the clustering result according to his purpose.

References

1. Bi, J., Chen, Y., Wang, J.Z.: A sparse support vector machine approach to region-based image categorization. In: CVPR (2005) 4
2. Bosch, A., Zisserman, A., Muñoz, X.: Scene Classification Via pLSA. In: Leonardis, A., Bischof, H., Pinz, A. (eds.) ECCV 2006, Part IV. LNCS, vol. 3954, pp. 517–530. Springer, Heidelberg (2006) 1, 4
3. Cai, D., He, X., Li, Z., Ma, W.Y., Wen, J.R.: Hierarchical clustering of www image search results using visual, textual and link information. ACM Multimedia (2004) 1, 3
4. Chen, N., Prasanna, V.K.: A bag-of-semantics model for image clustering. Tech. rep., University of Southern California (August 2012), http://www-scf.usc.edu/~nchen/paper/bos.pdf 7
5. Chen, N., Zhou, Q.Y., Prasanna, V.: Understanding web images by object relation network. In: Proceedings of the 21st International Conference on World Wide Web (2012) 1, 2, 4
6. Chen, Y., Wang, J.Z.: Image categorization by learning and reasoning with regions. J. Mach. Learn. Res. (2004) 4
7. Chen, Y., Wang, J.Z., Krovetz, R.: Clue: Cluster-based retrieval of images by unsupervised learning. IEEE Transactions on Image Processing (2003) 1, 3
8. Deng, J., Dong, W., Socher, R., Li, L.J., Li, K., Fei-Fei, L.: Imagenet: A large-scale hierarchical image database. In: CVPR (2009) 6
9. Everingham, M., Gool, L., Williams, C.K., Winn, J., Zisserman, A.: The PASCAL Visual Object Classes Challenge 2011 (VOC 2011) Results (2011), http://www.pascal-network.org/challenges/VOC/voc2011/workshop/index.html 6
10. Felzenszwalb, P.F., Girshick, R.B., McAllester, D., Ramanan, D.: Object detection with discriminatively trained part based models. IEEE TPAMI 32(9) (2010) 6
11. Gao, B., Liu, T.Y., Qin, T., Zheng, X., Cheng, Q.S., Ma, W.Y.: Web image clustering by consistent utilization of visual features and surrounding texts. ACM Multimedia (2005) 1, 3
12. van Gemert, J.C., Geusebroek, J.-M., Veenman, C.J., Smeulders, A.W.M.: Kernel Codebooks for Scene Categorization. In: Forsyth, D., Torr, P., Zisserman, A. (eds.) ECCV 2008, Part III. LNCS, vol. 5304, pp. 696–709. Springer, Heidelberg (2008) 1, 4
13. Gordon, S., Greenspan, H., Goldberger, J.: Applying the information bottleneck principle to unsupervised clustering of discrete and continuous image representations. In: ICCV (2003) 1, 3
14. Jing, F., Wang, C., Yao, Y., Deng, K., Zhang, L., Ma, W.Y.: Igroup: web image search results clustering. ACM Multimedia (2006) 3
15. Li, F.F., Perona, P.: A bayesian hierarchical model for learning natural scene categories. In: CVPR (2005) 1, 4
16. Liu, Y., Chen, X., Zhang, C., Sprague, A.: Semantic clustering for region-based image retrieval. J. Vis. Comun. Image Represent. (2009) 4
17. Rodden, K., Basalaj, W., Sinclair, D., Wood, K.: Does organisation by similarity assist image browsing? In: Proceedings of the SIGCHI Conference on Human Factors in Computing Systems (2001) 1, 3
18. Wang, X.J., Ma, W.Y., Zhang, L., Li, X.: Iteratively clustering web images based on link and attribute reinforcements. ACM Multimedia (2005) 1, 3
19. Zheng, X., Cai, D., He, X., Ma, W.Y., Lin, X.: Locality preserving clustering for image database. ACM Multimedia (2004) 3

Efficient Solid Texture Synthesis Using Gradient Solids

Guo-Xin Zhang[1], Yu-Kun Lai[2], and Shi-Min Hu[1]

[1] Department of Computer Science and Technology, Tsinghua University, China
[2] School of Computer Science and Informatics, Cardiff University, UK
zgx.net@gmail.com,
Yukun.Lai@cs.cardiff.ac.uk,
shimin@tsinghua.edu.cn

Abstract. In this paper, we propose a novel solid representation called *gradient solids* to compactly represent solid textures, including a tricubic interpolation scheme of colors and gradients for smooth variation and a region-based approach for representing sharp boundaries. We further propose a novel approach to *directly* synthesize gradient solid textures from exemplars. Compared with existing methods, our approach avoids the expensive step of synthesizing the complete solid textures at voxel level and produces optimized solid textures using our representation. This avoids significant amount of unnecessary computation and storage with comparable quality to the state of the art.

1 Introduction

Solid textures represent color (or other attributes) over 3D space and are naturally suitable for modeling solid objects. Due to the extra dimension, solid textures represented as attributes sampled at regular 3D grids are extremely expensive to synthesize and store. To provide sufficient resolution in practice, a typical solution is to synthesize only a small cube (e.g. 128^3), and tile the cube to cover the 3D space. However, tiling may cause undesirable visual repetition and is possible only when the solid textures have no interaction with the underlying objects, and thus cannot respect any model features or user design intentions. To address this, previous approaches [1,2] synthesize solid textures on demand; however, handling high-resolution solid textures is still expensive.

Wang et al. [3] extend image vectorization to solid textures, which requires voxel-level solid textures as input and inherits similar advantages as image vectorization, such as being compact and resolution independent. It remains costly as raster solid textures need to be synthesized first. In this paper, we instead propose a novel approach to directly synthesize vectorized solid textures from exemplars. Inspired by gradient meshes in image vectorization [4], we propose a novel *gradient solid* representation that uses a tricubic interpolation scheme for smooth color variations within a region, and a region-based approach to represent sharp boundaries with separated colors. We treat solid texture synthesis as *optimizing control points* of gradient solids to produce synthesized solids with similar sectional images as given exemplars. Compared with traditional solid texture synthesis, we have *far less* control points than voxels, leading to a much more efficient algorithm. To the best of our knowledge, this is the first algorithm that synthesizes vector solid textures directly from exemplars.

S.-M. Hu and R.R. Martin (Eds.): CVM 2012, LNCS 7633, pp. 67–74, 2012.

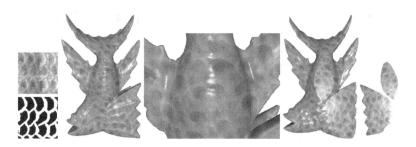

Fig. 1. High-resolution gradient solid texture synthesis. From left to right: the input exemplar, the synthesized gradient solid texture, a closeup and internal slices.

2   Related Work

Our work is closely related to example based texture synthesis and vector images/textures.

Early work on solid texture synthesis focuses on procedural approaches [5,6]. Since rules are used to generate solid textures, very little storage is needed. However, only restricted classes of textures can be effectively synthesized and it is inconvenient to tune the parameters. Exemplar-based approaches do not suffer from these problems, and thus received more attention. 2D non-parametric texture synthesis algorithms have been extended to solid texture synthesis [7,8,9]. These algorithms are generally expensive due to the extra dimension. To synthesize high resolution solid textures, Dong et al. [1] propose an efficient synthesis-on-demand algorithm based on deterministic synthesis of certain windows from the whole space [10] necessary for rendering, based on the fact that only 2D slices are needed at a time for normal displays. This work is extended in [2] that introduces user-provided tensor fields as guidance for solid texture synthesis.

Jagnow et al. [11] propose an algorithm based on stereological analysis which provides more precise modeling of solid textures. However, their approach only works for restricted types of solid textures with well separable pieces. Lapped textures have been extended to synthesize 3D volumetric textures [12]. 3D volumetric exemplars instead of 2D image exemplars are needed as input.

Different from raster images, vector graphics use geometric primitives along with attributes such as colors and their gradients to represent the images. Recent work proposes automatic or semi-automatic approaches to high-quality image vectorization using quadrilateral gradient meshes [4,13] or curvilinear triangle meshes for better feature alignment [14]. Diffusion curves [15] model vector images as a collection of color diffusion around curves. Some works consider combining raster images with extra geometric primitives [16,17,18] to obtain benefits such as improved editing and resizing.

Vector graphics have recently been generalized to solid textures [3,19]. Wang et al. [3] propose an automatic approach to vectorize the given solid textures using a Radial Basis Function(RBF)-based representation. This approach relies on raster solids as input, thus an expensive raster solid texture synthesis algorithm is needed if only 2D exemplars are given. Diffusion surfaces [19] generalized from diffusion curves [15] are also used to represent vector solids; their focus however is user design of solids rather than automatic generation.

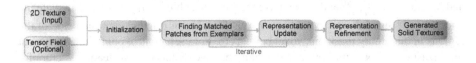

Fig. 2. Algorithm pipeline of gradient solid texture synthesis

We propose a novel algorithm that synthesizes gradient solids directly from 2D exemplars, leading to an efficient algorithm in both computation and storage that produces high quality solid textures by bypassing intermediate bitmap solid synthesis and subsequent bitmap-to-vector conversion.

3   Gradient Solid Representation

We give details of the gradient solid representation, allowing efficient representation of smooth regions and regions with boundaries.

We first consider representing regions with smoothly varying colors. We use an $n \times n \times n$ grid of control points with axes u, v, w to represent the solid textures. At each control point (i, j, k), we store a feature vector $\mathbf{f}$ including r, g, b color components and additional feature channels such as the signed distance [20]. In addition, the gradients of $\mathbf{f}$, i.e. $\frac{d\mathbf{f}}{du}, \frac{d\mathbf{f}}{dv}, \frac{d\mathbf{f}}{dw}$ are also stored allowing flexible control of variations in 3D space. 3D tricubic interpolation with gradients [21,22] is used to obtain the feature vector $\tilde{\mathbf{f}}$ for any voxel inside the grid. Similar tricubic interpolation has been used in isosurface extraction from volumetric data for visualization [23]. Assume that $p = 1, 2, \ldots, 8$ represents the 8 control points in the cube that covers the voxel and assume second or higher order derivatives of $\mathbf{f}$ to be zero, $\tilde{\mathbf{f}}$ at parameter (u, v, w) $(0 \leq u, v, w \leq 1)$ can be evaluated as $\tilde{\mathbf{f}}(u, v, w) = \sum_{i,j,k=0}^{3} \mathbf{a}_{ijk} u^i v^j w^k$. All the 64 coefficient vectors $\mathbf{a}_{ijk}$ are weighted sums of 32-dimensional vectors $V = (\cdots \mathbf{f}^{(p)}, \frac{d\mathbf{f}^{(p)}}{du}, \frac{d\mathbf{f}^{(p)}}{dv}, \frac{d\mathbf{f}^{(p)}}{dw} \cdots)$. Using the integer weights given in [22], C^1 continuity over the whole volume is guaranteed.

The geometric positions of control points in our representation are fixed, however, these points still carry other attributes such as color and gradients which control the appearance of the solids. Assuming the displacement between adjacent control points is d, the geometric position of the control point (i, j, k) is (id, jd, kd). The displacement determines the number of voxels located within each cube of the control grid. In all of our experiments we use $d = 4$ which means that the number of control points is roughly $\frac{1}{64} = 1.56\%$ of voxels. This simple representation has several significant advantages. For any fixed point with known parameter (u, v, w), since $u^i v^j w^k$ can be pre-computed, the expensive evaluation can be reduced to a weighted sum of elements in V.

Representing Region Boundaries. If the texture contains sharp boundaries that need to be preserved, a feature mask image is often used in texture synthesis as an additional component (other than color) to better preserve structures. Similar to previous work both in 2D and 3D textures [20,3], we assume regions can be separated using a binary mask. To represent the boundary in the solid textures, we also use a signed distance field stored at the *same* regular $n \times n \times n$ grid. We store both the signed distance $\bar{d}$

and its gradients $\frac{d\tilde{d}}{du}$, $\frac{d\tilde{d}}{dv}$ and $\frac{d\tilde{d}}{dw}$ and use the same tricubic interpolation to calculate the interpolated signed distance $\tilde{d}$ at each voxel. The sign of $\tilde{d}$ indicates which side of the regions in the binary mask this voxel belongs to. For each control point that is adjacent to at least one cube with both positive and negative distances, two feature vectors $\mathbf{f}^P$ (positive distance) and $\mathbf{f}^N$ (negative distance) and their gradients are stored.

4 Gradient Solid Texture Synthesis

Our algorithm synthesizes gradient solid textures directly from 2D exemplars, which may include optional binary masks (if sharp boundaries exist between regions). In addition, a smooth tensor field may be given to specify the local coordinate systems the exemplar images align with [2]. We use an optimization based approach to synthesize gradient solid textures, with local patches aligned to the field if given. The algorithm pipeline is summarized in Fig. 2, which involves several key steps: initialization, iterative optimization and final gradient solid refinement. We simply start from a randomized initialization. For each control point, we randomly select a pixel from the exemplar image, and assign the feature vector at the pixel to the control point. All the gradients are initialized to zero. During the optimization process, a coarse-to-fine strategy is used.

4.1 Optimization-Based Synthesis

Optimization is the key step in our gradient solid texture synthesis pipeline. It involves iterations of two alternating steps, namely choosing optimal patches from exemplars that best match the current representation and updating the representation to better approximate the exemplar patches. Unlike traditional texture optimization, we optimize the feature vectors in the control points of the gradient solids. New challenges exist due to the different nature of the representation.

Finding Matched Patches From Exemplars. We first identify those local patches from the exemplars that best match the current gradient solid. These patches will then be used to improve the representation. Since gradient solids have much sparser control points than voxels, we randomly choose a small number N_C of check points within each cube of the grid ($N_C = 3$ is used in the paper). At each check point, we sample three orthogonal planes each with $N \times N$ samples (denoted as $\mathbf{s}_x$, $\mathbf{s}_y$ and $\mathbf{s}_z$ respectively) which are evaluated based on our representation (as illustrated in Fig. 3). A fast approximate evaluation based on first-order Taylor expansion at the closest control point is used in the intermediate synthesis to significantly improve the performance without visually degrading the quality.

We then find three local patches from exemplars that best match these sampled patches. If all the three slices are equally important, we use three independent searches as [8]. Many practical solid textures are anisotropic and it is not possible to keep all three slices well matched with a single exemplar image. In such cases, it is known that matching two slices instead of three may lead to better results [8]. We propose a new approach that takes crossbar consistency into account, which works best when two slices are matched. Crossbars are those voxels shared by two or three slices (see Fig. 3) and inconsistent crossbars may result from independent best searches. For computational efficiency, we first search for the patch E_x from exemplars that best matches $\mathbf{s}_x$, as usual. We then search

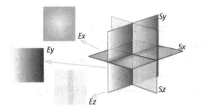

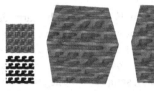

Fig. 4. Results without (left) and with (right) crossbar matching

Fig. 3. Illustration of crossbars

for the patch E_y that best matches $\mathbf{s}_y$ from a set of N_1 candidates with the most consistent crossbar voxels as E_x. If three slices are matched, we similarly search for the best match E_z of $\mathbf{s}_z$ from a set of N_2 candidates with the most consistent crossbars as E_x and E_y. $N_1 = 20$ and $N_2 = 50$ are used for all the experiments. This leads to improved synthesis results with better structure preservation (see Fig. 4). To speed up the computation, a PCA projection of the matching vectors is used, which effectively reduces dimensions from hundreds to 10-20 while keeping most of the energy.

Representation Update. Each matched patch at every check point gives $N \times N$ samples, which will be used to update the gradient solid representation. To efficiently collect samples, we conceptually build a bucket for each voxel in the grid that holds all the samples located in the voxel. After considering check points in all the cubes, each bucket may end up with none or a few samples. For buckets with more than one sample, in order to determine the feature vector, simply averaging all the samples in the bucket tends to produce blurred voxels. To avoid this, we propose a novel approach to first identify the color clusters from the given exemplar and only averages samples that belong to dominant clusters. Our representation itself is compact and during the synthesis process, only a small active front of buckets needs to be preserved, thus allows high resolution solids to be synthesized in full.

After obtaining the average feature vector for any bucket with at least one sample, we assign each non-empty bucket to the closest control point. The feature vector as well as gradients of the control point are updated by minimizing the fitting error in the least-squares sense. For a particular control point, assuming s buckets are related with relative coordinates du_t, dv_t, dw_t and feature vector $\mathbf{f}_t$ ($1 \leq t \leq s$), we find $\mathbf{f}_c$, $\frac{\mathbf{f}_c}{du}$, $\frac{\mathbf{f}_c}{dv}$, $\frac{\mathbf{f}_c}{dw}$ that minimize

$$E_C = \sum_{t=1}^{s} \left\| \mathbf{f}_c + \frac{\mathbf{f}_c}{du} du_t + \frac{\mathbf{f}_c}{dv} dv_t + \frac{\mathbf{f}_c}{dw} dw_t - \mathbf{f}_t \right\|^2 . \tag{1}$$

This can be considered as a local first-order Taylor expansion of our representation which can be efficiently solved by small linear systems. This approximation is sufficient for intermediate computation and we use the accurate evaluation only in the final stage.

4.2 Gradient Solid Representation Refinement

As the final step, we further optimize the gradient solid representation to better represent the synthesized gradient solids.

Region Separation. For solids with sharp region boundaries that need to be preserved, we differentiate regions with positive and negative signed distances for the computation of control point parameters during representation update. For each control point, we compute positive parameters ($\mathbf{f}^P$ and gradients) using samples with positive signed distance. Similarly, samples with negative signed distance contribute to negative parameters ($\mathbf{f}^N$ and gradients).

Control Point Optimization. To further improve the quality, instead of fitting with first order approximation, we minimize the fitting error between all the sample values and those evaluated using the gradient solid representation. For a sample point with sampled feature vector $\hat{\mathbf{f}}_i$ located in the cube c_i with corner control points collected as V_i and parameter (u_i, v_i, w_i), the evaluated feature vectors $\tilde{\mathbf{f}}$ are linear functions of V_i, denoted as $\mathbf{f}(V_i; u_i, v_i, w_i)$. We minimize the following quadratic energy

$$\bar{E}_C = \sum_{i=1}^{\#samp} \|\tilde{\mathbf{f}}_i - \hat{\mathbf{f}}_i\|^2 = \sum_{i=1}^{\#samp} \|\mathbf{f}(V_i; u_i, v_i, w_i) - \hat{\mathbf{f}}_i\|^2, \tag{2}$$

where $\#samp$ is the number of sample points. Minimization of $\bar{E}_C$ leads to a sparse linear system. As we have a good estimation from the previous approximation, the linear system can be effectively solved by a few iterations.

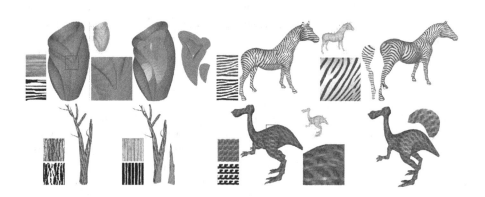

Fig. 5. Synthesized high-resolution solids following given directional fields with our algorithm: 'vase', 'horse', 'tree' and 'dinopet' with synthesized solids, close-ups and internal slices

5   Results and Discussions

We carried out our experiments on a computer with $2\times$Quad-Core 2.26GHz CPU and NVIDIA GTS 450 GPU.

Our algorithm directly synthesizes more compact and resolution-independent gradient solid textures from 2D exemplars. Solids with comparable quality to the state of the art can be synthesized, as shown in Figs. 1 and 5. As for other CPU-based algorithms that focus on synthesizing full solids of a 128^3 cube, the typical reported times have been tens of minutes, e.g. [8] uses 10-90 minutes (without tensor fields) and [24] (a CPU-based implementation similar to [1] with direction fields considered) reported about 30 minutes with a single core. For easier comparison, we consider gradient solids with equivalent raster resolution. Our current CPU-based implementation, after about 10 seconds preprocessing of the input exemplar (which is the same for arbitrarily sized output volumes), takes only 13 seconds. Even counting the different performance of CPUs, our algorithm is over 10 times faster. Due to the compactness in representation, we can synthesize high-resolution solid textures in full. Examples with about 512 samples in the longest dimension take 3-7 minutes. Region separation is not needed if the input texture does not contain sharp boundaries, as the 'vase' and 'tree' examples in Fig. 5. In these examples, the binary mask is used only as part of the feature vector, not for region separation. The 'tree' example shows that our synthesis algorithm can be generalized to synthesize solids with different exemplars covering different spaces, mimicking the real structure of a tree.

While our current *synthesis* implementation is CPU-based, gradient solids are *rendered* in real-time using the GPU. For each visible pixel, we obtain the interpolated texture coordinate using the vertex shader and evaluate the color using the fragment shader; the colors and gradients at control points are stored as textures for efficient GPU access. For solid textures with binary masks, the relevant set of feature vectors is used based on the evaluated signed distance.

Limitations. Although we can represent sharp boundaries with regions, similar to [3] using a single distance field we cannot in general recover sharp boundaries if more than two regions touch. Additional distance fields may be used in such situations. Our method may not reproduce textures with large amount of high-frequency details in the synthesized solids well. Nevertheless, we have demonstrated that our method works well on a variety of textures throughout the paper. Our representation is particularly suitable for solid textures having dominantly smooth color variations within each homogeneous region, as assumed by virtually all the vectorization methods.

6   Conclusions and Future Work

In this paper, we propose a novel gradient solid representation for compactly representing solids. We also propose an efficient algorithm for direct synthesis of gradient solid textures from 2D exemplars. Our algorithm is very efficient in both computation and storage, compared with previous voxel-level solid texture synthesis methods and thus allows high-resolution solid textures to be synthesized in full. Our current implementation of the synthesis algorithm is purely CPU based. The algorithm is highly parallel and we expect to implement this on the GPU to further improve the performance.

Acknowledgements. This work was supported by the National Basic Research Project of China (Project Number 2012CB316400), the Natural Science Foundation of China (Project Number 61120106007) and the National High Technology Research and Development Program of China (Project Number 2012AA011503).

References

1. Dong, Y., Lefebvre, S., Tong, X., Drettakis, G.: Lazy solid texture synthesis. Computer Graphics Forum 27(4), 1165–1174 (2008)
2. Zhang, G.X., Du, S.P., Lai, Y.K., Ni, T., Hu, S.M.: Sketch guided solid texturing. Graph. Mod. 73(3), 59–73 (2011)
3. Wang, L., Zhou, K., Yu, Y., Guo, B.: Vector solid textures. In: Proc. ACM SIGGRAPH, Article 86 (2010)
4. Sun, J., Liang, L., Wen, F., Shum, H.Y.: Image vectorization using optimized gradient meshes. ACM Trans. Graph. 26(3), Article 11 (2007)
5. Peachey, D.R.: Solid texturing of complex surfaces. In: Proc. ACM SIGGRAPH, pp. 279–286 (1985)
6. Perlin, K.: An image synthesizer. In: Proc. ACM SIGGRAPH, pp. 287–296 (1985)
7. Wei, L.Y.: Texture synthesis from multiple sources. In: SIGGRAPH 2003 Sketch (2003)
8. Kopf, J., Fu, C.W., Cohen-Or, D., Deussen, O., Lischinski, D., Wong, T.T.: Solid texture synthesis from 2D exemplars. ACM Trans. Graph. 26(3), Article 2 (2007)
9. Chen, J., Wang, B.: High quality solid texture synthesis using position and index histogram matching. The Visual Computer 26(4), 253–262 (2010)
10. Lefebvre, S., Hoppe, H.: Parallel controllable texture synthesis. ACM Trans. Graph. 24(3), 777–786 (2005)
11. Jagnow, R., Dorsey, J., Rushmeier, H.: Stereological techniques for solid textures. In: Proc. ACM SIGGRAPH, pp. 329–335 (2004)
12. Takayama, K., Okabe, M., Ijiri, T., Igarashi, T.: Lapped solid textures: filling a model with anisotropic textures. ACM Trans. Graph. 27(3), Article 53 (2008)
13. Lai, Y.K., Hu, S.M., Martin, R.R.: Automatic and topology-preserving gradient mesh generation for image vectorization. ACM Trans. Graph. 28(3), Article 85 (2009)
14. Xia, T., Liao, B., Yu, Y.: Patch-based image vectorization with automatic curvlinear feature alignment. ACM Trans. Graph. 28(5), Article 115 (2009)
15. Orzan, A., Bousseau, A., Winnemöller, H., Barla, P., Thollot, J., Salesin, D.: Diffusion curves: a vector representaiton for smooth-shaded images. ACM Trans. Graph. 27(3), Article 92 (2008)
16. Barrett, W., Cheney, A.S.: Object-based image editing. ACM Trans. Graph. 21(3), 777–784 (2002)
17. Tumblin, J., Choudhury, P.: Bixels: Picture samples with sharp embedded boundaries. In: Proc. Eurographics Symposium on Rendering, pp. 186–196 (2004)
18. Pavić, D., Kobbelt, L.: Two-colored pixels. Computer Graphics Forum 29(2), 743–752 (2010)
19. Takayama, K., Sorkine, O., Nealen, A., Igarashi, T.: Volumetric modeling with diffusion surfaces. ACM Trans. Graph. 29(6), Article 180 (2010)
20. Lefebvre, S., Hoppe, H.: Appearance-space texture synthesis. ACM Trans. Graph. 25, 541–548 (2006)
21. Ferguson, J.: Multivariable curve interpolation. J. ACM 11(2), 221–228 (1964)
22. Lekien, F., Marsden, J.: Tricubic interpolation in three dimensions. J. Numerical Methods Engin. 63, 455–471 (2005)
23. Kadosh, A., Cohen-Or, D., Yagel, R.: Tricubic interpolation of discrete surfaces for binary volumes. IEEE Trans. Vis. Comp. Graph. 9(4), 580–586 (2003)
24. Ma, C., Wei, L.Y., Guo, B., Zhou, K.: Motion field texture synthesis. ACM Trans. Graph. 28(5), Article 110 (2009)

A Robust Algorithm for Denoising Meshes with High-Resolution Details

Hanqi Fan[1], Qunsheng Peng[2], and Yizhou Yu[3]

[1] College of Information Engineering
North China University of Technology, Beijing, China
fhq@ncut.edu.cn
[2] State Key Lab. of CAD&CG
Zhejiang University, Hangzhou, China
peng@cad.zju.edu.cn
[3] Dept. of Computer Science
The University of HongKong
yzyu@cs.hku.hk

Abstract. In this paper, we present a robust and efficient mesh denoising algorithm which preserves high-resolution details very well. Our method is a three-stage algorithm. Firstly, we modify a robust density-based clustering method and apply it to the face neighborhood of each triangular face to extract a subset of neighbors which belong to the same cluster as the central face. Because the faces within the extracted subset are not distributed across high-resolution details, we filter the central face normal iteratively within this subset to remove noise and preserve such details as much as possible. Finally, vertex positions are updated to be consistent with the filtered face normals using a least-squares formulation. Experiments on various types of meshes indicate that our method has advantages over previous surface denoising methods.

Keywords: Mesh Denoising, High-Resolution Details, Face Neighborhood, Normal Clustering, Normal Filtering.

1 Introduction

A large portion of models are generated from finely scanned data of real 3D objects. However, noise from various sources is inevitably involved in this process. Such noise can severely impair the usability of mesh models. Therefore, denoising algorithms are required to improve the quality of the reconstructed meshes. With the progress of laser scanning technology, more and more high-resolution details of the physical models can be captured. High-resolution details present in noisy mesh models make denoising more challenging, because such signal cannot be easily distinguished from noise.

In this paper, we propose a mesh denoising method that can effectively preserve high-resolution details. Our method has two phases, face normal filtering and vertex reconstruction from filtered face normals. We perform normal filtering for triangle faces. Since there might be multiple high-res surface segments in a neighborhood,

S.-M. Hu and R.R. Martin (Eds.): CVM 2012, LNCS 7633, pp. 75–82, 2012.

for each face, our algorithm extracts a subset of faces in the neighborhood that belong to the same high-res segment as the central face. We call this subset uncluttered sub-neighborhood (USN). Normal filtering only occurs within the USN. This strategy can both remove noise and preserve the shape of the high-res local surface segment. Final vertex positions of the denoised mesh are reconstructed from the filtered face normals following a least-squares formulation.

In the remainder of the paper we first review previous work on mesh denoising before we present the method for computing USNs, filtering face normals and updating vertex positions in Section 3. In Section 4, we show experimental results.

2 Related Work

Many mesh smoothing methods have been proposed in the past[1–7]. Fleishman et al. [8] and Jones et al. [9] successfully extended the bilateral filter from image processing[10] to mesh denoising. These two methods consider the underlying geometry of a mesh as a single surface. Because of this, high frequency details, such as creases and corners, will be inevitably blurred, though at a much slower rate.

Hildebrandt and Polthier [11] introduced a prescribed mean curvature (PMC) flow to remove noise while preserving sharp geometric features. Other two-stage feature-preserving mesh denoising methods[12–15] have also been proposed. More recently, Fan et al. [16] have introduced a mesh denoising algorithm based on sub-neighborhoods. It considers a mesh surface piecewise smooth, and a sharp feature is the intersection of multiple smooth surface regions. This method can well preserve sharp features most of the time. However, it needs to classify vertices into three categories, and such classification is not very reliable. Furthermore, at sharp features, such as sharp edges and corners, vertex normals cannot be reliably defined.

3 The Algorithm

A triangle mesh M is a piecewise linear surface consisting of triangular faces with shared edges and vertices. The mesh geometry can be denoted by the tuple (V, E, F), where $V = \{\mathbf{v}_1, \ldots, \mathbf{v}_n\}$ is the set of vertices, $E = \{(\mathbf{v}_i, \mathbf{v}_j) | \mathbf{v}_i, \mathbf{v}_j \in V\}$ is the set of edges and $F = \{(\mathbf{v}_i, \mathbf{v}_j, \mathbf{v}_k) | \mathbf{v}_i, \mathbf{v}_j, \mathbf{v}_k \in V\}$ is the set of triangular faces. The normal of triangular face F_i is denoted as $\mathbf{n}_i$, and we denote the neighborhood of face F_i as N_i which is the collection of triangular faces near F_i. Since our algorithm extracts an USN from N_i, we denote it as $subN_i$. The one-ring neighborhood of vertex $\mathbf{v}_i$ is denoted as N_i^v, and the one-ring face neighborhood of the vertex, faces sharing vertex $\mathbf{v}_i$, is denoted as N_i^f. ΔF_i denotes the edges bounding face F_i.

3.1 Uncluttered Sub-neighborhood Extraction

Traditional Euclidean distance based clustering algorithms would be problematic since sometimes face normals across a feature may happen to be closer to each other than normals in the same smooth local region, as illustrated in Fig. 1, where point a is easily

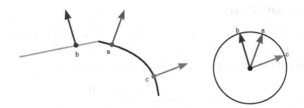

Fig. 1. Illustration of a typical scenario. There is a shallow discontinuity between point a and point b, while point c lies on the same smooth surface segment as point a. On the right, the three normals are mapped to a unit circle. The distance between the normals of point a and point b is smaller than that between the normals of point a and point c.

classified in the same cluster as point b using Euclidean distance between their normals. Even worse, since surface normals are corrupted with noise as well.

To overcome the limitations of Euclidean distance, We quantify the distance between two normals by defining a shared nearest neighbor (SNN) similarity. For each pair of normals, $\mathbf{n}_i$ and $\mathbf{n}_j$, if the distance between the two normals is less than r, that is $\|\mathbf{n}_i - \mathbf{n}_j\|_2 < r$, the *SNN similarity* between them is defined as:

$$\text{similarity}(\mathbf{n}_i, \mathbf{n}_j) = \text{size}(NN(\mathbf{n}_i) \cap NN(\mathbf{n}_j)), \tag{1}$$

where $NN(\mathbf{x}) = \{\mathbf{y} \mid \|\mathbf{y} - \mathbf{x}\| < r\}$. Since the SNN similarity reflects local configuration of the points on the Gaussian sphere, it is relatively insensitive to variations in density.

A SNN similarity graph is constructed to describe the similarities among all face normals in the neighborhood. We assign a link strength/weight to each edge which represents the similarity between the two nodes of the edge. Since many pairs of normals have zero SNN similarity, the resulting graph is very sparse.

In a SNN similarity graph, *SNN density* is defined by the number of connected neighbors with a link strength equal to or greater than Eps. Nodes in regions with either a high or low density typically have a relatively high SNN density, while nodes in regions where there is a transition between different densities have a low SNN density.

The points that have an SNN density greater than $MinPts$ are further defined as *core points*. Every subset of connected core points define a distinct cluster in the final result. All non-core points that have no link weight larger than Eps are eliminated. A border point, which is defined as a non-core and non-noise point, is assigned to the cluster where its nearest core point belongs.

There are two special cases where we directly take N_i as $subN_i$. The first one is $NN(\mathbf{n}_i) = N_i$, which means that all the normals do not differ too much from $\mathbf{n}_i$. This case makes our denoising algorithm work very efficiently by avoiding the relatively expensive clustering algorithm in neighborhoods. The second one is $\mathbf{n}_i$ is classified as an outlier, we take the entire neighborhood as its uncluttered sub-neighborhood in order to remove noise quickly.

3.2 Surface Normal Filtering

Once we have obtained the sub-neighborhood, $subN_i$, normal filtering can be much simpler yet more effective than that in previous work [12, 17, 14]. We update the normal $\mathbf{n}_i$ as the normalized weighted average of the normals in $subN_i$:

$$\mathbf{n}'_i = \frac{\sum_{\mathbf{n}_j \in subN_i} \mathbf{n}_j \, g(\|\mathbf{n}_i - \mathbf{n}_j\|)}{\|\sum_{\mathbf{n}_j \in subN_i} \mathbf{n}_j \, g(\|\mathbf{n}_i - \mathbf{n}_j\|)\|} \tag{2}$$

where $g(x)$ is the weighting function, which can be any suitable non-negative monotonically decreasing function for $x \geq 0$. We choose a simpler RMQ-type function, $g(x) = \frac{1}{(1+x^2)}$, which is fast to evaluate and performs well in all our experiments.

3.3 Vertex Position Updating

Since the three edges of a triangular face, F_m, should be perpendicular to the face normal, $\mathbf{n}_m$, the corresponding triangle vertices $\mathbf{v}_i, \mathbf{v}_j, \mathbf{v}_k$ can be updated after the face normal $\mathbf{n}_m$ has been filtered and demised. The orthogonality condition yields the following family of simultaneous linear equations:

$$\begin{cases} \mathbf{n}'_m \cdot (\mathbf{v}_i - \mathbf{v}_j) = 0 \\ \mathbf{n}'_m \cdot (\mathbf{v}_j - \mathbf{v}_k) = 0 \\ \mathbf{n}'_m \cdot (\mathbf{v}_k - \mathbf{v}_i) = 0 \end{cases} \tag{3}$$

The vertex positions can be updated as

$$\mathbf{v}'_i = \mathbf{v}_i + \lambda \sum_{\mathbf{v}_j \in N_i^v} \sum_{(\mathbf{v}_i, \mathbf{v}_j) \in \Delta F_m} \mathbf{n}'_m (\mathbf{n}'_m \cdot (\mathbf{v}_j - \mathbf{v}_i)) \tag{4}$$

where $\lambda > 0$ is the iteration step size. By taking the average valence of a vertex on a triangle mesh into account, λ can simply be $1/18$ according to [15].

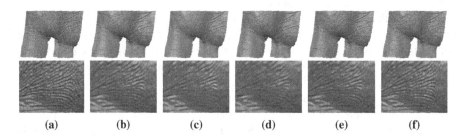

(a)   (b)   (c)   (d)   (e)   (f)

Fig. 2. A comparison of denoising results between our method and other feature-preserving methods on the real laser-scanned PALM model. The second row shows a locally zoomed view. Note that our result has the deepest skin wrinkles among all denoised results. (a) Original noisy model. (b) Fleishman et al. [8]. (c) Hildebrandt and Polthier [11]. (d) Sun et al. [15]. (e) Fan et al. [16]. (f) Our method.

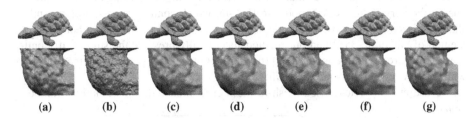

Fig. 3. A comparison of denoising results between our method and other feature-preserving methods on the TURTLE model with Gaussian noise ($\sigma = 0.15$ mean edge length) added. The bottom row shows a zoomed view of the leg, which clearly shows that our method better preserves surface details. (a) Original model. (b) Noisy model. (c) Fleishman et al. [8]. (d) Hildebrandt and Polthier [11]. (e) Sun et al. [15]. (f) Fan et al. [16]. (g) Our method.

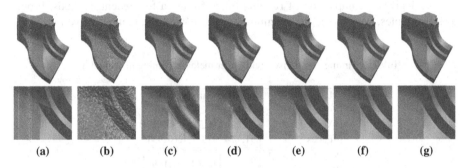

Fig. 4. A comparison between our method and other feature-preserving methods on the FAN-DISK model with Gaussian noise ($\sigma = 0.2$ mean edge length) added. The bottom row shows a zoomed view of the shallow discontinuity on the model. (a) Original model. (b) Noisy model. (c) Fleishman et al. [8]. (d) Hildebrandt and Polthier [11]. (e) Sun et al. [15]. (f) Fan et al. [16]. (g) Our method.

4 Experimental Results

In this section, we demonstrate our experimental results which shows the advantages of our method.

4.1 Denoising Results

Our experiments were carried out on generic meshes captured by laser scanners(Figs. 2), large meshes with synthetic noise (Figs. 3), CAD models with synthetic noise (Figs. 4).

In Figs. 2, we perform comparisons between our method and other feature-preserving denoising methods [8, 11, 15, 16]. The results there indicate that our method causes less blurring at high-resolution surface details than other methods. We have also performed similar comparisons over large meshes with synthetic noise. Figs. 3 clearly demonstrate that our method better preserves surface features than other methods.

We have also compared our method with recent feature-preserving denoising methods on the very typical CAD model in Fig. 4a, which contains edges, corners and a shallow discontinuity. Most of the methods keep edges and corners well, but only the method of Fan et al. [16] and our method successfully preserve the shallow discontinuity. Compared with the method in [16], our method spends much less time (Tab. 1), while achieving a higher-quality result.

We use the L^2 vertex-based mesh-to-mesh error metric in our numerical comparisons:

$$Error_v = \sqrt{1/(3 \sum_{k \in F} A_k) \sum_{i \in V} \sum_{j \in N_i^f} A_j dist(x_i', M)^2} \tag{5}$$

where $dist(x_i', M)$ is the L^2 distance between a new vertex x_i' and a triangle of a reference mesh M which is closest to x_i'. Table 2 shows errors measured in this metric for various algorithms. We can see that our denoised result is closest to the original noise-free model, which is consistent with the visual results.

Table 1 gives a comparison of running times among a few recent methods. From these two tables, we can see the running time grows with the number of vertices and

Table 1. Timing comparison with other methods (timing in seconds)

Model	Fandisk	Palm	Turtle
Figure	4	2	3
#Vertices	25,894	46,565	134,057
#Faces	51,174	92,054	267,931
Fleishman et al. [8]	0.197	0.361	1.149
PMC [11]	4.010	8.345	23.3301
Sun et al. [15]	0.201	0.398	1.118
Fan et al. [16]	2.975	4.773	13,349
Our method	0.582	1.154	1.872

Table 2. L^2 error comparison

Model	Fandisk	Turtle
Figure	4	3
#Verices	25,894	134,057
#Faces	51,174	267,931
Fleishman et al. [8]	2.197	1.774
PMC [11]	1.117	1.822
Sun et al. [15]	1.031	1.831
Fan et al. [16]	0.975	1.743
Our method	0.892	1.675

faces. Table 1 shows that our algorithm requires a little longer time than that of Sun et al. [15] and a much shorter time than that of Fan et al. [16]. In summary, our method can quickly generate high-quality denoised results.

5 Conclusions

We have presented a robust and efficient mesh denoising algorithm that preserves high-resolution details and shallow discontinuities very well. In our algorithm, we apply a revised density-based clustering method to a neighborhood of every face to extract a subset of neighboring faces which belong to the same cluster as the central face. By filtering the central face normal only within this subset, our method can preserve details while removing noise. Finally, vertex positions are updated to be consistent with the filtered face normals using a least-squares formulation. Experiments on various types of meshes indicate that our method has advantages over previous surface denoising methods.

Acknowledgement. This project was funded by the CNSF(61202229).

References

1. Field, D.: Laplacian smoothing and Delaunay triangulations. Communications in Applied Numerical Methods 4(6), 709–712 (1988)
2. Taubin, G.: A signal processing approach to fair surface design. In: Proceedings of the 22nd Annual Conference on Computer Graphics and Interactive Techniques, pp. 351–358 (1995)
3. Desbrun, M., Meyer, M., Schröder, P., Barr, A.: Implicit fairing of irregular meshes using diffusion and curvature flow. In: Proceedings of the 26th Annual Conference on Computer Graphics and Interactive Techniques, pp. 317–324 (1999)
4. Ohtake, Y., Belyaev, A., Bogaevski, I.: Polyhedral surface smoothing with simultaneous mesh regularization. In: Proceedings of Geometric Modeling and Processing 2000. Theory and Applications, pp. 229–237 (2000)
5. Clarenz, U., Diewald, U., Rumpf, M.: Anisotropic geometric diffusion in surface processing. In: Proceedings of the Conference on Visualization 2000, pp. 397–405 (2000)
6. Desbrun, M., Meyer, M., Schröder, P., Barr, A.: Anisotropic feature-preserving denoising of height fields and bivariate data. Graphics Interface 11(10), 145–152 (2000)
7. Bajaj, C., Xu, G.: Anisotropic diffusion of surfaces and functions on surfaces. ACM Transactions on Graphics (TOG) 22(1), 4–32 (2003)
8. Fleishman, S., Drori, I., Cohen-Or, D.: Bilateral mesh denoising. In: International Conference on Computer Graphics and Interactive Techniques, pp. 950–953 (2003)
9. Jones, T., Durand, F., Desbrun, M.: Non-iterative, feature-preserving mesh smoothing. ACM Transactions on Graphics 22(3), 943–949 (2003)
10. Tomasi, C., Manduchi, R.: Bilateral filtering for gray and color images. In: Proceedings of the Sixth International Conference on Computer Vision, p. 839 (1998)
11. Hildebrandt, K., Polthier, K.: Anisotropic filtering of non-linear surface features. In: Computer Graphics Forum, vol. 23, pp. 391–400. Blackwell Publishing (2004)
12. Yagou, H., Ohtake, Y., Belyaev, A.: Mesh denoising via iterative alpha-trimming and nonlinear diffusion of normals with automatic thresholding. In: Proc. Computer Graphics Intl., pp. 1–6 (2003)

13. Yu, Y., Zhou, K., Xu, D., Shi, X., Bao, H., Guo, B., Shum, H.: Mesh editing with poisson-based gradient field manipulation. ACM Transactions on Graphics (TOG) 23(3), 644–651 (2004)
14. Lee, K., Wang, W.: Feature-preserving mesh denoising via bilateral normal filtering. In: Ninth International Conference on Computer Aided Design and Computer Graphics, p. 6 (2005)
15. Sun, X., Rosin, P., Martin, R., Langbein, F.: Fast and effective feature-preserving mesh denoising. IEEE Transactions on Visualization and Computer Graphics 13(5), 925–938 (2007)
16. Fan, H., Yu, Y., Peng, Q.: Robust Feature-Preserving Mesh Denoising Based on Consistent Sub-Neighborhoods. IEEE Transactions on Visualization and Computer Graphics 16 (2010)
17. Shen, Y., Barner, K.: Fuzzy vector median-based surface smoothing. IEEE Transactions on Visualization and Computer Graphics 10(3), 252–265 (2004)

Mesh Segmentation for Parallel Decompression on GPU

Jieyi Zhao, Min Tang*, and Ruofeng Tong

College of Computer Science and Technology, Zhejiang University, Hangzhou, China
{su27,tang_m,trf}@zju.edu.cn

Abstract. We present a novel algorithm to partition large 3D meshes for GPU-based decompression. Our formulation focuses on minimizing the replicated vertices between patches, and balancing the numbers of faces of patches for efficient parallel computing. First we generate a topology model of the original mesh and remove vertex positions. Then we assign the centers of patches using geodesic farthest point sampling and cluster the faces according to geodesic distance. After the segmentation we swap boundary faces to fix jagged boundaries and store the boundary vertices for whole-mesh preservation. The decompression of each patch runs on a thread of GPU, we have evaluated its performance on various large benchmarks. In practice, the GPU-based decompression algorithm runs more than 48X faster with that on the CPU.

Keywords: Parallel decompression, Mesh segmentation, Connectivity compression, GPU, Edgebreaker.

1 Introduction

Various algorithms have been proposed to compress 3D meshes in computer graphics. Also many parallel algorithms have been proposed for accelerating mesh decompression on GPUs. In this paper, we mainly deal with designing algorithms that can exploit thread-level parallelism of GPUs. We present a novel mesh connectivity segmentation algorithm that can partition a large mesh into many patches to match the architecture of GPU for decompressing. Our formulation proves to accelerate mesh decompression significantly while only little increase of the compressed data. In practice, the GPU-based decompression algorithm runs more than 48X faster than the sequential algorithm on CPU.

2 Related Work

Rossignac's Edgebreaker [9] and its later improvements gives the best compression rate for triangle mesh connectivity. However, these mesh algorithms decompress through sequential encoding, which cannot be used for random access mesh

---

* Corresponding author.

S.-M. Hu and R.R. Martin (Eds.): CVM 2012, LNCS 7633, pp. 83–90, 2012.

traversal. Topraj [3] proposed the most efficient algorithm that can be used for random access mesh traversal.

Patch-type segmentation algorithms partition meshes into disk-like patches. Segmentation algorithms cluster small region with similar attributes into large regions. There are mainly three schemes: region-growing scheme, hierarchical-clustering scheme and the k-means based clustering scheme [10]. Categorized by applications, the features used in mesh segmentation can be curvature [6], normal [10] and geodesic distance [5], or symmetry [7].

Modern GPUs are regarded as high-throughput processors, which have a theoretical peak performance of a few Tera-Flops. The computations on GPUs are performed simultaneously by executing a large number of threads. GPUs consist of several multi-processors. To fully exploit the computational capabilities of GPUs, good task decomposition scheme needs to be designed.

3   Mesh Connectivity Segmentation

3.1   Motivation

Because of the limited memory of GPUs and the increasing size of 3D models, the compression and decompression of certain large 3D models still needs to be processed in non-random accessed algorithm. Our algorithm partitions 3D meshes into many patches, which will match the multi-thread architecture of GPUs. Then we use connectivity compression algorithm to compress each patch, thus the decompression can be highly accelerated to meet speed priority needs. The patches after the segmentation will share vertices, which will store more than the original 3D mesh. So we need to make the result of segmentation contain less replicate vertices. What's more, we need to make each patch have balanced number of faces so that the decompression speed will be optimized.

3.2   Evolution of Topology

Because our segmentation deals only with mesh connectivity, we can simplify the original mesh into a topology model without vertex positions. The center of a face is in the geometric center of the equilateral triangle. The distance between points are defined by geodesic distance of the topology model, we use 1 as the length of edges for the geodesic distance calculation.

The topology model cannot represent an actual mesh, but it can be use to judge the relationship among faces and vertices. As Figure 1 shows, the distance in the topology model is computed by geodesic distance. Given two faces, the distance between them is defined as the geodesic distance between their centers, where the center is in the geometric center of the equilateral triangle.

3.3   Center Assignment and Face Clustering

To obtain parallel execution of decompression across different threads of GPU, the mesh needs to be uniformly segmented so that the number of faces of each

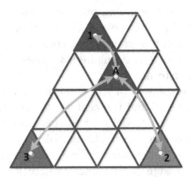

Fig. 1. The distance in the topology model: The distance is defined by the geodesic distance between the centers of faces

Fig. 2. Assignment of Centers: Using geodesic farthest point sampling on the topology model, 50 points are uniformly positioned on the Armadillo 3D mesh

patch is balanced. If one or more patch has many more faces than the others, the whole parallel decompression performance will slow down.

The algorithm to assign the centers of the patches is taken directly from previous works on geodesic remeshing [8]. A uniform sampling of points on a surface is obtained using a greedy farthest point sampling. A first point is picked then the geodesic distances to this point are computed. The Fast Marching algorithm [1] which was presented for finding 2D paths or for 3D extension and improvements is used to find the farthest point. The farthest point is selected as the next sampling point, then distance map is updated using a local propagation. The geodesic farthest points are generated from the distance map respectively.

The geodesic farthest point sampling procedure runs on the topology model, after that the sampled points will be refined to its nearest center of face. An example of center assignment is shown in Figure 2, 50 points are uniformly distributed on the surface of the Armadillo 3D mesh, these points make the centers of the following clustering step.

After the assignment of centers of the patches, we can cluster the faces using the distance between them and the centers. We use the distance defined in section 3.2, for each face of the model we find the nearest center point.

The clustering procedure can also run in multi-level to make the segmentation more flexible and accurate. For instance, if we want to partition the mesh into M patches, we can first assign $M*k$ centers where k is an integer. Then we can use clustering algorithm such as K-Means or Affinity Propagation [2] to further cluster the faces which will make higher correctness and quality of the segmentation. Figure 4 shows a partition example of the lucy 3D model in 50 clusters.

3.4   Postprocess on Boundary Elements

After the clustering step, the mesh is partitioned into several patches. Because the clustering only considers the distance between the faces and centers, the patches are likely to have jagged boundary. We need to refine such faces so that the replicate vertices can be further decreased. The refinement is done by swapping the cluster of the boundary faces. Figure 3 shows the swap of boundary faces and the refinement result of jagged boundary.

The goal of our algorithm is to generate mesh that is equivalent to the original one after parallel decompression, the patches need to connect with each other, accordingly the overall boundary information needs to be stored. We store the

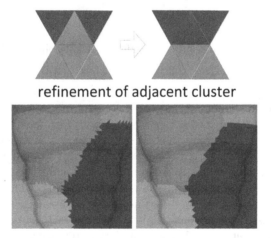

refinement of adjacent cluster

Fig. 3. Refinement of Faces: The faces on the jagged boundary need to be swapped in order to reduce replicate vertices

boundary vertices in a separate array. For each patch of the segmentation, the boundary vertices are stored in the format of their indices, while the other vertices are stored directly with their vertex coordinates. When parallel decompression process runs, the boundary vertices are directly indexed, while other vertices are indexed after a prefix-sum [4] operation. In this situation, the indices of the boundary vertices will be stored 2 more times, which will make the result mesh larger than the initial one before segmentation.

4   Implementation and Performance

In this section, we describe our implementation of the compression and decompression on the GPU, and highlight the performance of our algorithm on various benchmarks. We used Visual C++ for partitioning and later processes. We used CUDA toolkit 4.0 as the development environment for GPU. We use NVIDIA Visual Profiler to compute the kernel execution time, the data input/output time between GPU and host memory. The sequential version of decompression runs on a standard PC (AMD PhenomII 2.8Ghz CPU with 6 cores).

4.1   Compression

After the connectivity segmentation, the original mesh is partitioned into many patches. The segmentation result is stored in a specified file format, so that there are many patches in one file. Then for each patch, we use the Edgebreaker algorithm to compress its connectivity information.

The Edgebreaker algorithm [9] encodes the connectivity of triangle meshes homeomorphic to a sphere, produces an op-code describing the topological relation between the current triangle and the boundary of the remaining part of the mesh. Each triangle of the mesh is visited in a depth-first order using five different operations called C, L,E, R, and S. Each triangle is labeled according to the operation that processes it. The resulting CLERS string is a compact encoding of the connectivity of the mesh.

4.2   Decompression

We use the Edgebreaker decoding algorithm to decompress the compressed mesh file. The decompression procedure of each patch runs on a single thread of the GPU. As Figure 4 shows, Edgebreaker runs on each single partition of the Lucy 3D model.

After the decompression procedure, we will use the prefix-sum operator [4] to mark the vertices, so that different patches and faces of the mesh can be combined into a whole mesh.

4.3   Performance

We have tested several 3D models for segmentation and decompression, including the 41.6MB Happy Buddha,the 162MB Dragon and the 428MB Statue model.

Fig. 4. Edgebreaker Decompression: A large 3D model is partitioned into many patches, the Edgebreaker algorithm runs parallel on each patch on GPU

Table 1. Comparison: The size of compressed data for the benchmarks using different segmentation number

Patches	Original	512	2048	8192
Happy (41.6MB)	6.8MB	7.0MB	7.2MB	
Happy (Unprocessed)	6.8MB	7.6MB	8.5MB	
Dragon (162MB)	20.5MB	21.6MB	22.9MB	25.4MB
Statue (428MB)	44.9MB	47.1MB	49.2MB	52.7MB

As Figure 5 shows, the speedup gets higher when there are more partitions, we can get up to 48.5X speedup when the Dragon model is partitioned into 8192 patches. Because the unprocessed Happy Buddha is not uniformly partitioned and no jagged boundaries are swapped, the acceleration rate of it is much lower.

Table 1 shows the size of the compressed data resulting from the sequential Edgebreaker algorithm, the parallel algorithm with 512, 2048 and 8192 patches. The result of the unprocessed happy Buddha model is less optimized than the processed one. For the 3D models segmented into 8192 partitions, there are about 20% increase in the compressed size, this is because each patch has too few faces. If the patches have tens of thousands of faces, the influence of repeated vertices can be neglected.

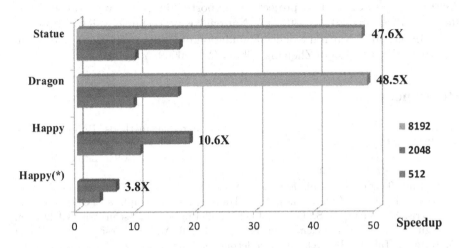

Fig. 5. Performance: The acceleration rate of the parallel decompression algorithm on GPU over the sequential algorithm on CPU. (*)Unprocessed Happy Buddha 3D model

5   Comparison and Analysis

Comparing with the sequential Edgebreaker decompression algorithm, we can get up to 48X decompressing speedup which can make further benefit for time sensitive uses.The data upload and download time from GPU to host memory is relatively a small part of the whole time for large 3D models. However, the segmentation procedure is relatively slow compared to that of decompression, we used several minutes to partition and compress these large 3D models.

The size of the compressed data will increase comparing to the sequential algorithms as there are many replicate boundary vertices whose indices will be stored twice. But this will go better when the size of each patch grows larger. If the decompression result is directly be used in GPU, it will get further benefit. Because the large 3D models are segmented into small patches, the partition and compression result can be used for out-of-core decompression for computers that does not have enough GPU memory.

6   Conclusion

We present an algorithm for parallel decompression of mesh connectivity on GPU. Our formulation focuses on the average segmentation of mesh connectivity for parallel connectivity decompression. Our approach is flexible and the decompression procedure maps well to commodity GPUs. In practice, our algorithm can improve the performance of mesh decompression on current GPU architectures.

Acknowledgement. The project is supported in part by National Basic Research Program (2011CB302205), National Key Technology R&D Program (2012BAD35B01), Natural Science Foundation of China (61170140), and Natural Science Foundation of Zhejiang, China (Y1100069, Y1100018).

References

1. Andrew, A.M.: Level set methods and fast marching methods. Robotica 18(1), 89–92 (2000)
2. Frey, B.J., Dueck, D.: Clustering by passing messages between data points. Science 315, 972–976 (2007)
3. Gurung, T., Luffel, M., Lindstrom, P., Rossignac, J.: Lr: compact connectivity representation for triangle meshes. ACM Transactions on Graphics (TOG) 30 (2011)
4. Harris, M., Sengupta, S., Owens, J.D.: Parallel prefix sum (scan) with CUDA. In: Nguyen, H. (ed.) GPU Gems 3, ch. 39, pp. 851–876. Addison Wesley (August 2007)
5. Katz, S., Tal, A.: Hierarchical mesh decomposition using fuzzy clustering and cuts. ACM Trans. Graph. 22(3), 954–961 (2003)
6. Lavoué, G., Dupont, F., Baskurt, A.: A new cad mesh segmentation method, based on curvature tensor analysis. Computer-Aided Design 37(10), 975–987 (2005)
7. Mitra, N.J., Guibas, L.J., Pauly, M.: Partial and approximate symmetry detection for 3d geometry. ACM Trans. Graph. 25(3), 560–568 (2006)
8. Peyré, G., Cohen, L.D.: Geodesic remeshing using front propagation. Int. J. Comput. Vision 69(1), 145–156 (2006)
9. Rossignac, J.: Edgebreaker: connectivity compression for triangle meshes. IEEE Transactions on Visualization and Computer Graphics 5, 84–115 (1998)
10. Yamauchi, H., Lee, S., Lee, Y., Ohtake, Y., Belyaev, A.G., Seidel, H.-P.: Feature sensitive mesh segmentation with mean shift. In: SMI, pp. 238–245 (2005)

Modeling Residential Urban Areas
from Dense Aerial LiDAR Point Clouds

Qian-Yi Zhou and Ulrich Neumann

University of Southern California

Abstract. We present an automatic system to reconstruct 3D urban models for residential areas from aerial LiDAR scans. The key difference between downtown area modeling and residential area modeling is that the latter usually contains rich vegetation. Thus, we propose a robust classification algorithm that effectively classifies LiDAR points into trees, buildings, and ground. The classification algorithm adopts an energy minimization scheme based on the 2.5D characteristic of building structures: buildings are composed of opaque skyward roof surfaces and vertical walls, making the interior of building structures invisible to laser scans; in contrast, trees do not possess such characteristic and thus point samples can exist underneath tree crowns. Once the point cloud is successfully classified, our system reconstructs buildings and trees respectively, resulting in a hybrid model representing the 3D urban reality of residential areas.

1 Introduction

Urban modeling from aerial LiDAR scans has been an important topic in both computer graphics and computer vision. As researchers mainly focus on downtown areas containing various building structures such as skyscrapers, modern office buildings, stadiums and convention centers; *building reconstruction* is believed to be the core of urban modeling, which has attracted much attention such as [4,5,8,10,15,18,19,20,21]. In these efforts, trees are usually considered as an interference to the urban modeling problem, and thus are detected and removed from the input by classification in pre-processing. Existing classification algorithms apply heuristics or machine learning approaches on point features including height, intensity, and local geometry information.

However, two new challenges emerge when the urban modeling problem extends to residential areas. First, as shown in Figure 1(a), vegetation is a major component of urban reality in residential areas. An urban modeling method for residential areas should detect and reconstruct both buildings and trees, *e.g.*, as we did in Figure 1(b). The second challenge lies in the classification method: dense LiDAR scans capture the detailed geometry of tree crowns, which may have similar height and local geometry features as rooftops of residential buildings. Figure 2 shows such an example where part of the tree crown shows similar or even better *planarity* than part of the rooftop (see closeups illustrating local points as spheres together with the optimal plane fitted to them). Classification

S.-M. Hu and R.R. Martin (Eds.): CVM 2012, LNCS 7633, pp. 91–98, 2012.
© Springer-Verlag Berlin Heidelberg 2012

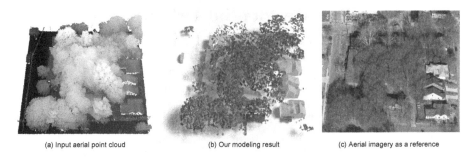

(a) Input aerial point cloud   (b) Our modeling result   (c) Aerial imagery as a reference

Fig. 1. Given (a) a dense aerial LiDAR scan of a residential area (point intensities represent heights), we reconstruct (b) 3D geometry for buildings and trees respectively. (c) Aerial imagery is shown as a reference.

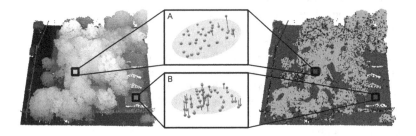

Fig. 2. Local geometry features become unreliable when dealing with residential areas with rich vegetation. In closeups of (A) a tree crown region and (B) a rooftop region, points are rendered as spheres while a locally fitted plane is rendered in yellow. Right: classification results of [18], trees in green, buildings in purple, and ground in dark grey.

algorithms based on local geometry features may fail and produce significant modeling errors. *E.g.*, Figure 2 right.

To address these two challenges, we present a robust classification method to classify input points into trees, buildings, and ground. Building models and trees are created from these points using a state-of-the-art building reconstruction algorithm [19] and a novel leaf-based tree modeling approach, respectively. The heart of our classification method is a simple, intuitive, but extremely effective measurement. In particular, we observe that residential buildings usually show a strong 2.5D characteristic, *i.e.*, they are composed of skywards roofs and vertical walls; both are opaque and thus prevent the laser beams from penetrating the building structure. Therefore, there is no point sample inside the building structure. The rooftops (or ground) become the lowest visible surface at a certain x-y position, as illustrated in Figure 3 left. In contrast, trees, composed of branches and leaves, do not have this 2.5D structure. With multiple passes of scanning from different angles, the point cloud captures not only the top surface of the tree crown, but also surfaces inside and underneath the crown, as shown in Figure 3 right.

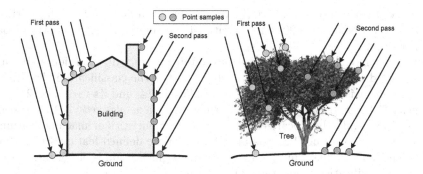

Fig. 3. While building structures have a 2.5D characteristic, trees do not possess such property. Dense laser scans may capture surface points under the tree crown (right).

Contributions: To the best of our knowledge, we are the first to address the urban modeling problem for residential areas with rich vegetation from aerial LiDAR scans. We specifically list our novelties as follows:

1. We observe the key difference between building structures and trees from the perspective of the 2.5D characteristic. Based on this observation, we propose an effective algorithm to classify trees, building roofs, and ground.
2. We propose a complete system for urban reconstruction of residential areas. A hybrid model containing both 2.5D building models and leaf-based tree models is generated in an automatic and robust manner.

2 Related Work

Urban modeling from aerial LiDAR is an important topic that has drawn much attention in both computer graphics and computer vision communities. Recent research work [8,10,15,18] introduces an automatic urban modeling pipeline involving three key steps: *classification* detects and removes trees from the input point cloud; *segmentation* splits individual building roof patches out of the ground; and *building reconstruction* focuses on creating compact and accurate mesh models to represent the geometry of building structures.

Since downtown areas are usually the main target of reconstruction, modern urban modeling methods emphasize on building structures. For instance, Verma *et al.*[15] explore the roof topology graph connecting planar roof patches. Lafarge *et al.*[4] find the optimal configuration of 3D building primitives using a RJMCMC sampler. Matei *et al.*[8] and Poullis and You [10] create building models adapted to Manhattan-World grammars via different approaches. Zebedin *et al.*[17] generate both planar roof patches and surfaces of revolution. Toshev *et al.*[14] propose parse trees as a semantic representation of building structures. Lafarge and Mallet [5] combine primitives and a general mesh representation to achieve hybrid reconstruction. Zhou and Neumann develop both data-driven modeling approaches [19,20] and primitive-based method that supports global regularities [21].

In urban modeling systems, trees are often recognized as outliers and thus are classified and removed in the first step. Most of the classification algorithms rely on point-wise features including height [5,7,11,14] and its variation [2,7,11], intensity [7,11], and local geometry information such as *planarity* [5,15,18], *scatter* [5,14,18], and other local geometry features. Heuristics or machine learning algorithms are introduced as classifiers based on the defined feature set. To further identify individual building roof patches, segmentation is either introduced in a post-classification step, or combined with classification in the form of energy minimization such as [5].

Computer graphics and remote sensing communities have made great efforts in modeling trees from ground LiDAR and imagery, such as [3,6,9,12,13,16]. A general tree model is broadly adopted in these literatures, composed of skeletal branches and leaves attached to them. Inspired by these efforts, we propose leaf-based tree modeling from aerial LiDAR scans.

The **2.5D characteristic of building models** is first formally observed and defined in [19], as "building structures being composed of detailed roofs and vertical walls connecting roof layers". Many research efforts exploit this characteristic to help building reconstruction either implicitly [8,10,15] or explicitly [5,19,20,21]. Nevertheless, we are the first to introduce the 2.5D characteristic of building structures into the classification problem. We propose a simple, efficient and effective classification algorithm that gains great accuracy in residential areas with rich vegetation.

3   Point Cloud Classification

Given an aerial LiDAR point cloud of a residential area as input, the objective of classification is to classify points into three categories: trees, buildings, and ground. As mentioned in Section 1 and illustrated in Figure 3, the 2.5D characteristic is the key difference between trees and buildings (or ground). In order to formulate this concept, we discretize the point cloud by embedding it into a uniform 2D grid G. In each grid cell c, the point set $P(c)$ is segmented into multiple *layer fragments* $L(c)$, using local distance-based region growing. Ideally, a layer fragment $l_{building} \in L(c)$ lying on a 2.5D object (rooftop or ground) must have the lowest height among all layer fragments in $L(c)$, because the rooftop (or ground) is always the lowest visible surface to laser beams at a certain x-y position, as analyzed in Section 1. On the other hand, a tree layer fragment l_{tree} can exhibit any height. However, as there is usually a ground or rooftop surface underneath tree samples, l_{tree} is not expected to be the lowest layer fragment in $L(c)$. Therefore, we check all the layer fragments in each cell, assign only the lowest layer fragment as non-trees (rooftop or ground), and classify the rest layer fragments as trees. From an energy minimization perspective, this 2.5D characteristic criterion can be quantized with a data energy term $E_d(x_l)$ for each $l \in L(c)$ as:

$$E_d(x_l) = \begin{cases} \alpha & \text{if } x_l = building \text{ or } ground, \text{ and } l \text{ is not the lowest in } L(c) \\ \beta & \text{if } x_l = tree, \text{ and } l \text{ is the lowest layer fragment in } L(c) \\ 0 & \text{otherwise} \end{cases} \quad (1)$$

where x_l is the label of layer fragment l.

To further discriminate building and ground in the energy minimization framework, we introduce *elevation* of layer fragment $e(l)$ defined as the height difference between l and the ground elevation at c's center. Another data energy term $E_g(x_l)$ is defined accordingly:

$$E_g(x_l) = \begin{cases} \gamma \cdot max(1 - \frac{e(l)}{\sigma}, 0) & \text{if } x_l = building \\ \gamma \cdot min(\frac{e(l)}{\sigma}, 1) & \text{if } x_l = ground \\ 0 & \text{if } x_l = tree \end{cases} \quad (2)$$

where σ is the normalization factor. Empirically, $\sigma = 6m$, as suggested in [5].

With a smooth energy $E_s(x_{l_1}, x_{l_2})$ defined over all neighboring layer fragment pairs (*i.e.*, layer fragments belonging to neighboring cells and satisfying certain distance criteria), we build a Markov Random Field which leads to an energy minimization problem over the labeling x of the entire layer fragment set $\mathcal{L}$:

$$E(x) = \sum_{l \in \mathcal{L}} (E_d(x_l) + E_g(x_l)) + \lambda \sum_{(l_1, l_2) \in \mathcal{N}} E_s(x_{l_1}, x_{l_2}) \quad (3)$$

where $\mathcal{N}$ is the set of neighboring layer fragment pairs, and smooth energy $E_s(x_{l_1}, x_{l_2})$ is defined as characteristic function $1_{x_{l_1} \neq x_{l_2}}$.

With the energy minimization problem being solved using the well-known graph-cut method [1], point labels are determined as the label of the corresponding layer fragment. To further construct roof patches from building points, a region growing algorithm is applied based on certain distance criteria. While large building patches are adopted as rooftops, small patches are considered as outliers and removed henceforth.

4 Modeling of Urban Elements

Based on the successful classification of input points, we introduce different modeling approaches for trees, buildings, and ground respectively.

4.1 Tree Modeling

Modern tree modeling approaches adopt a general tree structure composed of skeletal branches and leaves attached to them. Tree reconstruction usually begins with a branch generation algorithm followed by a leaf modeling approach. However, unlike ground-based laser scans and imagery, aerial LiDAR data captures very few samples on branches, making branch generation a difficult task. Therefore, we choose to directly model tree leaves by fitting surface shapes around tree points having sufficient neighbors.

In particular, for each tree point p with sufficient neighbors, Principal Component Analysis is applied to its neighboring point set $N(p)$ to fit an ellipsoid. Eigenvectors $\mathbf{v}_0, \mathbf{v}_1, \mathbf{v}_2$ and eigenvalues $\lambda_0, \lambda_1, \lambda_2$ of the covariance matrix represent the axes directions and lengths of the ellipsoid respectively. We employ the inscribed octahedron of the ellipsoid to represent the local leaf shape around p. Specifically, an octahedron is created with six vertices located at $\{\mathbf{v}_p \pm s\lambda_0\mathbf{v}_0, \mathbf{v}_p \pm s\lambda_1\mathbf{v}_1, \mathbf{v}_p \pm s\lambda_2\mathbf{v}_2\}$, where $\mathbf{v}_p$ is the location of p and s is a user-given size parameter.

A uniform sampling over the tree point set P_{tree} can be applied to further reduce the scale of the reconstructed models.

4.2 Building Modeling

We adopt 2.5D dual contouring method [19] to create building models from rooftop patches through three steps: (1) sampling 2.5D Hermite data over a uniform 2D grid, (2) estimating a hyper-point in each grid cell, and (3) generating polygons.

The only challenge in applying 2.5D dual contouring to residential area data lies in rooftop holes caused by occlusion. To solve this problem, we add a hole-filling step right after 2.5D Hermite data is sampled from input points. In particular, we scan the entire 2D grid to detect rooftop holes, and solve a Laplace's equation $\nabla^2 z = 0$ to fill these holes, where z represents the heights of *surface Hermite samples* at grid corners. Existing surface Hermite samples serve as the boundary condition of the Laplace's equation.

4.3 Ground Modeling

Ground models can be easily created by rasterizing ground points into a DSM (digital surface model). Holes are filled via linear interpolation.

5   Experimental Results

Figure 4 shows our urban reconstruction results for a 520m-by-460m residential area in the city of Atlanta. The input contains 5.5M aerial LiDAR points with $22.9/m^2$ resolution. Our algorithm reconstructs 56K triangles for building models, and 53K octahedrons as tree leaves, in less than two minutes on a consumer-level laptop. As illustrated in the closeups of Figure 4, our classification algorithm successfully classifies points into trees, ground, and individual building patches (second column). A hybrid urban model is generated by combining 2.5D polygonal building models and leaf-based tree models (third column). Aerial imagery is given in the last column as a reference.

| Input point cloud | Classification results | Urban reconstruction | Aerial Imagery |

Fig. 4. Urban models reconstructed from 5.5M aerial LiDAR points for a residential area in the city of Atlanta

6   Conclusion

In this paper, we address the complicated problem of reconstructing urban models for residential areas with rich vegetation. We observe the key difference between buildings and trees in terms of the 2.5D characteristic: while buildings are composed of opaque skyward rooftops and vertical walls, trees allow point samples underneath the crown. This feature enables a powerful classification algorithm based on an energy minimization scheme. By combing classification, building modeling and tree modeling together, our system automatically reconstructs a hybrid model composed of buildings and trees from the aerial LiDAR scan of a residential area. Our experiments demonstrate the effectiveness and efficiency of our system.

References

1. Boykov, Y., Veksler, O., Zabih, R.: Fast approximate energy minimization via graph cuts. IEEE PAMI (2001) 5
2. Chen, G., Zakhor, A.: 2d tree detection in large urban landscapes using aerial lidar data. In: IEEE ICIP (2009) 4
3. Côté, J.F., Widlowski, J.L., Fournier, R.A., Verstraete, M.M.: The structural and radiative consistency of three-dimensional tree reconstructions from terrestrial lidar. Remote Sensing of Environment (2009) 4
4. Lafarge, F., Descombes, X., Zerubia, J., Pierrot-Deseilligny, M.: Building reconstruction from a single dem. In: CVPR (2008) 2, 3
5. Lafarge, F., Mallet, C.: Building large urban environments from unstructured point data. In: ICCV (2011) 2, 4, 5
6. Livny, Y., Pirk, S., Cheng, Z., Yan, F., Deussen, O., Cohen-Or, D., Chen, B.: Texture-lobes for tree modelling. In: ACM SIGGRAPH (2011) 4
7. Lodha, S.K., Fitzpatrick, D.M., Helmbold, D.P.: Aerial lidar data classification using adaboost. In: 3DIM (2007) 4
8. Matei, B., Sawhney, H., Samarasekera, S., Kim, J., Kumar, R.: Building segmentation for densely built urban regions using aerial lidar data. In: CVPR (2008) 2, 3, 4
9. Neubert, B., Franken, T., Deussen, O.: Approximate image-based tree-modeling using particle flows. In: ACM SIGGRAPH (2007) 4
10. Poullis, C., You, S.: Automatic reconstruction of cities from remote sensor data. In: CVPR (2009) 2, 3, 4
11. Secord, J., Zakhor, A.: Tree detection in urban regions using aerial lidar and image data. IEEE Geoscience and Remote Sensing Letters (2007) 4
12. Tan, P., Fang, T., Xiao, J., Zhao, P., Quan, L.: Single image tree modeling. ACM SIGGRAPH Asia (2008) 4
13. Tan, P., Zeng, G., Wang, J., Kang, S.B., Quan, L.: Image-based tree modeling. In: ACM SIGGRAPH (2007) 4
14. Toshev, A., Mordohai, P., Taskar, B.: Detecting and parsing architecture at city scale from range data. In: CVPR (2010) 3, 4
15. Verma, V., Kumar, R., Hsu, S.: 3d building detection and modeling from aerial lidar data. In: CVPR (2006) 2, 3, 4
16. Xu, H., Gossett, N., Chen, B.: Knowledge and heuristic-based modeling of laser-scanned trees. ACM Trans. Graph. (2007) 4
17. Zebedin, L., Bauer, J., Karner, K., Bischof, H.: Fusion of Feature- and Area-Based Information for Urban Buildings Modeling from Aerial Imagery. In: Forsyth, D., Torr, P., Zisserman, A. (eds.) ECCV 2008, Part IV. LNCS, vol. 5305, pp. 873–886. Springer, Heidelberg (2008) 3
18. Zhou, Q.Y., Neumann, U.: A streaming framework for seamless building reconstruction from large-scale aerial lidar data. In: CVPR (2009) 2, 3, 4
19. Zhou, Q.-Y., Neumann, U.: 2.5D Dual Contouring: A Robust Approach to Creating Building Models from Aerial LiDAR Point Clouds. In: Daniilidis, K., Maragos, P., Paragios, N. (eds.) ECCV 2010, Part III. LNCS, vol. 6313, pp. 115–128. Springer, Heidelberg (2010) 2, 4, 6
20. Zhou, Q.Y., Neumann, U.: 2.5d building modeling with topology control. In: CVPR (2011) 2, 4
21. Zhou, Q.Y., Neumann, U.: 2.5d building modeling by discovering global regularities. In: CVPR (2012) 2, 4

Constrained Texture Mapping
on Subdivision Surfaces

Yanlin Weng[1], Dongping Li[1], and Yiying Tong[2]

[1] Zhejiang University, Hangzhou, China
[2] Michigan State University, East Lansing, Michigan, USA

Abstract. We propose a texture mapping technique that allows user to directly manipulate texture coordinates of subdivision surfaces through adding feature correspondences. After features, or constraints, are specified by user on the subdivision surface, the constraints are projected back to the *control mesh* and a Polygon Matching/Embedding algorithm is performed to generate polygon regions that embed texture coordinates of *control mesh* into different regions. After this step, some *Steiner points* are added to the *control mesh*. The generated texture coordinates exactly satisfy the input constraints but with high distortions. Then a constrained smoothing algorithm is performed to minimize distortions of the subdivision surface via updating texture coordinates of the *control mesh*. Finally, an Iterative Closest Point (ICP)-based deformation algorithm is performed to remove subdivision errors caused by the added *Steiner points*.

Keywords: Parameterization, hard constraints, subdivision surfaces, texture mapping, mesh deformation.

1 Introduction

Texture mapping is widely used in computer graphics. It maps vertices of a given surface to specified positions on a given texture image. The common way to generate texture mappings is through a parameterization: a bijection from a texture space to a surface patch. Some additional requirements are usually needed, such as minimal angle/area distortions, feature correspondences, etc. Subdivision surfaces, serving as a standard for representing detailed, smooth shapes, are used in both non-real-time applications such as movies and real-time applications such as computer games. Recent work by He et al. [6] investigated parametrization directly on subdivision surfaces. However, only angle/area distortions are taken into account, other fundamental requirements in texture mapping, such as feature correspondences, are ignored. Our goal is to generate a valid parameterization that exactly satisfies a given set of feature correspondences, and to minimize distortions on the subdivision surface at the same time.

1.1 Related Work

Free Form Parameterization. This class of methods solves parameterization problem with no feature correspondences. Different "energy" terms are

S.-M. Hu and R.R. Martin (Eds.): CVM 2012, LNCS 7633, pp. 99–106, 2012.

minimized with different boundary conditions. Uniform Barycentric Coordinates [13] can generate valid parameterization for arbitrary convex shapes with fixed boundary conditions, but fails to minimize either angle or area distortions. Harmonic coordinates [3] [14] is another type of barycentric coordinates that stems from finite element methods, more precisely, from the standard piecewise linear discretization of the Laplace equation; it generates parameterization with small angle distortions, given fixed boundary conditions. Least Square Conformal Map(LSCM) [10] is a free boundary approach that minimizes angle distortions without any additional user input. The Local/Global method [11] develops LSCM and minimizes both angle and area distortions. We refer readers to the SIGGRAPH course for details [7].

Parameterization with Constraints. This class solves parameterization problem with feature correspondences. Feature correspondences are handled as *soft* constraints or *hard* constraints. [5] uses a learning theory approach to satisfy positional constraints. [9] incorporates soft positional constraints into formulation of the parameterization problem: the positional constraints are satisfied in a least squares sense. However, the constraints may not be satisfied exactly due to possible great distortions or conflicts among different constraints. [4] shows that hard constraints can always be guaranteed with introducing extra (*Steiner*) points. [8] provides a more robust solution, named MatchMaker, by automatically partitioning a mesh into several triangle regions, and allowing the user to set correspondences between the regions and input texture images.

Parameterization on Subdivision Surfaces. Subdivision surfaces, such as Catmull-Clark subdivision [1] and Loop subdivision [12] are de-facto standards used in computer graphics. Research on parameterization directly on subdivision surfaces is, however, only at its beginning. [6] shows that polygon parameterization methods produce suboptimal results when applied to subdivision surfaces and describes how these methods may be modified to operate on subdivision surfaces. They focus on how to reduce distortions on subdivision surfaces, but have ignored how to fit feature correspondences.

2   Algorithm Overview

To void possible confusions, we introduce the following notations:

- A *control mesh* is a mesh to be subdivided.
- The user-input *control mesh* is denoted by $C = \{\mathbf{V}_C, \mathbf{F}_C\}$, where $\mathbf{V}_C$ is its vertex set and $\mathbf{F}_C$ is its face set. The subdivision surface of C is denoted by $D = \{\mathbf{V}_D, \mathbf{F}_D\}$, where $\mathbf{V}_D$ is its vertex set and $\mathbf{F}_D$ is its face set.
- The *control mesh* after polygon matching (elaborated below) is denoted by $C^* = \{\mathbf{V}_C^*, \mathbf{F}_C^*\}$. The subdivision surface of C^* is denoted by $D^* = \{\mathbf{V}_D^*, \mathbf{F}_D^*\}$. Denote $\mathbf{T}(C^*)$ to be the texture coordinates of C^* and $\mathbf{T}(D^*)$ to be the texture coordinates of D^*;
- *Control points* are user-input hard constraints that map specified vertices on the *control mesh* to specified positions on the input texture image. Denote

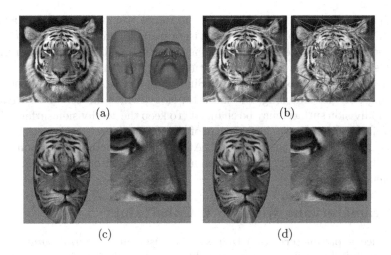

(a)   (b)

(c)   (d)

Fig. 1. Algorithm Pipeline. (a) Input texture and user specified constrained points on the subdivision surface. (b) The constrained points are projected to the coarse mesh; Polygon patches are generated and all coarse-mesh triangles are embedded to corresponding patches with no fold-overs. *Steiner* points may be added here. (c) A smoothing scheme is applied on the control mesh to minimizing distortions on the subdivision surface. (d) A mesh deformation follows to reduce subdivision errors caused by *Steiner* points.

the set of *Control points* to be CP. Denote $\mathbf{T}(CP)$ to be the target positions on texture images that the constrained points should be mapped to.

- A *subdivision matrix* is a linear operator that transforms vertices of *control mesh* to vertices of subdivision surface. Denote S, S^* such that:

$$\mathbf{V}_D = S * \mathbf{V}_C \tag{1}$$

$$\mathbf{V}_D^* = S^* * \mathbf{V}_C^* \tag{2}$$

- Angle/Area distortions: Defined exactly as in [6]

As shown in Figure 1, the overall process of our algorithm is as follows:

1. **Polygon Matching and Embedding:** After the user adds some control points on both texture image and subdivision surface, the control points are then projected to *control mesh*. A polygon matching algorithm similar with MatchMaker[8] is applied to generate paths among different control points on both texture image and control mesh. These paths cut up the texture image and texture coordinates of the *control mesh* into several convex polygon regions. Then an embedding algorithm is applied on the *control mesh* to put vertices' texture coordinates into different convex polygon regions with no foldovers.

2. **Constrained Smoothing on Subdivision Surface:** The texture coordinates after polygon matching and embedding are valid, but may result in

high angle distortion and area distortion. Hence, a smoothing scheme, aiming to minimize distortions on the subdivision surface while preventing foldovers, is performed to refine the 3D positions of vertices on the *control mesh*. After this step, a valid, low-distortion texture mapping can be obtained.

3. **Deforming the control mesh:** Since *Steiner points* may be generated during polygon matching, the mesh topology, which directly affects results of subdivision surface, may be changed. To keep the subdivision surface of the modified *control mesh* close to that of the input *control mesh*, we introduce a mesh deformation-based method. After applying mesh deformation to the modified *control mesh*, its subdivision surface is reasonably similar to the input *control mesh's*.

3   Parameterizing with Hard Constraints

To produce a parameterization that satisfies user-input *control points*, either soft constraints [9] or hard constraints [8] can be applied. Soft constraints, on the one hand, cannot exactly satisfy all constraints, especially if great distortions exist or conflicting *constraints* exist; it can also fail with large sets of constraints, resulting in an invalid parameterization [8]. Hard constraints, on the other hand, can always generate valid parameterizations, even with conflicting *control points*, through adding *Steiner points* [4]. In practice, especially when the number of *control points* is large, it is common to have conflicts. Thus parameterizing with hard constraints is our method of choice.

We derive our parameterization method from MatchMaker. However, our goal is to parameterize subdivision surface, which is sensitive to *Steiner points*: Different topologies of the control meshe, even with the same geometry shape, will lead to different subdivision surfaces. Hence, we must keep a minimal number of *Steiner points*. In fact, even though our Polygon Matching algorithm greatly reduces the number of *Steiner points*, they still have some influence on subdivisions. Such influence will be mitigated through our mesh deformation method, as is illustrated in Section 5.

Control Points Projection: C^* is initialized to C. Since *control points* are specified by the user on the subdivision surface D, we must first project them to *control mesh* C. Keeping track of the topology during the subdivision process, there are three types of control points after projection: (1). Belonging to the vertex set of C^*; this type can be added into set CP directly. (2). On an edge of C^*; then each triangle adjacent the edge should be split into two and the control point should be added. (3). In a triangle face of C^*; Then the face should be split into three and the control point should be added.

Initial Guess and Virtual Boundary: Directly following MatchMaker, the texture coordinates of *control mesh* C are first generated with the free boundary algorithm LSCM [10], and padded to create a triangulation of a bounding rectangle. The new vertices and faces are pushed into C^*. The vertices on the virtual boundary (boundary of the bounding rectangle) are then fixed in all the following processes.

Polygon Matching: The goal is to partition region inside the virtual boundary into several convex polygons with points in CP as polygon vertices. A *image line* is the line segment in texture image space connecting two points of $\mathbf{T}(CP)$; A *path* is a sequence of vertices (along with their 2D coordinates in the texture coordinate space) in the control mesh connecting the two points of CP. To make sure that corresponding *image line* and *path* are matched, several tests should be done:

1. **Self Intersection Test:** If a *path* is intersecting with any existing path, then it is not a legal path.
2. **Orientation Test:** If a newly added *path* results in a closed polygon, test its orientation and the orientation of polygon formed by corresponding *image lines*. If the orientations are different, it is not a legal path.
3. **Point Inside Region Test:** This test ensures that existed *path* will not block future paths. If a *path* divides a closed region into two closed subregions and there exists a point in CP located in different subregions in texture image space and texture coordinates space, then it is not a legal path.
4. **Convex Polygon Test:** This test guarantees that our matching results in convex polygons only, but not necessarily triangles. Consequently, fewer paths are generated by our Polygon Matching algorithm than those by MatchMaker. For each new *path*, first test whether it is diagonal of an existing closed convex polygon. If so, the *path* is not legal.
5. **Merge Polygons:** After all *paths* are generated, we merge polygon regions with the following rule: 1. push all *image lines* into a list with a random order; 2. For each *image line* in order, if its two adjacent convex polygons can be merged into a big convex polygon, delete it from the list. Perform this step until the list is no longer changing.

Polygon Embedding: We follow the same procedure as MatchMaker. Note that the embedding algorithm generates valid parameterization if the input is convex domains. Thus our Polygon Matching output, which results in convex polygons, can directly take advantage of the embedding method.

Polygon Smoothing: Described in Section 4.

Post-Processing and Output: Virtual boundaries and redundant faces are removed. The texture coordinates stored on the *control mesh C^** is our final mapping result.

4   Constrained Smoothing on Subdivision Surface

Polygon matching and embedding can generate a valid texture mapping, but the mapping result may not be visually pleasing: Great angle distortions and area distortions may exist. Our constrained smoothing method can minimizing distortions of subdivision surface D^* by updating vertex positions of the control mesh C^*. We compute the results with the following distortion energy function:

$$\min_{\mathbf{T}(C^*)} ||HS^*\mathbf{T}(C^*))||^2, \quad s.t. \quad \mathbf{T}(C^*) = \mathbf{T}(CP), \tag{3}$$

where H is a harmonic map matrix computed using LSCM [10] on subdivision surface D^* with fixed boundary(virtual boundary used in Polygon Matching).

Applying Equation 3 with exactly two constrained points and free boundary conditions will lead to texture mapping with minimal angle distortions. However, here we have more than two constraints and more importantly, we have to prevent triangle foldovers during the smoothing precess. We use the iterative Gauss-Seidel method, with some modifications. At each iteration, for each texture coordinate t_i^k, we firstly calculate a new coordinate that Gauss-Seidel formula leads to, denote it by t_g, then we update the texture coordinate as $t_i^{k+1} = t_i^k + \lambda(t_g - t_i^k)$; Where λ is step size. We use a small default step size: $\lambda = 0.1$. After updating texture coordinate of the vertex, we check its one-ring-neighbor faces, if any of them folds over, we will not updating its texture coordinate.

5   Mesh Deformation

After the constrained smoothing on subdivision surface, we nearly achieved the goal–a valid, smooth texture mapping that exactly satisfies our constraints. However, to obtain such a mapping, we may have to add *Steiner* points and result in a modified mesh topology, which can lead to difference (error) between subdivision surfaces D and D^*. To eliminate, or at least reduce, such errors, we introduce a mesh deformation scheme, which is widely used in shape modelings and mesh animations.

We adopt mesh deformation method of [15], combined with an ICP(Interactive Closest Points) procedure. At each iteration, we firstly find closest points on D for all vertices on D^*. Any closest distance below a certain threshold will result in a matched point-pair. Let M be the set of all matched point-pairs. Then we minimize the following energy function:

$$\min_{\hat{\mathbf{V}}_C^*} ||LS^*\hat{\mathbf{V}}_C^* - \delta^*(S^*\hat{\mathbf{V}}_C^*)||^2 + w_1 \sum_{i \in index(CP)} ||\hat{v}_i^* - v_i^*||^2 \\ + w_2 \sum_{i \in index(M)} ||S_i^*\hat{\mathbf{V}}_C^* - v_i^d||^2 \tag{4}$$

Where L is Laplacian operator matrix of input subdivision surface D^*, the cotangent formula [2] can be used to approximate it. v_i^* is vertex of control mesh C^*, v_i^d is matched point on subdivision surface D, $\hat{v}_i^*$ is deformed vertex to be calculated and $\hat{\mathbf{V}}_C^*$ is the vector form. S_i^* is the i'th row of matrix S^*. $\delta^*(S^*\hat{\mathbf{V}}_C^*)$ is the Laplacian vector of the deformed mesh. w_1 and w_2 are weights. we set $w_1 = 10000$ and $w_2 = 1$ by default. Recall that CP is the set of control points.

6   Experiment Results

We ran our tests in a PC with Intel(R) Core(TM) i5-2300 CPU 2.80 GHz, 4.0GB memory, 32 bits OS. Our experiments show convincing evidence that our

Table 1. Statistics & timing. #Vertices indicates number of vertices in input *control mesh*. #SubdivLevel is the levels of subdivision, generally one level leads to 4 times the number of vertices on the subdivision surface. #Control means number of *control points*. #Matching indicates timing for Polygon Matching and Embedding. #Smoothing indicates timing for smoothing on subdivision surfaces. #Deformation means timing for ICP-Deformation.

Models	#Vertices	#SubdivLevel	#Control	#Steiner	#Matching	#Smoothing	#Deformation
Face-Tiger	198	3	17	28	0.064 sec.	0.17 sec.	1.4 sec.
Monkey-Face	338	2	3	0	0.053 sec.	0.18 sec.	0 sec.
Monkey-Boot	114	2	11	6	0.043 sec.	0.20 sec.	0.05 sec.

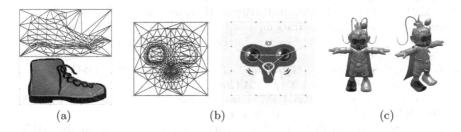

(a)   (b)   (c)

Fig. 2. (a) Polygons and texture mappings of Monkey-Boot. (b) Polygons and texture mappings of Monkey-Face. (c) Rendered result of Monkey King.

technique offers a flexible platform for constrained texture mapping on subdivision surfaces. Statistics of several experiment results are show in Table 1.

The first model, Face-Tiger, is used to illustrate our algorithm throughout the paper. The property of this model is that percentage of *control points* in the input vertices is high (nearly 10%). This will generally result in a high rate of *Steiner points* and the generated subdivision surface will significantly deviate from the original subdivision surface. Our deformation algorithm successfully reduces most of the differences.

The second and third models, Monkey-Face and Monkey-Boot, are parts of the model Monkey King. For this model, distortions are small and quite few control points are given. Our algorithm generated texture coordinates with quite few *Steiner points*. In this situation, a soft constraints method may give similar results. However, soft constraint method cannot constrain continuities along a texture seam such as the seam of the boot.

7   Conclusion

In this paper, we present a technique that provides users a simple and efficient way to manipulate texture coordinates on subdivision surfaces. We implemented our technique in an interactive system, allowing user to add/remove/move feature correspondences on both subdivision surfaces and input texture images and visualize the generated texture maps interactively. Our system can handle arbitrary number of features, producing valid and smooth results robustly.

References

1. Catmull, E., Clark, J.: Seminal graphics: Recursively generated B-spline surfaces on arbitrary topological meshes. ACM, New York (1998)
2. Desbrun, M., Meyer, M., Schröder, P., Barr, A.H.: Implicit fairing of irregular meshes using diffusion and curvature flow. In: Proceedings of the 26th Annual Conference on Computer Graphics and Interactive Techniques, pp. 317–324. ACM Press/Addison-Wesley Publishing Co., New York (1999)
3. Eck, M., DeRose, T., Duchamp, T., Hoppe, H., Lounsbery, M., Stuetzle, W.: Multiresolution analysis of arbitrary meshes. In: Proceedings of the 22nd Annual Conference on Computer Graphics and Interactive Techniques, pp. 173–182. ACM, New York (1995)
4. Eckstein, I., Surazhsky, V., Gotsman, C.: Texture Mapping with Hard Constraints. Computer Graphics Forum 20, 95–104 (2001)
5. Guenter, B., Grimm, C., Wood, D., Malvar, H., Pighin, F.: Making faces. In: ACM SIGGRAPH 2005 Courses. ACM, New York (2005)
6. He, L., Schaefer, S., Hormann, K.: Parameterizing subdivision surfaces. ACM Trans. Graph. 29, 120:1–120:6 (2010)
7. Hormann, K., Lévy, B., Sheffer, A.: Mesh parameterization: theory and practice. In: ACM SIGGRAPH 2007 Courses. ACM, New York (2007)
8. Kraevoy, V., Sheffer, A., Gotsman, C.: Matchmaker: constructing constrained texture maps. ACM Trans. Graph. 22, 326–333 (2003)
9. Lévy, B.: Constrained texture mapping for polygonal meshes. In: Proceedings of the 28th Annual Conference on Computer Graphics and Interactive Techniques, pp. 417–424. ACM, New York (2001)
10. Lévy, B., Petitjean, S., Ray, N., Maillot, J.: Least Squares Conformal Maps for Automatic Texture Atlas Generation. In: ACM SIGGRAPH Conference Proceedings (2002)
11. Ligang, L., Lei, Z., Yin, X., Craig, G., Steven, J.G.: A Local/Global Approach to Mesh Parameterization, pp. 1495–1504. The Eurographics Association and Blackwell Publishing Ltd., Copenhagen (2008)
12. Loop, C.: Smooth Subdivision Surfaces Based on Triangles. Master thesis, University of Utah (1987)
13. Tutte, W.T.: Convex representations of graphs. Proc. Lond. Math. Soc. 10, 304–320 (1960)
14. Ulrich, P., Strasse Des, J., Konrad, P.: Computing Discrete Minimal Surfaces and Their Conjugates. Experimental Mathematics 2, 15–36 (1993)
15. Zhou, K., Huang, X., Xu, W., Guo, B., Shum, H.: Direct manipulation of subdivision surfaces on GPUs. ACM Trans. Graph. 26 (2001)

Similar Region Contrast
Based Salient Object Detection

Qiang Fan and Chun Qi

School of Electronic and Information Engineering,
Xi'an Jiao Tong University, Xian, 710049, China
`qichun@mail.xjtu.edu.cn`

Abstract. Detection of visual saliency is an important issue in many computer vision tasks. In this paper, we propose a novel regional contrast based saliency detection method, generating a saliency map that enables high contrast between the foreground salient object and background. Our method mainly integrates four principles, which are based on psychological evidences, visual research and general observation. In order to suppress the homogeneous regions, and let the novel regions stand out, our method computes a region's saliency value based on the region's N closest regions defined in the $CIE\ L^*a^*b$ color space. We compared our method with the state-of-the-art saliency detection methods using a standard publicly available database. Experimental results show that our method has better performance on yielding higher precision and recall rates. In the application of image editing, we demonstrate that using our saliency map as energy map can achieve more appealing retargeting results with less distortions in the important regions.

Keywords: saliency detection, high contrast, closest regions.

1 Introduction

Human vision system is selecting and focusing on important regions that capture the attention from a variety of vision inputs every moment. We call such attracting regions *Visual saliency* or *Visual attention*. Saliency detection is an easy task for human beings while it is hard for automatic vision system. However, the computation of saliency is of significant importance in many computer vision tasks [1–3].

After the pioneering work by Itti et al. [4] on the rapid scene analysis, many saliency detection methods have raised in the following years. These methods mainly fall into two groups: bottom-up saliency detection and top-down saliency detection. Our proposed method is the first kind. It follows four basic principles as follows:

1. Local considerations, like contrast and color.
2. Global considerations, frequently occurred, homogeneous features will be less salient, while the rare features will be more salient.

S.-M. Hu and R.R. Martin (Eds.): CVM 2012, LNCS 7633, pp. 107–114, 2012.
© Springer-Verlag Berlin Heidelberg 2012

3. Human fixation rule, which states that human beings will more likely to focus their eyes on the center than the surround.
4. High-level considerations, the salient object always possesses smaller area than the background.

Principle 1 and 2 come up by psychological evidence [5–7], principle 3 is supported by a recent human vision research [8], and principle 4 is a generally accepted fact, we demonstrate it on one of the largest publicly available databases. We implement the four principles in a mathematical way. The formula mainly integrates four elements: color distance between image regions, area of the image regions, the distance between the center of the region to the center of the image, and zero setting. Our method firstly uses a segmentation step to partition the image into multiple regions. In order to let the salient region stand out, a region's saliency value is based on the color histogram contrast to its N similar regions defined in the *CIE L*a*b* color space. Besides, we introduce a weight indicating a bias to the center of the image. Moreover, it is generally accepted that background is always larger than the foreground, we propose a mechanism that if a continuous, homogeneous region is larger than 50% of the image area, we regard this region as background and set the saliency value of this region zero. In addition, in order to make the saliency map more robust, we introduce the multi-scale mechanism.

2   Similar Region Contrast Based Saliency

In this section, we elaborate our algorithm to realize the principle (1)-(4) proposed in Section 1. Consistent with principle (2), regions that have distinctive features should obtain high saliency, while those regions with frequently occured features should obtain low saliency, according to principle (1), we use color to represent this feature. According to principle (3), the salient object will more likely to be near the center of the image. Complying with principle (4), a salient object will not be too big.

This algorithm will be organized as follows (see Figure 1). We first sample the image into a prescribed size, and segment the image into regions. Then, we define a Global-based saliency based on principle (1)-(3). Next we adopt a mechanism based on principle (4) into our algorithm to enhance our saliency, Finally, we extend our saliency to multi-scale to make the saliency more robust.

2.1   Image Segmentation and Region Histogram Distance

For efficiency, we compute saliency based on region, we segment the input image into regions using a graph-based image segmentation method [9] like Cheng et al. [10]. After segmentation, we merge the ajacent regions if they are very similar.

We convert the image into *CIE L*a*b* color space, and quantize the L, a, b channel respectively. We quantize the number of $L \in [0, 100]$, $a, b \in [-128, 127]$ channel into 10, 15, 15 respectively in this paper. We choose *CIE L*a*b* color

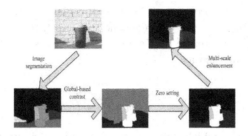

Fig. 1. The framework of the proposed method. There are four main steps in our method: segmenting the image into regions, computing Global-based saliency, setting the saliency of the region zero whose area is 50% more than the area of the image, and computing the multi-scale saliency. Note that, after the image segmentation, each region is represented by a gray value which is set arbitrary in this figure.

space due to its closeness to human vision perception compared to RGB color space. Then we build a color histogram for each region. Specifically, in our implement, the histogram of each region consists of 2250 components, each component denotes a color represented by the combination of the value of L, a, b channel respectively, we then normalize the histogram to 1.

Here, we use χ^2-distance to define the disparity between two histograms, which is more appropriate than Euclidean distance to compare histogram [11].

In our algorithm, for two region r_i^m and r_j^m, we define the χ^2-distance as [12],

$$d_{\chi^2}(r_i^m, r_j^m) = \sum_{i=1}^{d} \frac{(r_i^m - r_j^m)^2}{2(r_i^m + r_j^m)} \tag{1}$$

where the multiplication by $1/2$ is for the requirement of normalization.

2.2 Global-based Saliency

As mentioned in principle (2), if a region is considered to be salient, it may be distinctive with other regions, thus may not have many similar regions in the image. Unlike the salient object, background will always have larger areas and spread all over the image, so they have more chance to have similar background regions. Based on this observation, we define a region's saliency based on the color contrast to its N similar regions.

We denote a region as r_i^m, where i denotes the index of a region, $i \in \{1, 2, ..., I\}$, m denotes the index of scale, $m \in \{m_1, m_2, ..., m_M\}$.

For a region r_i^m, we compute $d_{\chi^2}(r_i^m, r_j^m)$ for each j, and select N similar regions with the smallest χ^2-distance between the two regions' histogram. Then, the saliency of region r_i^m is defined as:

$$S(r_i^m) = w_i^m \sum_{j=1}^{N} w_j^m d_{\chi^2}(r_i^m, r_j^m) \tag{2}$$

w_j^m means the ratio between the area of r_i^m and the total area of the N regions.

According to [8], human photographers tend to place objects of interest in the center of photographs, and the average saliency map from human eye fixations denotes a bias to the center of the image, which is close to a Gaussian falloff weight. Here, w_i^m is defined as:

$$w_i^m = exp(-\delta \cdot \frac{(x^2 + y^2)}{(w/2)^2 + (h/2)^2})$$ (3)

where w and h are the width and height of the image respectively, x^2 and y^2 are the square of average Euclidean distance of all pixels in r_i^m to the center of the image. δ controls the decent speed from the center to the surround of the image. We set $\delta = 5$ in this paper, since it is a moderate parameter. As for N, we suppose that the number of regions after segmentation and ajacent region merging is Num, we have done an experiment, varying N from $Num/4$ to $Num \cdot 2/3$, and found the influence of N is very small, but if N is too small, the number of similar region is not enough to separate the salient object from the background, in all the experiment below, if $Num < 10$, we set $N = \lceil Num/2 \rceil$, otherwise, $N = \lceil Num/4 \rceil$. The reason is that if the Num is too small, we choose more similar regions to make the saliency map more robust.

2.3   Zero Setting

Through the observation of natural images, it is generally accepted that the area of salient object is always small compared with background. Even though the salient object accounts for a large area of the image, it will generally be complex instead of homogeneous and continuous. We suppose that if the size of a region after merge is more than 50% of the image size, it is considered to be background and we set 0 for the saliency of this region,

$$S(r_i^m) = \begin{cases} S(r_i^m) & \frac{area(r_i^m)}{\sum_j area(r_j^m)} < 50\% \\ 0 & \frac{area(r_i^m)}{\sum_j area(r_j^m)} >= 50\% \end{cases}$$ (4)

2.4   Multi-scale Saliency Enhancement

As we don't know about the prior knowledge of the size of the salient object, and the single scale segmentation will not always generate a rational segmentation result through our experiment. We segment the image into different level of sizes using different parameters, thus obtain different scales. Let C denote the set of the scales, i.e., $C = \{m_1, m_2, ..., m_M\}$.

We represent each pixel by the set of multi-scale image regions centered at it. The saliency at pixel i is denoted as the mean of its saliency at different scales:

$$\bar{S}_i = \frac{1}{M} \sum_{m \in C} S_i^m$$ (5)

Finally, in order to get a more visually satisfactory result, we normalize the saliency as follows:

$$\bar{S}_i = \frac{\bar{S}_i - \min(\bar{S}_i)}{\max(\bar{S}_i) - \min(\bar{S}_i)} \tag{6}$$

3 Experiments

In this section, we tested our method on one of the largest publicly available standard databases provided by Achanta et al [13]. The experimental method we use is Segmentation by fixed thresholding as do by Achanta et al. [13] and Cheng et al. [10]. Firstly, we will do some validation experiments about steps of our methods.

3.1 Influence of the Number of Scales and Zero Setting

As stated in the segmentation method [9], the author uses a Gaussian filter to smooth the image slightly before computing the edge weights, and suggest $\delta = 0.8$, which does not produce any change to the image but helps remove artifacts. In this paper, we segment the image into regions using different δ to achieve different segmentation results, thus realize the multi-scale scheme. In this experiment, we vary M from 1 to 7. From Figure 2, we can see the performance of our saliency map improved with the increase of M.

As to zero setting, first, we will demonstrate the rationality of zero setting. According to the analysis of 1000 ground truth of the database, there is no region whose area is more than 50% of the image in the object, thus no zero setting is performed in the salient object.

From the contrast between red line and black line in the right curve of Figure 2, we can see that after adding zero setting, the performance of our method improves by some degrees.

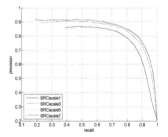 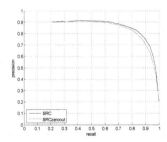

Fig. 2. The left curve shows the influence of M, the right curve shows the influence of zero setting. SRCscale1, SRCscale3, SRCscale5, SRCscale7 represent the saliency maps that are generated by $M = 1, 3, 5, 7$ respectively. SRC means the method that involves Zero Setting. SRCzeroout means the method that without zero setting.

3.2 Experimental Performance

We compared our method with other 9 state-of-the-art saliency detection methods on this dataset. Following [13], [10], the choice of these methods is motived by the following reasons: citation in literature(IT [4], SR [14]), recency(GB [15], SR [14], AC [16], FT [13], CA [17], HC [10], RC [10]), variety(IT is biologically motivated, MZ [18] is purely computational, GB is hybrid, SR estimates saliency in frequency domain, AC and FT output full resolution saliency maps), and being related to our approach(RC [10]). Qualitative comparison can be seen in Figure 3. We can seen, the saliency map generated by our method possess a high contrast between salient object and background.

The quantitative comparison can be seen from the precision and recall curves in Figure 4. The SRC method we used here is 7 scales. Our method achieves higher precision and recall rates compared with other methods.

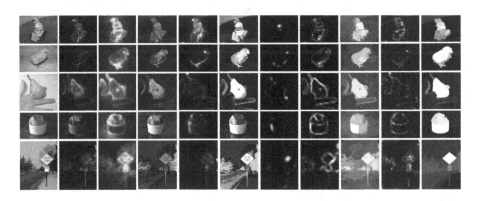

Fig. 3. qualitative comparison of saliency maps. The images from left to right columns are: original images, saliency maps produced using Achanta et.al [16], Goferman et al. [17], Achanta et.al [13], Harel et al. [15], Cheng et al. [10], Itti et al. [4], Ma et al. [18], Cheng et al. [10], Hou et al. [14], Our SRC method.

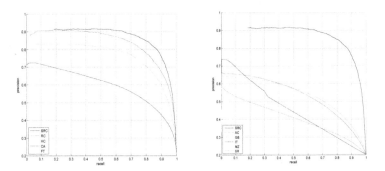

Fig. 4. Quantitative comparison between our method and other 9 state-of-the-art saliency detection methods

3.3   Content-Aware Image Retargeting

Image retargeting aims at resizing an image by expanding or shrinking the non-informative regions [1], while protecting the salient regions. The type of energy function in [1] is gradient magnitude, we replace the gradient magnitude map in [1] with our saliency map as the energy map, for comparison, we also add two most recently methods [17] and [10], from Figure 5, we can see that our methods can achieve the most eye-appealing image retargeting result.

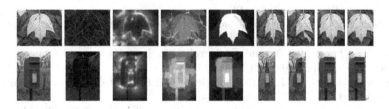

Fig. 5. Comparison of our saliency based seam carving with other methods' saliency based seam carvings on natural scene. From left to right, original image, saliency map of [1], saliency map of [17], saliency map of [10], our saliency map, result of [1], result of [17], result of [10], our method's result.

4   Conclusion

In this paper, we propose a novel salient region detection method. This saliency is based on four principles: low-level observation, global observation, human fixation observation, high-level observation. We propose an algorithm to realize these four principles. We did some verification experiments to demonstrate the setup of our algorithm. We also compared our method with other methods, experimental results show the superiority of our method. In application, we apply our saliency map on image retargeting. In the future, we will incorporate some other high level factors into our saliency map, like human face, pedestrian, vehicle detection.

Acknowledgments. We thank the anonymous reviewers for their helpful comments. This work was supported in part by the National Natural Science Foundation of China (No. 61133008), in part by the National Natural Science Foundation of China (No. 60972124) and in part by the Specialized Research Fund for the Doctoral Program of Higher Education (Grant No.20110201110012).

References

1. Avidan, S., Shamir, A.: Seam carving for content-aware image resizing. ACM Transactions on Graphics 26(3), 2462–2470 (2007)

2. Han, J., Ngan, K.N., Li, M.J., Zhang, H.J.: Unsupervised extraction of visual attention objects in color images. IEEE Transactions on Circuits and Systems for Video Technology 16, 141–145 (2006)

3. Rutishauser, U., Walther, D., Koch, C., Perona, P.: Is bottom-up attention useful for object recognition? In: IEEE CVPR, pp. 37–44 (2004)

4. Itti, L., Koch, C., Niebur, E.: A model of saliency-based visual attention for rapid scene analysis. IEEE TPAMI 20(11), 1254–1259 (1998)

5. Koch, C., Poggio, T.: Predicting the visual world: silence is golden. Nature Neuroscience 2(1), 9–10 (1999)

6. Treisman, A., Gelade, G.: Predicting the visual world: silence is golden. Cognitive Psychology 12(1), 97–136 (1980)

7. Wolfe, J.M.: A revised model of visual search. Psychonomic Bulletin & Review 1(2), 202–238 (1994)

8. Judd, T., Ehinger, K., Durand, F., Torralba, A.: Learning to predict where humans look. In: ICCV, pp. 2106–2113 (2009)

9. Rother, Felzenszwalb, P.F., Huttenlocher, D.P.: Efficient Graph-Based Image Segmentation. IJCV 59(2), 167–181 (2004)

10. Cheng, M.M., Zhang, G.X., Mitra, N.J., Huang, X.L., Hu, S.M.: Global contrast based salient region detection. In: CVPR, pp. 409–416 (2011)

11. Gorisse, D., Cord, M., Precioso, F.: Locality-Sensitive Hashing for Chi2 Distance. IEEE TPAMI 34(2), 402–409 (2012)

12. Rubner, Y., Tomasi, C., Guibas, L.J.: The Earth Mover's Distance as a Metric for Image Retrieval. IJCV 40(2), 99–121 (2000)

13. Achanta, R., Hemami, S., Estrada, F., Susstrunk, S.: Frequency-tuned salient region detection. In: CVPR, pp. 1597–1604 (2009)

14. Hou, X.D., Zhang, L.Q.: Saliency Detection: A Spectral Residual Approach. In: CVPR, pp. 1–8 (2007)

15. Harel, J., Koch, C., Perona, P.: Graph-based visual saliency. In: NIPS, pp. 545–552 (2006)

16. Achanta, R., Estrasda, F., Wils, P., Susstrunk, S.: Salient Region Detection and Segmentation. In: Gasteratos, A., Vincze, M., Tsotsos, J.K. (eds.) ICVS 2008. LNCS, vol. 5008, pp. 66–75. Springer, Heidelberg (2008)

17. Goferman, S., Zelnik-Manor, L., Tal, A.: Context-aware saliency detection. In: CVPR, pp. 2376–2383 (2010)

18. Ma, Y.F., Zhang, H.J.: Contrast-based image attention analysis by using fuzzy growing. In: ACM MM, pp. 374–381 (2003)

A Shape Enhancement Technique
Based on Multi-channel Salience Measure

Yongwei Miao[1,*], Jieqing Feng[2], Jinrong Wang[2], and Renato Pajarola[3]

[1] College of Computer Science and Technology,
Zhejiang University of Technology, Hangzhou 310023, China
[2] State Key Lab. of CAD&CG, Zhejiang University, Hangzhou 310027, China
[3] Department of Informatics, University of Zürich, Zürich CH-8050, Switzerland

Abstract. In this paper, we develop a novel visual saliency based shape enhancement technique for relief surfaces. It consists of three steps. Firstly, we calculate the multi-channel salience map of the underlying shape by combining three feature maps, i.e., the feature map of local height distribution, normal difference, and mean curvature variation. Secondly, we manipulate the original relief surface by a salience-domain shape manipulation function. Finally, we adjust surface normals of the original shape as the corresponding final normals of the manipulated surface. The experimental results show that our proposed algorithm can adjust the shading of the original shape and thus for improving its shape depiction.

Keywords: Shape Enhancement, Multi-Channel Salience, Salience-Domain Shape Modeling.

1 Introduction

Relief surfaces are now becoming widely used because of their efficiency for representing complex highly detailed models in computer graphics applications [1]. Based on the research on the visual depiction of 3D complex shapes [2–4], artists and illustrators usually employ the principles of visual perception for guiding the viewer's attention to visually salient regions. Due to its efficiency of visual persuasion in traditional art and technical illustrations, the visual saliency has been widely used in saliency-guided 3D shape enhancement for object visualization [5–7].

By incorporating the visual salience measure into the graphics modeling and rendering, the 3D shape depiction can be enhanced by bringing out its visually salient features. In fact, in the field of computer graphics, two types of shape enhancement technique have been proposed.

One type of shape enhancement approach is to adjust the geometric vertex positions to improve the illustration of 3D complex shapes. Displacement mapping [8] is the first technique that represents high frequency geometric details by adding mesostructure properties to the underlying shapes. The view-dependent displacement mapping proposed by Wang et al. [9] can synthesize the real 3D

---

* This is a paper for Computational Visual Media Conference 2012 (CVM2012), November 08—November 10, 2012, Tsinghua University, Beijing, China.

S.-M. Hu and R.R. Martin (Eds.): CVM 2012, LNCS 7633, pp. 115–121, 2012.

highly-detailed geometry by modeling the surface displacements along the viewing direction. Building upon the Lee's mesh saliency measure [4], Kim and Varshney [7] developed a technique to alter vertex position information to elicit greater visual attention.

Another type of shape enhancement technique is to enhance the visualization of 3D complex shapes by perturbing the surface normals or altering reflection rules based on local surface information. The normal perturbation technique proposed by Cignoni et al. [10] can enhance the surface features by a simple high-frequency enhancement operation of the surface normals. Inspired by the principals for cartographic terrain relief, the exaggerated shading of Rusinkiewicz et al. [11] locally adjusted the light direction over different areas of the underlying surfaces to depict the surface relief at grazing angles.

In this paper, owing to the multi-channel salience measure, we develop a novel visual saliency based shape enhancement technique to exaggerate surface geometric details of the underlying relief shape. The advantage of our shape enhancement technique is that it can adaptively alter surface shading to reveal visually salient features by perturbing the surface normals whilst keeping the desired appearance unimpaired.

2   Multi-channel Salience Measure of Relief Shapes

As a classical definition of image saliency, Itti et al. [12] calculated the saliency map by applying center-surround filtering to different multi-scale image feature maps. Inspired by Itti's model, Lee et al. [4] presented a computational framework of mesh saliency based on the multi-scale center-surround filters with Gaussian-weighted mean curvatures. However, as a local shape descriptor, the mean curvature can only characterize the differential property in an infinitesimal neighborhood of the underlying surface.

Here, in order to guide the viewer's attention to the fine-scale geometric details and thus exaggerate the visually salient features, we take the multi-channel salience measure as an input of our shape depiction algorithm. Different from the previous definitions, our salience definition of complex shapes is based on the multi-channel scheme, that is, the combination of three different feature maps, such as the 0-order feature map in terms of local height distribution, the 1-order feature map in terms of normal difference, and the 2-order feature map in terms of mean curvature variation.

Given an original complex surface, we can determine the Gaussian-weight average of three types of varied difference between each vertex and its neighboring vertices as follows,

$$\zeta_k^*(\mathbf{v}) = \frac{\sum\limits_{\mathbf{x} \in N_k(\mathbf{v})} \delta(\mathbf{v}, \mathbf{x}) exp[-\|\mathbf{x} - \mathbf{v}\|^2/(2\sigma^2)]}{\sum\limits_{\mathbf{x} \in N_k(\mathbf{v})} exp[-\|\mathbf{x} - \mathbf{v}\|^2/(2\sigma^2)]} \tag{1}$$

where N_k means the k-ring neighbors of vertex $\mathbf{v}$, σ is the standard deviation of the Gaussian filter and it is set as 1.0 in our practice. Thus, the three feature maps can be expressed as the absolute difference between the Gaussian weighted averages of three types of geometric information computed at fine and coarse scales, that is,

$$S^*(\mathbf{v}) = \|\zeta_2^*(\mathbf{v}) - \zeta_1^*(\mathbf{v})\| \tag{2}$$

In detail, the three feature maps can be calculated by the above equation (1) and (2) as follows.

- **Feature map of local height distribution** $S^h(\mathbf{v})$: It can be determined as $S^h(\mathbf{v}) = \|\zeta_2^h(\mathbf{v}) - \zeta_1^h(\mathbf{v})\|$. Here, the Gaussian-weighted average of the local height distribution $\zeta_k^h(\mathbf{v})$ can be calculated by equation (1) if we take the varied difference as $\delta(\mathbf{v}, \mathbf{x}) = \langle \mathbf{n_v}, \mathbf{v} - \mathbf{x} \rangle$. The term $\mathbf{n_v}$ means the normal vector of vertex $\mathbf{v}$.
- **Feature map of normal difference** $S^n(\mathbf{v})$: It can be computed as $S^n(\mathbf{v}) = \|\zeta_2^n(\mathbf{v}) - \zeta_1^n(\mathbf{v})\|$. Here, the Gaussian-weighted average of the surface normal difference $\zeta_k^n(\mathbf{v})$ can be determined by equation (1) if we take the varied difference as $\delta(\mathbf{v}, \mathbf{x}) = \triangle n(\mathbf{v}, \mathbf{x})$. The term $\triangle n(\mathbf{v}, \mathbf{x})$ means the normal difference between vertex $\mathbf{v}$ and its neighboring one $\mathbf{x}$, which can be computed as $\frac{1.0 - \langle \mathbf{n_v}, \mathbf{n_x} \rangle}{1.0 + \|\mathbf{v} - \mathbf{x}\|/C}$. The constant C can be chosen as $d/10.0$, and d is the diagonal length of the bounding box for whole model.
- **Feature map of mean curvature variation** $S^c(\mathbf{v})$: It can be calculated as $S^c(\mathbf{v}) = \|\zeta_2^c(\mathbf{v}) - \zeta_1^c(\mathbf{v})\|$. Here, the Gaussian-weighted average of the surface mean curvature variation $\zeta_k^c(\mathbf{v})$ can be computed by equation (1) if we take the varied difference as $\delta(\mathbf{v}, \mathbf{x}) = c(\mathbf{v}) - c(\mathbf{x})$. The term $c(\mathbf{v})$ denotes the mean curvature at vertex $\mathbf{v}$ that is estimated by the Taubin's method [13].

Finally, similar to the definition of image saliency developed by Itti et al. [12], a non-linear suppression operator $\mathfrak{N}(\cdot)$ is adopted to reduce the number of salient points of the above three feature maps before combining them. It can help the user to define what makes something unique, and therefore potentially salient features. For each feature map S^*, we first normalize it to $[0.0, 1.0]$, and then compute the maximum value M^* and the average m^* of the local maxima excluding the global maximum. The suppression step $\mathfrak{N}(S^*)$ will multiply S^* by the factor $(M^* - m^*)^2$, that is,

$$\mathfrak{N}(S^*)(\mathbf{v}) = S^*(\mathbf{v}) \cdot (M^* - m^*)^2$$

The final multi-channel mesh salience $S(\mathbf{v})$ can thus be determined by averaging all of the three maps after applying the non-linear normalization of suppression [12], that is,

$$S(\mathbf{v}) = \frac{1}{3}\mathfrak{N}(S^h)(\mathbf{v}) + \frac{1}{3}\mathfrak{N}(S^n)(\mathbf{v}) + \frac{1}{3}\mathfrak{N}(S^c)(\mathbf{v})$$

Figure 1 gives our multi-channel salience computation steps for Lion model. The final multi-channel salience map (see Figure 1(e)) combines three feature maps, which are in terms of local height distribution (see Figure 1(b)), normal difference (see Figure 1(c)), and mean curvature variation (see Figure 1(d)) respectively.

3 Multi-channel Salience Based Shape Enhancement Technique

Now, guided by the multi-channel salience definition of relief surfaces, a novel shape enhancement technique is proposed in this section. The original relief surface is firstly decomposed as the low frequency base surface and the high frequency detail surface. The detail layer is then manipulated by a special salience-domain enhancement function, and the enhanced surface can finally be obtained by adjusting its surface normals as the corresponding normals of the manipulated surface. The advantage of our shape enhancement technique is that it can adaptively alter surface shading to reveal visually salient features by perturbing the surface normals whilst keeping the desired appearance unimpaired.

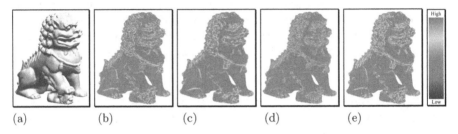

(a)   (b)   (c)   (d)   (e)

Fig. 1. Multi-channel salience computation steps for Lion model. (a): Original Lion model; (b),(c),(d): The feature map of local height distribution, normal difference, and mean curvature variation, respectively; (e) The final combined multi-channel salience map.

3.1 Shape Decomposition of Relief Surfaces

According to Zatzarinni et al.'s indirect approach [14] of surface relief extraction, the original relief surface S (be represented as the triplet $\{V|S = (\mathbf{v}_S, \mathbf{N}_S); E|S; F|S\}$ of vertices $V|S$, edges $E|S$, and facets $F|S$) is composed of a smooth base surface $B \subset \mathbb{R}^3$ and a height function $h : S \to \mathbb{R}$, that is,

$$S(\mathbf{v}) = B(\mathbf{v}) + h(\mathbf{v})\mathbf{N}_B(\mathbf{v}) \tag{3}$$

where the height function $h(\mathbf{v})$ represents the signed distance from the base surface B to the surface S along the direction of the base's unit normal $\mathbf{N}_B(\mathbf{v})$. For calculating the height field, normals of the base surface should be pre-computed via a normal smoothing operation. In practice, we employ the adaptive and anisotropic Gaussian mesh filtering scheme to estimate the face normals of base surface proposed by Ohtake et al. [15]. Here, the vertex normals of base surface can then be calculated as the normalized average of the normals of the incident faces. Furthermore, by using the estimated vertex normals $\{\mathbf{N}_B(\mathbf{v}_i), i = 1, 2, ..., n\}$, the height function $h(\mathbf{v})$ of each vertex $\mathbf{v}$ can be determined implicitly by the energy minimization step for the relative height differences of its neighboring vertices along the base surface normals. The reader can refer to their paper [14] for the technical details to calculate the height function $h(\mathbf{v})$ of each vertex $\mathbf{v}$.

Now, if taking the estimated relief height distribution of an original surface $S = \{V|S = (\mathbf{v}_S, \mathbf{N}_S); E|S; F|S\}$ as input, we can determine the base surface as $B(\mathbf{v}) = S(\mathbf{v}) - h(\mathbf{v})\mathbf{N}_B(\mathbf{v})$. The complex shapes can then be considered as made up of two layers, i.e., the large features (low frequency base surface $B(\mathbf{v})$) defining its overall shape, plus small features (high frequency detail surface $h(\mathbf{v})\mathbf{N}_B(\mathbf{v})$) accounting for the relief details.

3.2   Salience Based Shape Enhancement Operation

Inspired by the Gaussian high-pass filtering and enhancement filtering used in traditional image processing tasks [16], our salience-domain shape manipulation function can be defined as $H_{hp}(s) = 1 - exp[-(s-s_0)^2/(2\mu^2)]$, where s_0 means the average of the multi-channel salience of the whole model, and the parameter μ is the user-defined standard deviation of the Gaussian function (We set $\mu = 0.001$ in all of our experiments). The salience-domain shape enhancement function can then be expressed as follows:

$$R(s) = a + bH_{hp}(s) \tag{4}$$

Here, $H_{hp}(s)$ is the Gaussian high-pass shape manipulation function. The two manipulation parameters (a, b) can control final shape enhancement results. Finally, the surface normal $\mathbf{N}_{enhance}$ of the enhanced surface can be estimated by averaging the face normals incident to each vertices.

According to the section 3.1, we decompose the original surface into base layer and detail layer, and incorporate our multi-channel salience to influence its detail layer in the manipulated surface as follows.

$$E(\mathbf{v}) = B(\mathbf{v}) + R(s(\mathbf{v}))h(\mathbf{v})\mathbf{N}_B(\mathbf{v}) \tag{5}$$

where $E(\mathbf{v})$ represents the manipulated surface, and the $R(s(\mathbf{v}))$ is the user specified shape manipulation function defined on the multi-channel salience domain.

However, to keep the desired appearance unimpaired, it should be emphasized that we will enhance the shape depiction of 3D complex surfaces by adaptive perturbing surface normals. Now, it is easy for us to perturb the original surface normals, that is, by assigning the final normal $\mathbf{N}_{enhance}$ of the above manipulated surface $E(\mathbf{v})$ to the corresponding original surface vertex. The final enhanced surface $S' = \{V|S' = (\mathbf{v}_S, \mathbf{N}_{enhance}); E|S; F|S\}$ will improve the shape depiction of the original relief surface.

Figure 2 gives our shape enhancement framework for Lion model. The multi-channel salience map of Lion model is firstly calculated (see Figure 2(b)) and the relief height distribution is also extracted (see Figure 2(c)). The enhanced surface (see Figure 2(d)) can then be obtained in a non-photorealistic shading scheme.

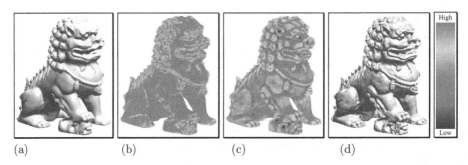

(a)   (b)   (c)   (d)

Fig. 2. Our shape enhancement framework. (a) Original Lion model; (b) The multi-channel salience map of Lion model; (c) The extracted relief height distribution of Lion model; (d) The shape enhancement result for Lion using manipulation parameters $(a, b) = (3.0, 2.0)$.

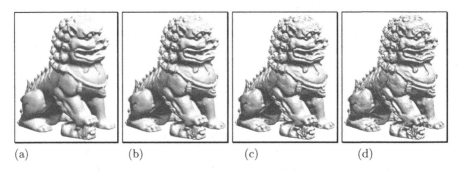

(a)   (b)   (c)   (d)

Fig. 3. Shape enhancement results for Lion model using different manipulation parameters. The two manipulation parameters (a, b) are taken as $(1.0, 2.0)$ in (b), $(3.0, 2.0)$ in (c) and $(3.0, 4.0)$ in (d), respectively.

Furthermore, in our saliency-based shape enhancement scheme, the two manipulation parameters (a, b) introduced in the salience-domain shape manipulation function $R(s) = a + bH_{hp}(s)$ will always effect the final shape enhancement results. Figure 3 shows some shape enhancement results for Lion model using different manipulation parameters (a, b) respectively, in which the surface details have been exaggerated whilst keeping the desired appearance unimpaired. Here, the large parameters a and b will bring out more fine-scale salient geometric details of the underlying shape and can convey both detail and overall shape as clearly as possible.

4   Conclusion and Future Work

In this paper, by incorporating our multi-channel salience measure into the salience-domain shape manipulation operation, we develop a novel visual saliency based shape enhancement technique to exaggerate surface geometric details of the underlying relief shape. The experimental results demonstrate that our proposed algorithm can enhance the surface geometric details effectively and thus for improving the shape depiction of the relief shape. Here, we have considered the role of surface salience measure in the context of 3D shape depiction. It will also be interesting in the future to see how other modeling and rendering tasks can benefit from our multi-channel salience measure, such as saliency-guided lighting, saliency-guided remeshing and saliency-based mesh segmentation, etc.

References

1. Botsch, M., Pauly, M., Kobbelt, L., Alliez, P., Levy, B., Bischoff, S., Rossl, C.: Geometric modeling based on polygonal meshes. In: Proc. of ACM SIGGRAPH 2007, Course Notes 23 (2007)
2. Tood, J.T.: The visual perception of 3D shape. TRENDS in Cognitive Sciences 8(3), 115–121 (2004)
3. Agrawala, M., Durand, F.: Smart depiction for visual communication. IEEE Computer Graphics and Applications 25(3), 20–21 (2005)
4. Lee, C., Varshney, A., Jacobs, D.: Mesh saliency. ACM Transactions on Graphics 24(3), 659–666 (2005)
5. Viola, I., Feixas, M., Sbert, M., Gröller, M.: Importance-driven focus of attention. IEEE Transactions on Visualization and Computer Graphics 12(5), 933–940 (2006)
6. Kim, Y., Varshney, A.: Saliency-guided enhancement for volume visualization. IEEE Transactions on Visualization and Computer Graphics 12(5), 925–932 (2006)
7. Kim, Y., Varshney, A.: Persuading visual attention through geometry. IEEE Transactions on Visualization and Computer Graphics 14(4), 772–782 (2008)
8. Cook, R.L.: Shade trees. Computer Graphics 18(3), 223–231 (1984)
9. Wang, L., Wang, X., Tong, X., Lin, S., Hu, S., Guo, B., Shum, H.-Y.: View-dependent displacement mapping. ACM Transactions on Graphics 22(3), 334–339 (2003)
10. Cignoni, P., Scopigno, R., Tarini, M.: A simple normal enhancement technique for interactive non-photorealistic renderings. Computers & Graphics 29(1), 125–133 (2005)
11. Rusinkiewicz, S., Burns, M., DeCarlo, D.: Exaggerated shading for depicting shape and detail. ACM Transactions on Graphics 25(3), 1199–1205 (2006)
12. Itti, L., Koch, C., Niebur, E.: A model of saliency based visual attention for rapid scene analysis. IEEE Transactions on Pattern Analysis and Machine Intelligence 20(11), 1254–1259 (1998)
13. Taubin, G.: Estimating the tensor of curvature of a surface from a polyhedral approximation. In: Proc. of the Fifth International Conference on Computer Vision, pp. 902–907 (1995)
14. Zatzarinni, R., Tal, A., Shamir, A.: Relief analysis and extraction. ACM Transactions on Graphics 28(5), 136: 1–136: 9 (2009)
15. Ohtake, Y., Belyaev, A., Seidel, H.-P.: Mesh smoothing by adaptive and anisotropic Gaussian filter applied to mesh normals. In: Proc. of Vision, Modeling and Visualization, pp. 203–210 (2002)
16. Gonzalez, R.C., Woods, R.E.: Digital Image Processing, 2nd edn. Prentice Hall, New Jersey (2002)

Multi-scale Salient Feature Extraction on Mesh Models

Yong-Liang Yang[1,2] and Chao-Hui Shen[2]

[1] King Abdullah University of Science and Technology, Thuwal, KSA
[2] TNList, Tsinghua University, Beijing, China

Abstract. We present a new method of extracting multi-scale salient features on meshes. It is based on robust estimation of curvature on multiple scales. The coincidence between salient feature and the scale of interest can be established straightforwardly, where detailed feature appears on small scale and feature with more global shape information shows up on large scale. We demonstrate this multi-scale description of features accords with human perception and can be further used for several applications as feature classification and viewpoint selection. Experiments exhibit that our method as a multi-scale analysis tool is very helpful for studying 3D shapes.

1 Introduction

Due to the fast development of 3D scanning and modeling technology, triangular meshes are now widely used in computer graphics. Objects with fruitful surface details can be well captured and constructed into mesh form. The interests in analyzing the geometric information of meshes are ever increasing. This is the most important step for a variety of applications in computer graphics, computer vision and geometric modeling, such as shape retrieval, shape alignment, feature preserved simplification etc.

In shape analysis, the key is how to define intrinsic features which can well represent the model's characteristic. To ensure the intrinsic property, the features are often required to be invariant under rigid transformation and uniform scaling. Moreover, the extracted feature should be discriminative to other models especially with different type. Based on different feature definition, shape analysis method can be generally classified into two categories: *global* and *local* [1]. The former one focuses on describing the entire shape of the model with a so-called "shape descriptor". The methodology of 3D statistics like shape distribution and histogram is usually involved, while local geometric details are not concerned much. On the other hand, local method defines features based on local surface properties. Curvature and its related quantities are often used here.

There have been several publications about determining saliency or extracting salient features on meshes in the recent years. [2] defined a measure of mesh saliency using a center-surround operator on Gaussian-weighted mean curvatures. This work incorporates insights from human perception, while the extraction of interesting feature parts is not their concern. [3] defined salient feature as

S.-M. Hu and R.R. Martin (Eds.): CVM 2012, LNCS 7633, pp. 122–129, 2012.

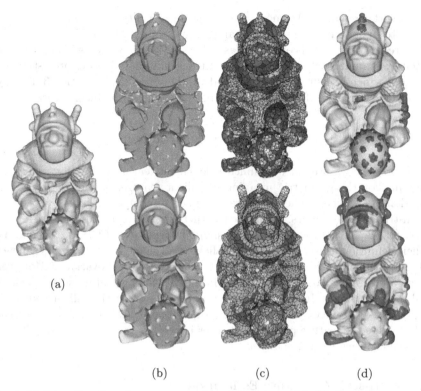

Fig. 1. Multi-scale salient feature extraction. (a) Grog model; (b) Gaussian curvature on small and large scales (from top to bottom, similarly hereinafter); (c) Local surface descriptors on small and large scales; (d) Salient features extracted accordingly.

region with high importance and non-trivial local shapes. They proposed to extract salient features based on curvature from local fitting, but there is no scale specialty of features considered here. Shilane et al. [4] presented a novel method to select regions that distinguish a shape by not only judging the shape itself. It is based on performing a shape-based search using each region as a query into a database. This method can reasonably select the regions which successfully discriminate the model with others, but the precondition is the availability of a shape retrieval environment. Recently, Chen et al. [5] investigated the so-called 'schelling points' on 3D surface. These points have to be manually selected by the users beforehand on a training data set. Then features can be predicted on new shapes based on the prior knowledge.

In this paper, we present a method of extracting salient geometric features on multiple scales. It is more likely to analyze local shape properties, while global shape information is taken into account when the scale of interest becomes large (see Fig. 1). Although the definition of salient feature is also based on curvature and its variance, the curvature estimation is performed in a multiscale way. The salient features extracted on different scales represent different level of surface details. We show that the scale specialty of salient features can help us to understand the surface shape more comprehensively.

The rest of the paper is organized as follows: In Section 2, we will describe the procedure of multi-scale salient feature extraction in detail. Two interesting applications which benefit from our method will be presented in Section 3. Finally, we conclude our paper in Section 4 and discuss some of the future work.

2   Multi-scale Salient Feature Extraction

In this section, we present our multi-scale salient feature extraction algorithm in detail. For the geometric meaning of salient feature, we adapt to use the definition in [3], where salient feature is defined as compound high-level feature of non-trivial local shapes. Compared with the features represented per mesh vertex (cf. [2]), it conveys much more shape information of the local geometry. In their definition, the criterion of the salient local shape is related to its saliency and interestingness which is determined by curvature and its variance. However, the curvature information they used is from local fitting and no scale specialty is taken into account. In our paper, we propose to extract the salient geometric feature based on curvature estimated on different scales. In this way, we can further judge the feature property whether it belongs to the surface detail or it represents surface more globally.

2.1   Multi-scale Curvature Estimation

Instead of computing curvature based on local quadric fitting, we use multi-scale curvature estimation in [6]. The principal curvatures and the principal frame are estimated by principal component analysis (PCA) of local neighborhoods defined via spherical kernels centered on the given surface. The neighborhood radius r can be naturally treated as the scale of interest. In this paper, we use PCA of the ball neighborhood for multi-scale curvature estimation for all examples. Fig. 2 shows the maximal principal curvature of the Asian Dragon model estimated on two different scales. Note that the scale features are more apparently recognized on the small scale.

2.2   Local Surface Descriptor Generation

Based on the multi-scale curvature information which has been successfully estimated, a sparse set of local surface descriptors (LSD) will be built across the mesh surface afterwards. Each LSD is a surface point p and its associated quadric patch that approximate the surface in a local neighborhood of p [3]. This kind of LSD has many advantages: adaptive to the geometry of the shape, independent of the underlying triangulation, heavily reduce the complexity of the original triangle mesh representation and ease of clustering non-trivial salient features.

In [3], the LSD of a surface point p is built based on the geometric error between the local surface patch and the fitting quadric. However, in our method,

Fig. 2. Multi-scale maximal principal curvatures on the Asian Dragon model, with two different kernels centered at one of its horn. The red color depicts the highest curvature value, blue color is for lowest value.(upper: small scale; bottom: large scale.)

the curvatures are estimated using PCA of local neighborhoods. In this case, the small shape variance can be neutralized on a large scale (see Fig. 2), which means the geometry itself can not reflect the change of the scale. So instead of using vertex coordinates, we build the LSD based on the curvature information, which is correlated with the scale of interest.

We also use the region-growing technique to iteratively generate the LSDs. First, we sort all the mesh vertices according to their curvature function value $Curv(p)$ in descending order. The curvature function can be chosen depending on the model's property. Commonly we choose the absolute Gaussian curvature, and for CAD models, the maximal absolute principal curvature will be used (see [3]). Then we build the LSDs one by one from the sorted list. For a vertex p in the list which hasn't been in any LSD, we extract its associated quadratic patch in a way different from local fitting.

As discussed in Section 2.1, based on PCA of local neighborhood of a surface point p, we get three eigenvectors which form its local principal frame on scale r besides principal curvatures κ_1 and κ_2. Then we form the paraboloid $P : z = \frac{1}{2}(\kappa_1 x^2 + \kappa_2 y^2)$ in principal frame as the second order approximation of the surface at p on the given scale. To generate the LSD from p, we greedily involve its neighbor vertices and integrate the error of Gaussian curvature over the local area until the prescribed threshold is reached. Suppose q is one of its neighbor, we can get the local coordinates of q by projecting it into p's principal frame. Then we only use the local $\mathbf{x}$, $\mathbf{y}$ coordinates q_x and q_y to compute the Gaussian curvature $\hat{K}_G^q$ of the local osculating paraboloid as in Equ. (1).

$$\hat{K}_G^q = \frac{\kappa_1 \kappa_2}{[1 + (\kappa_1 q_x)^2 + (\kappa_2 q_y)^2]^2} \tag{1}$$

The error of the Gaussian curvature can then be estimated as the difference between $\hat{K}_G^q$ and $K_G^q = \kappa_1^q \cdot \kappa_2^q$, where κ_1^q and κ_2^q are the principal curvatures of q estimated in Section 2.1. Note that in this way, we don't involve local $\mathbf{z}$ coordinate, this can eliminate the error of LSD caused by the local shape variance when the scale becomes large.

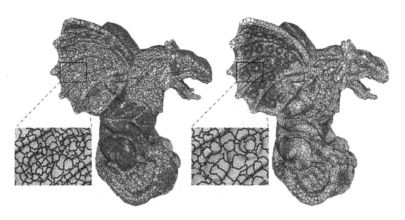

Fig. 3. Local surface descriptors of Gargoyle model on two different scales. Red is high curvature function value and blue is low. Zoomed figures show the tiny structure and starting point of each LSD. (left: small scale; right: large scale.)

In our implementation, for the model less than 100K faces, we use 0.3 of its largest absolute Gaussian curvature times the average area per-vertex as the threshold. For large models, we set the ratio to 1.0. After a single *LSD* with starting point p is extracted, we assign it with the largest curvature function value, i.e. $Curv(p)$, as the representative curvature value.

Fig. 3 shows the local surface descriptors of Gargoyle model on two different scales. We can find the *LSD*s on small scale follow the surface detail (the ring-like shape) better, while descriptors representing global curved shape are salient on large scale (see also zoom-in parts).

2.3   Salient Feature Extraction

The definition of saliency or salient feature is the foundation of distinctiveness analysis of 3D shapes. Due to its generality and our purpose of extracting multi-scale salient feature regions, we adapt to use the definition and measurement of salient feature in [3]. They define salient feature as a cluster of *LSD*s that locally describe a non-trivial region of the surface.

For each *LSD*, we grow a cluster of descriptors by recursively adding its neighboring descriptors until the saliency grade of the clustered feature is maximized. This greedy process stops when the contribution of a candidate descriptor is insignificant. The saliency grade of a feature cluster is determined by the curvature function value of each *LSD* and its variance over the cluster. We refer readers to [3] for the details.

When the whole surface has been decomposed into feature clusters, the ones with high saliency grade will be extracted as salient geometric features. This can be done by a prescribed threshold of the saliency grade value or the percentage of salient features among all clusters. Since concave feature is usually generated by adjacent meaningful convex parts [7], we suppress its saliency grade so that

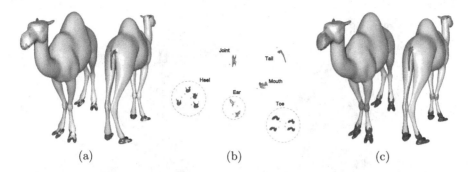

Fig. 4. Feature classification of camel model based on salient feature extraction on two different scales. (a) the classified salient features with different colors on small scale; (b) the 2D projection of the salient feature space computed using classical multidimensional scaling; (c) the classified salient features on large scale.

the inherent salient feature can be successfully extracted. The results of salient feature extraction of Grog model on two different scales can be found in Fig. 1.

3 Results and Discussion

3.1 Multi-scale Feature Classification

Our feature classification is based on multi-scale salient features in Section 2. The goal is to classify salient features on different scales according to their global shapes, i.e. the salient features which have similar shape will be grouped into the same class. We believe this way of multi-scale salient feature extraction and classification will give us a comprehensive understanding of 3D models.

In our method, we use spin-image [8] as the shape signature for each salient feature extracted from a 3D model. The resemblance between salient features is measured by their spin-images. A full distance matrix is generated afterwards. Then we extract a 2D embedding of the salient feature space using multi-dimensional scaling [9]. From the feature space, we obtain a meaningful classification of salient features.

Fig. 4(a) shows the salient feature classification results of Camel model on small scale. We can see the meaningful body parts like ears, toes, heels, mouth, tail and joint of front legs are successfully classified as in Fig. 4(b). The classification results on large scale of the same Camel model can be found in Fig. 4(c). The salient features capture more global interesting shape of the surface. Toes and heels are merged to whole foot features.

3.2 Multi-scale Viewpoint Selection

Based on our multi-scale salient feature extraction, we can do the viewpoint selection on multiple scales. In our approach, different viewpoint is determined

Fig. 5. Multi-scale viewpoints selected on two different scales for Gargoyle model (left: large scale; right: small scale)

by visible surface saliency on different scales. The visual effect is like observing an object from far to near. On large scale, features with some global shape information show up, while more details of an object are revealed on small scale. The intuition behind our approach is that people tend to notice global shape features of an object at first and then pay attention to more detailed ones. Thus, our approach helps to provide an informative illustration of a 3D object, with global and detailed features visible on different scales.

In our method, we define the saliency of a mesh vertex v as $S(F)/Size(F)$, where F is the salient feature which contains vertex v, $S(F)$ is the saliency grade of F, $Size(F)$ is the number of vertices that belong to F. For vertex which doesn't belong to any salient feature, the saliency value is 0. After that, we search for the viewpoint which maximizes the sum of saliency of all visible vertices. To avoid the sharp variance of saliency between neighboring viewpoints, here we set top 50% feature clusters as salient features.

Fig. 5 shows two optimal salient viewpoints of the Gargoyle model, which are selected on large and small scale respectively. Note that the two wings of Gargoyle model are more visible on large scale, while the detailed features (e.g. the rings) are more attractive on small scale.

3.3   Implementation Details

Our multi-scale salient feature extraction algorithm is implemented in C++ on a windows platform. In all our experiments, we scaled the models to fit into a bounding box with maximal length 2. On small scale, the radius of the ball neighborhood is set to 0.03 and on large scale it is $3 \sim 4$ times larger.

We test our algorithm on an Intel Core2 Duo 2.66GHz computer with 2GB RAM. For Camel model with 70K triangles, the average cost of salient feature extraction on a single scale is 38.9s. For Grog model with 200k triangle, the cost is 40.5s. The curvature estimation step takes most of the time. On the other hand, the extraction of local surface descriptors and salient features are much more efficient due to the greedy approach, these two processes can be done within 5 seconds for all test models.

4 Conclusion and Future Work

In this paper, we presented a new method of multi-scale salient feature extraction. The salient features extracted on small scale represent the surface detail while more global interesting salient regions can be extracted on large scale. This kind of multi-scale description of features accords with human perception from different scales of interest. We also applied the multi-scale salient feature extraction to feature classification and viewpoint selection, both applications show that our method as a multi-scale analysis tool is very helpful for studying 3D shapes.

We want to apply the multi-scale salient feature extraction to a wider usage like in shape matching, where different models can be compared on different scales. Models have details in common have more similarity on small scale while models with similar global features are expected to be matched on large scale. We believe this kind of multi-scale feature based shape matching is favorable of further applications like modeling by example and shape retrieval.

References

1. Tangelder, J.W., Veltkamp, R.C.: A survey of content based 3d shape retrieval methods. SMI, 145–156 (2004)
2. Lee, C.H., Varshney, A., Jacobs, D.W.: Mesh saliency. ACM Trans. Graph. 24(3), 659–666 (2005)
3. Gal, R., Cohen-Or, D.: Salient geometric features for partial shape matching and similarity. ACM Trans. Graph. 25(1), 130–150 (2006)
4. Shilane, P., Funkhouser, T.: Distinctive regions of 3d surfaces. ACM Trans. Graph. 26(2), 7 (2007)
5. Chen, X., Saparov, A., Pang, B., Funkhouser, T.: Schelling points on 3D surface meshes. ACM Trans. Graph. 31(3) (2012)
6. Yang, Y.L., Lai, Y.K., Hu, S.M., Pottmann, H.: Robust principal curvatures on multiple scales. In: Symposium of Geometry Processing, pp. 223–226 (2006)
7. Katz, S., Tal, A.: Hierarchical mesh decomposition using fuzzy clustering and cuts. ACM Trans. Graph. 22(3), 954–961 (2003)
8. Johnson, A.: Spin-Images: A Representation for 3-D Surface Matching. PhD thesis, Robotics Institute, Carnegie Mellon University, Pittsburgh, PA (August 1997)
9. Cox, T., Cox, M.: Multidimensional Scaling. Chapman & Hall, London (2001)

Global Contrast of Superpixels
Based Salient Region Detection

Jie Wang[1], Caiming Zhang[1,2,*], Yuanfeng Zhou[1], Yu Wei[1], and Yi Liu[1]

[1] Shandong University, School of Computer Science and Technology, Jinan, China
[2] Shandong University of Finance and Economics,
Shandong Provincial Key Laboratory of Digital Media Technology, Jinan, China
wangjiesweets@gmail.com, czhang@sdu.edu.cn

Abstract. Reliable estimation of visual saliency has become an essential tool in image processing. In this paper, we propose a novel salient region detection algorithm, superpixel contrast (SC), consisting of three basic steps. First, we decompose a given image into compact, regular superpixels that abstract unnecessary details by a new superpixel algorithm, hexagonal simple linear iterative clustering (HSLIC). Then we define the saliency of each perceptually meaningful superpixel instead of rigid pixel grid, simultaneously evaluating global contrast differences and spatial coherence. Finally, we locate the key region and enhance its saliency by a focusing step. The proposed algorithm is simple to implement and computationally efficient. Our algorithm consistently outperformed all state-of-the-art detection methods, yielding higher precision and better recall rates, when evaluated on well-known publicly available data sets.

Keywords: saliency detection, superpixel, global contrast, focusing.

1 Introduction

A profound challenge in computer vision is to make the computer understand the surrounding scene via image or video. To achieve this goal, three vital tasks need to be resolved: focusing on the key object, detecting its shape and contour, and capturing the context information. Therefrom saliency detection technology comes into being and provides an alternative methodology. Reliable saliency estimation breaks down the barrier between the content understanding and underlying characteristics, making the higher level understanding of image possible; what's more, it furnishes valuable information for various applications including content-aware image editing [1] and image restoration [2, 3].

Existing saliency detection algorithms can be broadly categorized into local and global schemes. Local methods [4–7] estimate the saliency of a particular image region based on immediate neighborhoods, and tend to produce higher saliency values near edges instead of uniformly highlighting salient objects.

* This project was supported by NSFC (No. 61020106001 and No. 61202148), Ph.D. Programs Foundation of Ministry of Education of China (No. 20110131130004), and Shandong Provincial Natural Science Foundation (No. ZR2011FM031).

S.-M. Hu and R.R. Martin (Eds.): CVM 2012, LNCS 7633, pp. 130–137, 2012.

Global methods [8, 9] take contrast relations over the complete image into account. While these algorithms are more consistent in terms of global structures, they suffer from the involved combinatorial complexity, hence they are applicable only to relatively low resolution images, or they need to operate in spaces of reduced dimensionality, resulting in loss of small, potentially salient detail. FT [10] and SR [11] are the methods based on frequency analysis, which belong to the global scheme. RC [9] is one of the best existing methods, which simultaneously evaluates global contrast differences and spatial coherence. However, RC cannot boast excellent boundary adherence, mainly because the graph-based image segmentation preprocessing [13] RC uses cannot do this easily.

In this paper, we propose a superpixel-based global contrast method (SC) to measure saliency. Our SC method first groups pixels into perceptually meaningful atomic regions, superpixels, via a new superpixel algorithm, hexagonal simple linear iterative clustering (HSLIC). HSLIC uses hexagon to control superpixel's shape and size, and exploits new search mechanism and merge mechanism as well. Note that superpixels HSLIC generates are more compact, more uniform in size, and adhere to object boundaries better. Furthermore, it is easy to use and computationally efficient. Then SC assigns saliency values to superpixels of high quality above, instead of the huge number of rigid structures of the pixel grids, simultaneously evaluating global contrast differences and spatial coherence. In this way, our algorithm not only separates the object-of-interest from its surroundings with excellent boundary adherence, but also makes the saliency measure sufficiently efficient for real-time applications.

We have extensively evaluated our algorithm on the largest publicly available benchmark data sets [10], and compared it with nine state-of-the-art methods [4–12]. The experiments show SC outperformed existing saliency detection methods, yielding higher precision and better recall rates, while still being simple and efficient. We also present applications of the extracted saliency maps to segmentations and non-photorealistic rendering.

2   Superpixels Based Global Contrast

Our saliency detection method SC consists of the following three basic steps.

2.1   Superpixels Based Preprocessing

The pixel-based processing is usually inefficient owing to the huge number of pixels. In order to reduce computational complexity, we introduce a preprocessing step based on superpixels.

SLIC approach [14], as one of the best existing methods, clusters pixels in the combined five-dimensional color and image plane space. It could generate compact, nearly uniform superpixels efficiently with linear complexity.

$$D_{S_o} = \sqrt{(l_k - l_i)^2 + (a_k - a_i)^2 + (b_k - b_i)^2} + \frac{m}{S_o}\sqrt{(x_k - x_i)^2 + (y_k - y_i)^2} \quad (1)$$

where D_{S_o} is the sum of the color distance in CIELAB color space between two pixels and the xy plane distance, S_o is the grid interval, and m controls the compactness of a superpixel. However, as for SLIC, the arrangement of cluster centers and the search neighborhood are both squares, which may not be able to achieve the best effects when we cluster pixels or do saliency detections. So we propose a new method for generating superpixels, HSLIC, which is memory efficient, boasts excellent boundary adherence, and improves the performance of saliency measure. Our algorithm consists of the following steps.

Seeds Initialization. For color images in the CIELAB color space, the clustering procedure begins with an initialization step where K initial seeds are sampled according to hexagons on a regular grid spaced $\sqrt{3}s$ pixels apart, as illustrated in Fig.1. K, as the only parameter of the algorithm, is the desired number of approximately equally-sized superpixels. s is the length of side of hexagonal superpixels, and $s = \sqrt{2\sqrt{3}N/9K}$, where N is the number of pixels.

The arrangement of seeds determines the shape of superpixels, so our method will produce hexagonal superpixels. The well-known honeycomb conjecture [15] has been proved. This conjecture, put simply, states that the best way to partition a plane into regions of equal area is with a region that is a regular hexagon. Hexagonal superpixels have many advantages, such as more balanced adjacency relations and higher isotropy. Meanwhile, because cells in the foveal region of retina are packed in nearly perfect hexagons [16], so hexagonal superpixels can simulate the eyes of human better, and are more suitable for saliency detection.

Besides, edges of our hexagonal superpixels could fit image boundaries better. In SLIC, as for a superpixel, eight adjacent cluster centers (color, distance) could affect its shape, in addition to its own. We should pay more attention to the color attribute when we cluster pixels if we want edges of superpixels to fit edges of objects better. Simply increasing the weight of color distance in distance measure function (Eq. (1)) will cause a series of problems, for instance pixels' cluster may be scattered. The best solution is to make the distribution of cluster centers more balanced (in accordance with hexagons).

Searching Matching Pixels Iteratively. We treat the seeds as cluster centers, then associate each pixel with the nearest cluster center whose search region

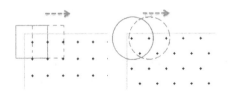

Fig. 1. Clustering pixels schematic diagram of SLIC and HSLIC

Fig. 2. An example of KRF. Left to right: Input image, basic saliency map, focal superpixels, saliency change schematic, and refined saliency map.

overlaps its location. Since the expected length of side of a hexagonal superpixel is approximate s, the search for similar pixels is done in a round neighborhood whose radius is $2s$ around the superpixel center, as shown in Fig. 1. After this, an update step adjusts cluster centers to be the mean $[l\ a\ b\ x\ y]^T$ vector of all pixels belonging to the cluster. And then the L1 norm is used to compute a residual error E between the new cluster center locations and previous ones. Assignment and update steps can be repeated iteratively until the error converges.

Note that, we search the best matching pixels from a round neighborhood rather than a square neighborhood of SLIC. Updating the shortest distance from the pixel to the cluster centers in the round neighborhood of each cluster center, could ensure that numbers of pixels we optimize are the same in all directions, could make the boundary adherence of superpixels more accurate, and furthermore could deal with the situation of complex edges better.

Besides, at the initial period of HSLIC, as for any seed, the distances between it and six adjacent seeds are the same, and so do the influence spheres of the search neighborhoods. In this way, pixels in the flat areas could reach a steady state with relatively few iterations. But SLIC, with different distances and influence spheres above, cannot do this. Residual error E of HSLIC drops sharply in a few iterations, so we use 2 iterations for all the results in this paper.

Enforcing Connectivity. At the end of the clustering procedure, some orphaned pixels that do not belong to the same connected component as their cluster center may remain. To correct for this, SLIC relabels disjoint segment with the label of the largest neighboring cluster, but both may have a large color deviation, so we change the merge criterion, relabling small disjoint block with the label of the closest color neighboring cluster.

Fig. 3 provides a visual comparison of our output against SLIC. We note that superpixels HSLIC generates are more compact, more uniform in size, adhere to object boundaries better and have more balanced adjacency relations and higher isotropy. Moreover, for typical natural images, HSLIC needs $O(N)$ computation time and is sufficiently efficient for real-time saliency detection.

Fig. 3. Visual comparison of SLIC and HSLIC. Left to right: Input image, superpixels obtained by SLIC, superpixels obtained by HSLIC, saliency map obtained by SC based on SLIC superpixels, and saliency map obtained by SC based on HSLIC superpixels.

Fig. 4. Visual comparison of saliency maps. Left to right: Input image, IT, GB, AC, MZ, LC, FT, SR, CA, RC and SC.

2.2 Superpixels Based Global Contrast

Contrast is a measure of color difference, but it is influenced by spatial relationship as well. High contrast attracts people's attention; moreover, high contrast to its surrounding regions is usually stronger evidence for saliency of a region than high contrast to far-away regions. Since directly introducing spatial relationships when computing pixel-level contrast is computationally expensive, we define the saliency of each superpixel r_k instead of pixel simultaneously evaluating global contrast differences and spatial coherence. In this way, we get basic saliency maps, as illustrated in Fig. 2.

$$S(r_k) = \sum_{r_i \neq r_k} \frac{\sqrt{(l_k - l_i)^2 + (a_k - a_i)^2 + (b_k - b_i)^2}}{\sqrt{(x_k - x_i)^2 + (y_k - y_i)^2}} \tag{2}$$

where the numerator is the color distance in CIELAB space between two superpixels, and the denominator is the xy plane distance. Note that as for a superpixel, if another superpixel is far away, even if the two have large color difference, the salient contribution another superpixel to this one is still small.

2.3 Key Region Focusing

The basic saliency map usually highlights more than one region. But when people view the image, only one region can get their first attention. As the Gestalt law [17] goes, the region close to the focal point should be more prominent than that away from. So we propose a new method, key region focusing (KRF), to highlight the main region, consisting of two basic steps.

At first, we determine the focal superpixels via an adaptive value T_α, while the adaptive method can adapt to changes of images well.

$$T_\alpha = \frac{\alpha}{K} \sum_{r_i \in R} S(r_i) + (1 - \alpha) \max_{r_i \in R} S(r_i) \tag{3}$$

where R is the set of all superpixels in the image, $K = |R|$. The greater α, the more focal superpixels. In our implementation, we use $K = 300$ and $\alpha = 0.7$.

Then the saliency of each superpixel r_i can be reset according to focal superpixels. $\bar{d}_{foci}(r_i)$ is the sum of Euclidean distances between r_i and all the focal superpixels. We normalize $\bar{d}_{foci}(r_i)$ to $[0, 1]$, then recalculate the saliency map.

$$\hat{S}(r_i) = S(r_i)(1 - \bar{d}_{foci}(r_i)) \tag{4}$$

Fig. 2 shows the effect of optimizing the basic saliency map by our KRF method. It can be seen that KRF only emphasizes the main region of the image, and further weakens the saliency of small regions and other regions.

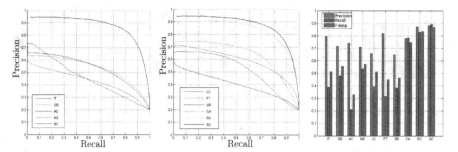

Fig. 5. (Left and middle)Precision-recall curves for naive thresholding of saliency maps using 1000 publicly available benchmark images. (Right) Precision-recall bars for our saliency cut algorithm using different saliency maps as initialization.

3 Experimental Comparisons

We compared our algorithm SC with 9 state-of-the-art saliency detection methods, among which four were local methods (IT [4], GB [5], AC [6], MZ [7]), and five were global methods (LC [8], FT [10], SR [11], CA [12], RC [9]). Comparisons mainly consisted of three aspects: segmentation by fixed thresholding, saliency cut and non-photorealistic rendering. Fig. 4 shows a visual comparison of saliency maps obtained by the various methods.

3.1 Segmentation by Fixed Thresholding

We evaluate the performance of our algorithm SC measuring its precision and recall rate. Set a threshold $T_f \in [0, 255]$, then we can get a binary segmentation of salient region. We vary the threshold T_f from 0 to 255, to reliably compare how well various saliency detection methods highlight salient regions in images. We use the largest publicly available database [10] provided by Achanta et al., which has ground truth in the form of accurate human-marked labels for salient regions. Fig. 5 shows the precision-recall curves of ten methods. SC is very outstanding compared to four local methods. Relative to five global methods, SC still has significant progress compared to the best RC. The precision and recall curves clearly show that SC outperforms the other nine methods.

3.2 Saliency Cut

The extracted saliency map can be used to assist in object-of-interest segmentation. Firstly, we binarize the saliency map using an adaptive value T_α (Eq. (3)). Then we use this binarization result to automatically initialize GrabCut. And then we iteratively run GrabCut to improve the saliency cut result.

Average precision, recall, and F-Measure are compared over the entire ground-truth database [10], with the F-Measure defined as:

$$F_\beta = \frac{(1 + \beta)Precision \times Recall}{\beta \times Precision + Recall} \tag{5}$$

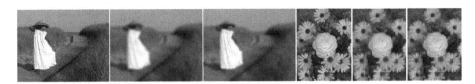

Fig. 6. Left to right: Input image, stylized drawing result, and non-photorealistic rendering result. Effects are produced using lens blur and mosaic pixelate respectively.

We use $\beta = 0.3$ to weigh precision more than recall. As can be seen from the comparison (see Fig. 5-right), saliency cut using our SC saliency maps significantly outperforms other methods. Compared with the state-of-the-art results on this database of RC ($Precision = 0.871$, $Recall = 0.829$), our method achieves better accuracy and integrity ($Precision = 0.884$, $Recall = 0.892$).

3.3 Non-photorealistic Rendering

Non-photorealistic rendering (NPR) is the abstraction of the real world. This technology highlights meaningful parts of an image while masking out unimportant regions. Inspired by this observation, a number of NPR efforts use saliency maps to generate interesting effects [1]. However, it is difficult to combine the saliency detection with various rendering methods one by one. So our strategy is to restore details of the key object according to the saliency map after rendering. We define the final non-photorealistic rendering result $\hat{I}_{NPR}$ as,

$$\hat{I}_{NPR}(p_i) = w(p_i) \cdot I(p_i) + [1 - w(p_i)] \cdot I_{NPR}(p_i)$$
$$w(p_i) = \begin{cases} 0 & S(p_i) < T_{low}, \\ \alpha \cdot S(p_i) & T_{low} \leq S(p_i) < T_{high}, \\ \alpha \cdot T_{high} & S(p_i) \geq T_{high}. \end{cases} \tag{6}$$

where I is the original image, I_{NPR} is the stylized drawing result, and $w(p_i)$ is the weight of pixel p_i. In our implementation, we use $T_{low} = 0.2$, $T_{high} = 0.8$ and $\alpha = 0.5$ with the pixel's saliency normalized to $[0, 1]$. Fig. 6 shows NPR results of lens blur and mosaic pixelate. As can be seen, our NPR method better preserves details in important image parts while smoothing out others, and generates interesting effects under the premise of keeping the rendering style consistent.

4   Conclusions and Future Work

We presented a new saliency computation method, namely SC. The SC method is based on compact and regular superpixels, simultaneously evaluates global contrast differences and spatial coherence, and generates high quality saliency maps with relatively low computational cost. We evaluated our method on the largest publicly available data set and compared our scheme with nine other state-of-the-art methods. Experiments indicate that the proposed scheme is superior in terms of both precision and recall, while still simple and efficient.

In the future, we plan to further refine our saliency maps to eliminate artificial marks and improve visual effects. Also, it is desirable to incorporate higher-level features such as human faces, symmetry into saliency maps. Finally, it may be beneficial to detect real time, as thus saliency detection technology can be broadly used to video processing, rapid scene analysis and other capacious fields.

References

1. Cong, L., Tong, R., Dong, J.: Selective image abstraction. Visual Comput. 27(3), 187–198 (2010)
2. Fu, S., Zhang, C.: Adaptive bidirectional diffusion for image restoration. Sci. China Inform. Sci. 53(12), 2452–2460 (2010)
3. Fu, S., Zhang, C.: Image denoising and deblurring: non-convex regularization, inverse diffusion and shock filter. Sci. China Inform. Sci. 54, 1184–1198 (2011)
4. Itti, L., Koch, C., Niebur, E.: A model of saliency-based visual attention for rapid scene analysis. IEEE T. Pattern Anal. 20(11), 1254–1259 (1998)
5. Harel, J., Koch, C.: Graph-based visual saliency. In: Advances in Neural Information Processing Systems 19, pp. 545–552 (2007)
6. Achanta, R., Estrada, F.J., Wils, P., Süsstrunk, S.: Salient Region Detection and Segmentation. In: Gasteratos, A., Vincze, M., Tsotsos, J.K. (eds.) ICVS 2008. LNCS, vol. 5008, pp. 66–75. Springer, Heidelberg (2008)
7. Ma, Y., Zhang, H.: Contrast-based image attention analysis by using fuzzy growing. In: 11th ACM International Conference on Multimedia, pp. 374–381. ACM Press, New York (2003)
8. Zhai, Y., Shah, M.: Visual attention detection in video sequences using spatiotemporal cues. In: 14th Annual ACM International Conference on Multimedia, pp. 815–824. ACM Press, New York (2006)
9. Cheng, M., Zhang, G., Mitra, N., Huang, X., Hu, S.: Global contrast based salient region detection. In: IEEE Conference on Computer Vision and Pattern Recognition 2011, pp. 409–416. IEEE Press, New York (2011)
10. Achanta, R., Hemami, S., Estrada, F., Susstrunk, S.: Frequency-tuned salient region detection. In: IEEE Conference on Computer Vision and Pattern Recognition 2009, pp. 1597–1604. IEEE Press, New York (2009)
11. Hou, X., Zhang, L.: Saliency detection: A spectral residual approach. In: IEEE Conference on Computer Vision and Pattern Recognition 2007, pp. 1–8. IEEE Press, New York (2007)
12. Achanta, R., Susstrunk, S.: Saliency detection for content-aware image resizing. In: 16th IEEE International Conference on Image Processing, pp. 1005–1008. IEEE Press, New York (2009)
13. Felzenszwalb, P., Huttenlocher, D.: Efficient graph-based image segmentation. Int. J. Comput. Vision 59(2), 167–181 (2004)
14. Achanta, R., Shaji, A., Smith, K., Lucchi, A., Fua, P., Süsstrunk, S.: SLIC superpixels. Technical Report, 149300 EPFL (2010)
15. Hales, T.: The honeycomb conjecture. Discrete Comput. Geom. 25(1), 1–22 (2001)
16. Williams, D.: Topography of the foveal cone mosaic in the living human eye. Vision Res. 28(3), 433–454 (1988)
17. Koffka, K.: Principles of Gestalt Psychology. Routledge and Kegan Paul (1955)

Incremental Shared Subspace Learning
for Multi-label Classification

Lei Zhang, Yao Zhao*, and Zhenfeng Zhu

Institute of Information Science, Beijing Jiaotong University
Beijing Key Laboratory of Advanced Information Science and Network Technology
No. 3 Shang Yuan Cun, Hai Dian District Beijing, 100044, China
{10112061,yzhao,zhfzhu}@bjtu.edu.cn

Abstract. Multi-label classification plays an increasingly significant role in most applications, such as semantic scene classification. In order to exploit the related information hidden in different labels which is crucial for lots of applications, it is essential to extract a latent structure shared among different labels. This paper presents an incremental approach for extracting a shared subspace on dynamic dataset. With the incremental lossless matrix factorization, the proposed algorithm can be incrementally performed without using original existing input data so that to avoid high computational complexity and decreasing the predictive performance. Experimental results demonstrate that the proposed approach is much more efficient than the non-incremental methods.

Keywords: Multi-label classification, incremental learning, shared subspace, singular value decomposition.

1 Introduction

So-called multi-label classification [4] is that multiple labels are associated with a single object. It plays an increasingly significant role in most applications. For example, in protein function classification [8], multiple functional labels are associated with each protein; in text categorization [9], each text document is assigned to multiple categories. As all the labels share the same input space, the semantics conveyed by different labels are usually correlated. Hence, to capture the intrinsic relationships among different labels, it is essential to exploit the related structures among them.

At present, there are several existing classical algorithms to mine correlation between sets of observed variables, such as CCA (Canonical Correlation Analysis) [5] and ASO (Alternating Structure Optimization) [6]. These methods calculate low-dimensional embedding of the input data directed by relevant label information. In addition, a supervised learning framework based on the least

---

* Corresponding author.

S.-M. Hu and R.R. Martin (Eds.): CVM 2012, LNCS 7633, pp. 138–145, 2012.

squares loss has been proposed in [7] recently, called Shared-Subspace Learning for Multi-Label Classification (SSLMC) method. The approach seeks a linear transformation to discover a shared subspace.

However, the above-mentioned algorithms need to use all the input data during the learning process. So these methods will face an enormous challenge in the real-world applications for the following reasons. For one thing, with the rapid increase in the amount of data, the data may be dispersedly stored in different places, and hence it is commonly difficult to collect them together simultaneously. In addition, many online applications will continuously generate new data like stream data. Consequently, it is nearly impossible for us to obtain all the input data before the learning. As a result, this causes an expensively relearning by way of repeating a whole non-incremental training that involves the new data and the original existing data. Therefore, low computational complexity is hardly achieved for the above-mentioned approaches due to the lack of the scalability.

To overcome the above-mentioned shortcomings, this paper proposes an incremental approach for extracting a shared subspace on dynamic dataset, called ISSLMC (Incremental Shared Subspace Learning for Multi-Label Classification) algorithm. This method combines the ideas of SSLMC method with the incremental lossless matrix factorization without using the original existing input data so that to avoid high computational complexity and decreasing the predictive performance. Experimental results demonstrate that the proposed approach is much more efficient than the non-incremental methods.

Notation: Let $X_0 = [x_1, \cdots, x_n]^T \in \mathbb{R}^{n_1 \times d}$ denote the original input data matrix, where n_1 is the number of the initial training instances, d is the dimensionality of the input space, and $x_i \in \mathbb{R}^d$ is the i-th instance. $Y_0 = [y_1, \cdots, y_n]^T \in \mathbb{R}^{n_1 \times m}$ denotes the label indicator matrix, where m is the number of labels, $y_i \in \mathbb{R}^m$ is the label vector of the i-th instance, and $y_{ij} = 1$ if and only if x_i is associated with label j, $y_{ij} = -1$ otherwise. $X_0 = U_1 \Sigma_1 V_1^T$ is used to denote the compact singular value decomposition (SVD) [3] of X_0, where $rank(X_0) = k_1$, $U_1 \in \mathbb{R}^{n_1 \times k_1}$ and $V_1 \in \mathbb{R}^{d \times k_1}$ have orthonormal columns, Σ_1 is a $k_1 \times k_1$ diagonal matrix with non-zero singular values of X_0 on the principal diagonal. Let $\{x_i\}_{i=1}^{n_2} \in \mathbb{R}^d$ denote a set of the newly-collected input data, where n_2 is the number of the new instances. These data constitute the data matrix $X_N \in \mathbb{R}^{n_2 \times d}$. The corresponding label information is provided by the label indicator matrix $Y_N \in \mathbb{R}^{n_2 \times m}$.

2 Brief Review on SSLMC Algorithm

Recently, a supervised learning framework for extracting a shared subspace among different labels is proposed in [7] as follow:

$$\min_{U,V,\Theta} \| X_0 U - Y_0 \|_F^2 + \alpha \| U - \Theta^T V \|_F^2 + \beta \| U \|_F^2$$
$$s.t. \quad \Theta \Theta^T = I \tag{1}$$

where $U = [u_1, \cdots, u_m]^T \in \mathbb{R}^{d \times m}$, $u_l = w_l + \Theta^T v_l$, $V = [v_1, \cdots, v_m]^T \in \mathbb{R}^{r \times m}$, $w_l \in \mathbb{R}^d$ and $v_l \in \mathbb{R}^r$ are the weight vectors, the linear transformation Θ is common for all labels and it projects the input data onto a low-dimensional shared subspace, α and β are the regularization parameter, and $\| \bullet \|_F^2$ denotes the Frobenius norm.

The procedure for computing Θ is summarized in Algorithm 1. In the first step, the computational complexity for the SVD of the $n_1 \times d$ matrix X_0 is $O(dn_1^2)$ assuming $d > n_1$. In the sixth step, the computational complexity for the SVD of the $m \times k_1$ matrix C is $O(k_1 m^2)$ assuming $k_1 > m$. In the seventh step, the computational complexity for the QR decomposition of the $d \times k_1$ matrix $V_1 D B_2$ is $O(dk_1^2)$. Because m and k_1 are usually both small, the computational cost of SSLMC algorithm depends mostly on the cost for computing the compact SVD of the input data matrix X_0.

Algorithm 1. Shared-Subspace Learning for Multi-label Classification (**SSLMC**)

Input: X_0 and Y_0
Output: Θ
1: Calculate the compact SVD of X_0 as $X_0 = U_1 \Sigma_1 V_1^T$.
2: $D_1 = (\Sigma_1^2 / n + \beta I)^{-1} \Sigma_1$.
3: $D_2 = \Sigma_1 (\Sigma_1^2 / n + (\alpha + \beta) I)^{-1}$.
4: $D = (D_1 D_2^{-1})^{1/2}$.
5: $W = D^{-1} D_1$.
6: Calculate the SVD of $C = Y_0^T U_1 W$ as $C = B_1 \Lambda B_2^T$.
7: Calculate the QR decomposition of $V_1 D B_2$ as $V_1 D B_2 = QR$.
8: Set $\Theta = Q^T$.

---

3   The Proposed Algorithm

In this section, we will present our proposed Incremental Shared Subspace Learning for Multi-Label Classification (ISSLMC) algorithm.

3.1   Incremental Lossless Matrix Factorization

We propose an incremental lossless matrix factorization method to update the compact SVD of the input data matrix with the newly-collected data. Suppose that we can obtain an augmented input data matrix $M = [X_0^T, X_N^T]^T$ by inserting X_N into the original input data matrix X_0. Further, M can be factorized into

$$M = \begin{bmatrix} X_0 \\ X_N \end{bmatrix} = \begin{bmatrix} U_1 \Sigma_1 V_1^T \\ X_N \end{bmatrix} = \begin{bmatrix} U_1 \\ & I \end{bmatrix} \begin{bmatrix} \Sigma_1 V_1^T \\ X_N \end{bmatrix} \qquad (2)$$

by virtue of $X_0 = U_1 \Sigma_1 V_1^T$, where $I \in \mathbb{R}^{n_2 \times n_2}$ is an identity matrix. Assume the compact SVD [3] of block matrix $N = [(\Sigma_1 V_1^T)^T, X_N^T]^T$ as

$$N = H_1 \Lambda_1 G_1^T \qquad (3)$$

where $rank(N) = k$, $H_1 \in \mathbb{R}^{(k_1+n_2) \times k}$ and $G_1 \in \mathbb{R}^{d \times k}$ have orthonormal columns and Λ_1 is an $k \times k$ diagonal matrix with non-zero singular values of N on the principal diagonal. Thereby, M can be factorized into

$$M = \begin{bmatrix} U_1 \\ & I \end{bmatrix} H_1 \Lambda_1 G_1^T \tag{4}$$

The following Lemma 1 shows that Eq.(4) is the compact SVD of M.

Lemma 1. *Given an augmented input data matrix $M = [X_0^T, X_N^T]^T$, the compact SVD of X_0 as $X_0 = U_1 \Sigma_1 V_1^T$, the compact SVD of block matrix $N = [(\Sigma_1 V_1^T)^T, X_N^T]^T$ as $N = H_1 \Lambda_1 G_1^T$, and $I \in \mathbb{R}^{n_2 \times n_2}$. Define three matrices:*

$$P_1 = \begin{bmatrix} U_1 \\ & I \end{bmatrix} H_1, S_1 = \Lambda_1, and\ Q_1 = G_1$$

Then the compact SVD of M is $M = P_1 S_1 Q_1^T$.

Proof. Because $P_1 \in \mathbb{R}^{(n_1+n_2) \times k}$ and $Q_1 \in \mathbb{R}^{d \times k}$ have orthonormal columns, there exists two matrices $E \in \mathbb{R}^{(n_1+n_2) \times ((n_1+n_2)-k)}$ and $F \in \mathbb{R}^{d \times (d-k)}$ such that $[P_1, E] \in \mathbb{R}^{(n_1+n_2) \times (n_1+n_2)}$ and $[Q_1, F] \in \mathbb{R}^{d \times d}$ are orthogonal matrices [3, Chapter 2.5, page 69], that is

$$I_{(n_1+n_2)} = [P_1, E][P_1, E]^T \quad and \quad I_{(n_1+n_2)} = [P_1, E]^T[P_1, E] \tag{5}$$
$$I_d = [Q_1, F][Q_1, F]^T \quad and \quad I_d = [Q_1, F]^T[Q_1, F] \tag{6}$$

In addition, according to Eq.(4), M can be further factorized into the product of three matrices P_1, S_1, and Q_1^T, i.e., $M = P_1 S_1 Q_1^T$. We use P_1, S_1, and Q_1 to construct three new matrices:

$$P = [P_1, E], S = \begin{bmatrix} S_1 \\ & 0 \end{bmatrix}, and\ Q^T = [Q_1, F]^T$$

As $P_1 S_1 Q_1^T = PSQ^T$, we can obtain

$$M = PSQ^T \tag{7}$$

As P and Q are obviously unitary matrices, they are invertible matrices. Accordingly, Eq.(7) indicates that M and S are equivalent to each other. Thus M and S have the same singular values. Since S is a diagonal matrix, the entries on the principal diagonal of S are its singular values. Hence these entries are also the singular values of M. So the entries on the principal diagonal of Λ_1 are the non-zero singular values of M. In addition, according to Eq.(7), we can obtain

$$Q^T M^T M Q = S^2 \tag{8}$$

From Eq.(8), it follows that because Q is an unitary matrix, $M^T M$ is a Hermitian matrix, and S^2 is a diagonal matrix, the column vectors of $Q = [Q_1, F]$ are the eigenvectors of $M^T M$. That is to say, the column vectors of Q are the right singular vectors of M, and the column vectors of Q_1 are corresponding to the non-zero singular values of M. Moreover, in a similar way, the column vectors of P_1 are corresponding to the non-zero singular values of M. Therefore, $M = P_1 S_1 Q_1^T$ is the compact SVD of M. So the proof is completed. $\square$

3.2   The Proposed ISSLMC Algorithm

Following Lemma 1, we propose an Incremental Shared Subspace Learning for Multi-Label Classification (ISSLMC) algorithm. The computing procedure of the proposed ISSLMC method can be summarized in Algorithm 2.

Algorithm 2. Incremental Shared Subspace Learning for Multi-label Classification (**ISSLMC**)

Input: $U_1, \Sigma_1, V_1, X_N, Y_N$, and Y_0
Output: Θ
1: Calculate the compact SVD of $N = [(\Sigma_1 V_1^T)^T, X_N^T]^T$ as $N = H_1 \Lambda_1 G_1^T$
2: Update $Y_0 = [Y_0^T, Y_N^T]^T$, $U_1 = [U_1^T, I^T]^T H_1$, $\Sigma_1 = \Lambda_1$, and $V_1 = G_1$.
3: Calculate $\Theta = \mathbf{SSLMC}(U_1, \Sigma_1, V_1, Y_0)$.

3.3   Analysis of Computational Complexity

In this subsection, we will discuss the computational complexity of the proposed ISSLMC algorithm in two cases. The first case is aimed at the large sample size problem, in which the number of the training instances is far greater than the dimensionality of the input space. The second case is aimed at the small sample size problem, in which the number of the training instances is far less than the dimensionality of the input space. As the original input data matrix is typically not a full row rank matrix, its rank k_1 is less than the number of the initial training instances n_1, that is $n_1 > k_1$.

For the first case with $n_1 > k_1$, we can have $d \ll (k_1 + n_2) < (n_1 + n_2)$. Thus for the SSLMC algorithm, the computational complexity for the SVD of the $(n_1 + n_2) \times d$ matrix M is $O((n_1 + n_2)d^2)$. However, for the ISSLMC algorithm, the computational complexity for the SVD of the $(k_1 + n_2) \times d$ block matrix N is $O((k_1 + n_2)d^2)$. Due to $n_1 > k_1$, ISSLMC method has lower time complexity than SSLMC algorithm in the first case.

For the second case with $n_1 > k_1$, we can have $d \gg (n_1 + n_2) > (k_1 + n_2)$. Hence, for the SSLMC algorithm, the computational complexity for the SVD of the $(n_1 + n_2) \times d$ matrix M is $O(d(n_1 + n_2)^2)$. Nevertheless, for the ISSLMC algorithm, the computational complexity for the SVD of the $(k_1 + n_2) \times d$ block matrix N is $O(d(k_1 + n_2)^2)$. Owing to $n_1 > k_1$, ISSLMC method has lower time complexity than SSLMC algorithm in the second case. In addition, because $(n_1 + n_2)^2$ is larger than $(k_1 + n_2)^2$, the proposed ISSLMC algorithm is more suitable for the small-scale samples.

4   Experimental Study

Two experiments are presented in this section. We will evaluate the performance of the proposed ISSLMC algorithm with other five non-incremental methods, namely SSLMC, CCA+Ridge, CCA+SVM, SVM, and ASO, where CCA+Ridge denotes that CCA is performed first before ridge regression [1] and CCA+SVM denotes that CCA is performed first before linear support vector machines [2]. The codes of the five non-incremental methods are publicly available at the website (http://www.public.asu.edu/~sji03/multilabel/).

4.1 Experimental Setup

The two experiments are conducted on two publicly available multi-label datasets (http://www.csie.ntu.edu.tw/~cjlin/libsvmtools/datasets/), namely mediamill and rcvlv2. The brief description of the datasets is in Table 1.

Table 1. Statistics of the multi-label datasets

Dataset	Dimensionality	Total samples
mediamill	120	43907
rcvlv2	47236	30000

In addition, each dataset is separated into a training set, a test set, and an incremental set, where each subset is constructed by way of random sampling. We use 5-fold cross-validation to tune the regularization parameters of the six methods based on AUC (area under the receiver operating characteristic curve) from the candidate set $\{10^i | i = -6, -5, \cdots, 2\}$ on the training set.

4.2 Experiment A : Performance Evaluation for Large Sample Size Problem

This experiment is to evaluate the performance of the proposed ISSLMC algorithm for the large sample size problem on mediamill datasets, in which the training samples account for 20 percent of the original dataset, another 20 percent of the original dataset is used as the incremental data, and the remaining instances act as the test data. We pick out 100 attributes occurring most frequently from the original dataset such that the number of the training instances is far greater than the dimensionality of the input space. Fig.1 illustrates the performance of the six methods with fixed number of dimensions.

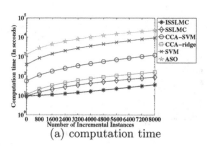
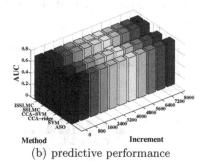

(a) computation time   (b) predictive performance

Fig. 1. Comparison of performance with fixed number of dimensions

From Fig.1(a), we can observe that the proposed ISSLMC approach is the fastest and with the increasing amount of the incremental instances the superiority of the proposed ISSLMC algorithm in computational cost is more obvious. In the aspect of the predictive performance, it can be seen from Fig.1(b) that despite the unceasing insertion of new samples into the initial training set, the proposed ISSLMC approach always achieves the same AUC as the SSLMC algorithm. This indicates that no matter what structure the input data matrix has, no error will be introduced in the proposed ISSLMC algorithm in comparison with the SSLMC method.

4.3   Experiment B : Performance Evaluation for Small Sample Size Problem

In this experiment, we will demonstrate the performance of our proposed ISSLMC algorithm for the small sample size problem. It is to compare the performance of our proposed ISSLMC algorithm and SSLMC method with varied number of dimension on the basis of the randomly-selected data features on the rcvlv2 datasets. The first 200 ones of the randomly-selected attributes are used as the initial data features of the instances. Afterwards, the number of data features is increased gradually to 2000. We randomly sample 5 percent of the data from the original dataset as the training samples and another 1 percent of the data from the original dataset as the incremental data such that the number of the training instances is far less than the dimensionality of the input space.

Fig.2 displays the comparison of computational time of the proposed ISSLMC algorithm and SSLMC approach and the rank of the original input data matrix with varied number of dimension. In Fig.2(a), the red dashed line indicates the number of the initial training instances, and hence if a rectangle in the pictures touches the red dashed line, this means that the original input data matrix is a full row rank matrix for the corresponding dimensionality of the input space.

We can observe from Fig.2 that if the rank of the original input data matrix is always less than the number of the initial training instances, the proposed ISSLMC approach is faster than the SSLMC method. Furthermore, as is exhibited in the Fig.2(b), with the increasing dimensionality of the input space, the proposed ISSLMC algorithm wins an increasingly predominance over SSLMC algorithm on condition that the original input data matrix is not a full row rank matrix.

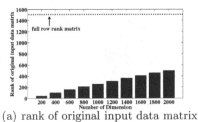
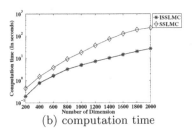

(a) rank of original input data matrix   (b) computation time

Fig. 2. Comparison of computation time and the rank of the original input data matrix

5   Conclusion

This paper proposes an Incremental Shared Subspace Learning for Multi-Label Classification (ISSLMC) approach. With the incremental lossless matrix factorization, the proposed ISSLMC algorithm can be incrementally performed so that to avoid high computational complexity and decreasing the predictive performance. Experimental results demonstrate that the proposed approach is much more efficient than the non-incremental methods.

Acknowledgment. This work was supported in part by 973 Program (No.2012CB316401), National Science Foundation of China (No.61025013, No.61172129), Beijing Municipal Natural Science Foundation (No.4112043), and Fundamental Research Funds for the Central Universities (No.2012JBZ012).

References

1. Hoerl, A., Kennard, R.: Ridge regression: Biased estimation for nonorthogonal problems. Technometrics 12(3), 55–67 (1970)
2. Burges, C.J.C.: A Tutorial on Support Vector Machines for Pattern Recognition. Data Mining and Knowledge Discovery 2(2), 121–167 (1998)
3. Golub, G.H., Van Loan, C.F.: Matrix Computations. The Johns Hopkins University Press (1996)
4. Tsoumakas, G., Katakis, I.: Multi-Label Classification: An Overview. International Journal of Data Warehousing and Mining 3(3), 1–13 (2007)
5. Hotelling, H.: Relations between two sets of variates. Biometrika 28(3/4), 321–377 (1936)
6. Ando, R.K., Zhang, T.: A framework for learning predictive structures from multiple tasks and unlabeled data. Journal of Machine Learning Research 6(2), 1817–1853 (2005)
7. Ji, S., Tang, L., Yu, S., Ye, J.: Extracting shared subspace for multi-label classification. In: SIGKDD, pp. 381–389 (2008)
8. Barutcuoglu, Z., Schapire, R.E., Troyanskaya, O.G.: Hierarchical multi-label prediction of gene function. Bioinformatics 22(7), 830–836 (2006)
9. Yang, Y., Pedersen, J.O.: A comparative study on feature selection in text categorization. In: ICML, pp. 412–420 (1997)

2D-Line-Drawing-Based 3D Object Recognition

Yong-Jin Liu[1], Qiu-Fang Fu[2], Ye Liu[2], and Xiao-Lan Fu[2]

[1] TNList, Department of Computer Science and Technology,
Tsinghua University, Beijing, China
[2] State Key Lab of Brain and Cognitive Science, Institute of Psychology,
Chinese Academy of Sciences, Beijing, China

Abstract. 3D object recognition has attracted considerable research in computer vision and computer graphics. In this paper, we draw attentions from neurophysiological research that line drawings trigger a neural response similar to natural color images, and propose a line-drawing-based 3D object recognition method. The contribution of the proposed method includes a feature defined for line drawings and a similarity metric for object recognition. Experimental results on McGill 3D shape benchmark show that the proposed method has the best performance when compared to five classic 3D object recognition methods.

1 Introduction

3D object recognition has attracted considerable attentions in both computer vision and neurophysiological research. Many recognition algorithms have been proposed in computer science and graphics research (e.g., [2,4,6,7,9,10]). Compared to state-of-the-art computational algorithms for object recognition in computer science area, human brain still has a distinct advantage in object recognition, i.e., human being can accurately recognize unlimited variety of objects within a fraction of a second.

In our study, we based on neurophysiological finding that line drawings trigger a neural activity pattern similar to color natural images [5,14]. The human vision system (with normal visual acuity and normal color vision) views 3D objects in the physical environment as color natural images at the retina. However, it is well known that the natural images are statically redundant. For example, the results in [5] show that the low level 2D image features used in human vision system are not specific to the type of stimuli such as color photographs, but appear to be definitive information sufficient for object recognition. Since line-drawings capture some essential structure of objects [14], it is interesting to apply line drawings as a concise and economical representation of the natural images [12,13].

Line drawing is a set of sparse, simple two-dimensional featured lines, without hatching lines or stippling for shading or tone effects. Line drawings are a convention of art that even untrained children can easily recognize them. Lines in line drawings include not only those edges that can be detected by object silhouette, intensity contrast and color gradients, but also some perceptually

S.-M. Hu and R.R. Martin (Eds.): CVM 2012, LNCS 7633, pp. 146–153, 2012.

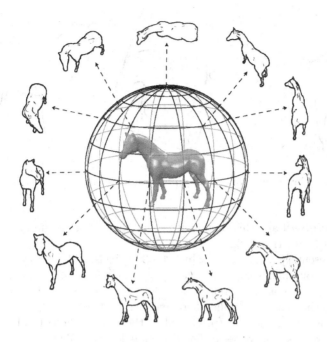

Fig. 1. Viewpoint distribution over a spherical domain using an interval of 5 degree in both longitude and latitude. For each viewpoint, a line drawing is generated using the CLD method [8].

important lines that currently can only be captured by artists in a ambiguous way. In this paper, we first present a visual circular feature representation using both excitatory and inhibitory components, to extract distinct information from line drawings. Then a codebook-based matching method is used for 3D object recognition.

2   Line Drawing Representation of 3D Objects

Object recognition is to identify an observed object from a set of known labels. In our study, we represent a set of known 3D objects by a codebook of line drawing forms. Then, when observing a novel 3D object, we convert the observation into the same line drawing form and determine its identity by matching the codebook.

Given a viewpoint and viewing direction, a 3D object projects an image on the retina. To simulate this process, we place the 3D object model by coinciding the center of gravity with the center of a sphere which bounds the 3D object (Figure 1). A dense sampling of viewpoints are applied on the spherical surface in which the sampling density is 5 degree in both longitude and latitude. For each viewpoint, a standard Lambertian light model is applied to generate a shading

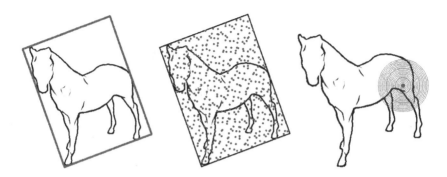

Fig. 2. A local feature representation of line drawings

image of that object and this shade image is further converted into a line drawing using the CLD algorithm [8].

If we represent each line drawing by 320×320 pixels, all line drawings sampling from the surrounding sphere are clearly a 2-manifold point cloud embedded in a very high-dimensional (more than 100k) feature space. Many dimensional reduction methods can be applied here and in this study we apply a complexity-dependent clustering method (presented in the next section) to obtain a small yet effective representative set of line drawings for each 3D object.

3 Local Circular Feature of Line Drawings

Given a line drawing representation P, let $B(P)$ be the minimum-area bounding box of all black pixels in P (Figure 2 left). The Halton's quasi-random point sequence is applied to uniformly sample n_p points in $B(P)$ (Figure 2 middle). At each sample point, a circular histogram is established (Figure 2 right), in which each circular bin has the same difference of radii and the maximal circle has radius of one fifth of diagonal length of $B(P)$. The reasons that we use such a circular feature representation are as follows:

- Random sampling provides a maximal entropy of point locations. For 3D object models, random sampling on object surfaces has been demonstrated to be an effective tool [4].
- Circular histogram makes the feature representation rotation invariant and less sensitive to the shape distortion: this is important since line drawings are not an accurate form and human used to matching them with elastic deformation (cf. two horses in Figure 3).

The feature histogram of each sample point has n_f bins. In our experiment, $n_p = 300$ and $n_f = 20$ are sufficient to make the proposed recognition method have a good performance.

Denote n_{tl} be the total number of black pixels fell into the circular histogram. For each bin, if the number of black pixels fell into the bin is larger than a

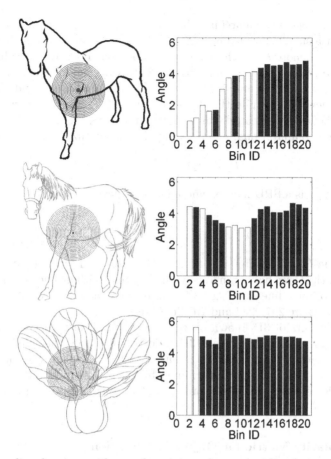

Fig. 3. Three line drawings with sample points and corresponding feature histogram. The top horse line drawing is converted from projection of 3D object (Figure 1). The middle horse line drawing is provided by a paid artist. The bottom vegetable line drawing presents a different object representation. For the feature histograms, the blue solid bins are activated ones. Hollow bins are not activated.

threshold[1], then that bin is activated (akin to neuron firing). We index the bins $1, 2, \cdots, n_f$ from innermost to outmost and denote the first activated bin as b_f. Each black pixel in b_f corresponds to an angle in polar coordinate and the average of all angles of all black pixels in b_f is denoted by A_{aver}. We use A_{aver} to setup a local coordinate system for the feature histogram h. Each of all later activated bins (other than the first activated one) has an average angle and we use this angle as the bin values. Three examples are illustrated in Figure 3. Only activated bins are involved in the feature matching.

---

[1] The threshold gives a measures of signal intensity and in our experiment we set it as 5% of n_{tl}.

For feature histogram matching, due to inaccurate forms of line drawings, it is desired that a small deformed histogram has a small distance to the original one. For example, denote h_a as the histogram which has nonzero bin values $\pi/2$ at bins 4 and 16, h_b has nonzero bin values $\pi/2$ at bins 5 and 17, and h_c has nonzero bin values $\pi/2$ at bins 4 and 5. Intuitively, h_a and h_b is similar and should have small distance value, while the distance between h_a and h_c should be large. However, the L_2 Euclidean distance $L_2(h_a, h_b) = \pi > L_2(h_a, h_c) = \sqrt{2}\pi/2$. In the proposed computational model, we apply a generalized distance [15]:

$$D(h_1, h_2) = h_1^T M_{n_f \times n_f} h_2 \tag{1}$$

where $M_{n_f \times n_f}$ is a SPD matrix whose elements are

$$m_{ij} = \frac{1}{2\pi\sigma^2} e^{-(i-j)^2/2\sigma^2}, \quad \sigma = 0.5$$

Using metric (1), $D(h_a, h_b) = 0.4252 < D(h_a, h_c) = 1.7834$, giving us desired results. For the three histograms shown in Figure 3, with metric (1), the distance between two horse line drawings is 209.3710, and the distances of vegetable to the two horses are 267.0254 and 297.2649, respectively.

Given a set M of 3D known objects, let F be all feature histograms of all line drawings projected by these 3D objects. We apply the affinity propagation (AP) method [3] to classify F into m clusters, where the number m is automatically and optimally determined by the AP method. For each cluster, its center is selected as a codeword c_i and m clusters constitute a codebook $C = \{c_1, c_2, \cdots, c_m\}$.

3.1   Similarity Metric for Object Recognition

Recall that for each line drawing projected by a 3D object, n_p sample points are sampled in a Halton's quasi-random sequence and a feature histogram is generated for each point. Given the codebook $C = \{c_1, c_2, \cdots, c_m\}$, a line drawing l can be presented by $l = (n_1 c_1, n_2 c_2, \cdots, n_m c_m)$, $n_1 + n_2 + \cdots + n_m = n_p$, by finding the clusters (corresponding to codes) in which the feature histograms of l fall; e.g., n_i means that there are n_i feature histograms of l fall into the cluster represented by the code c_i.

Let m_j be a 3D model in the database $M = \{m_1, m_2, \cdots, m_n\}$ and $L(m_j)$ be all line drawings of m_j. The frequency of occurrence of the code c_i in the model m_j, denoted as $f_{i,j}$, is the number of times that c_i appears in $L(m_j)$. Not all codes in C have equally usefulness for describing a 3D model. Obviously, the larger $f_{i,j}$ is, the more important the code c_i is to the model m_j. On the other hand, if a code c_j appears in most or all models in M, then it is less discriminative than a code that just appears in a few models in M. We thus use the TF-IDF weight [1]

$$w_{i,j} = \begin{cases} (1 + \log f_{i,j}) \times \log \frac{n}{r_i} & \text{if } f_{i,j} > 0 \\ 0 & \text{otherwise} \end{cases}$$

where $w_{i,j}$ is the weight assigned to the pair (c_i, m_j), r_i is the number of 3D models in M in which a code c_i occurs, and n is the total number of models in M.

Given the codebook $C = \{c_1, c_2, \cdots, c_m\}$ and the TF-IDF weights, a 3D model m_j in M is encoded as a m-vector

$$C(L(m_j)) = (w_{1,j}, w_{1,j}, \cdots, w_{m,j})$$

Given a query model q, after the same encoding process

$$C(L(q)) = (w_{1,q}, w_{1,q}, \cdots, w_{m,q}),$$

the models in M are sorted by the similarity value

$$S(m_j, q) = \frac{C(L(m_j)) \cdot C(L(q))}{\|C(L(m_j))\| \|C(L(q))\|} \tag{2}$$

and the semantic tags in the model that has the largest similarity value are used for recognizing the query model. Note that in the similarity metric (2), the encoding vectors are normalized since different models may have different complexity and thus have the different vector magnitudes.

4 Experiment

In this experiment, we compare the proposed method to two classic methods (EGI [6] and SPIN [7]) and three state-of-the-art methods (D2 [4], G2 [2], VSKL [9]). We use McGill 3D Shape Benchmark [11] to test the above methods and our method. The McGill Benchmark contains articulated and non-articulated objects. Ten classes are included in articulated objects: they are ants (30), crabs (30), hands (20), humans (30), octopus (25), pliers (20), snakes (25), spectacles (25), spiders (31), and teddy (20). The number in the bracket is the number of models in that class. Nine classes are included in non-articulated objects: they are airplanes (26), birds (21), chairs (23), cups (25), dinosaurs (19), dolphins (12), fishes (23), four-limbs (31), and tables (22).

We use the precision and recall (PR) metric to compare the different recognition methods. Let I be a 3D object in a class C_i of the McGill Benchmark. We use I as input to get a set of recognized objects R. Ideally, if R is much closer to C_i, the better recognition performance we obtained. The precision value is defined as $p = \frac{|R \cap C_i|}{|R|}$ and the recall value is defined as $p = \frac{|R \cap C_i|}{|C_i|}$, where $|S|$ is the cardinality of set S. We rank the recognized objects and define the set R to be top matched objects with increased set cardinality. We use each of the 3D objects in the benchmark in turn as input and the final PR curve is the average of all individual PR curves. The corresponding PR curves of different methods are summarized in Figure 4. From the data presented in Figure 4, it is clearly shown that the proposed method has the best recognition performance.

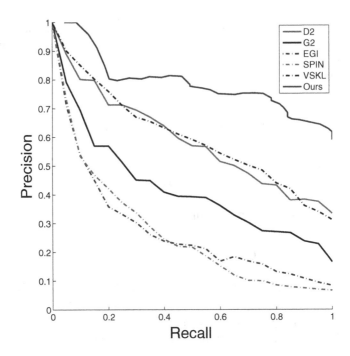

Fig. 4. The PR curves of five methods (EGI, SPIN, D2, G2, VSKL) and the proposed method, tested on the McGill 3D Shape Benchmark

5   Conclusions

In this paper, we present a 2D-line-drawing-based 3D object recognition method. Compared to previous object recognition methods in computer science area, the proposed model has two distinct characteristics: (1) a concise line drawing representation is used for 3D object recognition; (2) a codebook defined by a circular feature representation of line drawings is used for object recognition. Object recognition performance is tested using the McGill 3D Shape Benchmark and the comparison among our method and five representative methods shows that the proposed method has a better performance.

Acknowledgments. This work was supported in part by the National Basic Research Program of China (2011CB302201), the Natural Science Foundation of China (61272228) and the 863 program of China (2012AA011801). The work of Y.J. Liu was supported in part by the Program for NCET and TNList Cross-discipline Foundation.

References

1. Baeza-Yates, R., Ribeiro-Neto, B.: Modern Information Retrieval. ACM Press (1999)
2. Elbaz, A., Kimmel, R.: On bending invariant signatures for surfaces. IEEE Trans. Pattern Analysis and Machine Intelligence 25, 1285–1295 (2003)
3. Frey, B., Dueck, D.: Clustering by passing messages between data points. Science 315, 972–976 (2007)
4. Funkhouser, T., Min, P., Kazhdan, M., Chen, J., Halderman, A., Dobkin, D., Jacobs, D.: A search engine for 3D models. ACM Trans. Graphics 22, 83–105 (2003)
5. Haxby, J., Gobbini, I., Furey, M., Ishai, A., Schouten, J., Pietrini, P.: Distributed and overlapping representations of faces and objects in ventral temporal cortex. Science 293, 2425–2430 (2001)
6. Horn, B.: Extended Guassian images. Proc. IEEE 72, 1671–1686 (1984)
7. Johnson, A., Hebert, M.: Using spin images for efficient object recognition in cluttered 3D scenes. IEEE Trans. Pattern Analysis and Machine Intelligence 21, 433–449 (1999)
8. Kang, H., Lee, S., Chui, C.: Coherent Line Drawing. In: ACM Symp. Non-Photorealistic Animation and Rendering, pp. 43–50 (2007)
9. Liu, Y., Chen, Z., Tang, K.: Construction of iso-contours, bisectors, and Voronoi diagrams on triangulated surfaces. IEEE Trans. Pattern Analysis and Machine Intelligence 33, 1502–1517 (2011)
10. Liu, Y., Zheng, Y., Lv, L., Xuan, Y., Fu, X.: 3D Model retrieval based on color+geometry signatures. The Visual Computer 28, 75–86 (2012)
11. McGill 3D Shape Benchmark, http://www.cim.mcgill.ca/~shape/benchMark/
12. Simoncelli, E., Olshausen, B.: Natural image statistics and neural representation. Annual Review of Neurosicnece 24, 1193–1216 (2001)
13. Liu, Y., Luo, X., Xuan, Y., Chen, W., Fu, X.: Image retargeting quality assessment. Computer Graphics Forum (Regular Issue of Eurographics 2011) 30, 583–592 (2011)
14. Walther, D., Chai, B., Caddigan, E., Beck, D., Fei-Fei, L.: Simple line drawings suffice for functional MRI decoding of natural scene categories. Proceedings of the National Academy of Sciences, USA 108, 9661–9666 (2011)
15. Wang, L., Zhang, Y., Feng, J.: On the Euclidean distance of images. IEEE Trans. on Pattern Analysis and Machine Intelligence 27, 1334–1339 (2005)

Graph Regularized ICA
for Over-Complete Feature Learning

Yanhui Xiao, Zhenfeng Zhu, and Yao Zhao

Institute of Information Science,
Beijing Jiaotong University,
Beijing, China
xiaoyanhui@gmail.com, {zhfzhu,yzhao}@bjtu.edu.cn

Abstract. Independent Component Analysis with a soft Reconstruction cost (RICA) has been recently presented to learn highly over-complete sparse features even on unwhitened data. However, RICA failed to consider the geometrical structure of the data space, which has been shown essential for classification problems. To address this problem, we propose a graph regularized ICA model with Reconstruction constraint for image classification, called gRICA. In particular, we construct an affinity graph to encode the geometrical information, and thereby learn a graph regularized over-complete basis which makes sparse representations respect the graph structure. Experiments conducted on several datasets show the effectiveness of gRICA for classification.

1 Introduction

Independent Component Analysis (ICA) is an efficient tool for unsupervised feature learning, which transforms an observed multidimensional random vector into non-gaussian components statistically as independent from each other as possible. In order to estimate an ICA model, a general principle is the maximization of non-Gaussianity[1]. This is based on the central limit theorem that sum of non-Gaussian independent random variables is closer to Gaussian than the original random variables. Furthermore, sparseness is one form of non-Gaussianity [2], which is dominant in natural images. Then maximization of non-Gaussianity is basically equivalent to maximization of sparseness in natural images. Thus, ICA can be successfully applied to learn sparse representations for classification tasks by maximizing sparseness[3].

However, there are two main drawbacks to standard ICA. First, ICA is hard to learn over-complete basis set(i.e., the number of basis vectors is greater than the dimensionality of input data). Whereas Coates et al.[4] showed that several approaches with over-complete basis, e.g., sparse autoencoder[5], K-means [4] and RBM[6], obtain an improvement for the performance of classification. This puts ICA at a disadvantage compared to these methods. Second, ICA is sensitive to whitening, which is an important preprocessing step in ICA to extract efficient features. In addition, standard ICA is difficult to exactly whiten high dimensional data. For example, an input image of size $200{\times}200$ pixels could be

S.-M. Hu and R.R. Martin (Eds.): CVM 2012, LNCS 7633, pp. 154–161, 2012.

exactly whitened by principal component analysis(PCA), while it has to solve the eigen-decomposition of the $40,000 \times 40,000$ covariance matrix.

Both drawbacks are mainly due to the hard orthonormality constraint in standard ICA. Mathematically, that is $WW^T = I$, which is utilized to prevent degenerate solution for the basis matrix W where each basis vector is a row of W. While this orthonormalization cannot be satisfied when W is over-complete. Specifically, the optimization problem of standard ICA is generally solved by using gradient descent methods, where W is orthonormalized at each iteration by symmetric orthonormalization(i.e. $W \leftarrow (WW^T)^{-1/2}W$) which doesn't work for over-complete learning. In addition, although alternative orthonormalization methods could be employed to learn over-complete basis, they not only are expensive to calculate but also may arise from the cumulation of errors.

To address the above issues, V. Le et al.[7] replaced the orthonormality constraint with a robust soft reconstruction cost for ICA(RICA). Then RICA can learn sparse features with highly over-complete set even on unwhitened data. However, this model didn't take into account the geometrical structure of the data space, which is essential for classification and clustering problems[8,9]. In particular, Zheng et al.[9] showed that exploiting the geometrical information in the data and preserving the local structure invariance could improve the performance of classification.

Motivated by the graph regularized model[9] for classification, we propose an unsupervised graph regularized ICA model with Reconstruction constraint, named gRICA. The gRICA utilizes the local geometrical information of the data to preserve the local manifold structure. In particular, we firstly build a k-nearest neighbor graph to encode the geometrical information in the data. Then, based on techniques from spectral graph theory[10], we incorporate the graph Laplacian as the structure inconsistency regularizer into the RICA framework to preserve the local manifold structured. This leads to the learned sparse representations respect the geometrical structure of the data space, and thereby facilitates classification tasks.

2   A Brief Review of RICA

Since sparseness is one form of non-Gaussianity, maximization of sparseness for ICA is equivalent to maximization of independence[2]. Given the unlabeled data set $\{x_i\}_{i=1}^m$ where $x_i \in R^n$, the optimization problem of standard ICA[1] is generally defined as:

$$\underset{W}{\text{minimize}} \sum_{i=1}^{m} \sum_{j=1}^{k} f(W_j x_i) \tag{1}$$
$$s.t. \ WW^T = I,$$

where $f(\cdot)$ is a nonlinear convex function, $W \in R^{k \times n}$ is the basis matrix, k is the number of basis vectors and W_j is j-th row basis vector in W. Additionally, the orthonormality constraint $WW^T = I$ is traditionally utilized to prevent the basis vectors in W from becoming degenerate. Meanwhile, a good general purpose smooth L1 penalty is: $f(\cdot) = \log(\cosh(\cdot))$ [2].

However, as above pointed out, the orthonoramlity constraint makes standard ICA difficult to learn over-complete basis set. In addition, ICA is sensitive to whitening. These drawbacks restrict ICA to scale to high dimensional data. Consequently, RICA[7] used a soft reconstruction cost to replace the orthonormality constraint in ICA. Applying this replacement to Equ.1, RICA can be formulated as the following unconstrained problem:

$$\underset{W}{\text{minimize}} \frac{\lambda}{m} \sum_{i=1}^{m} ||W^T W x_i - x_i||_2^2 + f(W x_i), \qquad (2)$$

where parameter λ controls the relative importance of the two terms and $W x_i$ could be regarded as the sparse representation of sample x_i[7]. Swapping the orthonormality constraint with a reconstruction penalty, the RICA optimization problem can be allowed to employ fast unconstrained optimizers (such as L-BFGS[11]) instead of slower constrained optimizers (e.g., projected gradient descent) which is generally used to solve the standard ICA optimization problem. In addition, the reconstruction penalty works well even on the data without whitening when W is over-complete. However, RICA just simply learned the over-complete basis set with reconstruction cost without considering the intrinsic geometrical and discriminating structure of the data space, which may not be good enough for classification tasks. Thus, in this work, we focus on learning a structure preserved over-complete basis for sparse representation.

3   Graph Regularized ICA with Reconstruction Constraint

As above pointed out, RICA failed to utilize the geometrical structure of the data space, which is essential to classification tasks[9]. In this Section, we introduce our graph based ICA model with Reconstruction constraint(gRICA) algorithm which avoids this limitation by incorporating a structure based regularizer. This regularizer can be formulated as follows.

3.1   Model Formulation

Given the unlabeled data matrix $X = [x_1, \ldots, x_m] \in R^{n \times m}$ where each column of X is a sample vector, we can construct a nearest neighbor(undirected) graph G with m vertices. In graph G, each vertex corresponds to a data point, and edge weight matrix $P \in R^{m \times m}$. If x_i is among the k-NN of x_j or x_j is among the k-NN of x_i, $P_{ij} = 1$, otherwise, $P_{ij} = 0$. Additionally, we define graph Laplacian matrix $L = D - P$, where $D = diag(d_1, \ldots, d_m)$ is the degree matrix with the diagonal elements defined as $d_i = \sum_{j=1}^{m} P_{ij}$.

For convenience, we denote sparse coefficient matrix $S = [s_1, \ldots, s_m] \in R^{k \times m}$ where $s_i = W x_i \in R^k$ as the sparse representation of sample x_i with the basis matrix $W \in R^{k \times n}$. Based on spectral graph theory[10], we transform the problem, i.e. preserving the geometrical structure of data for the sparse representation, into minimizing the following objective function

$$\frac{1}{2} \sum_{i,j=1}^{m} (s_i - s_j)^2 P_{ij}$$

$$= \frac{1}{2} (\sum_{i=1}^{m} s_i{}^2 D_{ii} + \sum_{j=1}^{m} s_j{}^2 D_{jj} - 2 \sum_{i,j=1}^{m} s_i s_j P_{ij})$$

$$= \mathbf{Tr}(SLS^T)$$

$$= \mathbf{Tr}(WXLX^TW^T). \tag{3}$$

This formulation can be regarded as a kind of dimensionality reduction of coefficient matrix S. For convenience, we term Equ.3 as structure inconsistency regularizer. That is, if two data points x_i and x_j are close (i.e. P_{ij} is big), the s_i and s_j should be similar to each other.

By incorporating the structure inconsistency regularizer into the original RICA model, we can get the following objective function

$$\underset{W}{\text{minimize}} \frac{\lambda}{m} ||W^TWX - X||_2^2 + f(WX)$$

$$+ \alpha \mathbf{Tr}(WXLX^TW^T), \tag{4}$$

where λ and α are the scalars controlling the relative contribution of the corresponding terms. Given a test sample, Equ.4 means that the learned basis set can sparsely represent it while requiring its representation to respect the geometric structure in the data.

3.2 Norm Ball Projection

Note that if the basis set W is over-complete ($k \gg n$), it may reconstruct the data with only a complete subset of the rows of W while setting the rest to zero. Thus, to learn an over-complete basis without degenerate(zero) vectors, we have to enforce each row of W as

$$||W_i||_2^2 = 1, \forall i = 1 \ldots k. \tag{5}$$

However, Equ.5 results in the optimization problem of Equ.4 have to be solved by constrained optimizers which are much slower than unconstrained solvers (e.g., L-BFGS and CG[11]). To utilize L-BFGS/CG to solve this constrained optimization problem, we employ the L_2-norm ball projection as [7]. The main idea is to map the basis vectors onto the norm ball during each iteration of the optimization. In particular, we denote $\hat{W}_i = W_i/||W_i||_2^2$. Furthermore, we have to take the projection in the gradient computation into account since the supplied gradient vector is employed to evaluate the objective function in L-BFGS or CG. Specifically, we will backpropagate the gradients through the projection and thereby considering the projection during the optimization. Therefore, the

Table 1. Gradient Computation

1. Projection: $\hat{W}_{ij} = \dfrac{W_{ij}}{\sqrt{\varepsilon+\sum_{t=1}^{n} W_{it}^2}}, \forall i = 1 \ldots k.$
2. Calculate the gradient g of Equ.4 with $\hat{W}$.
3. Inverse Projection: $g_{ij} = \dfrac{g_{ij}}{\sqrt{\varepsilon+\sum_{t=1}^{n} W_{it}^2}} - \hat{W}_{ij}\dfrac{\sum_{t=1}^{n} g_{it} W_{it}}{\varepsilon+\sum_{t=1}^{n} W_{it}^2}.$

constrained optimization problem becomes unconstrained. The gradient computation with inverse projection is described in Table 1 and ε is a small constant to prevent division by zero.

4 Experiments

In this section, we will firstly introduce the feature extraction for image classification. Then, we evaluate the performance of gRICA model for image classification on three public databases: Caltech 101[12], CIFAR-10[4] and STL-10 [4]. In all the experiments, if no specific mentioned, the tuning parameters in gRICA, i.e. α and λ in the objective function, are verified by cross validation to avoid over-fitting. The test values for the α and λ are $\{0.0001, 0.001, 0.01, 0.1, 1\}$.

4.1 Feature Extraction for Classification

Given a $p \times p$ input image patch (with d channels) $x \in R^n$ ($n = p \times p \times d$), gRICA can transform it to a new representation $s = Wx \in R^k$, where p is termed as the 'receptive field size'. For an image of $N \times M$ pixels (with d channels), we could obtain a $(N - p + 1) \times (M - p + 1)$(with k channels) feature following the same setting in [4], by estimating the representation s for each $p \times p$ 'subpatch' of the input image. To reduce the dimensionality of the image representation, we utilize similar pooling method in [4] to form a reduced $4k$-dimensional pooled representation for image classification. Given the pooled feature for each training image, we utilize linear SVM for classification.

4.2 Classification on Caltech 101

Caltech 101 dataset consists of 9144 images which are divided among 101 object classes and 1 background class including animals, vehicles, etc. Following the common experiment setup[13], we implement our algorithm on 15 and 30 training images per category with basis size $K = 1020$ and 10×10 receptive fields, respectively. Comparison results are shown in Table 2. We compare our classification accuracy with ScSPM[13] and LC-KSVD[14]. Table 2 shows that gRICA outperforms the other competing approaches.

Table 2. Image classification Accuracy on Caltech 101

Training size	15	30
ScSPM[13]	67.0%	73.2%
LC-KSVD[14]	67.7%	73.6%
RICA[7]	67.1%	73.7%
gRICA	67.3%	74.1%

4.3   Classification on CIFAR-10

The CIFAR-10 dataset includes 10 categories and 60000 32×32 color images in all with 6000 images per category, such as airplane, automobile, truck and horse etc. In addition, there are 50000 training images and 10000 testing images. Specifically, 1000 images from each class are randomly selected as test images and the other 5000 images from each class as training images. In this experiment, we utilize the size of basis set to 4000 with 6×6 receptive fields followed by[4]. We compare our approach with RICA[7] and K-means (Triangle, 4000 features)[4] etc. Table 3 shows the effectiveness of the proposed gRICA.

Table 3. Test Classification Accuracy on CIFAR-10

Model	Accuracy
Improved Local Coord. Coding[15]	74.5%
Sparse autoencoder[4]	73.4%
Sparse RBM[4]	72.4%
K-means (Hard)[4]	68.6%
K-means (Triangle)[4]	77.9%
K-means (Triangle, 4000 features)[4]	79.6%
RICA[7]	81.4%
gRICA	81.9%

4.4   Classification on STL-10

In STL-10, there are 10 classes(e.g., airplane, dog, monkey and ship etc), where each image is 96x96 pixels and colorful. In addition, this dataset is divided into 500 training images (10 pre-defined folds), 800 test images per class and 100,000 unlabeled images for unsupervised learning. In our experiments, we set the size of basis set $K= 1600$ and 8×8 receptive fields in the same manner described in [7]. Table 4 shows the classification results of the raw pixels[4],K-means [4], RICA[7] and gRICA.

As can be seen, although RICA tried 10×10 receptive fields and achieved 52.9% on the test set, our algorithm gRICA performs best in all cases. This means that gRICA implies more discriminative power for classification by preserving the local invariance.

We also investigate the effects of basis set size on the gRICA algorithm. In our experiments, we try seven sizes: 50, 100, 200, 400, 800, 1200 and 1600. As

Table 4. Test Classification Accuracy on STL-10

Model	Accuracy
Raw pixels[4]	31.8%
K-means(Triangle 1600 features)[4]	51.5%
RICA(8x8 receptive fields)[7]	51.4%
RICA(10x10 receptive fields)[7]	52.9%
gRICA	53.4%

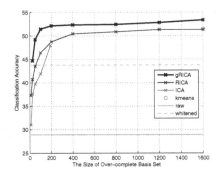

Fig. 1. Performance on the STL-10 with varying basis set size and 8×8 receptive fields

shown in Fig.1, the classification accuracy of gRICA continues to increase when the basis size goes up to 1600.

5   Conclusions

In this paper, we propose a graph regularized ICA model with Reconstruction constraint, called gRICA. The gRICA can learn an over-complete basis on the data manifold, and thereby learn the sparse representations consistent with this manifold. Consequently, gRICA could have more discriminative power than the original RICA model which only considers the Euclidean structure of the data. Furthermore, based on norm ball projection, we transform the constrained optimization problem into faster unconstrained problem. The experimental results on image classification have demonstrated the effectiveness of the proposed gRICA algorithm.

Acknowledgments. This work was supported in part by 973 Program (No. 2012CB316400), the National Science Foundation of China (No. 61025013, 61172129), Beijing Municipal Natural Science Foundation (No. 4112043), and Fundamental Research Funds for the Central Universities (No.2012JBZ012).

References

1. Hyvärinen, A., Karhunen, J., Oja, E.: Independent component analysis, vol. 26. Wiley-Interscience (2001)
2. Hyvärinen, A., Hurri, J., Hoyer, P.: Natural image statistics, vol. 1. Springer (2009)
3. Le, Q., Ngiam, J., Chen, Z., Chia, D., Koh, P., Ng, A.: Tiled convolutional neural networks. In: NIPS, vol. 23 (2010)
4. Coates, A., Lee, H., Ng, A.: An analysis of single-layer networks in unsupervised feature learning. In: AISTATS, vol. 1001 (2010)
5. Bengio, Y., Lamblin, P., Popovici, D., Larochelle, H.: Greedy layer-wise training of deep networks, vol. 19 (2007)
6. Hinton, G., Osindero, S., Teh, Y.: A fast learning algorithm for deep belief nets. Neural Computation 18(7) (2006)
7. Le, Q., Karpenko, A., Ngiam, J., Ng, A.: Ica with reconstruction cost for efficient overcomplete feature learning. In: NIPS (2011)
8. Cai, D., He, X., Han, J., Huang, T.: Graph regularized nonnegative matrix factorization for data representation. IEEE Transactions on Pattern Analysis and Machine Intelligence 33(8) (2011)
9. Zheng, M., Bu, J., Chen, C., Wang, C., Zhang, L., Qiu, G., Cai, D.: Graph regularized sparse coding for image representation. IEEE Transactions on Image Processing 20(5) (2011)
10. Chung, F.: Spectral graph theory, vol. 92. Amer. Mathematical Society (1997)
11. Schmidt, M.: minfunc. (2005)
12. Fei-Fei, L., Fergus, R., Perona, P.: Learning generative visual models from few training examples: An incremental bayesian approach tested on 101 object categories. Computer Vision and Image Understanding 106(1) (2007)
13. Yang, J., Yu, K., Gong, Y., Huang, T.: Linear spatial pyramid matching using sparse coding for image classification. In: CVPR. IEEE (2009)
14. Jiang, Z., Lin, Z., Davis, L.: Learning a discriminative dictionary for sparse coding via label consistent k-svd. In: CVPR. IEEE (2011)
15. Yu, K., Zhang, T.: Improved local coordinate coding using local tangents. In: ICML (2010)

Real-Time Recombination Method of Complex 3D Tree Model Information on Visual Perception Preserving

Tianyang Dong, Yunyi Fan, Jing Fan[*], and Lei Ji

School of Computer Science and Technology,
Zhejiang University of Technology, Hangzhou 310023, China
fanjing@zjut.edu.cn

Abstract. For the rapid visualization of large-scale forest scene, this paper proposes a real-time recombination method of complex 3D tree model information. This method adopts visual attention model and the visual characteristic of tree structures, then uses geometry-based and image-based methods to simplify tree models and construct a hybrid representation model for the 3D tree models based on the visual perception. It reflects the visual perception features of 3D tree models that can embody topological semantics in dynamic simulation. Finally, the method in this paper is applied to the simplification of several tree models, and compared with some existing tree model simplification methods. The experimental results show that this method can not only preserve better visual perception of 3D tree models, but also effectively decrease the geometric data of the forest scene, and improve the rendering efficiency and real-time walkthrough speed of forest scene.

Keywords: visual perception, model simplification, 3D trees, real-time recombination, hybrid representation.

1   Introduction

Real-time rendering a large-scale forest scene is an extremely challenging problem in computer graphics [1]. While modeling large-scale forest scene, tree models with abundant details of geometric information are very large and difficult to be rendered rapidly [2-3]. So, how to efficiently simplify the complex geometric details and preserve the visual perception of tree models in real time has become a hotspot in the research of virtual reality.

The rest of the paper is organized as follows. The related work is discussed in Section 2. Section 3 presents a hybrid representation method for considering visual features of tree structure. Then, the view-dependent and real-time recombination method is described in Section 4. In Section 5 the experimental results are discussed and an objective metric is developed to evaluate the quality of the method. Finally, conclusions are presented in Section 6.

---

[*] Corresponding author.

S.-M. Hu and R.R. Martin (Eds.): CVM 2012, LNCS 7633, pp. 162–169, 2012.

2   Related Work

The existing simplification methods of tree model include: geometry-based static simplification and view-dependent progressive representation. In order to simplify the geometric models of a large number of discrete leaves, a foliage simplification algorithm [4] (FSA) was proposed by Remolar. Xiaopeng Zhang proposed a method for hierarchical union of organs, introducing the botanical knowledge about leaf phyllotaxy and flower anthotaxy [5] (HUO). Then Qingqiong Deng adopted a hybrid polygon/line model to represent leaves according to the morphological characteristics of leaves (broad leaf or conifer) in 2010 [6]. In 2011, Guanbo Bao and Xiaopeng Zhang proposed a new leaf modeling method that uses the texture to simplify triangular mesh models of leaves [7]. The method of geometry-based static simplification is a good way to reduce the complexity of tree models. However, the simplified model still contains many meshes, which still will be a heavy burden in the rendering process of large-scale forest scene.

Cook et al. proposed a stochastic simplification of aggregate detail [8]. Gumbau presented a view-dependent multi-resolution model for the foliage of the trees in 2010 [9]. The existing method of view-dependent progressive representation can solve the hopping problem, but it can't reflect the visual perception features of 3D tree models that can embody topological semantics in dynamic simulation.

In addition, Hujun Bao et al. presented an image-based approach to simplify tree models and reconstruct depth meshes in different LOD levels in 2010 [10]. Baoquan Chen et al. presented a lobe-based tree representation for modeling trees in 2011 [11].

3   Constructing Hybrid Representation Model of 3D Trees Based on Visual Perception

The hybrid representation method of tree models in this paper adopts triangular meshes to represent the shape of trees and the important visual areas of the crown, and uses textures to represent the branches, twigs and the unimportant visual areas of the crown. This method not only maintains the importance of visual perception, but also meets the integrity expression of 3D tree models.

3.1   The Partition of Important Visual Areas of Crown

In partitioning the important visual areas of crown, this method firstly chooses 8 typical visual perception directions surrounding the model according to the spatial structure of tree. Then, it extracts the visual saliency maps from the original images with the 8 visual perception directions based on the Itti visual attention model into consideration [12-13]. Finally, according to the correlation between visual saliency maps and original tree models, the method constructs the important visual areas of the crown. The leaves composing the important visual areas of the crown are named as important visual leaves in this paper, and the other leaves are named as unimportant visual leaves.

3.2   Hybrid Representation Method for Considering Visual Features of Tree Structure

Tree usually has certain hierarchical structure and topological form, including trunk, main branches, branches, twigs and so on. And the shape of tree is mainly represented by the trunk and the main branches. To further compress the amount of tree model data and improve rendering efficiency, this paper simplifies the trees structure based on the hierarchy of tree models, and prunes the small branches and twigs.

According to the hierarchy of trees, the branches, twigs and unimportant visual leaves are divided into different clusters based on the main branches. The process of cluster partition is as follows:

Firstly, each main branch of tree model is identified, and the geometric centers of main branches are calculated. Secondly, the distance between the geometric center of each leaf and the geometric center of all main branches are calculated respectively, as shown in Equation (1).

$$centerdis \ (l,b) = \sqrt{(l_1 - b_1)^2 + (l_2 - b_2)^2 + (l_3 - b_3)^2} \tag{1}$$

Where, l is the geometric center point of leaf, and b is the geometric center point of main branch. Next, select the main branch for each leaf that gets the minimal $centerdis\,(l,b)$. Then, traverse all the unimportant visual leaves of crown to determine the main branches where each leaf grows. After that, different leaves clusters based on main branches are generated. Finally, the textures generated for different visual perception directions are used to replace the geometric representation of leaves and branches clusters.

In this paper, 3D meshes are used to represent the overall shape of tree model, like trunk and main branches. And geometric leaves culling method is adopted to simplify the important visual leaves. The textures are used to represent the branches, twigs and unimportant visual leaves, which are not in the region of human visual attention.

4   View-Dependent Real-Time Recombination Method of 3D Tree Model for Visual Perception Preserving

4.1   Dynamic Culling Factors of Leaves

This paper uses a geometry culling method for the simplification of important visual leaves to reduce the number of meshes of crown. For preserving the visual perception of pruned leaves, this method adopts the idea of Reference [14-15], and dynamically prunes the leaves according to the following culling factors:

- Distance ($dis(l,c)$): the distance between the geometric centers of leaves and the geometric center of crown.

- Orientation ($\cos(l, cam)$): the angle between the normal vector of leaf and visual perception direction.
- Area ($area(l)$): The area that observed in visual perception direction is used to represent the area of each leaf.

The sum of these weighted culling factors determines which leaves to be pruned, as Equation (2).

$$\varepsilon(l) = k_1 * dis(l,c) + k_2 * \cos(l,cam) + k_3 * area(l) \qquad (2)$$

Where, the value of each factor is between 0 and 1. k_1, k_2 and k_3 are the weight values of the indexes, and $k_1 + k_2 + k_3 = 1$. In this paper, the weight values of k_1, k_2 and k_3 are 0.3, 0.4 and 0.3 respectively.

4.2   Dynamic Culling Based on Visual Importance of Leaves

In dynamic culling of leaves based on visual importance, this method firstly calculates culling factors for each leaf and get the value of $\varepsilon(l)$ according to Equation (2). Then, it sorts the important visual leaves in descending order according to the value of $\varepsilon(l)$, and stores the information of sorted leaves into a queue, as shown in Figure 1.

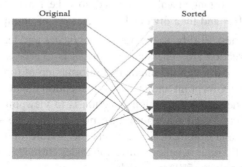

Fig. 1. The process of the leaves sorting

Finally, based on the distance d between the viewpoint and tree models, the rendering rate λ of the important visual leaves is calculated, as Equation (3).

$$\lambda = \frac{1}{In^d} \qquad (3)$$

If the number of important visual leaves is N, it will dynamically render the first λN leaves in the sorted queue as shown in Figure 2.

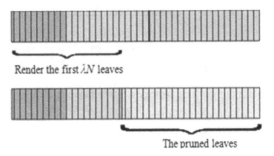

Render the first λN leaves

The pruned leaves

Fig. 2. Rendering of important visual leaves

4.3 Real-Time Recombination of 3D Tree Models for Visual Perception Preserving

Based on the visual perception features, this paper adopts a hybrid representation method of geometry and image to construct tree models for each visual perception direction.

Firstly, this method divides tree model into trunk, branches and crown, and establish the hierarchy of tree and the relationship between these parts. Secondly, this method retains the shape of trees and prunes the level of details based on the hierarchy of trees. Then, it divides the branches cluster based on the main branches. Thirdly, it selects some typical visual perception directions to generate original images of 3D trees and extracts visual saliency to form visual saliency maps. Fourthly, it calculates culling factors for important visual leaves and sort the leaves in descending order based the value of $\varepsilon(l)$, and then divides leaves clusters of unimportant visual leaves based on main branches. Fifthly, the textures of branches and leave clusters for each visual perception direction are generated. Sixthly, it is to access the viewpoint position of the virtual scene through the interactive information of forest scene, and calculate the angle between viewpoint and all visual perception directions. The smaller the angle is, the closer the visual perception direction is to viewpoint direction. Finally, this method selects the visual perception direction that has the smallest angle with viewpoint direction, and automatically extracts the texture of leaves and branches clusters based on that visual perception direction under current viewpoint to complete the real-time recombination of 3D tree model.

5   Experiment Result

To verify the validity about real-time recombination method of complex 3D tree models information for visual perception preserving, this paper adopts VC++ and OpenGL to develop a 3D tree model simplification system for supporting real-time recombination. The experiments were conducted on a computer with Intel(R) Core(TM) i3 CPU 550@3.20GHz, 2048 MB (DDR2 SDRAM) memory, ATI Radeon HD 4550 Graphics hardware and Microsoft Windows 7 Operating System.

5.1   The Data Analysis of Real-Time Recombination Method

This paper compared the FSA [4], stochastic simplification [8] and our method to show the compression ratio of simplified model. Figure 3 shows the simplification results of ilex aquifolium model. Figure 3 (a)-(d) respectively show the original model, the simplified model of FSA, the simplified model of stochastic simplification and the simplified model of our method for the ilex aquifolium model. In Figure 3, the geometric patches number of crown in ilex aquifolium model is 26872, 7860, 5374 and 5952 respectively; the geometric patches number of trunk in ilex aquifolium model is 150864, 150864, 150864 and 16362 respectively. Based on the result in Figure 3, the proposed real-time recombination method of 3D tree model has a better visual effect under the subjective judgment of human vision, and can generate the simplified models with a higher compression ratio.

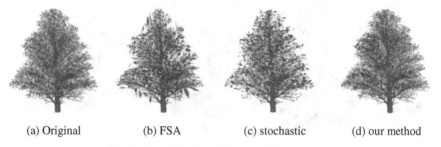

(a) Original   (b) FSA   (c) stochastic   (d) our method

Fig. 3. Simplification of ilex aquifolium model

5.2   Visual Quality Analysis

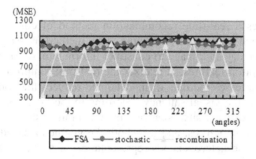

Fig. 4. Visual quality analysis of simplified ilex aquifolium model

This paper adopted a computational model of the saliency map [16-17] in visual quality analysis. To verify whether our method effectively preserves appearance in different viewing angles, series of screenshots are taken around the tree and compared with those obtained from the original model. We compared three simplification methods from Figure 4, where the x-axis is the viewpoints around those tree models and the y-axis plots the MSE (mean-squared error) values of the saliency map of each simplification method (with respect to the original model). The three methods under comparison are: foliage simplification algorithm [4], stochastic simplification method [8] and our method. From the Figure 4, it can be seen clearly that the proposed real-time recombination method of 3D trees model gives a better performance near the visual perception direction.

5.3   Application in Forest Scene

In the visualization of forest scene, the system recombines tree models according to the positional relation between the viewpoint and trees in real time. Figure 5 shows a forest scene, which contains 13 tree models, and the total number of geometric patches is 150758. The forest scene rendering frame rate is 13 fps.

Fig. 5. Application in forest scene

6   Conclusions

This paper proposes a real-time recombination method of complex 3D tree model information for visual perception preserving. This method uses a hybrid representation method of geometry and image to construct information of 3D tree models based on the visual perception features. It realizes the real-time simplification of tree models, effectively compresses the data of models, and reduces the complexity of scene. This method extracts the visual saliency according to the visual attention model, and distinguishes the important visual areas of crown. On this basis, it considers the visual characteristics of tree structures, and uses both the geometry-based and image-based methods to achieve the heterogeneous representation of tree models for their leaves and branches. This method not only maintains the hierarchy of trees and visual perception features, but also effectively decreases the geometric complexity of forest scene and improves rendering efficiency.

Acknowledgements. This work is sponsored by National Natural Science Foundation of China (No. 61003265, 61173097, 61202202), Key Science and Technology Innovation Team of Zhejiang Province (No.2009R50009), Zhejiang Science and Technology Planning Project of China (No.2010C33046) and Zhejiang Natural Science Foundation of China (No.Z1090459, Y1101102) and Tsinghua - Tencent Joint Laboratory for Internet Innovation Technology.

References

1. Tu, C.: Real-Time Rendering of Realistic Trees in Virtual Reality System. Computer Technology and Development 19, 206–209 (2009)
2. Liu, X.Q., Cao, W.Q., Zhang, L.: The Modeling and Animation of Complex 3D Forestry Scenarios. Journal of Image and Graphics 15, 136–141 (2010)
3. Huang, Y.L.: Study and Implement of Forest Landscape Visualization based on OpenSceneGraph. Beijing Forestry University, Beijing (2009)
4. Remolar, I., Chover, M., Belmonte, O., Ribelles, J., Rebollo, C.: Geometric Simplification of Foliage. Eurographics 2, 397–404 (2002)
5. Zhang, X.P., Blaise, F., Jaeger, M.: Multiresolution Plant Models with Complex Organs. In: Proceedings of the 2006 ACM International Conference on Virtual Reality Continuum and its Applications, pp. 331–334. ACM, Hong Kong (2006)
6. Deng, Q.Q., Zhang, X.P., Yang, G., Jaeger, M.: Multiresolution Foliage for Forest Rendering. Computer Animation and Virtual Worlds 21, 1–23 (2010)
7. Bao, G.B., Li, H.J., Zhang, X.P., Che, W.J., Jaeger, M.: Realistic Real-Time Rendering for Large-Scale Forest Scenes. In: 2011 IEEE International Symposium on VR Innovation (ISVRI), pp. 217–223. IEEE, Singapore (2011)
8. Cook, R.L., Halstead, J., Planck, M., Ryu, D.: Stochastic Simplification of Aggregate Detail. ACM Transactions on Graphics 26, 79 (2007)
9. Gumbau, J., Chover, M., Remolar, I., Rebollo, C.: View-Dependent Pruning for Real-Time Rendering of Trees. Computers & Graphics 35, 364–374 (2011)
10. Liu, F., Hua, W., Bao, H.J.: Quad Mesh Based Dynamic Simulation of Large-Scale Forest on GPU. Journal of Computer-Aided Design & Computer Graphics 22, 1701–1708 (2010)
11. Livnyl, Y., Pirk, S., Cheng, Z.L., Yan, F.L., Deussen, O., Cohen-Or, D., Chen, B.Q.: Texture-Lobes for Tree Modeling. ACM Transactions on Graphics 30, 53 (2011)
12. Wang, Y.: Research and Application of Visual Attention Model. Shanghai Jiao Tong University, Shanghai (2012)
13. Ma, R.N., Tu, X.P., Ding, J.D., Yang, J.Y.: To Evaluate Salience Map towards Popping Out Visual Objects. Acta Automatica Sinica 38, 870–876 (2012)
14. Lee, J., Kuo, C.C.J.: Fast and Flexible Tree Rendering with Enhanced Visibility Estimation. In: Tenth IEEE International Symposium on Multimedia, pp. 452–459. IEEE, California (2008)
15. Lee, J., Kuo, M., Kuo, C.C.J.: Enhanced 3D Tree Model Simplification and Perceptual Analysis. In: IEEE International Conference on Multimedia and Expo., pp. 1250–1253. IEEE, Hilton Cancun (2009)
16. Itti, L., Koch, C.: A Saliency-based Search Mechanism for Overt and Covert Shifts of Visual Attention. Vision Research 40, 1489–1506 (2000)
17. Lee, J., Kuo, C.C.J.: Tree model simplification with hybrid polygon/billboard approach and human-centered quality evaluation. In: 2010 IEEE International Conference on Multimedia and Expo., pp. 932–937. IEEE, Singapore (2010)

Efficient Spherical Parametrization Using Progressive Optimization

Shenghua Wan[1], Tengfei Ye[2], Maoqing Li[2], Hongchao Zhang[3], and Xin Li[1,*]

[1] School of Electrical Engineering and Computer Science, Louisiana State University
(LSU), Baton Rouge, LA 70803, USA
xinli@lsu.edu
[2] Department of Automation, Xiamen University, Xiamen 361005, China
[3] Department of Mathematics, LSU, Baton Rouge, LA 70803, USA

Abstract. Spherical mapping is a key enabling technology in modeling and processing genus-0 close surfaces. A closed genus-0 surface can be seamless parameterized onto a unit sphere. We develop an effective progressive optimization scheme to compute such a parametrization, minimizing a nonlinear energy balancing angle and area distortions. Among all existing state-of-the-art spherical mapping methods, the main advantage of our spherical mapping are two-folded: (1) the algorithm converges very efficiently, therefore it is suitable for handling huge geometric models, and (2) it generates bijective and lowly distorted mapping results.

Keywords: Spherical Parametrization, Hierarchical Optimization.

1 Introduction

Spherical parametrization seeks a bijective map $f : M \to S$ between a closed genus-0 surface M and a unit spherical domain S. For a very wide category of solid models without handles or voids, their boundary surfaces are closed and genus-0. The sphere is a natural parametric domain for these surfaces, on a sphere domain their seamless parametric representations can be constructed directly. A parameterization introducing small metric distortion is desirable. Isometry (preserving both angle and area) is ideal but usually not possible for a generally given M. We therefore seek for a map that minimizes either angle distortion, or area distortion, or a balancing between both of them.

Computing a map on a non-flattened domain, however, is often formulated as a non-linear optimization problem, and cannot be computed efficiently [6]. For example, a harmonic spherical map is conformal [2,7]. The resultant mapping is angle-preserving. However, its area distortion could be very large, especially in the long and thin protrusion regions (e.g. ears of the Stanford bunny). A map balancing angle and area distortions is therefore often desirable. Zayer et al. [11] proposed a Curvilinear Spherical Parametrization which better reduces area-distortion efficiently. Another state-of-the-art spherical mapping algorithm is

---

[*] Corresponding author.

S.-M. Hu and R.R. Martin (Eds.): CVM 2012, LNCS 7633, pp. 170–177, 2012.

proposed by Praun and Hoppe [9]. They used the progressive mesh to iteratively optimize the $L2$ stretching energy [10] defined piecewise on the mesh of M. Such a coarse-to-fine solving scheme can effectively overcome the local minima issue existing in most spherical mapping formulations that aim to minimize angle and area distortion together. Inspired by this, we also adopt the progressive simplification and develop a hierarchical optimization scheme. But unlike [9], we utilize the distortion energy [1] which is shown converged to the continuous energy. Furthermore, we develop an effective hierarchical optimization scheme over the mesh (with different resolutions) from both local and global aspects, to improve the mapping efficiency and efficacy significantly.

We present a hierarchical optimization framework for the spherical parametrization problem. Compared with other state-of-the-art spherical mapping algorithms, our method generates a bijective and lowly-distorted mapping, and converges efficiently. Therefore, our algorithm can be applied on large geometric models with complex geometry (e.g. with long branches) robustly.

2   Hierarchical Spherical Parametrization

2.1   Mapping Distortion

The angle distortion per triangle can be measured [4] on the map of each triangle $f_T : T \to t$ by $E_D(T) = \cot \alpha |a|^2 + \cot \beta |b|^2 + \cot \gamma |c|^2$ where T and t are the triangle of mesh M and its image on the parametric sphere S respectively; α, β, γ are the angles in T and a, b, c are the corresponding opposite edge lengths in t. The area distortion can be measured by $E_A(T) = \frac{Area(t)}{Area(T)}$. The integrated (over the area of parameter triangle t) angle and area distortions of the entire spherical parametrization $f : M \to S$ are therefore $\bar{E}_D(M) = \sum_{i=1}^{N_F} E_D(T_i) Area(t_i)$ and $\bar{E}_A(M) = \sum_{i=1}^{N_F} E_A(T_i) Area(t_i)$, where N_F is the number of faces in M. Following the modification proposed by [1], we use formulations in Eqs (1) and (2) for new distortions, which provide upper bounds of the spherical integrals and avoid degeneracy during the optimization:

$$E_D(M) = \sum_{i=1}^{N_F} d_i^{-2} \cdot E_D(T_i) Area(t_i), \tag{1}$$

$$E_A(M) = \sum_{i=1}^{N_F} d_i^{-2} \cdot E_A(T_i) Area(t_i). \tag{2}$$

where d_i is the minimum distance from the origin to triangle t_i. And the objective function is their weighted sum:

$$E = \lambda E_D(M) + \mu E_A(M) \tag{3}$$

where λ and μ are parameters balancing angle and area distortions. Area distortion is a common issue for spherical mapping, leading to under-sampling, especially for the models with long and thin protrusions, which could cause undesirable artifacts in applications. We found that a relatively large weight on area distortion usually provides stable and desirable mappings; hence in our experiments, we set $\lambda = 0.1$ and $\mu = 1.0$ by default.

2.2   Algorithm Overview

The distortion energy introduced in Section 2.1 is nonlinear and nonconvex. Generally, directly optimizing the energy will get trapped in local minima inevitably. We therefore adopt the progressive mesh [3] to simplify the mesh into coarser resolutions and solve the optimization hierarchically while we gradually refine the mesh back to the original tessellation. The progressive scheme is similar to [9], but our optimization is developed differently and is more efficient and effective. Given a genus-0 mesh M with n vertices, we first progressively simplify it to a tetrahedron with 4 vertices, denoted as M^4. We then use M^k to denote the resolution of M with k vertices, and v_i^k to denote the vertex which will split during the refinement process. v_i^k is a vertex on M^k and it splits into v_i^{k+1} and v_{k+1}^{k+1} (suppose the newly inserted vertex is always given the id $k+1$) in the new mesh M^{k+1}. Based on above definitions, the algorithm pipeline is as follows:

1. Simplify M^n to a tetrahedron M^4 using progressive mesh;
2. Map M^4 onto a unit sphere domain S^4, get $f^4 : M^4 \rightarrow S^4$;
3. Following the vertex split order that refines M^4 back to M^n, optimize the spherical mapping $f^k : M^k \rightarrow S^k$ hierarchically.

2.3   Global Hierarchical Optimization

We progressively refine M^k from $k = 4, \ldots, n$, and during each vertex split $v_i^k \rightarrow \{v_i^{k+1}, v_{k+1}^{k+1}\}$, we find a locally optimal spherical position as the image for each of these two vertices v_i^k, v_{k+1}^{k+1} while fixing images of all their one-ring neighboring vertices. After every η (a constant integer) vertex splits, we optimize all these newly placed vertices as well as their neighboring vertices.

Ideally, after each split, we can perform a local optimization on images of v_i^k, v_{k+1}^{k+1}, and all their neighboring vertices until we get to a local optimum. However, this precise local optimization per every vertex split is relatively expensive and sometimes not necessary. Therefore, we only conduct the optimization after a set of vertices are inserted.

2.4   Local Optimization on a Vertex

After the split of a vertex v_i^k, we need to embed the images of the two new vertices v_i^{k+1} and v_{k+1}^{k+1} on the sphere. Here we solve a simple local optimization to determine valid (non-flipped) spherical locations for them. Later, after each η vertex splits, we will perform such local optimizations on new vertices and their neighboring vertices together. When the mapping of a vertex is updated and the objective energy change is bigger than a threshold, its one-ring vertices may need to be optimized again. We propagate this local refinement to larger regions using a priority queue.

We develop a local optimization to find the most suitable spherical embedding of each vertex through an efficient great-circle search. In this algorithm, we do not update a vertex's spherical embedding if the energy reduction is not significant. A line search mechanism is employed on the great circle of the spherical domain.

Note even if the initial position introduces flip-over, the energy minimization would guide the movement of vertex's spherical image to a valid position free of flip-over. This local optimization is efficient and will converge within finite steps (see Section 2.7 for detailed analysis).

2.5   Priority Queue

When optimizing spherical images of the vertices, we iteratively pick a vertex to do its local optimization. The order of picking vertices is important and it could greatly affect the result and computation efficiency. Intuitively, we shall optimize the vertex whose movement potentially reduces the distortion energy most significantly. Both the magnitude of the first order KKT [8] violation and the distance the vertex can move are critical for the energy reduction. For example, in a region whose spherical mapping shrinks severely, KKT violations of the objective functions on vertices could be big, but spherical embedding of these vertices could not move much (since all these spherical triangles are already very small) before flipover appear. Then moving such vertices may not have high priority. We therefore use the first order KKT violation magnitude multiplying the potential moving distance as the key for this priority queue.

Therefore, for the priority queue we adopt the following priority function τ defined on v_i's spherical image p_i:

$$\tau(v_i) = \rho(v_i) \cdot d \tag{4}$$

where d is the distance from p_i (v_i's image on sphere) to the boundary of its *spherical kernel* (see Section 2.6) along the negative gradient direction. And ρ is the magnitude of the first order KKT optimality violation:

$$\rho(v_i) = \|\nabla E(p_i)\| \sqrt{1 - (\frac{\nabla E(p_i)^T \cdot p_i}{\|\nabla E(p_i)\|})^2} \tag{5}$$

where $\nabla E(p_i)$ is the gradient of the objective function E of eq (3) at vertex v_i. Note that the feasibility condition $\|p_i\| = 1$ is always guaranteed by the construction. In our experiments, we simply use the average distance from p_i to its spherical one-ring to approximate d. $\tau(v_i)$ therefore estimates the aforementioned potential function reduction at vertex v_i, measured via the first order KKT optimality condition violation ρ at p_i multiplied by d.

2.6   Spherical Kernel and the Mapping Bijectivity

The spherical kernel can be defined on the spherical polygon formed by the one-ring neighboring vertices of a vertex v_i. It is defined and can be computed as the intersection of the open hemispheres defined by the spherical polygon edges. To avoid the flip-over on the spherical parametrization, we shall maintain a valid spherical embedding. This can be guaranteed if every vertex is inside its spherical kernel. We generalize the planar kernel computation algorithm [5] onto the spherical triangle mesh. The computation is efficient and takes $O(k)$, where k is the number of vertices on the spherical polygon.

The **bijectivity** of the spherical mapping can be shown. First, during local optimization, a non-flipped local region will not be converted into a flipped local region. Therefore, if we can guarantee the initial spherical embedding during the entire progressive refinement is valid, then our final parametrization is non-flipped. Through induction, we can show that a valid initial spherical embedding can always be constructed during vertex split. (1) After the progressive simplification, the mesh is simplified to a tetrahedron M^4 with 4 vertices, which can be embedded on the sphere. (2) Suppose the mesh M^k with k vertices has a valid spherical embedding, and the next refinement is to do the vertex split from v_i^k to $(v_i^{k+1}, v_{k+1}^{k+1})$, then the spherical kernel for v_i^k is not empty. Then it can be shown that non-empty spherical kernel regions for v_i^{k+1}, v_{k+1}^{k+1} can always be constructed [9]. Therefore, a valid spherical embedding for the refined mesh M^{k+1} exists and can be used as the initial spherical positions for the next insertion and refinement. The mapping bijectivity is therefore guaranteed.

2.7   Analyzing Convergence of the Optimization

The first order KKT optimality condition of $\min E(p_i)$, subject to $\|p_i\| = 1$ can be written as

$$\nabla E(p_i) - \lambda p_i = 0, p_i^T p_i = 1. \tag{6}$$

where $\lambda \in R$ is Lagrange multiplier associated with the ball constraints. By considering $p^T p = 1$, which is guaranteed by the algorithm, we have $\lambda = \nabla E(p_i)^T p_i$. Then, the 2-norm residue of the left hand side of the first equation in Eq (6) can be written as

$$\rho(v_i) = \|\nabla E(p_i)\| \sqrt{1 - (\frac{\nabla E(p_i)^T \cdot p_i}{\|\nabla E(p_i)\|})^2} = 0 \tag{7}$$

which can be considered as the magnitude of the violation of KKT condition.

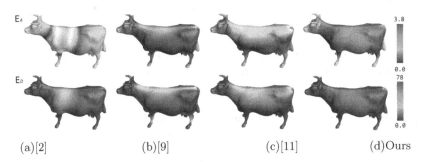

Fig. 1. Comparison of Other Spherical Parametrization Algorithms and Our Method on the Cow model. (a) is from [2]; (b) is from (b)[9]; (c) is from [11] and (d) is from our method. E_A and E_D indicate area distortion and angle distortion. Warmer color, e.g red, indicates larger distortion; while cooler color, e.g. blue, indicates lower distortion. The rightmost column shows our results, which exhibits lower angle and area distortion. Please refer to this paper's online version for the color-encoding.

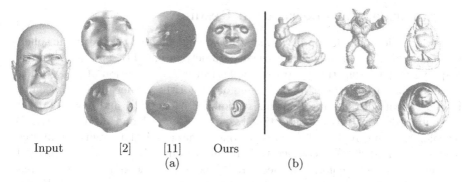

Input   [2]   [11]   Ours

(a)   (b)

Fig. 2. (a)Comparison of Other Spherical Parametrization Algorithms and Our Method on the Head model. The leftmost column is the input model. Our approach preserves the facial features like eyes, nose, mouth and ears more naturally. (b) Some results of our approach.

When $\rho(v_i)$ is not small, p_i is not close to a local minimum. Then, because the angle between the asymptotic searching directions and the negative gradient direction of the energy function is an acute angle, the Armijo-type great-circle back tracking line search will be successful within a finite number of steps and a sufficient energy value reduction relative to the KKT violation $\rho(v_i)$ will be obtained. This would force the first order KKT violation $\rho(v_i)$ goes to zero, since the energy function value is always bounded above from zero.

Globally, the objective energy is also bounded below, actually nonnegative, and monotonically decreasing. Furthermore, the great-circle back tracking line search conditions will prevent the step size getting too small and the energy will be reduced sufficiently when p_i is far away from local minimum. Therefore, globally, the total energy will decrease relatively rapidly to a minimum value.

The graphs of the total distortion energy per vertex in the optimization are depicted in Figure 3. In this figure we observe the energy drops severely in the beginning and the slope of the graph asymptotically goes towards zero with increasing number of iterations. This indicates our approach finally converges.

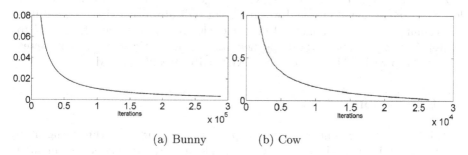

(a) Bunny   (b) Cow

Fig. 3. Energy (per vertex) with respect to iterations on Bunny and Cow. The y-axis shows the energy; the x-axis shows the iteration number.

3   Spherical Parametrization Results

To perform side-by-side comparisons, we have implemented the harmonic spherical mapping [2], curvilinear spherical parametrization [11], and we obtained mapping results from the progressive spherical parametrization of [9]. We also parameterize various input models using our algorithm under different weights. In experiments demonstrated in this section, we use $\lambda = 0.1$ and $\mu = 1.0$.

Figure 1 demonstrates the effectiveness of our approach on Cow(11K vertices) by color-encoding angle and area distortions of the spherical mappings computed by [2], [11], and [9]. We can see that results of our method in the rightmost column are in cooler color, and therefore it has lower angle and area distortions.

Figure 2-a demonstrates the results of our approach on the Head (13K vertices) model side by side compared with [2] and [11]. Our approach introduces smaller angle and area distortions, and hence better preserves the facial features like eyes, nose, mouth and ears on the sphere. Figure 2-b illustrates some more mapping results computed by our algorithm.

Table 1. Comparison of Statistics on Bunny

Bunny	#V=34K				Cow	#V=11K				Gargoyle	#V=100K			
	[2]	[11]	[9]	Ours		[2]	[11]	[9]	Ours		[2]	[11]	[9]	Ours
#FO	2585	0	3	0	#FO	2536	2	0	0	#FO	6106	9	0	0
E_D	50.8	63.6	78.1	61.4	E_D	51.2	73.2	117.3	69.9	E_D	51.7	78.8	81.2	81.8
E_A	22.8	25.5	14.0	14.2	E_A	32.9	23.8	14.4	15.5	E_A	93.6	141.7	41.5	47.7
T(s)	2397	91	600	58	T(s)	224	28	420	21	T(s)	24393	1151.4	1380	193

Table 2. Execution Time of Our Approach on Various Models

Models	Cow	Frog	Bunny	Horse	David	Venus	Gargoyle	Amardillo	Budda
#Vertices	11K	25K	34K	48K	50K	50K	100K	106K	400K
Time(s)	21	48	58	89	111	70	193	250	526

Numerically, the spherical mapping results of Bunny, Cow and Gargoyle, computed by [2], [9] and [11] are compared with our approach in Tables 1. The visualization of E_D and E_A for Cow is given in Figure 1, where cooler color indicates less distorted triangle map and warmer color indicates otherwise. Table 2 lists the running times of our method on 9 models (vertex sizes vary from 11K to 400K). Our experiments (the implementation is not optimized) are conducted on a desktop with AMD Athlon X2 2.9GHz CPU and 2GB RAM.

4   Conclusion

In this paper, we present an effective spherical mapping algorithm using hierarchical optimization scheme minimizing angle and area distortions. Compared with other state-of-the-art spherical mapping algorithms, our method generates a bijective and lowly-distorted mapping, and converges efficiently.

Our current spherical parametrization has not considered the preservation of any features or intrinsic structures of the given geometric model. For example, for local features such as semantic feature points, it is often desirable if the parametrization can flexibly control their distributions on the sphere; for global features such as symmetry, preserving such symmetric structure in its spherical image is also desirable for subsequent geometry processing tasks. These are currently not integrated in our mapping framework. We will explore the feature-preserving simplification (e.g. preserving both feature points and symmetry structure on the base domain) and consider the optimization satisfying such constraints.

References

1. Friedel, I., Schröder, P., Desbrun, M.: Unconstrained spherical parameterization. In: SIGGRAPH Sketches (2005)
2. Gu, X., Yau, S.T.: Global conformal surface parameterization. In: Proc. Symp. of Geometry Processing, pp. 127–137 (2003)
3. Hoppe, H.: Progressive meshes. In: SIGGRAPH, pp. 99–108 (1996)
4. Hormann, K., Greiner, G.: Mips: An efficient global parametrization method. In: Curve and Surface Design: Saint-Malo 1999, pp. 153–162 (2000)
5. Lee, D.T., Preparata, F.P.: An optimal algorithm for finding the kernel of a polygon. J. ACM 26(3), 415–421 (1979)
6. Li, X., Bao, Y., Guo, X., Jin, M., Gu, X., Qin, H.: Globally optimal surface mapping for surfaces with arbitrary topology. IEEE Trans. on Visualization and Computer Graphics 14(4), 805–819 (2008)
7. Li, X., He, Y., Gu, X., Qin, H.: Curves-on-surface: A general shape comparison framework. In: Proc. IEEE International Conf. on Shape Modeling and Applications, pp. 352–357 (2006)
8. Nocedal, J., Wright, S.J.: Numerical Optimization (2006)
9. Praun, E., Hoppe, H.: Spherical parametrization and remeshing. ACM Trans. Graph. 22, 340–349 (2003)
10. Sander, P.V., Snyder, J., Gortler, S.J., Hoppe, H.: Texture mapping progressive meshes. In: SIGGRAPH, pp. 409–416 (2001)
11. Zayer, R., Rossl, C., Seidel, H.P.: Curvilinear spherical parameterization. In: Proc. IEEE International Conf. on Shape Modeling and Applications (2006)

Curve Skeleton Extraction by Graph Contraction

Wei Jiang[1], Kai Xu[1], Zhi-Quan Cheng[1,*], Ralph R. Martin[2], and Gang Dang[1]

[1] School of Computer, National University of Defense Technology, P.R. China
cheng.zhiquan@gmail.com
[2] School of Computer Science and Informatics, Cardiff University, Wales, UK

Abstract. In this paper, we propose a practical algorithm for extracting curve skeletons from a 3D shape represented by a triangular mesh. We first construct an initial *skeleton graph* by copying the connectivity and geometry information from the input mesh. We then perform iterative skeletonization over the nodes of the skeleton graph using coupled processes of graph contraction and surface clustering. In the contraction step, the skeleton graph is simplified and regularized with surface clustering: mesh vertices are clustered, while the positions of nodes in the skeleton graph are updated at the same time. Eventually, the skeleton graph is automatically simplified to an approximately-centered curve skeleton. Our algorithm naturally produces a skeleton-to-surface mapping, making the output skeletons directly applicable to skinning deformation.

Keywords: curve skeleton extraction, graph contraction, clustering.

1 Introduction

A skeleton is a compact and effective representation of a solid shape [1,2], efficiently encoding both its geometry and topology. Skeleton extraction has been extensively studied, and many approaches have been proposed for computing medial structures. In general they either find a 2D medial surface [3], or a 1D curve skeleton [1]. In this paper, we aim to extract an curve skeleton, as it is a more concise representation, with generally wider application. As well as producing an approximately-centered curve skeleton, a secondary output is a skeleton-to-surface mapping, which is directly applicable to skeleton-driven shape deformation (see Figure 1).

Our practical curve skeleton extraction method is based on graph contraction. The *approximate centroidal Voronoi diagram* (ACVD) [4] lies at the core of our approach, as it provides a fast and efficient simplification and clustering algorithm. Although in the 2D case, the Voronoi diagram can be effectively used as a paradigm for producing a curve skeleton [5], as Amenta et al. [2,3] pointed out, direct extension of this result to 3D shapes is not trival: like other Voronoi-based algorithms [3], ACVD produces a medial surface, rather than a medial curve. Further processing is needed to produce a curve skeleton.

---

* Corresponding author.

S.-M. Hu and R.R. Martin (Eds.): CVM 2012, LNCS 7633, pp. 178–185, 2012.

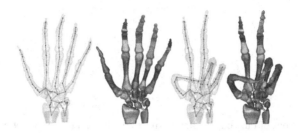

Fig. 1. Hand bone model. Left: extracted curve skeleton shown with nodes and edges, and the associated surfaces clustering. Right: a new configuration obtained by shape deformation driven by the extracted skeleton.

2   Related Work

Curve skeleton extraction and its applications have been studied both theoretically and algorithmically. One way of classifying approaches to the problem is as *volumetric* or *geometric* [6], according to whether an interior representation or only a surface representation is used. We focus on the most relevant *geometric* methods; see [1,6] for detailed reviews.

Direct *volumetric* approaches are based on thinning [7], producing a curve skeleton by iteratively removing voxels from the boundary of an object until the required thinness is obtained. The main volumetric alternative is to use distance-field methods [8,9,10]. The distance field or distance transform [8] is defined for each interior point of a 3D shape as the smallest distance from that point to the boundary. Other types of fields [9] generated by functions based on the distance transform can also be used to extract curve skeletons.

Geometric methods can be applied to objects represented by polygonal meshes or scattered point sets, e.g. [5,6,11,12,13,14]. A popular class of approach uses the Voronoi diagram [5,13] generated by the vertices of the 3D polygonal representation, or directly from a set of unorganized points [3]. Our algorithm is related to these approaches, but uses the *approximate centroidal Voronoi diagram* (ACVD) [4] to speed up the Voronoi computation. More importantly, we aim to produce a curve skeleton rather than the straightforward medial surface produced by e.g. [3,4].

Laplacian-based contraction was first developed by [6] to find skeletons of mesh surfaces, then extended for use with point sets [14]. Tagliasacchi et al. [15] proposed the notion of generalized rotational symmetry axis (ROSA) as a basis for extracting the skeleton for an oriented point set.

Other geometric methods use differing approaches to produce the curve skeleton. Several have some similarities with the ideas we present here. Li et al. [11] constructed a line segment skeleton by edge collapse. Katz and Tal [12] first decomposed a mesh surface into segments using minimal curvature cues and fuzzy clustering, and then used this segmentation to construct a skeleton. In the work of [16], curve skeleton extraction and mesh decomposition processes are simultaneously performed, using approximate convex decomposition. Our approach is similar to these algorithms in that it uses a relationship between skeletonization and decomposition. Although we also utilize

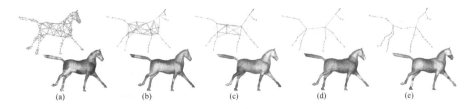

Fig. 2. Four iterations of our coupled graph extraction with surface clustering on a horse model (a-d). The final skeleton can be refined if necessary to give a more dense sampling (e).

ACVD for surface clustering, i.e. mesh decomposition, the fundamental difference between these algorithms and ours is that we *simultaneously* use graph contraction to extract the skeleton, rather than generating a shape decomposition and then *subsequently* extracting the skeleton.

3 Curve Skeleton Extraction Algorithm

Given a triangular mesh, we extract its curve skeleton by graph contraction. We first provide an overview of our algorithm, and in following sections, we further explain the main steps, including the graph contraction and surface clustering processes, as well as an optional skeleton refinement step.

3.1 Overview

Algorithm 1 gives pseudocode for our algorithm. We denote the input mesh by $\mathcal{M}$, the skeleton graph by $\mathcal{G}$ (which is initialized as a direct copy of $\mathcal{M}$), and the surface clusters by Ω. Initially each vertex of M is put in an independent cluster. The skeleton graph and clustering are consistent in the sense that the clustering Ω determines the graph $\mathcal{G}$, and the mapping from the mesh $\mathcal{M}$ to the skeleton $\mathcal{G}$. During iterative skeletonization, we perform graph contraction coupled with surface clustering. Graph contraction, running on $\mathcal{G}$, works similar to ACVD [4], but with topological and geometrical constraints to ensure that the skeleton meets various expectations described later. This progressively coarsens and contracts the initial graph into a medial structure of the input mesh. This graph contraction is coupled with a surface clustering process, which upodates the surface clusters Ω on $\mathcal{M}$. Surface clustering serves both to group mesh regions, *and* to provide good node distribution and connectivity of the skeleton graph for the subsequent graph contraction step. Iteration stops when no contractible nodes remain. If the user requires a more detailed skeleton and corresponding surface clusters, an optional refinement process may be used which places additional skeleton nodes between the ones already determined, and refines the clustering accordingly. As well as giving denser sampling, this can also help to provide better distributed skeleton points. Finally, the skeleton graph is contracted into the output curve skeleton. Figure 2 shows several iterations of skeletonization (a-d) and skeleton refinement (e).

Our contraction idea is based on noting that AVCD can simplify the input mesh and generate a medial structure [4]. ACVD mimics CVD via k-means clustering of mesh

---

Algorithm 1 Curve skeleton extraction by graph contraction

Require: A mesh $\mathcal{M}$
Ensure: Its skeleton $\mathcal{K}$ and surface clusters $\Omega = \{C_i | i = 1, ..., n\}$

1: Initialize skeleton graph $\mathcal{G}$ from $\mathcal{M}$;
2: Initialize surface clusters $\Omega = \{C_i | i = 1, ..., N_V\}$;
3: $N_{seeds} = 200$;
4: **repeat**
5:     $N_{seeds} = r \times N_{seeds}$;
6:     Graph contraction on $\mathcal{G}$ using N_{seeds};
7:     Surface clustering on Ω;
8:     Update contraction and clustering constraints;
9: **until** (no contractible node in $\mathcal{G}$);
10: $\mathcal{K} \leftarrow \mathcal{G}$;
11: Optionally refine skeleton $\mathcal{K}$;
   Note: C_i is the ith cluster. N_V is the number of vertices of $\mathcal{M}$. r is the cluster reduction ratio, experimentally set to 0.7. No contractible node in $\mathcal{G}$ means that there is no *inessential* triangle (explained later) in $\mathcal{G}$.

---

vertices to coarsen the input mesh. However, if ACVD is used in a straightforward way, it produces a medial *surface*-like mesh as the result, Like other popular methods. For example, Figure 3 shows medial structures for similar hand models computed using typical Voronoi-based approaches, including the *power crust* approach [3] and ACVD [4]: in neither case does a *one-dimensional* curve skeleton result. Our output is also shown in Figure 3. We thus have to modify AVCD.

3.2 Graph Contraction Coupled with Surface Clustering

Graph contraction and surface clustering are coupled steps. Each node in the skeleton graph is placed at the center of mass of its corresponding surface cluster; edges of the graph are deduced from the adjacency relations of the surface clusters. In each iteration, we first perform skeleton graph contraction using a subset of the current graph nodes as seeds. During contraction, graph nodes come from the associated surface clusters obtained in the last iteration. A contraction of two graph nodes causes their associated

Fig. 3. Hand model medial structure. Left to right: via power crust [3] (image after [3]), via ACVD [4] and using our approach.

surface clusters to be merged. The merged surface clusters are then optimized via surface clustering, which updates the skeleton graph (including both nodes and edges) to agree with the optimized surface clusters. Optimizing the surface clustering adjusts the contracted graph to provide a better placement of nodes.

To perform skeleton graph contraction, we utilize a revised version of ACVD on $\mathcal{G}$ whihc minimizes the following energy:

$$F_{\mathcal{G}} = \sum_{i=0}^{n-1} \left(\sum_{n_i \in C_j} \omega_i \|n_i - c_j\|^2 \right),$$ (1)

where n_i is a graph node within the Voronoi cell C_j with center of mass c_i, the weight of node n_i is $\omega_i = 1/\sum_{j \in N_1(i)} A_{ij}$, and $N_1(i)$ is the 1-ring neighboring triangles of node n_i while A_{ij} is the area of the corresponding triangle. If a node has no neighboring triangle, we simply set its weight to 10^6. Clustering is performed using classical Lloyd relaxation where we interleave cluster growing and center relocation. The process is bootstrapped with a set of seed points and the initial clusters associated with each seed point. The initial clusters are obtained by grass-fire region growing from each seed. Then in each iteration, we check those boundary edges $e_{ij} = (n_i, n_j)$ whose two end nodes lie in different clusters: $n_i \in C_1$ and $n_j \in C_2$. We then select one of the following three operations according to which decreases the energy $F_{\mathcal{G}}$ most: 1) merge n_i into cluster C_2, 2) merge n_j into cluster C_1 and, 3) keep the current configuration. When no further update of boundary edges is possible, we finish contraction and move on to surface clustering. On each iteration the number of seeds reduces by a factor r; we experimentally take $r = 0.7$ for all tested models.

Surface clustering works in a similar to the above except that it operates on the original mesh. The energy function to be optimised is given later in Equation 2, which has similar form to Equation 1; both are variations of the basic ACVD definition. Coupled contraction and clustering are iterated until no contractible nodes remain, i.e., all remaining nodes are selected as seeds and no inessential triangles (see later) remain.

Note that performing ACVD over the skeleton graph only leads to the coarsening of the graph. In order to eventually make it converge to an approximately-centered skeleton, we need to add constraints during graph contraction and surface clustering. Firstly, in order to avoid over-contraction, we add a constraint which prevents extreme nodes of the skeleton graph from being contracted. Secondly, in order to center the graph in the interior of the input surface, we constrain the surface clustering to favor an increase in eccentricity of the center of mass of the resulting clusters.

Eccentricity Control During Surface Clustering. The skeleton should be located as centrally in the shape as possible. This is achieved by controlling surface clustering, as the surface clusters determine the positions of the skeleton nodes. To do so, we constrain the growing direction of each surface cluster. Specifically, surface clustering optimizes the following energy function:

$$F_{\mathcal{G}} = \sum_{i=0}^{n-1} \left(\sum_{n_i \in C_j} \omega_i \|n_i - c_j\|^2 \right) + 1/d^2(c_j, C_j)$$ (2)

where $d(c_j, C_j)$ is the Euclidean distance from a cluster C_j's center of mass c_j to the surface patch of C_j. The second energy term is highly nonlinear. Fortunately, it can be optimized using Lloyd's relaxation framework. Specifically, in each iteration of Lloyd's algorithm, merging of boundary edges is not only determined by minimization of the ACVD energy but also by maximization of distance from the current center to the surface cluster; note that an approximate computation of surface distance suffices. In our implementation, we simply query the closest vertex on the surface mesh using a k-D-tree and compute the distance as the minimum distance from the center to all 1-ring neighbouring triangles of the closest vertex. Since skeleton nodes should be located in the interior of the surface mesh, the point to surface distance should only take into account interior distance. This is approximately achieved by filtering back-facing triangles (w.r.t. the center) based on normal. Our simple approach to eccentricity control is merely one possible solution. Other more complicated constraints could be used within the optimization framework of Lloyd relaxation.

3.3 Skeleton Refinement

After obtaining the skeleton, we can optionally perform geometric refinement to upsample it by inserting graph nodes into the skeleton graph. Given two neighboring graph nodes, we extract all mesh edges shared by the two surface clusters of the two nodes to form a new cluster. We then compute the center of mass of the new cluster and insert a new node (along with the corresponding surface cluster) in-between the two graph nodes. The location of the newly inserted node, is locally optimized by minimizing the energy in Equation 1. However, unlike in Section 3.2, we now perform grassfire growing where we grow the boundary one ring at a time instead of one triangle at a time. This is because we hope to keep the cluster in the shape of a ring to avoid introducing incorrect topology. Figure 2(e) demonstrates the effect of geometric refinement.

4 Results

We next present results of skeleton extraction for various input 3D shapes, and show how our approach can be used in skeleton-driven shape deformation.

4.1 Capability

Figure 4 demonstrates the capability of our method using eleven 3D shapes. Our method correctly captures the genus of the input shape and produces an approximately centered skeleton within each shape. All results shown in this paper were produced with the same parameter settings given earlier. Our algorithm takes about 1-2 mins to perform skeletonization for these models, on a PC with an Intel Core2Quad 2.4GHz CPU and 2GB memory.

4.2 Application: Deformation

Perhaps the most widespread application of skeletons is for skeleton-driven deformation, a key component of skinning animation. We show in Figure 1 that skeletons extracted with our method, although only approximately-centered, can be used to produce

Fig. 4. A gallery of results on various input shapes, including Dog, Dancing Children, Wood-thinker, Fertility, Pegasus, Elk, Neptune, Heptoroid, Raptor, Feline, and Dancer (top left to bottom right). Our method extracts good quality, approximately-centered, skeletons even for complex models with high-genus or flat regions.

visually pleasing deformation results. Skinning deformation was performed using the dual quaternion technique from [17].

5   Conclusions

We have presented a new algorithm for curve skeleton extraction from 3D shapes. Our algorithm makes use of graph contraction to produce the skeleton and surface cluster-ing on the input shape. Surface clustering serves to ensure uniformity during skeleton graph contraction, leading to an approximately-centered skeletonization process. We also output surface clusters associated with the skeleton, useful in applications such as skinning deformation.

Several improvements could be made to our algorithm. Graph contraction is guided by heuristic criteria and we cannot provide a theoretical guarantee on the uniqueness of the extracted skeletons. Another limitation is that our method may overlook small geometric protrusions due to the nature of the clustering method. Finally, our method does not work in 2D, because our surface clustering, which aims to form cylindrical clusters [15], does not have an analog for 2D contours.

Acknowledgement. We would like to thank Sebastien Valette, Nicu D. Cornea, and Oscar Kin-Chung Au for sharing their source code. All test shapes are from http://www-roc.inria.fr/gamma/download/ or the AIM@SHAPE Shape Repository. The work was supported by NSFC grants 60970094, 61103084.

References

1. Cornea, N.D., Silver, D., Min, P.: Curve-skeleton properties, applications, and algorithms. IEEE Transactions on Visualization and Computer Graphics 13(3), 530–548 (2007) 1, 2

2. Amenta, N., Choi, S.: Voronoi methods for 3d medial axis approximation. In: Siddiqi, K., Pizer, S.M. (eds.) Medial Representations. Computational Imaging and Vision, vol. 37, pp. 223–239. Springer, Netherlands (2008) 1

3. Amenta, N., Choi, S., Kolluri, R.K.: The power crust. In: ACM Symposium on Solid Modeling and Applications, pp. 249–266 (2001) 1, 2, 4

4. Valette, S., Chassery, J.-M.: Approximated centroidal voronoi diagrams for uniform polygonal mesh coarsening. Computer Graphics Forum 23(3), 381–389 (2004) 1, 2, 3, 4

5. Ogniewicz, R., Ilg, M.: Voronoi skeletons: Theory and applications. In: Proc. Computer Vision and Pattern Recognition, pp. 63–69 (1992) 1, 2

6. Au, O.K.-C., Tai, C.-L., Chu, H.-K., Cohen-Or, D., Lee, T.-Y.: Skeleton extraction by mesh contraction. ACM Transactions on Graphics 27, 44:1–44:10 (2008) 2

7. Bertrand, G., Malandain, G.: A new characterization of three-dimensional simple points. Pattern Recognition Letters 15, 169–175 (1994) 2

8. Ma, W.-C., Wu, F.-C., Ouhyoung, M.: Skeleton extraction of 3d objects with radial basis functions. In: Proc. Shape Modeling International, pp. 207–214 (2003) 2

9. Cornea, N.D., Silver, D., Yuan, X., Balasubramanian, R.: Computing hierarchical curve-skeletons of 3d objects. The Visual Computer 21(11), 945–955 (2005) 2

10. Hassouna, M.S., Farag, A.A.: Variational curve skeletons using gradient vector flow. IEEE Transactions on Pattern Analysis and Machine Intelligence 31, 2257–2274 (2009) 2

11. Li, X., Woon, T.W., Tan, T.S., Huang, Z.: Decomposing polygon meshes for interactive applications. In: Symposium on Interactive 3D Graphics and Games, pp. 35–42 (2001) 2

12. Katz, S., Tal, A.: Hierarchical mesh decomposition using fuzzy clustering and cuts. ACM Transactions on Graphics (Proc. SIGGRAPH) 22, 954–961 (2003) 2

13. Dey, T.K., Sun, J.: Defining and computing curve-skeletons with medial geodesic function. In: Eurographics Symposium on Geometry Processing, pp. 143–152 (2006) 2

14. Cao, J., Tagliasacchi, A., Olson, M., Zhang, H., Su, Z.: Point cloud skeletons via laplacian-based contraction. In: Proc. Shape Modeling International, pp. 187–197 (2010) 2

15. Tagliasacchi, A., Zhang, H., Cohen-Or, D.: Curve skeleton extraction from incomplete point cloud. ACM Transactions on Graphics 28, 71:1–71:9 (2009) 2, 7

16. Lien, J.-M., Keyser, J., Amato, N.M.: Simultaneous shape decomposition and skeletonization. In: ACM Symposium on Solid and Physical Modeling, pp. 219–228 (2006) 2

17. Kavan, L., Collins, S., Žára, J., O'Sullivan, C.: Skinning with dual quaternions. In: Proc. of Symposium on Interactive 3D Graphics and Games, pp. 39–46 (2007) 7

Robust Feature Extraction Based on Principal Curvature Direction

Jin-Jiang Li[1] and Hui Fan[2]

[1] Department of Computer Science and Technology, Tsinghua University,
Beijing, 100084, P.R. China
lijinjiang@gmail.com
[2] School of Computer Science and Technology, Shandong Institute of Business and
Technology,
Yantai, 264005, P.R. China
fanlinw@263.net

Abstract. In this paper, we propose a new robust feature extraction algorithm for 3D models based on principal curvature direction. After principal curvatures directional fuzzy filtering, it is a good description of the geometric discontinuity. Compared with of the curvatures value, the impact of noise on the principal curvature direction is small. Therefore, feature extraction based on principal curvature direction is more robust and more accurately.

Keywords: Feature extraction, Integral Invariants, Principal Curvature Direction.

1 Introduction

Feature takes an important position in reverse engineering CAD; it can improve the efficiency of reverse modeling and automation degree, improve the precision of the surface reconstruction, and be beneficial to the innovation of the product design. Around the core of feature extraction, domestic and overseas scholars made the research respectively from the different levels of the point, curve, and surface and so on. The feature point and feature curve can be used to partition measured data, namely it is used in data partitioning based on surface. While the extraction of feature surface can not only realize the data partitioning based on surface, but also finish the construction of the local surface model at the same time. This paper mainly introduces the extraction methods of feature point. Feature points are useful in many applications, including segmentation, metamorphosis, mesh retrieval, deformation transfer, cross-parameterization and texture mapping. Feature point is mainly reflected in the continuity of the surface. Features detection is primarily according to the given gradient threshold of curvature change, looking for boundary, fold, tip and other transiliences.

S.-M. Hu and R.R. Martin (Eds.): CVM 2012, LNCS 7633, pp. 186–193, 2012.
© Springer-Verlag Berlin Heidelberg 2012

2   Related Work

At present, the feature point extraction method is mostly based on curvature. Milroy [1] used Snake algorithm in the 3D OCS (Orthogonal Cross Section) model application, and used extreme value point of the curvature to define the feature point. Huy et al. [2] proposed a multi-scale feature extraction algorithm using a rotation and translation invariant local surface curvature measure known as the curvedness. Different values of the curvedness of a point are calculated at multiple scales by fitting a surface to its neighbourhood of different sizes. Prathap et al. [3] proposed an approach to accurately detect landmarks and segment regions on face meshes, which is based on 3D point distribution model (PDM) that is fitted to the region of interest using candidate vertices extracted from low-level feature maps. In order to characterize the curvature property of each vertex, two features maps are computed. These features maps are derived based on the principal curvature values. Fang et al. [4] think the feature points and feature regions can be expressed via the curvature parameter, and a local curvature extreme point could be regarded as a feature point. Wu et al. [5] detected feature point based on local entropy. Local entropy reflects the degree of dispersion of the mean curvature of all points in the point cloud. In the large local entropy, the mean curvature of the point is relatively uniform; on the contrary, the discrete of average curvature will be greater discrete.

Novatnack and Nishino et al. [6] presented a multi-scale corner and edge features from 3D meshes. The key idea of this approach is to analyze the geometric scale variability of a given 3D model in the scale-space of a dense and regular 2D representation of its surface geometry encoded by the surface normals. In order to detect salient features in the geometric scalespace, the first- and second-order partial derivatives of the normal map are derived. Novel corner and edge detectors are then derived using these partial derivatives. Demarsin et al. [7] used PCA (Principal component analysis) to calculate the normal direction of points, and feature point is extracted through the changed size of adjacent points.

The SUSAN(Smallest Univalue Segment Assimilating Nucleus) [8] principle is the basis for algorithms to perform edge detection, corner detection and structure-preserving image noise reduction. SUSAN method is based on a circular window in which the center pixel, named nucleus, is the analyzed pixel. In order to complete the work on the 3D SUSAN operator, Walter et al. [9] proposed an extraction of principal saliency degrees and direction. The homologous 3D operator to a circular pixellized window becomes a voxellized sphere.

3   Multi-scale Curvature Estimated Based on the Integral Invariants

At first integral invariants were put forward by Manay etc [10] and used for plane curve matching. They studied the situation integral invariants work on the planar curve. One of integral invariants is area invariant. In [11], integral invariants based on the principal component analysis (PCA) was proposed points not variables, and used to analyze local properties of the curved surface. The basic idea is that: the PCA of point set P, i.e., the covariance matrix is:

$$J(P) = \int_P (x - s) \cdot (x - s)^T dx$$

where s is its center of gravity.

The principal curvature directions of the surface, or primary components of P, can be got through calculating three eigenvectors and corresponding eigenvalues of the covariance matrix $J(P)$. Here the neighborhood of a point on surface can be ball neighborhood, spherical neighborhood, curved surface piece neighborhood and so on. The eigenvalues M_{b1}, M_{b2} (ball neighborhood) and M_{s1}, M_{s2} (spherical neighborhood) meet:

$$M_{bi}^r = \frac{2\pi}{15}r^5 - \frac{\pi}{48}(2k_i + k_1 + k_2)r^6 + O(r^7) \tag{1}$$

$$M_{si}^r = \frac{2\pi}{3}r^4 - \frac{\pi}{8}(2k_i + k_1 + k_2)r^5 + O(r^6) \tag{2}$$

where $i = 1, 2$, k_i are two corresponding principal curvature values. Using formula (1) and formula (2), principal curvature value of scale r can be defined, and it approaches to the classic definition when r approaches to 0. At this time, formula (1) and formula (2) also are used to reverse curvature value.

4   Feature Extraction Based on Principal Curvatures Direction

After estimated the principal curvature directions by integral invariants, the directions are smoothed through FVM filtering [12]. The generalized vector median $x_{(\delta)}$ is the sample that minimizes the distance metric $D(\cdot, \cdot)$ between itself and all others:

$$x_{(\delta)} = \arg\min \sum_{i=1}^{N} D(x, x_i)$$

where $D(x, x_i)$ is the angle of vector x and x_i.

A vector-based fuzzy membership function was defined, $\mu(u, v): IR^m \times R^m \mapsto [0, 1]$. The fuzzy vector median (FVM) is a natural extension of the fuzzy median, and the output can be defined as:

$$x_{FVM} = \frac{\sum\limits_{i=1}^{N} x_i R_{i,(\delta)}}{\sum\limits_{i=1}^{N} R_{i,(\delta)}}$$

where $R_{i,(\delta)} = \mu(x_i, x_{(\delta)})$.

We define the curvature direction values to characterize the change of curvature direction for each point, which can be defined as:

$$Q_i = \frac{\sum\limits_{j \in Neighbor_i} <t_{i,1}, t_{j,1}> + <t_{i,2}, t_{j,2}>}{2k}$$

where, $t_{j,1}$ and $t_{j,2}$ are two principal curvature direction of p_i's k neighborhood point. Therefore, Q_i can reflect the degree of consistency between principal direction and its neighborhood points.

To illustrate the principal curvature directions smoothing process, Figure 1 shows experiments on two model objects with different noise, which is described the curvature direction value.

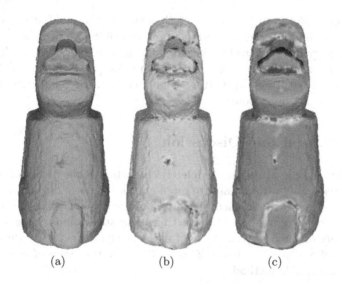

(a)   (b)   (c)

Fig. 1. Curvature map and curvature direction values map. (a)3d model with noise, (b)Gauss curvatures map, (c) Principal curvature direction values map.

It can be seen from the figure that principal curvature direction after fuzzy mean filter can effectively extract the model characteristics, which is more robust to noise and better than curvature graph. Note that the curvature direction values processed by the FVM are very close to the feature of original model.

For point p_i , density function defined for the point of its K-nearest neighbor data points affect the sum of the function.

$$F(p_i, p_j) = e^{-\frac{||Q_{p_i} - Q_{p_j}||^2}{2\sigma^2}}$$

$$D(p_i) = \frac{1}{k} \sum_{j=1}^{k} F(p_i, p_j), p_j \in Nb(p_i)$$

where, Q_{p_i} is curvature direction values; the density parameter σ is also called the window width size. The window width size of σ determines the influence range of each point.

Determine the density function $D(p_i)$ exceeds a set threshold ξ, if $D(p_i) \geq \xi$, the point p_i is a possible noise point.

Let t_1^i and t_2^i be the principal curvatures direction of p_i. p_j is the neighborhood point. t_1^i and t_2^i as a benchmark, we computer the *cos* value between t_1^j and t_1^i,

t_2^j and t_2^i, that is $< t_1^i, t_1^j >$ and $< t_2^i \cdot t_2^j >$. Two sequences $C^1 = \{c_1^1, c_2^1, ..., c_k^1\}$ and $C^2 = \{c_1^2, c_2^2, ..., c_k^2\}$ are get.

To calculate the standard deviation of C:

$$\sigma_{C^i} = \sqrt{\frac{1}{k} \sum_{j=1}^{n} (C_j^i - \overline{C^i})}, \overline{C^i} = \frac{1}{k} \sum_{j=1}^{n} c_j^i, i = 1, 2$$

If the standard deviation σ_C is greater than the set threshold, it can determine that the distribution of p_i nearest point is non-uniform, so p_i is a boundary characteristic point; conversely, you can judge p_i is an internal point. The difference of principal curvature direction between noise point and its neighborhood is larger, and $\overline{C^i}$ will be larger. If $\overline{C^i}$ is greater than the set threshold, p_i may be considered as a noise point.

5   Experiment and Discussion

In geometry, the curvature can completely characterizes the degree of bending of the surface. Because variance able to represent the degree of deviation of data, so the curvature variance can reflect the impact of the noise. The larger the variance and is more sensitive to noise. Constructing a unit sphere and adding some noise, the curvature of the noise immunity of different algorithms are analyzed. For a sphere model added noise, figure 2 shows the curvature map of quadric fitting and integral variable method.

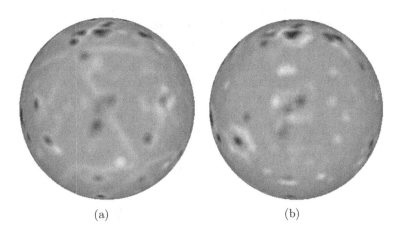

(a)   (b)

Fig. 2. Curvature map (a) Quadric Fitting, (b) Integral variable

Table 1 shows the comparison the noise variance among quadric fitting, Taubin and integral variable. The variance of curvature estimated by integral variable is the smallest, which is more robust to noise.

Table 1. Noise variance comparison

	Quadric fitting	Taubin	Integral variable
mean	0.013712	0.159160	0.008029
gauss	0.056238	0.703499	0.006204

Table 2. Principal curvature direction accuracy comparison

noise strength A	Quadric Fitting	Taubin	Integral variable
0	0.766888	0.756622	0.805285
0.005	0.743970	0.756797	0.792268
0.01	0.730486	0.758294	0.780363
0.02	0.712991	0.730826	0.754611

According to the surface parameters equation, we can calculate the accurate information of the principal curvatures direction, surface normal, curvature etc. In order to test the robustness of different algorithm, we add different ranges of noise. Table 2 shows the estimated error of principal curvatures direction increases with the noise for the implicit surface $x \cdot x + y \cdot y - z = 0$. We propose to add pseudo-random noises on vertex coordinates according to the following equation: $x_i = x_i + a_i \cdot R$; where R denotes the average distance from vertices to object center, and a_i is a pseudo-random number uniformly distributed in interval $[-A, A]$. The values in the table are the cosine of the angle between estimated curvature direction and the true direction. It can be seen from the experiment, the principal curvature direction estimated by integral variable to be reliable. Especially when the data points with a lot of noise, this performance is more excellent.

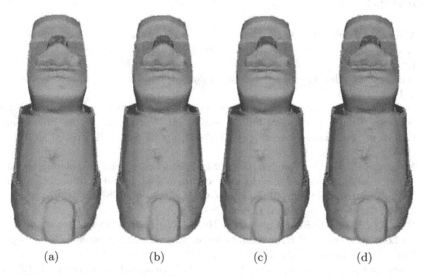

| (a) | (b) | (c) | (d) |

Fig. 3. Feature points extraction. (a)curvature value, (b) fitting method (c) Taubin method (d) Integral variable.

Figure 3 shows the example graph of feature point extraction. If there is no noise points, the effect of these methods to extract characteristic points are quite satisfactory. However, the curvature value method introduces a small amount of non-feature points (fig. 3 (a)); Quadric fitting and Taubin method lost part of the feature points (fig. 3 (b), (c)).

After the analysis of experimental results for different data, in the case of noise, curvature-based approach will incorrectly judged some noise points as feature points, and it is more robust to noise for the method of principal curvature direction.

6   Conclusions

In this paper, the 3D model feature point extraction algorithm has been improved to obtain satisfactory results from the experimental results. Integral invariants based on principal component analysis (PCA) points can estimate robustly principal curvature size and direction of each point on curved surface under different scales. Because the area invariant is unrelated to the coordinate selection and rigid transformation, it can be regarded as characteristic quantity to measure the shape of curve in different scale. Experimental results show that the proposed method can effectively extract the feature points, especially in the case of noise.

Acknowledgments. This work was supported in part by the National Natural Science Foundation (Grant No: 61173173 and 61272430).

References

1. Milroy, M.J., Bradley, C., Vickers, G.W.: Segmentation of a wraparound model using an active contour. Computer Aided Design 29(4), 299–320 (1997)
2. Huy, T.H., Danny, G.: A Curvature-based Approach for Multi-scale Feature Extraction from 3D Meshes and Unstructured Point Clouds. IET Computer Vision 3(4), 201–212 (2009)
3. Prathap, N., Andrea, C.: Region segmentation and feature point extraction on 3d faces using a point distribution model. In: Proceedings of the International Conference on Image Processing (ICIP 2007), pp. 85–88. IEEE Press, San Antonio (2007)
4. Yuanmin, F., Jie, C., Yonghua, X.: A Study of feature points extraction based on point cloud data sets and model simplification in goaf. In: International Conference on Geo-spatial Solutions for Emergency Management (GSEM 2009), pp. 84–87. ISPRS Archives Production, Beijing (2009)
5. Wu, J.J., Wang, Q.F., Huang, Z.D., Huang, Y.: Feature Point Detection Based on Local Entropy and Repeatability Rate. Journal of Computer-Aided Design & Computer Graphics 17(5), 1046–1053 (2005)
6. Novatnack, J., Nishino, K.: Scale-Dependent 3D Geometric Features. In: IEEE 11th International Conference on Computer Vision, pp. 1–8. IEEE Press, Philadelphia (2007)

7. Demarsin, K., Vanderstraeten, D., Volodine, T., Roose, D.: Detection of Closed Sharp Feature Lines in Point Clouds for Reverse Engineering Applications. Technical Report, Department of Computer Science, Katholieke University Leuven, Belgium (2006)
8. Smith, S.M., Brady, J.M.: Susan - a new approach to low level image processing. International Journal of Computer Vision 23(1), 45–78 (1997)
9. Aubreton, O., Fougerolle, Y.D., Laligant, O.: Susan 3d operator, principal saliency degrees and directions extraction and a brief study on the robustness to noise. In: Proceedings of the 16th IEEE International Conference on Image Processing (ICIP 2009), pp. 3493–3496. IEEE Press, Le Creusot (2009)
10. Manay, S., Hong, B., Yezzi, A., Stefano, S.: Integral Invariant Signatures. In: Pajdla, T., Matas, J. (eds.) ECCV 2004. LNCS, vol. 3024, pp. 87–99. Springer, Heidelberg (2004)
11. Yang, Y.L., Lai, Y.K., Hu, S.M., Pottmann, H.: Robust principal curvatures on multiple scales. In: Proceedings of Eurographics Symposium on Geometry Processing, Eurographics Association 2006, pp. 223–226. ACM Press, Sardinia (2006)
12. Yuzhong, S., Kenneth, E.B.: Fuzzy Vector Median-Based Surface Smoothing. IEEE Transactions on Visualization and Computer Graphics 10(3), 252–265 (2004)

Compact Combinatorial Maps in 3D

Xin Feng[1], Yuanzhen Wang[1], Yanlin Weng[2], and Yiying Tong[1]

[1] Michigan State University, USA
[2] Zhejiang University, China

Abstract. We propose a compact data structure for volumetric meshes of arbitrary topology and bounded valence, which offers cell-face, face-edge, and edge-vertex incidence queries in constant time. Our structure is simple to implement, easy to use, and allows for arbitrary, user-defined volume cells, while remaining very efficient in memory usage compared to previous work.

Keywords: 3D mesh data structure, Combinatorial maps, Cell complex.

1 Introduction

Volumetric meshes are now ubiquitous in solid modeling, physics-based simulation, computational science, and even rendering of translucent materials. However, the ever-increasing size and complexity of meshes impose undue stress on both memory access times and usage, especially since mesh size typically grows as a cubic function of the resolution. A data structure with small memory footprint that can efficiently handle queries of incidence and adjacency would thus benefit a wide range of applications in graphics and scientific computing.

While our data structure is based on the compact, array-based mesh data structure [1], we provide a simple but generic method for defining volume cell types, *complete the data structure with a list of edges, and improve incidence queries within each volume cell.*

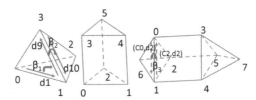

Fig. 1. From left to right: tetrahedron cell type; prism cell type; a mesh with 3 cells

Related work. We limit our discussion of previous work to closely related 3D data structures— for a survey of 2D mesh data structures, see, e.g., [2,3]. Note, however, that the 2D version of our compact combinatorial map data structure is equivalent to HEDS [1], which is known to be similar in memory usage to a number of compact implementations of the half-edge data structure.

S.-M. Hu and R.R. Martin (Eds.): CVM 2012, LNCS 7633, pp. 194–201, 2012.

In scientific computing, 3D volumes are often assumed to be 3D manifolds. Thus, a table of mesh element connectivity that maps volume cells to their corner vertices provides *complete* information about incidence among vertices, edges, faces, and volume cells. While this can be sufficient for various geometry processing algorithms [4,5], many computational applications require constant-time incidence queries, which cannot be achieved without auxiliary connectivity information. This requirement was referred to as *comprehensiveness* in [1]. To address this issue, several data structures were proposed to store sufficient adjacency information to be comprehensive, e.g. [6–9]. Among these, combinatorial maps [8] can be extended to generalized *d*-maps to encode non-orientable manifolds [10], and be compressed [11], but the adjacency information will only be restored through decompression.

Recently, a number of compact data structures have been proposed. For instance, [12] introduced a method only applicable to simplicial meshes. [1] presented a compact array-based data structure for 3D orientable manifold cell complexes. However, while they can produce incident cell representations such as an edge represented by two vertex indices, *it is impossible to find an identifier for the edge using only the proposed connectivity representation.* [13] independently developed a similar data structure.

There are a number of libraries providing practical implementations of volume mesh data structures. [14] already contains an implementation of Combinatorial Maps; OpenVolumeMesh [15], released recently, is based on OpenMesh [16], which stores incidence information for cells with those with one dimension less; libMesh [17] provides a complete but *not* comprehensive connectivity description; CGoGN [18] provides an implementation of Generalized Maps. However, none of these existing implementations are optimized for storage.

Contributions. Our main contributions include:

- a concise local connectivity description of generic 3-cell (volume cell) types;
- an efficient way to store all the combinatorial maps in volume meshes;
- a straightforward way of associating attributes to k-cells ($k \in \{0, 1, 2, 3\}$);
- a constant time complexity access to adjacency information (e.g., *face-edge*).

Note that unique edge identifiers and the face-edge incidence are the main missing components in the compact array-based mesh data structures [1], compared to our implementation.

The rest of the paper is organized as follows. In Sec. 2, we briefly introduce the combinatorial maps data structure for volume meshes. In Sec. 3, we describe our compact array-based data structure, and briefly analyze its space complexity. In Sec. 4, we discuss adjacency queries and typical operations that our data structures can efficiently handle, before concluding in Sec. 5.

2   Combinatorial Maps

In order to introduce the notion of combinatorial maps, we loosely follow the notation used in [14] and call k-dimensional cells k-*cells*. Hence, vertices are 0-cells, edges are 1-cells, faces are 2-cells, and volume cells (such as tetrahedra, prims, etc) are 3-cells. Two cells of different dimensions are defined to be *incident* if one is a subset of the other. Two k-cells of the same dimension are *adjacent* if they share a common $(k-1)$-cell.

A combinatorial map describes the incidence and adjacency relations among cells of the mesh using a basic type of element called *dart*, and a group of relations between darts. For an orientable 3D manifold, a 3D dart corresponds to a cell tuple (v, e, f, c), where v is a starting vertex of an edge e that lies in a face f of 3-cell c. For 2D orientable surfaces, a 2D dart would be the same as the usual half-edge.

An abstract way to define a whole 3D combinatorial map M is to use a 4-tuple $M = (D, \beta_1, \beta_2, \beta_3)$, with:

- D is a finite set of darts;
- for $i = 1, 2, 3$, $\beta_i : D \to D$ is a mapping;
- β_1 is a permutation;
- β_2, β_3, and $\beta_1 \circ \beta_3$ are involutions, i.e., $\forall d \in D$, $\beta_2 \circ \beta_2(d) = d$, $\beta_3 \circ \beta_3(d) = d$, and $(\beta_1 \circ \beta_3) \circ (\beta_1 \circ \beta_3)(d) = d$.

3   Compact Data Structure

3.1   Overview

File format. For a 2D polygonal mesh, the complete connectivity information can be encoded by a face list, with each entry corresponding to the list of vertices in the polygon face. However, for a polyhedral mesh, the same list of vertices can correspond to different polyhedra. For instance, both an octahedron and a prism have six vertices each. As there are only a handful of 3-cell types in most 3-dimensional meshes used in practice, we opt to describe all the 3-cell types in the header part of the file, and to describe each polyhedron by an ordered vertex list and its 3-cell type.

Comprehensive data structure. All low dimensional (≤ 2) relations (β_1, β_2) map darts within the same 3-cell. Given the type of a 3-cell, we may assign each dart in that cell a local id, and the maps among the darts can be precomputed when the 3-cell type is known. One can easily assemble a global ID for each dart by (C, d), where C is the global ID of the 3-cell, and d is the local dart ID.

β_3 maps a dart in one 3-cell C_1 to another dart in an adjacent 3-cell C_2. Noticing the relation among β's, we only store β_3 for one dart in the common 2-cell in C_1. Thus, the size of β_3 is reduced to one dart per (C_2, C_1) pair (also called *half-face*).

The relation between 3-cells and darts is implicitly given in the way we express a global ID for each dart (C, d). The mapping from darts to vertices (0-cells) is implicitly stored in the vertex lists for 3-cells, also called the element connectivity in array-based methods such as [1], denoted $Cv2V$ below. The map from each vertex to one of its darts is stored in a table, denoted by $V2D$ below.

We propose to build a minimal set of additional connectivity tables to provide these incidence relations crucial to real world applications. We describe them as optional, since one may only need some of the tables in this set, although at least one of them is, in many cases, indispensable.

3.2   Details

To illustrate the detailed actual data structure, we use as a running example the description of the simple meshes shown in Figure 1, as found in a mesh file—skipping the list of vertex coordinates since our focus is on connectivity information. As in the compact array-based half-face data structure (HFDS) [1], we leverage the fact that there are only a few types of cells typically used in engineering or graphics applications.

Local information within each 3-cell. Each 3-cell is treated locally as a 2-manifold cell complex, which can be represented by a local half-edge structure, i.e., a 2D combinatorial map. For a given type of 3-cell with n_v vertices, n_e edges, n_f faces:

- locally denote each vertex by v_i, with $i \in \{0, \ldots, n_v - 1\}$;
- locally label each face as $f_m = (v_i, v_j, v_k, \ldots)$, with $m \in \{0, \ldots, n_f - 1\}$.
- locally label each of the $2n_e$ darts as $e_k = (v_i, v_j)$, with $k \in \{1, \ldots, 2n_e\}$;

Darts are indexed starting from 1, as 0 is reserved for boundaries.

The mesh file for Figure 1 would thus contain the following information:

Cell type 0 (tetrahedron):

faces	0:(0,2,1)	1:(0,1,3)	2:(1,2,3)	3:(2,0,3)		
darts	1:(0,1)	2:(1,0)	3:(0,2)	4:(2,0)	5:(0,3)	6:(3,0)
	7:(1,2)	8:(2,1)	9:(1,3)	10:(3,1)	11:(2,3)	12:(3,2)

Cell type 1 (prism):

faces	0:(0,2,1)	1:(0,1,4,3)	2:(1,2,5,4)	3:(2,0,3,5)	4:(3,4,5)				
darts	1:(0,1)	2:(1,0)	3:(0,2)	4:(2,0)	5:(0,3)	6:(3,0)	7:(1,2)	8:(2,1)	9:(1,4)
	10:(4,1)	11:(2,5)	12:(5,2)	13:(3,4)	14:(4,3)	15:(3,5)	16:(5,3)	17:(4,5)	18:(5,4)

Cells:

type 0	C0:(1,0,2,6)	C1:(3,4,5,7)
type 1	C2:(0,1,2,3,4,5)	

In all the tables we list, the information before ":" is for illustration purposes only, and is thus not stored in memory or files. For each 3-cell type, defining only the faces would be necessary and sufficient, since we can build the darts based on faces and give them labels. We then build a lookup table for β_1 and β_2 of all darts, with $2n_e$ entries and $2n_e$ possible values in the range for each entry. In our running example, the β_1 and β_2 tables for 3-cell type 0 are

d	1	2	3	4	5	6	7	8	9	10	11	12
$\beta_1(d)$	9	3	8	5	12	1	11	2	6	7	10	4
$\beta_2(d)$	2	1	4	3	6	5	8	7	10	9	12	11

We denote local incidence mappings as follows:

- $d2f(d)$ maps a dart d to its local face ID;
- $f2d(f, i)$ is the i-th dart of the local face f;
- $d2v(d)$ maps a dart d to its starting vertex.

We use lower (resp., upper) case in the name of a map to denote whether the index is local (resp., global).

Global information. We load the connectivity table that contains, for each 3-cell, the global indices of its vertices. We denote this table by $Cv2V(C, v)$ since it maps the v-th vertex of 3-cell C to its global index V. Once we have the 3-cell connectivity, a dart can be globally indexed by an ordered pair $D = (C, d)$, where C is the global 3-cell ID, and d is the local dart index. Note that instead of using a local face index with a starting vertex (called anchored half face) as in HFDS, we use local indices of darts; for the common case of tetrahedron meshes, this means we can cope with meshes twice as large for the same amount of memory.

To complete incidence and adjacency information in the combinatorial map, we need to construct β_3. We save space by noticing that $\beta_3 = \beta_1 \circ \beta_3 \circ \beta_1$, which means that $\beta_3(D)$ can be inferred if $\beta_3(\beta_1(D))$ is known. Thus, we only store β_3 for the *first* dart in each half face $H = (C, f)$, and denote this additional table by $H2D(C, f)$. If the application requires the use of boundary darts, their β_3 can be stored in a separate list $B2D(B)$, mapping the first dart of each boundary face B to its corresponding dart in the 3-cell adjacent to it. We also need to map from a vertex to one of its darts $V2D(v)$; but the map from a dart to its starting vertex is trivially found by $D2V(C, d) = Cv2V(C, d2v(d))$.

The tables for the 3-cell example are:

β_3	C0	f0d3:(2,8) f1d1:(0,0) f2d7:(1,0) f3d4:(2,0)
	C1	f0d3:(2,16) f1d1:(3,0) f2d7:(4,0) f3d4:(5,0)
	C2	f0d3:(0,8) f1d1:(6,0) f2d7:(7,0) f3d4:(8,0) f4d13:(1,2)

B2D	BF0:(0,1)	BF1:(0,7)	BF2:(0,4)	BF3:(1,1)	BF4:(1,7)	BF5:(1,4)	BF6:(2,1)	BF7:(2,7)	BF8:(2,4)

V2D	V0:(0,7)	V1:(0,1)	V2:(0,4)	V3:(1,1)	V4:(1,7)	V5:(1,4)	V6:(0,10)	V7:(1,6)

Boundary. The map β_3 usually returns an internal dart (C, d) with $d > 0$. However, if the opposite is a boundary dart, it will return $(B, 0)$, i.e., the boundary half-face ID. We carefully choose $V2D$ so that whether a vertex V is on boundary can be determined by examining $\beta_3(V2D(V))$. Darts belonging to boundary half-face do not need to be explicitly maintained in most cases .

Edge and face incidence information. If we need to use unique edge identifiers, a table for $E2D(E)$ is maintained to map an edge to one of its darts. We sort the edges in the $E2D$ table by lexicographic order of their vertices (V_{start}, V_{end}) assuming that it always points from the vertex with a smaller index to the one with a larger index. A backward mapping $D2E$ can be implemented by a table $V2E(V)$, mapping vertex V to the first edge starting from it. We can avoid sorting the edges by using a linked list at the cost of storing another n_1 integers. The map $V2E$ would then be made to map a vertex to a linked list of edges starting from it.

If only half faces need identifiers, (C, f) can be used directly. Otherwise, a table $F2D(F)$ is required. Similar to the edge case, we can sort the faces by their first three vertices, assuming vertices are in ascending order within each face F. Then the backward mapping $D2F$ can be implemented by $V2F(V)$, mapping vertex V to the first face that has V as its smallest-indexed vertex.

For our running example, the (optional) edge tables are

E2D	E0(V0,V1):(0,2)	E1(V0,V2):(2,3)	E2(V0,V3):(2,5)	E3(V0,V6):(0,9)	E4(V1,V2):(0,3)
	E5(V1,V4):(2,9)	E6(V1,V6):(0,5)	E7(V2,V5):(2,11)	E8(V2,V6):(0,11)	E9(V3,V4):(2,13)
	E10(V3,V5):(1,3)	E11(V3,V7):(1,5)	E12(V4,V5):(2,17)	E13(V4,V7):(1,9)	E14(V5,V7):(1,11)

V2E	V0:0 V1:4 V2:7 V3:9 V4:12 V5:14 V6: V7:

The construction of most tables is straightforward since the mesh connectivity information is complete.

Spatial complexity. Tetrahedron meshes are the easiest to establish comparisons between various data structures—for such meshes, we can approximate all k-cell counts n_k as a function of the number of tetrahedra n_3 and boundary faces n_b—other mesh types must be analyzed using the count of darts, and its estimated relation with k-cell numbers. Based on similar assumptions as in [9], we have for tetrahedron meshes

$$n_0 \approx 0.175n_3, \quad n_1 \approx 1.175n_3 + 0.5n_b, \quad n_2 = 2n_3 + 0.5n_b.$$

For the models shown in Table 1, these estimates are very close to the actual k-cell counts.

In the following analysis, we assume that the lowest four or more bits are sufficient to encode the local dart index or the local half face index; thus we need only one integer for (C, d) or (C, f). The memory size required for the various connectivity tables are listed below:

Table	V2XYZ	Cv2V	H2D	V2D	B2D
Space	$3n_0$	$4n_3$	$4n_3$	n_0	n_b
Table(optional)		E2D	V2E	F2D	V2F
Space		n_1	n_0	n_2	n_0

By tallying up these numbers, we find that $8n_3 + n_0 + n_b \approx 8.175\,n_3 + n_b$ integers are required for the basic tables, in par with the bare minimal data structures. Data structures capable of handling generic polytope meshes require more memory space when used for simplicial meshes, e.g., Dobkin and Laszlo's structure [19] would require around $18n_3$ pointers, while radial-edge, cell-tuple, and G-map representations, as well as CGAL's combinatorial map, would use even more memory.

HFDS [1] uses the same amount of basic space ($8.175\,n_3 + n_b$). However, their encoding of a local dart (anchored face) identifier (C, f, v) uses a separate local index f for a face within the tetrahedron and a local index v of a vertex within the face. Thus, it would be less memory efficient when dealing with generic 3-cells, for example, 3-cells that have 5-edge faces or more. In addition, even in the common case of tetrahedron meshes, HFDS requires 5 bits for local indices ($f = 0$ is reserved for boundary), while we only need 4 bits, enabling us to handle meshes with 256M 3-cells with a 32-bit integer representation, instead of their 128M limit. Furthermore, and *key to runtime efficiency*, we provide a simple way to give edges and faces unique identifiers. This enables constant time incidence queries, and allows appending attributes to edges and faces, which are important in simulation and other computational tasks. The HFDS data structure does not actually provide any means to get unique adjacent edge IDs in constant time.

4   Incidence/Adjacency Queries

As our data structure can be seen as an internal representation of a combinatorial map, it can directly leverage any implementation of combinatorial maps to get

Table 1. Actual memory usage for a variety of meshes

model name	n_0	n_1	n_b	n_3	V2XYZ+Connectivity	est.	Edges included
1mag	95,156	648,969	48,308	529,652	19,858k	18,625k	23,006k
Armadillo	189,919	1,314,767	77,704	1,085,997	39,502k	38,103k	44,634k
david	140,592	965,377	65,402	792,038	29,486k	27,824k	33,334k
dc-wt	550,770	3,819,288	224,024	3,156,497	111,286k	110,742k	125,702k
emd1590	23,419	150,930	19,540	117,736	5,346k	4,175k	6,110k
fertility	341,924	2,385,564	125,450	1,980,912	70,098k	69,438k	79,490k
neptune	358,647	2,498,975	133,476	2,073,588	73,622k	72,695k	83,442k

incidence and adjacency information in constant time. In addition, with integer IDs, additional attributes associated to vertices, darts, half faces, cells, edges, and faces, can be directly allocated as arrays with the appropriate sizes, making them highly efficient and flexible for static meshes. For instance, to map a dart to a unique edge ID, we find the end vertices (V_{start}, V_{end}) with $V_{start} < V_{end}$. We then perform a linear search in $E2D$ starting from $V2E(V_{start})$, this again would terminate in constant time.

5 Conclusion

We presented an efficient internal representation of combinatorial maps. All necessary components in combinatorial maps can be implemented in compact form. Compared to previous work, our data structure can handle arbitrary 3-cell types, and it provides adjacency and boundary inquiries in constant time. Appending attributes to *cells of any dimension* is also straightforward.

One limitation of the compact combinatorial map data structure we described is its apparent inability to deal gracefully with dynamically changing connectivity, in particular with possible changes of 3-cell types. (On the other hand, if 3D cells are kept intact as in the case of cutting or merging meshes along faces, the mesh can be easily modified accordingly.) However, we believe that our data structure can be readily altered to efficiently handle connectivity changes as well: one could use pointers instead of integers for the IDs of 3-cells and vertices—and the last few bits of the pointer can actually be used to encode local dart index as in the integer case. The linked list version of $V2E$ will be necessary, increasing the memory space by $n_1 = 1.175\,n_3$.

Thus, a possible research direction worth exploring is the design of admissible local connectivity changes (such as edge removal or 2-3 flip) that maintain the validity of our compact data structure. Compression of neighboring information (β_3) using difference coding after sorting the cells along space-filling curves could also lead to further reduction of memory usage. Additionally, the extension to dimension $n > 3$ could be done by encoding the local connectivity $(\beta_1, \ldots, \beta_{n-1})$ of n-cell types, and store only β_n.

Acknowledgments. This work was supported in part by NSF grants CCF-0936830, IIS-0953096, CMMI-0757123 and CCF-0811313.

References

1. Alumbaugh, T.J., Jiao, X.: Compact Array-Based Mesh Data Structures. In: Hanks, B.W. (ed.) Engineering, IMR 2005, pp. 485–503. Springer, Heidelberg (2005)
2. Sieger, D., Botsch, M.: Design, Implementation, and Evaluation of the Surface Mesh Data Structure. In: Quadros, W.R. (ed.) Proceedings of the 20th International Meshing Roundtable, vol. 90, pp. 533–550. Springer, Heidelberg (2011)
3. Serna, S.P., Stork, A., Fellner, D.W.: Considerations toward a Dynamic Mesh Data Structure. In: SIGRAD Conference, pp. 83–90 (2011)
4. Tautges, T.J., Blacker, T., Mitchell, S.A.: The Whisker Weaving Algorithm: a Connectivity-Based Method for Constructing All-Hexahedral Finite Element Meshes. Int. J. for Numer. Methods in Eng. 39(19), 3327–3349 (1996)
5. Murdoch, P.: The spatial twist continuum: A connectivity based method for representing all-hexahedral finite element meshes. Finite Elements in Analysis and Design 28(2), 137–149 (1997)
6. Guibas, L., Stolfi, J.: Primitives for the manipulation of general subdivisions and the computation of voronoi. ACM Trans. Graph. 4(2), 74–123 (1985)
7. Brisson, E.: Representing geometric structures in d dimensions: topology and order. In: Proceedings of the Fifth Annual Symposium on Computational Geometry, SCG 1989, vol. 9, pp. 218–227. ACM Press (1989)
8. Edmonds, J.R.: A combinatorial representation for polyhedral surfaces. Notices Amer. Math. Soc. 7, 646 (1960)
9. Beall, M.W., Shephard, M.S.: A general topology-based mesh data structure. Int. J. for Numer. Methods in Eng. 40(9), 1573–1596 (1997)
10. Lienhardt, P.: Topological models for boundary representation: a comparison with n-dimensional generalized maps. Computer-Aided Design 23(1), 59–82 (1991)
11. Prat, S., Gioia, P., Bertrand, Y.: Connectivity compression in an arbitrary dimension. The Visual Computer 21(8-10), 876–885 (2005)
12. Blandford, D.K., Blelloch, G.E., Cardoze, D.E., Kadow, C.: Compact Representations of Simplicial Meshes in Two and Three Dimensions. International Journal of Computational Geometry and Applications 15(1), 3–24 (2005)
13. Celes, W., Paulino, G.H., Espinha, R.: A compact adjacency-based topological data structure for finite element mesh representation. International Journal for Numerical Methods in Engineering 64(11), 1529–1556 (2005)
14. Damiand, G.: Combinatorial maps. In: CGAL User and Reference Manual, 4.0 edn., CGAL Editorial Board (2012)
15. OVM: OpenVolumeMesh - A Generic and Versatile Index-Based Data Structure for Polytopal Meshes (2012), http://www.openvolumemesh.org/
16. Botsch, M., Steinberg, S., Bischoff, S., Kobbelt, L.: OpenMesh - a generic and efficient polygon mesh data structure. Structure (2002)
17. Kirk, B.S., Peterson, J.W., Stogner, R.H., Carey, G.F.: libmesh: a c++ library for parallel adaptive mesh refinement/coarsening simulations. Eng. with Comput. 22(3), 237–254 (2006)
18. CGoGN: Combinatorial and Geometric modeling with Generic N-dimensional Maps (2012), http://cgogn.u-strasbg.fr/Wiki/index.php/CGoGN
19. Dobkin, D.P., Laszlo, M.J.: Primitives for the manipulation of three-dimensional subdivisions. In: Proceedings of the third annual Symposium on Computational Geometry, SCG 1987, pp. 86–99. ACM, New York (1987)

Towards Large Scale Cross-Media Retrieval via Modeling Heterogeneous Information and Exploring an Efficient Indexing Scheme

Bo Lu, Guoren Wang, and Ye Yuan

Key Laboratory of Medical Image Computing, Ministry of Education
School of Information Science & Engineering, Northeastern University, China
mrcooler1982@gmail.com, {wanggr,yuanye}@ise.neu.edu.cn

Abstract. With the rapid development of Internet and multimedia technology, cross-media retrieval is concerned to retrieve all the related media objects with multi-modality by submitting a query media object. In this paper, we propose a novel method which is dedicate to achieve effective and accurate cross-media retrieval. Firstly, a Multi-modality Semantic Relationship Graph (MSRG) is constructed by using the semantic correlation amongst the media objects with multi-modality. Secondly, all the media objects in MSRG are mapped onto an isomorphic semantic space. Further, an efficient indexing MK-tree based on heterogeneous data distribution is proposed to manage the media objects within the semantic space and improve the performance of cross-media retrieval. Extensive experiments on real large scale cross-media datasets indicate that our proposal dramatically improves the accuracy and efficiency of cross-media retrieval, outperforming the existing methods significantly.

1 Introduction

Cross-media retrieval is coming as a new trend along with the rapid development of Internet and multimedia technology. Compared with the traditional content-based multimedia retrieval with single modality, cross-media retrieval is more in accordance with the user's experience. Because the modality of query example and returned results are often different, which is propitious to satisfy the various requirements of users [6,7].

Traditional content-based multimedia retrieval method generally extract low-level features of media object, which can be utilized to measure the similarity among media objects with single-modality [1]. However, it's difficult to measure the similarity of media objects with multi-modalities by only exploring low-level features of different media types, because low-level features of media objects with multi-modalities can not be computed in an uniform feature space. Thus, one of the major challenges associated with cross-media retrieval is to find the semantic correlations among different types of media objects and construct a uniform semantic correlation model. In order to solve these issues, we use semantic concepts as the high-level semantic features to measure semantic correlation

S.-M. Hu and R.R. Martin (Eds.): CVM 2012, LNCS 7633, pp. 202–209, 2012.
© Springer-Verlag Berlin Heidelberg 2012

amongst media objects with multi-modality. Since the media objects of different modalities, such as text, image and video, generally exist some information of latent semantic correlation among each other. In addition, semantic concept is certainly closer to the natural representation of human and benefit to unify the features of media objects with multi-modality.

For the cross-media retrieval, the other one major challenge is to manage and retrieve various types of media objects which store in the large scale multimedia database. When faced with the large scale dataset, most of existing retrieval methods ignore the retrieval cost of cross-media retrieval, which usually lead to degrade the performance of cross-media retrieval. Therefore, it is important to effectively retrieve the results associated with the user request from large scale multimedia database. Specifically, there is an urgent need of indexing techniques which can manage the cross-media database and support execution of similarity queries.

According to the above mentioned, in this paper, we propose a novel method which is dedicated to solving these difficulties to achieve effective and accurate cross-media retrieval. Firstly, a multi-modality semantic relationship graph is constructed by using the semantic correlation information of media objects with multi-modality. Specifically, semantic correlation among media objects with multi-modality is learned by canonical correlation analysis [5]. Further, all the media objects are mapped onto an isomorphic semantic space. To manage and retrieve all the media objects, an efficient indexing MK-tree based on heterogeneous data distribution is proposed to manage media objects within semantic space and improve the performance of cross-media retrieval with the large scale cross-media database. Finally, we execute the *range* query to examine the performance of cross-multimedia retrieval.

The rest of the paper is organized as follows. Section 2 briefly reviews the related work. In section 3, we introduce the construction of Multi-modalities Semantic Relationship Graph (MSRG) in details. In section 4, we discuss cross-media retrieval based on MK-tree indexing. In section 5, we present our experiments and results. Finally, we offer our conclusions and describe future work in Section 6.

2 Related Work

In recent years, the academic community has proposed concept-based multimedia retrieval by pooling a set of pre-trained semantic concept detectors which can be regarded as intermediate descriptors to bridge the semantic gap. The semantic concepts generally cover a wide range of topics which include objects, scenes, people, events and etc. Some multimedia research communities have put tremendous efforts into manual annotating and releasing a large number of ground truth annotations, such as *TRECVID* [2], *imageCLEF* [3], and *LSCOM* [4], involving image or video data complemented with annotations, close-caption information, or speech recognition transcripts.

The intrinsic problem of Cross-media retrieval is to mine the semantic correlations among the heterogeneous multimedia data. Yang et al.[7] proposed a two-level manifold learning method for cross-media retrieval. They first constructed three independent graphs for images objects, audio objects and text objects respectively. According to the graphs, media objects were projected into three spaces which were then combined to obtain the final data representation in Multimedia document semantic space. However, the semantic correlations among heterogeneous multimedia objects were not exploited when constructing the independent spaces for image, audio and text objects. In addition, the two-level manifold learning method is very complex and more than 10 parameters must be simultaneously tuned, making it less applicable in the real applications.

3   Construction of Multi-modalities Semantic Relationship Graph

As we know from above, in order to effectively address the issues of the heterogeneity of media objects with multi-modality, we construct a unified and compact semantic correlation model. In this section, we describe the main steps of construction of Multi-modality Semantic Relationship Graph (MSRG). The details of each step are then explained sequentially.

We consider the problem of cross-media retrieval from a database which contains components of text, image and video, respectively. Each media objects is represented as a high-level semantic feature vector, such as the text object t_i is denoted as $t_i = \{f_1^{t_i}, f_2^{t_i}, ..., f_n^{t_i}\}$. The representation of image object and video object is followed by the same way. Furthermore, the MSRG can be represented a affinity matrix, which indicates the semantic correlation amongst different media objects.

3.1   Measure Semantic Correlation

Let R be a n-by-n affinity matrix to represent the MSRG, in which r_{ij} represents the semantic correlation among media objects with multi-modality. Here, semantic correlation among media objects is learned by canonical correlation analysis [5].

The mathematical formulation of semantic correlation metric is described as follows. Given arbitrary two types media objects X and Y, denoted as

$$X = [f_1^X, f_2^X, ..., f_n^X]^T, Y = [f_1^Y, f_2^Y, ..., f_n^Y]^T \qquad (1)$$

We extract the correlated modes between vectors X and Y by searching for a set of transformation vector pairs as α_i and β_i respectively. Then, the maximum semantic correlation is defined as

$$\rho_i = \max_{\alpha_i \neq 0, \beta_i \neq 0} \frac{\alpha_i^T C_{XY} \beta_i}{\sqrt{\alpha_i^T C_{XX} \alpha_i} \sqrt{\beta_i^T C_{YY} \beta_i}} \qquad (2)$$

where C_{XY} is the cross-covariance matrix of X and Y, C_{XX} and C_{YY} are auto-covariance matrix. To maximize the Equation (2), we obtain the partial derivative of ρ_i with respect to α_i and β_i, and set the derivative to be zero. We have

$$\begin{cases} C_{XX}^{-1}C_{XY}C_{YY}^{-1}C_{YX}\alpha_i = \rho_i^2\alpha_i \\ C_{YY}^{-1}C_{YX}C_{XX}^{-1}C_{XY}\beta_i = \rho_i^2\beta_i \end{cases} \tag{3}$$

By solving the eigenvalue in Equation (3), we obtain the ascending ordered correlation values $\{\rho_1, \rho_2, ..., \rho_n\}$ and the corresponding transformation vectors, $\overline{\alpha} = [\alpha_1, \alpha_2, ..., \alpha_n]$ and $\overline{\beta} = [\beta_1, \beta_2, ..., \beta_n]$. Note that, the semantic correlation values $\{\rho_1, \rho_2, ..., \rho_n\}$ is the pairwise correlation among the high-level semantic features of media objects. As a result, we have $\rho_i = [r_{ij}]$, such as $\rho_1 = [r_{11}, r_{12}, ..., r_{1n}]^T$. Then, we obtain the semantic correlation matrix R.

3.2   Media Objects Mapping

In order to efficiently manage and retrieve all the media objects, we need to map the media objects onto an isomorphic semantic space. As mentioned above, we derive the semantic correlation of all the media objects from the MSRG. In this section, we decompose the semantic correlation matrix R and construct an isomorphic semantic space.

The eigenvalue decomposition of semantic correlation matrix R by calculating

$$R = O\Lambda O^T = O \begin{pmatrix} \lambda_1 & & \\ & \ddots & \\ & & \lambda_v \end{pmatrix} O^T, 0 \le v \le k \tag{4}$$

where Λ is the diagonal matrix. Its elements of diagonal corresponding to the eigenvalues of correlation matrix R. O is the orthogonal eigenvector matrix corresponding to all the eigenvalue, which is defined by $O = (q_1, q_2, ..., q_v)^T$. O^T represents the transpose of O. q_i is the normalized eigenvectors of semantic correlation matrix R corresponding to the eigenvalue λ_i.

We denote that $(q_1, q_2, ..., q_v)^T$ is an orthogonal basis vector of semantic space. Thus, the isomorphic semantic space can be defined as:

$$\text{SemanticSpace} \rightarrow span(q_1, q_2, ..., q_v)^T$$

which is a orthogonal space generated by linear combinations of $(q_1, q_2, ..., q_v)^T$.

4   Cross-Media Retrieval

The cross-media dataset is usually large scale, it is inefficient to retrieve over large scale cross-media dataset by only using linear scan. In this section, we propose an efficient indexing MK-tree based on heterogeneous data distribution to index all the media objects which are mapped onto the isomorphic semantic space.

4.1   Data Partition Based on Data Distribution and Key Dimension

MK-tree is a dynamically index structure, which can be used to index large scale multimedia objects dataset. Specifically, we both consider heterogeneous data distribution and key dimension to improve the efficiency of data space partition and reduce the response time of similarity search for various media objects.

As we know, heterogeneous media types have different data distributions. For example, the set of video data may be normal distribution and the set of text data may be uniform distribution. In [9], it is confirmed that the optimal query processing depends not only on the number of objects stored in the database but also on the underlying data distribution. Therefore, data distribution is an important factor for influencing query processing.

In an isomorphic semantic space, a key dimension is a dimension that affects mostly similarity computation. Meanwhile, it is crucial to select the key dimension for filtering irrelevant data. In addition, a key dimension can be used to minimize the overlap, and thus avoid a lot of unnecessary path traversals over the index.

In this paper, data partition of semantic space is performed as follows: (1) according to heterogenous data distribution, we firstly segment the original semantic space based on key dimension, (2) the partitioned subspace is split by m-RAD-2 way [8], (3) the subspace is further segmented into twin subspace. An overview of steps of data partition of semantic space is shown in Figure 1.

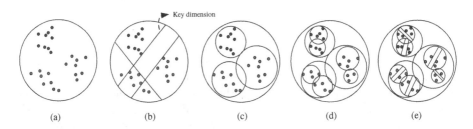

Fig. 1. Overview of data partition with regard to different data distribution in semantic space. (a) the original isomorphic semantic space. (b) considering heterogenous media types have different data distribution, partition the original semantic space based on key dimension. (c)and(d) partitioned subspace is split by m-RAD-2 way. (e) the subspace is further partitioned into twin subspace based on key dimension.

4.2   Query Algorithms

In this section, we cover the details of the algorithms on *range* query. Given a query object q and a query radius r, the *range* query starts from the root node and recursively traverses all the paths in which the objects match the search condition. The search algorithm is described in algorithm 1.

As shown in algorithm 1, *range* query begins from root firstly. For all subspaces in the current space, those subspaces not containing any query result can be

Algorithm 1: *Range*-query (*N*:node, *Q*:query object, $r(Q)$:query radius)

1: **if** N is not leaf node **then**
2:   o_r in N, do:
3:     **if** $|d(o_p - Q) - d(o_r - o_p)| \leq r(Q) + r(o_r)$ **then**
4:       compute $d(o_r, Q)$
5:       **if** $d(o_r, Q) \leq r(Q) + r(o_r)$ **then**
6:         **if** $key \dim Val(Q) \leq ML_{\max} + r(Q)$ **then**
7:           $range - query(*lTwinPtr(Tlt(o_r)), Q, r(Q))$
8:           **if** $key \dim Val(Q) \geq MR_{\min} - r(Q)$ **then**
9:             $range - query(*rTwinPtr(Trt(o_r)), Q, r(Q))$
10: **else**
11:    **if** $|d(o_p - Q) - d(x_i - o_p)| \leq r(Q)$ **then**
12:      compute $d(x_i, Q)$
13:    **else**
14:      **if** $d(x_i, Q) \leq r(Q)$ **then**
15:        add $oid(x_i)$ to the result

---

filtered according to the property of triangular inequality. If the sub-tree is active and cannot be filtered, the distance between the querying object and the routing object is calculated, and further filtering can be done still based on the property of triangular inequality. Then, filtering based on the key dimension is performed on the twin nodes. The process is done recursively till the leaf node. In a leaf node, the results can be obtained by computation and comparison.

5 Experiments

In this section, we report the results of an extensive performance study conducted to evaluate the proposed methods on large-scale real multimedia datasets.

5.1 Experiments Setup

To test the effectiveness and efficiency of the proposed method: Effective Indexing-based Cross-media Retrieval(IBCR), we experiment with a large-scale multimedia datases. The experimental data includes 2000 texts,35000 images and 5000 video clips. All the experiments are executed on Intel Core2 2.4GHz CPU, 4G RAM and 500G hard disk.

5.2 Effectiveness of Cross-Media Retrieval Method

Figure 2 illustrates a recall-precision curve for the performance comparisons between the our approach (IBCR) and CIndex [10]. In [10], the research employ a one dimension index structure like B+-tree by reduction the dimension of the original space and the low level features of media object is used to measure the correlation of heterogenous media types. But the drawback of CIndex is that drop out some important correlation information when reduction the dimension

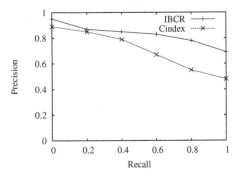

Fig. 2. Recall vs. Precision

of the data space, and the low level features can not well represent the semantic correlations of heterogenous media objects. In particular, we compares the average retrieval result (indicates the average precision rate under the average recall rate) of 20 media objects queries randomly chosen from the multimedia datasets. From the Figure 2, the retrieval effectiveness of our proposed method is better than that of CIndex by a large margin.

5.3   Experiments on Range Query

In this section, we discuss the impact of query radius of range query on the querying CPU time and I/O cost. As shown in Figure 3, we can see the performance of our proposed method is superiority over the CIndex and sequential scan. At the same time, we considering the average precision of range query, the accuracy of retrieval by exploring our method is not to change more along with the larger query radius. Especially, when the query radius is smaller, more twin nodes in indexing tree can be filtered by the key dimension. The runtime of our method is averagely four times faster than sequential scan.

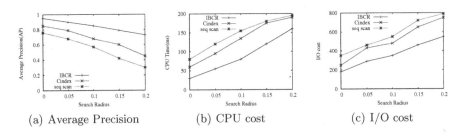

(a) Average Precision   (b) CPU cost   (c) I/O cost

Fig. 3. Analysis of the performance of *Range* query

6   Conclusion

In this paper, we present a novel and efficient method for cross-media retrieval. We firstly construct a multi-modality semantic relationship graph (MSRG) by exploring the semantic correlation of media objects with multi-modality. Further, all the media objects within MSRG are mapped onto an isomorphic semantic space, which used to encapsulate the heterogenous media objects. Finally, an efficient indexing MK-tree is proposed to manage media objects and effectively speedup the cross-media retrieval performance for facilitate to cope with the large scale multimedia datasets. In order to effectively index the heterogenous media objects, MK-tree partitions the data space based on the different media data distribution and key dimensions. Extensive experiments on real large scale multimedia datasets indicate that our proposal dramatically improves the accuracy and efficiency of cross-media retrieval, outperform existing methods significantly.

Acknowledgments. This research are supported by the NSFC (Grant No. 61025007, 60933001 and 61100024), National Basic Research Program of China (973, Grant No. 2011CB302200-G), National High Technology Research and Development Program of China (863, Grant No. 2012AA011004) and the Fundamental Research Funds for the Central Universities (Grant No. N110404011).

References

1. Lew, M., Sebe, N., Djeraba, C., Jain, R.: Content-based multimeida information retrieval: State-of-the-art and challenges. ACM Trans. Multimeida Comput., Commun., Applic. 2(1), 1–19 (2006)
2. Smeaton, A.F., Over, P., Kraaij, W.: Evaluation campaigns and TRECVid. In: Proc. of MIR (2006)
3. Paramita, M., Sanderson, M., Clough, P.: Diversity in photo retrieval: overview of the Image CLEF photo task 2009. CLEF Working Notes (2009)
4. Naphade, M., Smith, J.R., Tesic, J., Chang, S.-F., Hsu, W., Kennedy, L., Hauptmann, A., Curtis, J.: Large-Scale Concept Ontology for Multimedia. IEEE Multimedia Magazine 13(3) (2006)
5. Hotelling, H.: Relations between two sets of variates. Biometrike 28, 321–377 (1936)
6. Zhang, H., Zhuang, Y., Wu, F.: Cross-modal correlation learning for clustering on image-audio dataset. In: ACM Multimeida (2007)
7. Yang, Y., Zhuang, Y., Wu, F.: Harmonizing hierarchical manifolds for multimedia document semantics understanding and cross-media retrieval. IEEE Transactions on Multimedia 10, 437–446 (2008)
8. Ciaccia, P., Patella, M., Zezula, P.: M-tree: An efficient access method for similarity search in metric spaces. In: Proc of the VLDB Conference, pp. 426–435 (1997)
9. Christian, B.: A cost model for query processing in high dimensional data spaces. ACM Transactions on Database Systems 25, 129–178 (2000)
10. Zhuang, Y., Li, Q., Chen, L.: A Unified Indexing Structure for Efficient Cross-Media Retrieval. In: Zhou, X., Yokota, H., Deng, K., Liu, Q. (eds.) DASFAA 2009. LNCS, vol. 5463, pp. 677–692. Springer, Heidelberg (2009)

Robust Place Recognition by Avoiding Confusing Features and Fast Geometric Re-ranking

Mingying Gong, Lifeng Sun, Shiqiang Yang, and Yun Yang

Department of Computer Science and Technology,
Tsinghua University, Beijing, China
gongmingying07@gmail.com,
{sunlf,yangshq}@tsinghua.edu.cn, yyun20@126.com

Abstract. There are millions of mobile phone applications based on location. Using a photo to precisely locate users location is useful and necessary. However, real-time location recognition or retrieval system is a challenging problem due to the really big differences between the query and the dataset in scale, viewpoint and lighting, or the noise existed in the foreground or background etc. To address this problem, we design a place recognition system and a new famous buildings dataset with ground truth labels. By adding a fast geometric image matching procedure before using RANSAC and applying a relative camera orientation calculation algorithm to filter the dataset collected from the Internet, we can substantially improve the efficiency of spatial verification and recognition accuracy.

Keywords: Image Recognition, Confusing Features Detection, Geometric Verification, Relative Camera Orientation.

1 Introduction

With the popularity of the smartphones, people can get photos anytime and anywhere. The prevalence of digital photography devices leads to huge volume of images accessible online which makes it difficult for users to find what they need or are interested in. For example, when you upload a photo to Flickr, you may want to know who has the same interest with you; or when you get lost in an unfamiliar place, its helpful to have an application to find where you are based on the photo you shot in that place. Due to the big differences between the query and the dataset in scale, viewpoint and lighting, real-time photo match is a really challenging problem. Besides, not only the dataset we have but also the query we shot have all kinds of noises which affect the search result very much. We can see from Fig. 1 (bottom), that's the standard view of a pinpoint, however, what we have as the queries are mostly like Fig. 1 (top).

So in this paper, we focus on the difficulties and propose solutions. Considering the noise existed in the photo, we propose the relative camera orientation calculation algorithm [1,2] to first filter the dataset, and then in view of immediacy we need in real-time application, a fast geometric image matching procedure [3,4] is added before using RANSAC to verify the result. Combining the solutions with existing techniques, we get a more precise result using the dataset we built which has more than 200K images.

S.-M. Hu and R.R. Martin (Eds.): CVM 2012, LNCS 7633, pp. 210–217, 2012.
© Springer-Verlag Berlin Heidelberg 2012

Fig. 1. Example of place recognition images. Given a query image (top), we aim to find an image shot at the same place as the query from a geotagged database (bottom).

The following of this paper will be organized as follows. In Section 2, we will discuss the framework of our system, and in Section 3 and 4, confusing feature detection and spatial verification are discussed in more detail to see how to search the similar photo more precisely in our system. In Section 5, the experiments will show the effectiveness and efficiency in our system compared with SVM and other methods. Finally, we summarize results and our work in Section 6.

2   Place Recognition Framework

This section overviews the baseline of place recognition approach based on the bag-of-words (BoW) model. With a pre-collected dataset, when the query image comes, the query image features are extracted and each feature is quantized by the visual vocabulary. Then a relative camera orientation calculation algorithm is used to predict whether it fails in tf-idf retrieval. After a confusing feature detection step, image similarity is evaluated by calculating the distance between the query vector and each document vector of the corpus. The spatial verification composed of a fast geometric re-ranking and RANSAC is applied in the top n most similar results. Further, we use a query expansion strategy to achieve final visual place recognition results.

Image representation: Detecting the image features in the dataset is the first step. For the excellent performance of SIFT [5] in invariance to image transformations, we use it as the feature detector. RootSIFT may be a better choice, which acquires a dramatic performance boost by replacing the standard Euclidean distance of SIFT descriptors measuring method with a square root (Hellinger) kernel [6]. A vocabulary of 10K visual words is generated from a subset of 1000 images (about 2M features) of the image dataset using a k-means clustering algorithm [7,8].

Retrieval failure prediction: we use a relative camera orientation calculation algorithm [1,2] to judge whether the query contains a qualified subject. A qualified subject means most parts of the subject are not occluded by other objects, such as trees, cars, or bill-boards, or is just a small part of the whole subject. An unqualified subject often leads to angle calculation failure. The orientation undetectable queries are likely to have a mass of confusing features which are the dominating reason for the BoW retrieval failure. When a possible retrieval failure is predicted, a preprocessing automatic tf-idf failure recovery [9] is applied before the retrieval scheme. Unfortunately, limited by the algorithm, we can only predict queries containing EXIF information now [1].

Retrieval Scheme: Similar to [10,9,11], the search engines are based on the corpus retrieval method. We use the occurrences of virtual word as terms to generate tf-idf weighted vector and rank the image by the cosine value of angle between the query vector and each dataset image. The retrieval procedure using inverted files [12] has been illustrated to perform well on datasets as large as 1M images [10,11]. We remain up to a maximum of the top 1000 results for the next stage.

Spatial verification: For matching features between image I and J, a kd-tree is created from the feature extracted from I, then we find the nearest neighbor of each feature in I from the kd-tree. Using the strategy promoted by Low [5], we search for the two nearset neighbors in J. After finding matched features, a fast geometric re-ranking [3,4] is conducted between the image pair (I, J). More details will be discussed in Section 4. This process can greatly reduce the number of images needed to be verified by RANSAC [13,14], or otherwise will spend too much time. Up to 100 verified results from the fast geometric re-ranking are finally evaluated by the affine homography calculated from image pairs. After the RANSAC iteration, we compute a maximum of inliers. If the number of remaining matches (inliers) is less than the threshold (20) [10,11,15], we consider the image pair is not matched and remove it from the candidate list.

Query expansion: Since images after spatial verification are reliable, it is possible to expand the original query to form a new more robust query. The query expansion is put forward by Chum and Philbin and Sivic et al. [10]. It brings a significant boost in almost all image retrieval approaches up to now [10,16,17].

3   Confusing Features Detection and Avoidance

A problem that image localization often faces is either a query image or dataset contains significant amount of non-informative objects, such as trees, roadblocks etc.. Recent work [11,9] has proposed approaches to remove the confusing feature in the query image or datasets. In [11] the confusing words are detected by using a sliding window. When the local confusion score is high, the corresponding region is considered as a confusing part and is removed from the dataset. However, as the confusing part removed, useful information maybe lose at some special cases (e.g. landscape images). Another strategy is put forward in [9]. It is a solution to the problem that the retrieval based on BoW often fails to return expected results when too many visually confusing words appear in the query tf-idf vector.

If expected images arent included in the results because of the confusing features, it is called a tf-idf failure [9]. When this situation happens, a re-querying is required after removing these confusing words and obviously double time will be spent. Our approach goes further in two respects: first the query image quality is evaluated, and a high quality image can be used to promote the dataset, second it can predict a probable tf-idf failure and thus greatly reduce the cost time and enhance the retrieval efficiency.

Our approach could be separated into two parts: (i) retrieval failure prediction and (ii) confusing feature removing and tf-idf recovery.

In the retrieval failure prediction part, a relative camera orientation calculation algorithm is adapted. The focal length of each image is extracted from the EXIF information and the shooting angle is calculated. A query or image from dataset has too many confusers, it is very likely to fail the algorithm. A correct calculated angle needs a proper max rectangle detected from the image, so we can infer that objects contained in the image have a clear structure. Empirically, it means that the front of a subject is well shot. In this work we opt for a simple threshold of the angle precision.

For a query failed to calculate the angle, a tf-idf recovery process is conducted. The goal of this part is to remove the confusing feature and retrieval the most similar image to the query in the dataset. To achieve this goal, we compute the query confusion score. We assume $P(w|Q)$ and $P(w)$ are the distribution of visual words in the query and the whole dataset. A query confusion score ρ is then measured over the tf-idf vector of query and dataset. For a visual word w at query we determine the score as:

$$\rho_w = \frac{P(w|Q)}{P(w)}. \tag{1}$$

In other words, the score measures the occurrences of visual word between query and dataset. If the query has abundant confusing features, the score is high which means the visual word w is probably a confusing word.

After that, we aim at localization improvement by assigning confusing words negative weights rather than simply remove them from the query. The recovery query is then matched to dataset with negative weighted confusing word. Thus the new query avoids the influence of confusing features and the whole scheme is less computationally expensive than without prediction.

4   Geometrical Consistency Re-ranking

The goal of this stage is to decide whether the returned image from the previous stage is correct. To find more correct image, we verify the top-ranked image as many as 1000 from the spatial filter. However, this verification is much more time expensive using RANSAC. A weak geometrical consistency method is proposed in [3,4,18]. It uses a vocabulary tree to match feature pairs and confirm the matching pairs using the angle, scale and location information. It has been shown that angle and scale contain more useful geometrical information.

Unlike [3], we use the approximate nearest neighbors kd-tree to match feature. So the method is orthogonal to previously used RANSAC and a fast geometric re-ranking scheme can be well used in conjunction with previous work. We have implemented a two-stage space verification approach. In the first stage, the goal is to find a small set of most likely expected candidate images from the top 1000 results of retrieval scheme. This is achieved by verifying the consistency of the angle, scale and location differences. In the second stage, the candidate images are re-ranked by the number of inliers. In the following we describe details of the two space verification stage.

A fast geometric re-ranking scheme is built upon weak geometrical information from SIFT. For an image pair (I, J), we use the histogram to represent the angle, scale and location differences. The angle geometric score (S_a), scale geometric sore (S_s) and location geometric score (S_l) are formed as follow:

$$S_a = \max_\alpha \left(\sum_{(m,n) \in M} I \left(\frac{2 \cdot \pi \cdot \alpha}{c} \leq a_{i,m} - a_{j,n} < \frac{2 \cdot \pi \cdot (\alpha+1)}{c} \right) \right)$$

$$S_s = \max_\alpha \left(\sum_{(m,n) \in M} I \left(\frac{\alpha}{c} \leq log \left(\frac{s_{i,m}}{s_{j,n}} \right) < \frac{\alpha+1}{c} \right) \right) \tag{2}$$

$$S_l = \max_\alpha \left(\sum_{(m,n),(p,q) \in M} I \left(\frac{\alpha}{c} \leq log \left(\frac{dist(l_{i,m}, l_{i,p})}{dist(l_{j,n}, l_{j,q})} \right) < \frac{\alpha+1}{c} \right) \right),$$

where M is the matched feature set between image I and J, $I(\cdot)$ is the indicator function, and a, s, l represent the angle, scale and location value of SIFT feature. α/c corresponds to the geometric difference and c is a tolerance threshold.

Therefore, the final score (S_f)

$$S_f = \min(S_a, S_s, S_l) \tag{3}$$

is a reasonable estimate of the geometrical consistency. By using the SIFT geometric, we can confirm the image pair well and reduce the number of candidate images verified by hypothesize transformations.

After this stage, using RANSAC we robustly estimate a fundamental matrix in the small candidate image set. During RANSAC iteration, a normalization step is conducted to improve robustness [19]. Only images of which the number of inliers is more than 20 are taken into consideration. And remaining images are used for the query expansion.

5   Experiments

A series of experiments have been conducted to evaluate our system we propose. We have three different kinds of datasets which makes our evaluation more precisely.

5.1   Dataset

We use the Oxford dataset [7], Tsinghua dataset and Bing dataset to evaluate our system. The first one is a relatively small dataset of 5K collected from Flickr by searching for the landmarks in Oxford with a ground truth. The second one is the images shot in Tsinghua which are manually annotated. The last one is a relatively large dataset which can evaluate our system well. More details can be found below in Table 1.

The Oxford Dataset. The dataset is crawled from Flickr by searching for the landmarks in Oxford, such as "Cornmarket Oxford" and "Bodleian Oxford". It includes 5062 high

Table 1. The number of images for each dataset

Dataset	Number of images
Oxford	5,062
Tsinghua	4,012
Bing	209,826

resolution images. This dataset has been manually annotated into 11 landmarks with 4 possible labels: Good, OK, Bad and Junk. More details can be found in [7].

The Tsinghua Dataset. This dataset is shot in Tsinghua University including most famous spots such as "Tsinghua Gate" and "Lotus Pond". It consists of 4K high resolution images with manually annotated.

The Bing Dataset. This dataset is crawled from the Bing image search engine which include 5 categories: location, people, art, object, and nature. Each category contains 210 sub-categories. The Bing dataset has more than 200K images. So in this large dataset we can evaluate our system more precisely.

5.2 Experimental Results

We use the above datasets to demonstrate the performance of the system we proposed. First, extract the image features for each one in the dataset. We use a variant of multi-scale Hessian regions-of-interest [20] to detect the affine regions. For each of these regions, a 128-dimensional SIFT descriptor is computed which is vector quantized into visual words. Then, when given a query image, the highest scoring 1000 images were returned. Get the mean score from the Average Precision scores as the Mean Average Precision (MAP). We test the MAP score using 10 query images.

Compared the system we proposed with Vocabulary tree (VT) + SVM and Query expansion (QE) methods, we get Table 2. As we can see in Table 2, the MAP in our system boosts significantly compared with VT + SVM and is close to QE results by just verifying a small set of top candidates.

Besides the outstanding MAP performance in the top n candidate list, our system has the advantages in the time costing. Instead of directly using the RANSAC algorithm, we adopt the fast geometric re-ranking method to filter the results which can reduce the

Table 2. Performance comparison. The left column represent the number of used top candidates for spatial verification.

	MAP		Time	
VT+SVM	0.76		-	
	QE		Ours	
	MAP	Time	MAP	Time
100	0.924	0.55	0.924	0.24
200	0.942	0.78	0.937	0.49
800	0.944	1.39	0.956	0.81

processing time greatly. The average time for the three different methods can be seen in Table 2. As we can see, our method is ahead of others.

6   Conclusion

We have demonstrated a novel system which can perform better in real-time location recognition or retrieval system. The innovation can be concluded into 3 points: (1) the efficiency of spatial verification and recognition accuracy have been substantially improved by adding a fast geometric image matching procedure before using RANSAC; (2) reduce the influence of confusing features in the photos by applying a relative camera orientation calculation algorithm; (3) a large place recognition system is built with ground truth. The experiments prove that compared with VT + SVM and QE methods, our system achieves significant improvement both in precision and search time in large scale applications.

Acknowledgment. This work was supported by 973 Program under Grant No. 2011CB302206, NSFC under Grant No. 61272231/60833009 and Tsinghua-Tencent Joint Lab Research Grant.

References

1. Wang, Z., Sun, L., Yang, S.: Efficient relative camera orientation detection for mobile applications. In: Proceedings of the 1st International Workshop on Mobile Location-Based Service, pp. 53–62. ACM (2011)
2. Jacobs, N., Roman, N., Pless, R.: Toward fully automatic geo-location and geo-orientation of static outdoor cameras. In: IEEE Workshop on Applications of Computer Vision, WACV 2008, pp. 1–6. IEEE (2008)
3. Jégou, H., Douze, M., Schmid, C.: Improving bag-of-features for large scale image search. International Journal of Computer Vision 87(3), 316–336 (2010)
4. Tsai, S., Chen, D., Takacs, G., Chandrasekhar, V., Vedantham, R., Grzeszczuk, R., Girod, B.: Fast geometric re-ranking for image-based retrieval. In: 17th IEEE International Conference on Image Processing (ICIP), pp. 1029–1032. IEEE (2010)
5. Lowe, D.: Distinctive image features from scale-invariant keypoints. International Journal of Computer Vision 60(2), 91–110 (2004)
6. Zisserman, A., Arandjelovic, R.: Three things everyone should know to improve object retrieval. In: IEEE Conference on Computer Vision and Pattern Recognition, pp. 2911–2918. IEEE (2012)
7. Philbin, J., Chum, O., Isard, M., Sivic, J., Zisserman, A.: Object retrieval with large vocabularies and fast spatial matching. In: IEEE Conference on Computer Vision and Pattern Recognition, CVPR 2007, pp. 1–8. IEEE (2007)
8. Quack, T., Leibe, B., Van Gool, L.: World-scale mining of objects and events from community photo collections. In: Proceedings of the 2008 International Conference on Content-Based Image and Video Retrieval, pp. 47–56. ACM (2008)
9. Chum, O., Mikulik, A., Perdoch, M., Matas, J.: Total recall ii: Query expansion revisited. In: IEEE Conference on Computer Vision and Pattern Recognition (CVPR), pp. 889–896. IEEE (2011)

10. Chum, O., Philbin, J., Sivic, J., Isard, M., Zisserman, A.: Total recall: Automatic query expansion with a generative feature model for object retrieval. In: IEEE 11th International Conference on Computer Vision, ICCV 2007, pp. 1–8. IEEE (2007)

11. Knopp, J., Sivic, J., Pajdla, T.: Avoiding Confusing Features in Place Recognition. In: Daniilidis, K., Maragos, P., Paragios, N. (eds.) ECCV 2010, Part I. LNCS, vol. 6311, pp. 748–761. Springer, Heidelberg (2010)

12. Zobel, J., Moffat, A.: Inverted files for text search engines. ACM Computing Surveys (CSUR) 38(2), 6 (2006)

13. Chum, O., Matas, J., Obdrzalek, S.: Enhancing ransac by generalized model optimization. In: Proc. of the ACCV, vol. 2, pp. 812–817 (2004)

14. Fischler, M., Bolles, R.: Random sample consensus: a paradigm for model fitting with applications to image analysis and automated cartography. Communications of the ACM 24(6), 381–395 (1981)

15. Snavely, N., Seitz, S., Szeliski, R.: Modeling the world from internet photo collections. International Journal of Computer Vision 80(2), 189–210 (2008)

16. Philbin, J., Chum, O., Isard, M., Sivic, J., Zisserman, A.: Lost in quantization: Improving particular object retrieval in large scale image databases. In: IEEE Conference on Computer Vision and Pattern Recognition, CVPR 2008, pp. 1–8. IEEE (2008)

17. Jégou, H., Douze, M., Schmid, C.: On the burstiness of visual elements. In: IEEE Conference on Computer Vision and Pattern Recognition, CVPR 2009, pp. 1169–1176. IEEE (2009)

18. Jégou, H., Douze, M., Schmid, C.: Hamming Embedding and Weak Geometric Consistency for Large Scale Image Search. In: Forsyth, D., Torr, P., Zisserman, A. (eds.) ECCV 2008, Part I. LNCS, vol. 5302, pp. 304–317. Springer, Heidelberg (2008)

19. Hartley, R.: In defense of the eight-point algorithm. IEEE Transactions on Pattern Analysis and Machine Intelligence 19(6), 580–593 (1997)

20. Mikolajczyk, K., Schmid, C.: Scale & affine invariant interest point detectors. International Journal of Computer Vision 60(1), 63–86 (2004)

Design and Implementation
of a Context-Based Media Retrieval System

Liang Zhao, Tangjian Deng, Hao Wang, Qingwei Liu, and Ling Feng

Dept. of Computer Science & Technology, Tsinghua University, Beijing, China
{zhaoliang0415,dengtangjian,wanghaomails,liuqingwei2019}@gmail.com,
fengling@tsinghua.edu.cn

Abstract. Multimedia information has greatly enriched our digital life. Every day we freely scan and download different media objects on the local computer or through the Internet. With the explosion of the individual-related media data, the need of easily re-locating the visited media objects becomes more and more urgent. We design and implement a media retrieval system called *M-ReFind* that enables users to re-find the previously accessed media information by relevant contexts. In this paper, we demonstrate how a user adds associate contexts to the media objects s/he stores or accesses in daily life and re-finds them by certain context. We show that *M-ReFind* supports a convenient context-based media retrieval experience, allowing users to re-find local, removable or global media objects more easily.

1 Introduction

With the development of information technology, multimedia data rapidly booms and greatly enriches our digital life in this information era for its vitality. Beyond scanning and downloading the lively media objects, we also frequently look back for previously visited ones. However, the explosion in the amount of personally accessed multimedia information has made the process of re-finding certain media targets a time-consuming task. To illustrate, let's see a real case.

[case 1]*I want to recommend a nameless music to my friend which I encountered in a web page last month at home during a paper writing, but have no idea its title and also cannot remember its melody clearly.*

Information re-finding is often affected by fast content changes and frequently updated result ranking of the search engines [17]. Currently, techniques of media retrieval mainly concentrate on content-based keywords. Traditional keyword-based searching and ranking strategies developed for the general-purpose search engines may not be applicable. Moreover, sometimes a re-finding request cannot simply be formulated by content-based keywords. Psychological studies show that context under which information was accessed in the past can serve as a powerful cue for information recall, as it is always easier to remember and formulate [4, 7, 8, 10–12, 17]

S.-M. Hu and R.R. Martin (Eds.): CVM 2012, LNCS 7633, pp. 218–225, 2012.
© Springer-Verlag Berlin Heidelberg 2012

Existing Solutions. Web search and personal information management (PIM) communities make substantial efforts to improve information recall with contextual search [5, 10, 14]. Google's *Web History* [1] keeps and classifies users' web access information including search requests and clicked pages into different topics such as images, news, etc., It allows users to browse their historically accessed pages at a selected date or during a different (newest, newer, older, oldest) time period. Keyword-based searching over the accessed page titles and contents is also allowed. *YouPivot* system [9] bookmarks a moment in time, and allows a user to access all activities that was ongoing at a particular moment rather than manually keep track of individual files, websites, and bookmarks. *SearchBar* tool [15] accommodates user's recent search topics, queries, results visited, and notes, which can be re-acquired later. The *Contextual Web History* tool [18] employs user's visiting time and visual appearance of the accessed web pages to assist web re-visitation. *Stuff I've Seen* system [7] builds an index for what a person has seen, and uses file type, access date, and author information for result filtering and sorting. XSearcher desktop search system [4] exploits semantic association/lineage among files to enhance full-text keyword-based search. The file search tool *Connections* [16] expands and reorders traditional content-based search results by the contextual temporal locality information. SEMEX system [2] enables a user to browse the personal information via semantic associations (i.e., AuthoredBy, Cites, AttachedTo, MentionedIn) among data items as well as objects (i.e., person, publication, and message) on one's desktop. [12] proposed a query method to re-find referenced files, given some file items as input, where three types of reference relations (*temporal adjacent, inclusive,* and *lineage*) are exploited. [3] also developed a system to support multi-level associative retrieval of desktop information. [13] presented a theoretical model of user context. The context is obtained by multi-sensory knowledge and applied in an image retrieval system.

Inspired by human memory and its recalling characteristics (memory decay and reinforcement), [6] developed a context-based re-finding query model upon a well-organized and evolving context memory. Each context instance in the personal context memory links to the media objects accessed before. Context instances are organized in a hierarchical, clustering, and associative manner. They evolve dynamically in life cycles to mimic the amnesia of human memory that some prominent events can last for very long or even a life long, while the majority will gradually degrade and finally disappear. Memory reinforcement is also incorporated by adjusting the decay rates of certain well-remembered context instances. Based on the context memory model, a recall-by-context query model was built and two algorithms (i.e., cluster-based re-finding and association-based re-finding) were devised to evaluate context-based re-finding queries upon a personal database.

Our Contribution. So in this paper, we design *M-ReFind*, a context-based media retrieval system that implements and extends the techniques of [6] in the following three important ways.

- Since it is often difficult to properly extract and formulate content-based keywords from media information, we apply the context-based method in [6] to the media retrieval scenario. Using context, *M-ReFind* achieves a more flexible and easy user experience.
- Beyond the single personal relational database, A windows right-button plug-in and an Internet browser plug-in are embeded into *M-ReFind* to realize context annotation of local and online media objects respectively.
- While all the parameters influencing context degradation are heuristically predefined in [6], *M-ReFind* opens the black box of context memory and allows users to maintain context hierarchies to make the context memory more consistent with users' memory and hence their context-based re-finding requests.

We will illustrate the overall architecture of *M-ReFind* in Section 2. Demonstration scenarios are presented in Section 3. And section 4 discusses several future work in schedule.

2   Overall Architecture

M-ReFind contains two parts, namely, *context annotation* and *media re-location*.

2.1   Context Annotation for Visited Media Information

This part facilitates users to annotate their interesting media files/web pages with the access context. The local media annotation is realized by a CSharp-based right-button plug-in on Windows OS. When encountering interesting local media files, as shown in Figure 1, the user can click the right mouse button and select *ContextAnnotation* operation just like other system-defined operations(i.e., open file, copy, paste, etc.), which is natural enough without bringing any learning burden to users.

For web media annotation, a cross-platform Internet browser plug-in is in service. The user can click the icon of *M-ReFind* on the tool bar of the web browser to annotate the current web page with media objects as Figure 2 shows. To better serve users, the multi-platform web annotation of *M-ReFind* supports currently dominating web browsers, such as Microsoft Internet Explorer, Firefox, Google Chrome and so on.

Responding the user's operation, the two plug-ins will record the file paths/web URLs into a personal database and meanwhile provides a pop-up window to get user-input contextual information. *M-ReFind* considers three typical kinds of contextual attributes, namely, access *Time*, *Place*, and concurrent *Activity*. The domain of each attribute forms a hierarchy of levels of abstraction. The access *Time* is the current date automatically filled in by *M-ReFind*. The user can either manually input *Location* and concurrent *Activity*, or select appropriate values from the pre-defined *Location* and *Activity* hierarchies, respectively. *M-ReFind* allows the user to maintain the contextual hierarchies by inserting, deleting, or renaming attribute values. For *case 1*, the user can briefly annotate that music web page with the following context instance:

[Time: [2011-11-26], Place: Home, Activity: PaperWriting]

Fig. 1. Local media file annotation

Fig. 2. Web media annotation

M-ReFind organizes user's context instances into a context memory, possessing a clustering and associative structure with dynamic evolution. Each context instance is linked to the corresponding accessed media objects via file paths or URLs stored in the personal database.

2.2   Context-Based Media Re-location

To re-find previously accessed media files or web pages, the user just indicates the previous access context via the *M-ReFind* interface in Figure 3. The user selects contextual values in the hierarchies to form a context-based query. In this step, the user can also freely modify the contextual hierarchies to reflect his memory and preference change.

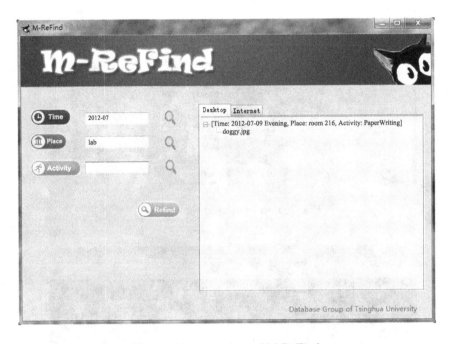

Fig. 3. Main interface of M-ReFind

M-ReFind's context memory manager is responsible to identify those closely matching context units from the personal context memory, and return the linked file(s) and web page(s) via the *M-ReFind*'s interface. The user can simply double-click the returned file paths/URLs to re-visit the media objects. *M-ReFind* ensures the smallest yet correct policy for information re-finding. That is, the target information that the user demands must be in the result set, and the size of the result is the minimal one.

Organization and Maintenance of Context Memory. Simulating human memory, the personal context memory is organized into a short-term memory and a long-term memory. There are two types of long-term context memory: *permanent* and *general*. The former records life-long experiences and is immutable, while the latter will decay. *M-ReFind* concentrates on the general long-term context memory (abbreviated as context memory for short). A context memory is a graph $CM = (VCC, ECC)$, where VCC is a set of vertices (representing context instance clusters) and ECC is a set of edges on vertices (representing association relationships of context instances). The clustering of context instances is based on an instance similarity calculation. Let $A_1 = time$, $A_2 = place$, and $A_3 = activity$, and let $C = (c_1, c_2, c_3)$ and $C = (c'_1, c'_2, c'_3)$ be two context instances. $Sim^I(C, C') = \sqrt{\frac{1}{3} \sum_{i=1}^{3} sim^2(A_i, c_i, c'_i)}$, where $sim(A_i, c_i, c'_i)$ is the value similarity of c_i and c'_i on contextual attribute A_i, which is subject to their level distance in the contextual hierarchy, as well as their ordering distance when prompted to the same hierarchical level. When a user modifies a contextual hierarchy by adding, deleting, or renaming certain contextual attribute values, the context manager will re-calculate such similarity, hence re-cluster context instances. Each context instance points to the accessed file paths and web URLs in the *information resource*.

Decay and Reinforcement of Context Memory. Like our human memory, the context memory evolves with time. Each contextual attribute value of a context instance is bounded with a memory retention strength $r \in [0, 1]$, determining the value's retention/degradation along its contextual hierarchy. The computation of the retention strength r is subject to the original retention strength, the decay rate, and the age (i.e., lasting time):

$$r = r_0 \cdot e^{-\lambda \sqrt{t}}$$

where r_0 is the original value of retention strength in $[\theta_1, \theta_2]$, λ is the decaying rate coefficient, t is the age, θ_{max} and θ_{min} are two system-defined thresholds. An attribute value r will be permanently remembered if $r > \theta_2$ and will be forgotten and discarded when $r < \theta_1$.

The context memory also experiences reinforcement by user's context-based recalling. In this case, the decay rate of the refreshed contextual attribute value will be adjusted according to user's queries and feedbacks. If a contextual attribute value decays too fast, the system will slow down the degradation speed; and if it decays too slowly, the system will speedup the degradation to catch up with user's recalling requests.

Match/Query of M-ReFind. Compared with conventional keyword search of SQL query, *M-ReFind* executes its match/query function in a different way. The user's query request Q is formulated as a context instance. The personal context memory CM is the query target. And the query returns a ranked list of matched context instances as the intermediate query result, whose ranking is based on simple Euclidean similarity between query Q and context instance C in CM. The intermediate query result is obtained by the association-based matching method [6]. Note that Q may or may not exactly match C due to the dynamic evolution of CM. Three kinds of match between Q and C are considered and included in the result list, namely, *exact match* (C is equal to Q), *specific match* (C is specific than Q), and *general match* (C is general than Q).

Linked files or web pages as the final result will then be identified and returned to the user.

3   Demonstration

Attendees will be invited to interact with *M-ReFind* to re-find any media information from the local computer or global Internet based on the previous access context. The demonstration will proceed in two steps.

Annotating media objects. A user will access (scan, download, etc.) several media files or web pages. Then he can annotate the interesting ones with the current access context - Place (e.g., *Home*) and Activity (e.g., *PaperWriting*). The Time context will be filled in by the system date (e.g., *2011-10-26*) automatically. *M-ReFind* keeps some hierarchical context values for the user to select. The user can also modify them by inserting, deleting, or changing the contextual values to reflect his interest and context memorization status.

Re-finding visited media files/web pages. Entering the main interface of *M-ReFind*, the user can re-find the previously visited media files/web pages by inputing the corresponding context information. Sometimes, it is hard for users to precisely memorize the access context (e.g., [Time: *2011-10-26*, Place: *Home*, Activity: *PaperWriting*]), particularly when that information access happened long time ago. *M-ReFind* allows the users to input some vague or even missing contextual values (like [Time: -, Place: *Home*, Activity: *Working*]) instead. And sometimes a user may recall the very precise context information (e.g., [Time: *2011-10-26*, Place: *Home*, Activity: *PaperWriting*]), while the corresponding contextual information in the personal context memory has already degraded to more general ones (e.g., [Time: *2011*, Place: *Home*, Activity: -]). *M-ReFind* will return a superset of the wanted media files/web pages and internally adjust the decay rates of *Time* and *Activity* properly. Once the same contextual information is reinforced by the user, its decay rate will decrease as well.

For better user experience, we design a top window of *M-ReFind* floating on the screen (Figure 2). Clicking it and select the corresponding operations (*Annotate, ReFind, Exit*), the user can either annotate the current media object, enter the main interface of *M-ReFind*, or exit the top window respectively.

4   Conclusion and Future Work

In this paper, we demonstrate *M-ReFind*, a context-based media retrieval system which supports users to contextually annotate interesting media files and web pages and re-find them by context. Beyond the user artificial annotation, we will further investigate the automatic machinary annotation. One key is to predict the retrieval potential of encountered media files and web pages, especially for web pages containing media objects. We are now making efforts in web page retrieval prediction. We assume to extract some content features of the accessed web pages and employ a naive bayes classifier to make prediction. Also, some machine learning models are also supposed to be as the predictor.

Acknowledgement. The work is supported by Chinese Major State Basic Research Development 973 Program (2011CB302203-2), Important National Science & Technology Specific Program (2011ZX01042-001-002-2), research fund of Tsinghua-Tencent Joint Laboratory for Internet Innovation Technology, and National Natural Science Foundation of China (60773156, 61073004).

References

1. Google web history, http://www.google.com/history
2. Cai, Y., Dong, X.L., Halevy, A., Liu, J.M., Madhavan, J.: Personal information management with semex. In: SIGMOD (2005)
3. Chau, D.H., Myers, B., Faulring, A.: What to do when search fails: finding information by association. In: CHI (2008)
4. Chen, J., Guo, H., Wu, W., Xie, C.: Search your memory! - an associative memory based desktop search system. In: SIGMOD (2009)
5. Chen, Y., Jones, G.: Integrating memory context into personal information re-finding. In: The 2nd BCS-IRSG Symposium on Future Directions in Information Access (2008)
6. Deng, T., Zhao, L., Feng, L., Xue, W.: Information re-finding by context: A brain memory inspired approach. In: CIKM (2011)
7. Dumais, S., Cutrell, E., Cadiz, J., Jancke, G., Sarin, R., Robbins, D.C.: Stuff i've seen: a system for personal information retrieval and re-use. In: SIGIR (2003)
8. Fuller, M., Kelly, L., Jones, G.J.F.: Applying contextual memory cues for retrieval from personal information archives. In: PIM, Workshop at CHI (2008)
9. Hailpern, J., Jitkoff, N., Warr, A., Karahalios, K., Sesek, R., Shkrob, N.: Youpivot: improving recall with contextual search. In: CHI (2011)
10. Kelly, L., Chen, Y., Fuller, M., Jones, G.J.F.: A study of remembered context for information access from personal digital archives. In: Proceedings of the Second International Symposium on Information Interaction in Context (2008)
11. Lamming, M., Flynn, M.: "forget-me-not"-intimate computing in support of human memory. In: FRIEND21 International Symposium on Next Generation Human Interface (1994)
12. Li, Y., Meng, X.: Supporting context-based query in personal dataspace. In: CIKM (2009)
13. Mani, A., Sundaram, H.: Modeling user context with applicatins to media retrieval. Springer (2006)
14. Mayer, M.: Web history tools and revisitation support: A survey of existing approaches and directions. Foundations and Trends in HCI 2(3), 173–278 (2009)
15. Morris, D., Morris, M.R., Venolia, G.: Searchbar: a search-centric web history for task resumption and information re-finding. In: CHI (2008)
16. Soules, C.A.N., Ganger, G.R.: Connections: using context to enhance file search. In: SOSP (2005)
17. Teevan, J.: The re:search engine: simultaneous support for finding and re-finding. In: UIST (2007)
18. Won, S., Jin, J., Hong, J.: Contextual web history: using visual and contextual cues to improve web browser history. In: CHI, pp. 1457–1466 (2009)

Determining Personality Traits from Renren Status Usage Behavior

Shuotian Bai, Rui Gao, and Tingshao Zhu*

Institute of Psychology, University of Chinese Academy of Sciences, CAS,
Beijing 100101, China
{baishutian10,gaorui11}@mails.gucas.ac.cn, tszhu@psych.ac.cn

Abstract. Social Networks have developed so fast recently, and the most popular one in China is Renren, with 200 million members until 2012. In this study, we propose to determine personality traits based on Renren status usage behavior. Renren status is a short text published by the user like micro-blog and is available for all registered users. We extract behavior features from Renren status, and calculate the correlation between "Big Five" personality traits and the status usage. More than two hundred graduate students participated in our experiment. We get their authorizations to collect their status content using Renren APIs. Comparing to the classical self-reported personality analysis, we demonstrate via experimental studies that users' personalities have a significant correlation with status usage. Results show that some significant correlations exist between status content and personality type.

Keywords: Personality Traits, SNS Usage, RenRen Status.

1 Introduction

Social Networking Site (SNS) like Facebook and RenRen(http://www.renren.com) is a part of normal life nowadays. It is reported that China has 370 million registered SNS users in 2011. Currently, RenRen has the largest market share in China, with 200 million registered users (http://www.iresearch.cn/). A recent study on Facebook[6] investigated on the correlation between users' personal profile and personality. It tends to find out the correlation between personality traits and personal profiles.

Personality uniquely characterizes an individual, and profoundly influences his/her mental status as well as social behaviors[1]. The trait theory suggests that individual personalities are composed of broad dispositions[12] (e.g., Cattell's 16-PF). Currently the mostly influential one is the *Big-Five* theory[5], which proposes five basic traits that interact to form human personality. In Big-Five theory, personality is characterized by *agreeableness, conscientiousness, extraversion, neuroticism* and *openness* (e.g.[11]). Agreeableness refers to being helpful and cooperative; Conscientiousness is determined by being disciplined and

---

* Corresponding author.

S.-M. Hu and R.R. Martin (Eds.): CVM 2012, LNCS 7633, pp. 226–233, 2012.

achievement-oriented; Extraversion is displayed through a higher degree of sociability and talkativeness; Neuroticism refers to emotional stability and anxiety; Openness is reflected in a strong intellectual curiosity and novelty[5][4][13][14].

Some empirical studies reported that personality could be a major influencing variable toward web usage behaviors[8][9], including behaviors on SNSs[15][18]. Therefore, in this paper, we propose to find the correlations between users' status usage behavior with their personality traits.

RenRen status is short messages less than 240 words which published by users to share their attitudes, experiences or moods. The big amount of status have a strong link to their personality traits. There are also many mood compositions in status. Status publishing frequency and time distribution can be a hint of their preferences. This motivates us to do content analysis on status to help us identify the user's personality.

The rest of the paper is organized as following: Section 2 will talk about some related work by other researchers. Then we will show our experiment method and system in detail in Section 3. Section 4 mainly discusses the experiment results and some analysis corresponding with comparison between different dataset. Section 5 concludes our whole work with a discussion on future work.

2   Related Work

Much research work on SNS has been conducted, such as topological characteristics[19], web community mining[17] and psychology related topic[7].

Orr et al. found that shyness is significantly positively associated with the time online, and negatively correlated with the number of friends[18]. Meanwhile, Correa et al. [3] find that openness and extraversion is positively related with social media usage, while neuroticism associates negatively.

Gosling et al. [7] reported a mapping between personality and SNS online behaviors on personality with self-reported Facebook usage and observable profile information. However, their features are all based on statistical characteristics, instead of the psychological properties of user.

Chris Sumner et al. [2] find the correlations of users' Facebook posts activities and personality traits. They take not only the Facebook usage into account but also the posts content and emotion. They find that openness is significantly positively correlated with words to do with negative emotion and anger as well as traditionally taboo subjects of money, religion and death.

In short, previous SNS personality-related research mostly focus on English environment. These research investigate the SNS status usage instead of the status content. The status content contains users' attitudes, moods and preferences which may be correlated with personality traits. Facing these weakness, this study tries to design emotion-related, content-related and preference-related features and find out the correlations between status content and personality traits in the Chinese SNS environment.

3   Methods

We have developed an experimental platform *Dao*(http://dao.gucas.ac.cn) where participants can log in by his/her RenRen account, and complete the experiment online. 335 participants all over China with average age of 23.8 took part in this study during January and February of 2012. The participant is an active user, if he has more than 100 friends and at least 50 status published.

At the same time, participants need to complete the 44-question big five inventory. It providing measures of the five personality dimensions. The platform downloads RenRen status data and extracts 25 features shown in Tab.1. F is key number of each feature, symbol "-" denotes "negative" and "+" denotes "positive".

Table 1. Features description

F	Name	Description	No.	Name	Description
1	count	status number	2	zz	status republishing number
3	word	word number of status	4	expression	expr. number of status
5	expr1	1-word expr. number	6	exprover2	>2-word expr. number
7	sentence	sent. number of status	8	WPS	average word per sent.
9	Pstate	statements proportion(prop.)	10	Pexclm	exclamatory sent. prop.
11	Pques	interrogative sent. prop.	12	EWd	emotion word count
13	1sts	1st person singular	14	1stpl	1st person plural
15	2nds	2nd person singular	16	2ndpl	2nd person plural
17	3rds	3rd person singular	18	3rdpl	3rd person plural
19	num	numeral words count	20	PEW	+ emotion word number
21	NEW	- emotion word number	22	PEvW	+ evaluation word number
23	NEvW	- evaluation word number	24	AWN	advocating word number
25	FWN	frequency word number			

Some users are eliminated since they seldom publish status or just pure emoticon without any word. After checking qualification, 209 qualified participants (72 females and 137 males) left. The content of each participant's RenRen status is analyzed by using several dictionaries, including the extended lexicon of TongYiCi CiLin[10], the original TongYiCi CiLin[16], and HowNet (http://www.keenage.com/). We use six emotion dictionaries with more than one thousand four hundred key words in total. The whole work flow is depicted in Fig. 1.

4   Results

We aim to investigate whether users' RenRen status relates to his/her Big Five personality Agreeableness (A), Conscientiousness (C), Extraversion (E), Neuroticism (N) and Openness (O). In the following result tables, F is the feature number corresponds to Tab.1

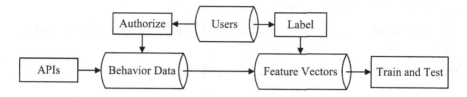

Fig. 1. Flow chart

4.1   Recent Status Analysis

The Pearson correlation is conducted on the Big Five personality traits and users status within one month (January 13th to February 13th, 2012). The results are shown in Tab. 2.

Table 2. Pearson correlation matrix of the Big Five personality and recent status

F	A	C	E	N	O	F	A	C	E	N	O
1	.0026	.0246	-.1525	.1477*	.0276	2	-.0002	.0644	.0228	.0141	-.0639
3	-.0152	.0540	-.1797*	.1747*	-.0151	4	-.0197	.0605	-.1938*	.1788*	-.0244
5	-.0081	.0480	-.1625*	.1624*	-.0053	6	-.0244	.0342	-.1579*	.1734*	-.0338
7	-.0083	.0221	-.1873*	.1780*	-.0095	8	.0565	.1129*	.1124*	-.0728	.0191
9	.0558	.0971	.0247	-.0400	.0564	10	.0478	.0207	.0325	.0243	.0903
11	.1324*	.0843	-.1031*	-.0300	.1249*	12	.0142	.0594	-.1477*	.1246*	.0176
13	.0003	.0063	-.1781*	.1826*	-.0034	14	-.0755	-.0291	-.1123*	.0925	.0475
15	-.0103	.0500	-.1001*	.1615*	-.0119	16	.0018	.0516	-.1774*	.0566	-.0387
17	-.0323	.0115	-.1039*	.1017*	-.0091	18	-.0204	.0117	-.1226*	.1110*	.0210
19	-.0187	.0047	-.1260*	.1604*	-.0042	20	-.0298	.0300	-.1545*	.1673*	-.0139
21	.0343	.0418	-.0929	.1246*	.0138	22	.0211	.0578	-.1200*	.1228*	-.0137
23	-.0175	.0409	-.1618*	.1602*	-.0288	24	.0144	.0652	-.1543*	.0921	.0100
25	-.0210	.0204	-.1260*	.1643*	-.0595						

In "recent" status, *Agreeableness* is positively correlated with the proportion of interrogative sentence ($r = .1324$). The more interrogative sentences, the more agreeable he is and the more friends he would like to make. *Conscientiousness* is positively correlated with words per sentence ($r = .1129$). It means that the more conscientious, the more likely he would write sentences with multiple words. He tend to use clauses rather than simple sentences. *Extraversion* is negatively correlated with words ($r = -.1797$) and sentences ($r = .1938$), suggesting that the more extravert, the less words in status($r = -.1525$). Extroversive people have a large extent of friends, and are unnecessary to spend much time online. Results of *Neuroticism* provides that the more neurotic, the more likely he will use emotion words ($r = .1246$) such as "happy". It positively associated with the status publishing ($r = .1477$), words ($r = .1744$) and sentence ($r = .1788$). He'd like to use "I" rather than "we"($r = .1826$). *Openness* is positively correlated with the proportion of interrogative sentence ($r = .1249$).

4.2   Complete-Status Analysis

We also compute Pearson correlations on the Big Five personality traits and the users' complete status shown in Tab. 3.

Table 3. Pearson correlation matrix of the Big Five personality and complete-status

F	A	C	E	N	O	F	A	C	E	N	O
1	.0787	.1043*	-.0527	.0906	.1494*	2	.0681	.0162	-.0674	.0103	.0438
3	.1180*	.0945	-.0835	.0980	.1409*	4	.1127*	.0890	-.0926	.0987	.1283*
5	.1240*	.0946	-.0605	.0956	.1600*	6	.0965	.0912	-.0442	.0778	.1782*
7	.0788	.1043*	-.1198*	.1496*	.1013*	8	.0134	.0606	.0755	-.0806	.1773*
9	-.1113*	-.0602	.0225	.0348	.0375	10	.0965	-.0307	.0038	.0273	-.0359
11	.0702	.1030*	-.0515	-.0047	.1732*	12	.1495*	.1066*	-.0740	.0957	.1351*
13	.1630*	.0950	-.1091*	.0653	.0682	14	.1092*	.0790	-.0759	.1270*	.1629*
15	.0948	.1056*	-.1383*	.1320*	.0932	16	.1207*	.1014*	-.1365*	.0868	.1287*
17	.1258*	.0814	-.1069*	.0881	.1581*	18	.0303	.0377	.0099	.1344*	.1693*
19	.1032*	.0708	-.1063*	.0766	.1411*	20	.1330*	.1278*	-.0894	.1049*	.1118*
21	.1136*	.0769	-.0601	.0833	.1589*	22	.1420*	.0977	-.0615	.0894	.1586*
23	.1152*	.0832	-.0654	.0884	.1435*	24	.1751*	.1508*	-.0453	.0493	.1058*
25	.1147*	.1193*	-.0733	.1041*	.1069*						

Agreeableness is positively correlated with emotion word count ($r = .1495$), 1st person singular ($r = .1630$) and advocating word number ($r = .1751$). This suggests that the more emotion word the more agreeable. Agreeable people prefer "I" to "we" and they tend to use more advocating words showing that they like to advocate activities. *Conscientiousness* is positively correlated with positive emotion word number ($r = .1278$), advocating word number ($r = .1508$) and frequency word number ($r = .1193$), meaning that the more conscientious, the more likely he would use optimistic words and advocate activities. *Extraversion* is negatively correlated with sentence count of status ($r = -.1198$), 2nd person singular ($r = -.1383$) and 2nd person plural ($r = -.1365$), suggesting that the more extravert, the less sentences in his status. People with high extraversion do not use "you" quite often. *Neuroticism* is positively correlated with the sentence count of status ($r = .1496$), 1st person plural ($r = .1270$) and 2nd person singular ($r = .1320$), providing that the more neurotic, the more likely he publishes more sentences in status. They tend to use "we" and "you" when talking to others. *Openness* is positively correlated with 2-word or more expression number ($r = .1782$), average word per sentence ($r = .1773$) and 3rd person plural ($r = .1693$). People with high openness will use longer expressions in their sentences and have a high proportion in average word per sentence. They tend to use "they" or "their" in status.

4.3   Comparison

To identify whether complete-status dataset differs from recent status on the correlation, we compare the differences of their Pearson correlations with Big-Five traits, and the result is in Tab. 4. From the table, we find that most correlation coefficients change a lot (> 0.05). It means that the correlations rise when experiment personality traits on complete status than that of "recent" ones. Intuitively, personality is stable with respect of time and has little change with time passing by. It might suggest that we run experiment on the dataset that consists of user behavior as much as possible.

Table 4. Differences of Pearson correlations between complete and recent status

F	A	C	E	N	O	F	A	C	E	N	O
1	0.08 ↑	0.08 ↑	0.10 ↑	−0.06 ↓	0.12 ↑	2	0.07 ↑	-0.05−	-0.09 ↓	-0.00−	0.11 ↑
3	0.13 ↑	0.04−	0.10 ↑	-0.08 ↓	0.16 ↑	4	0.13 ↑	0.03−	0.10 ↑	-0.08 ↓	0.15 ↑
5	0.13 ↑	0.05−	0.10 ↑	-0.07 ↓	0.17 ↑	6	0.12 ↑	0.06 ↑	0.11 ↑	-0.10 ↓	0.21 ↑
7	0.09 ↑	0.08 ↑	0.07 ↑	-0.03−	0.11 ↑	8	-0.04−	-0.05−	-0.04−	-0.01−	0.16 ↑
9	-0.17 ↓	-0.16 ↓	-0.00−	0.07 ↑	-0.02−	10	0.05−	-0.05−	-0.03−	0.00−	-0.13 ↓
11	-0.06 ↓	0.02−	0.05−	0.03−	0.05−	12	0.14 ↑	0.05−	0.07 ↑	-0.03−	0.12 ↑
13	0.16 ↑	0.09 ↑	0.07 ↑	-0.12 ↓	0.07 ↑	14	0.19 ↑	0.11 ↑	0.04−	0.03−	0.12 ↑
15	0.11 ↑	0.06 ↑	-0.04−	-0.03−	0.11 ↑	16	0.12 ↑	0.05−	0.04−	0.03−	0.17 ↑
17	0.16 ↑	0.07 ↑	-0.00−	-0.01−	0.17 ↑	18	0.05−	0.03−	0.13 ↑	0.02−	0.15 ↑
19	0.12 ↑	0.07 ↑	0.02−	-0.08 ↓	0.15 ↑	20	0.16 ↑	0.10 ↑	0.07 ↑	-0.06 ↓	0.13 ↑
21	0.08 ↑	0.04−	0.03−	-0.04−	0.15 ↑	22	0.12 ↑	0.04−	0.06 ↑	-0.03−	0.17 ↑
23	0.13 ↑	0.04−	0.10 ↑	-0.07 ↓	0.17 ↑	24	0.16 ↑	0.09 ↑	0.11 ↑	-0.04−	0.10 ↑
25	0.14 ↑	0.10 ↑	0.05−	-0.06 ↑	0.17 ↑						

4.4 Discussion

We combine "recent" and "complete" tables together in Tab. 5. For each feature over each personality dimension, if the absolute value of correlation is great than 0.1 (greater then 0.1 or smaller then -0.1), we mark it '+' and put them as "recent"/"complete" respectively. The correlation marks are shown in Tab. 5.

"+/+" Features From Tab.5, we find a few double '+/+' features. These features show a relatively greater correlation with personality traits. Extraversion has a significant correlation with sentence count, 1st person singular, 2nd

Table 5. Correlations on recent and complete status

F	A	C	E	N	O	F	A	C	E	N	O	F	A	C	E	N	O
1		/+	+/	+/	/+	2						3	/+		+/	+/	/+
4	/+		+/	+/	/+	5	/+		+/	+/	/+	6			+/	+/	/+
7		/+	+/+	+/+	/+	8		+/	+/		/+	9	/+				
10						11	+/	/+	+/		+/+	12	/+	/+	+/	+/	/+
13	/+		+/+	+/		14	/+		+/	/+	/+	15		/+	+/+	+/+	
16	/+	/+	+/+		/+	17	/+		+/+	+/	/+	18			+/	+/+	/+
19	/+		+/+	+/	/+	20	/+	/+	+/	+/+	/+	21	/+			+/	/+
22	/+		+/	+/	/+	23	/+		+/	+/	/+	24	/+	/+	+/		/+
25	/+	/+	+/	+/+	/+												

person, 3rd person singular and the number of numeral words. Neuroticism is significantly correlated with sentence count, 2nd person singular, 3rd person plural, positive emotion word and frequency word usage. People with high score in neuroticism like to use positive emotional words and frequency words("happy", "never"). Openness is significantly correlated with the interrogative sentences proportion.

" /+" Features   Some ' /+' labeled features will make better sense in the long run, and have a higher correlation with personality over a long period. For agreeableness, word and expression count, statement proportion, 1st person, 2nd person plural, 3rd person singular and emotion, evaluation advocating and frequency usage make more correlation in long period. For conscientiousness, status and sentence count, 2nd person, positive emotion count, advocating and frequency word count will get more correlated with personality with time passing by. For openness, status, word, expression and sentence count, 1st and 2nd person plural, emotion, numeral, advocating and frequency word count show more correlation with personality in long time period, meaning that open people publishes more status in long time period than in short time.

"+/ " Features   There are some '+/ ' features correlated with personality in recent period. Recent interrogative sentence proportion is significantly related with agreeableness. The agreeable person may use more interrogative sentences. Conscientious person may have a high average word per sentence. Their status will contain more long sentences. Extroverts publish more status and interrogative sentences. They use more "we/they", more emotional words and advocating words. People with high score in neuroticism also tend to publish more status, but they tend to use "I/he/she" instead of "we/they".

5   Conclusions and Future Work

This study finds the correlation between RenRen status usage and personality traits. In the long time, agreeableness relates to interrogative sentence count; conscientiousness has significantly positive correlation with the advocating word number; extraversion has significantly negative correlation with 2nd person singular usages; neuroticism has significantly positive correlation with the sentence count, 1st person singular usage and openness has a positive correlation with positive evaluation word number. These results help us conduct further research. Some features correlate with personality in short period, while others prefer to status over a long period. In the future, we can design more suitable features in both "recent" and "long-time" aspects. With these strongly personality-related features, an application that predicts users' personality will be developed.

Acknowledgments. The authors gratefully acknowledges the generous support from NSFC (61070115), Institute of Psychology(113000C037), Strategic Priority Research Program (XDA06030800) and 100-Talent Project(Y2CX093006) from Chinese Academy of Sciences.

References

1. Burger, J.: Personality, 7th edn. Thomson Wadsworth, Belmont (2008)
2. Chris Sumner, M.S., Byers, A.: Determining personality traits and privacy concerns from facebook activity. Black Hat Briefings 11 (2011)
3. Correa, T., Hinsley, A., Ziga, H.: Who interacts on the web? the intersection of users personality and social media use. CMB 26(2), 247–253 (2010)
4. Costa, P., McCrae, R.: Four ways five factors are basic. PID 13, 653–665 (1992)
5. Funder, D.C.: Personality. Annu. Rev. Psychol. 52, 197–221 (2001)
6. Golbeck, J., Robles, C., Turner, K.: Prediciting personality with social media. In: Proceedings of the 2011 Annual Conference Extended Abstracts on Human Factors in Computing Systems, pp. 253–262. ACM (2011)
7. Gosling, S., Augustine, A., Vazire, S., Holtzman, N., Gaddis, S.: Manifestations of personality in online social networks: Self-reported facebook related behaviors and observable profile information. CBSN 14(9), 483–488 (2011)
8. Hamburger, Y.A.: Internet and personality. CHB 18, 1–10 (2002)
9. Hamburger, Y.A., Artzi, E.B.: The relationship between extraversion and neuroticism and the different uses of the internet. CHB 16, 441–449 (2000)
10. HIT-IRLab. Extended tongyici cilin, http://ir.hit.edu.cn/demo/ltp/Sharing_Plan.html
11. Matthews, G., Deary, I., Whiteman, M.: Personality Traits. Cambridge University Press (2006)
12. McAdams, D., Olson, B.: Personality development: Continuity and change over the life course. ARP 61, 517–542 (2010)
13. McCrae, R., Costa, P.: An introduction to the five factor model and its applications. JP 60, 175–215 (1992)
14. McCrae, R., Costa, P.: Toward a new generation of personality theories: Theoretical contexts for the five factor model. In: The Five Factor Model of Personality: Theoretical Perspectives, pp. 51–87 (1996)
15. Mehdizadeh, S.: Self-presentation 2.0: Narcissism and self-esteem on facebook. CBSN 13, 357–364 (2010)
16. Mei, J., Zhu, Y., Gao, Y., Yin, H.: TongYiCi CiLin. Shanghai CiShu Press (1996)
17. Mucha, P., Richardson, T., Macon, K., Porter, M., Onnela, J.: Community structure in time-dependent, multiscale, and multiplex network. Science 328(5980), 876–878 (2010)
18. Orr, E., Sisic, M., Ross, C., Simmering, M., Arseneault, J., Orr, R.: The influence of shyness on the use of facebook in an undergraduate sample. CB 12(3), 337–340 (2009)
19. Yong-Yeol, A., Han, S., Kwak, H., Moon, S., Jeong, H.: Analysis of topological characteristics of huge online social networking services. In: WWW 2007: Proceedings of the 16th International Conference on WWW, pp. 835–844 (2007)

A Memory-Efficient KinectFusion Using Octree

Ming Zeng, Fukai Zhao, Jiaxiang Zheng, and Xinguo Liu*

State Key Lab of CAD&CG, Zhejiang University, Hangzhou, China, 310058
mingzeng85@gmail.com, xgliu@cad.zju.edu.cn

Abstract. KinectFusion is a real time 3D reconstruction system based on a low-cost moving depth camera and commodity graphics hardware. It represents the reconstructed surface as a signed distance function, and stores it in uniform volumetric grids. Though the uniform grid representation has advantages for parallel computation on GPU, it requires a huge amount of GPU memory. This paper presents a memory-efficient implementation of KinectFusion. The basic idea is to design an octree-based data structure on GPU, and store the signed distance function on data nodes. Based on the octree structure, we redesign reconstruction update and surface prediction to highly utilize parallelism of GPU. In the reconstruction update step, we first perform "add nodes" operations in a level-order manner, and then update the signed distance function. In the surface prediction step, we adopt a top-down ray tracing method to estimate the surface of the scene. In our experiments, our method costs less than 10% memory of KinectFusion while still being fast. Consequently, our method can reconstruct scenes 8 times larger than the original KinectFusion on the same hardware setup.

Keywords: Octree, GPU, KinectFusion, 3D Reconstruction.

1 Introduction

3D reconstruction for real scenes is an important research area in computer vision and computer graphics. For decades, researchers have developed all kinds of methods for efficient and accurate reconstruction. One popular method reconstructs scenes by fusing depth maps from different views. Especially, Newcombe et al. [9] and Izadi et al. [6] proposed KinectFusion, which used a commodity depth camera Kinect[8] to scan and model the dense surface of a room-size (about $4m \times 4m \times 4m$) scene in realtime. The algorithm leverages the parallel computing ability of the modern GPU to track the pose of the Kinect, and fuses the depth map of each frame into a scene volume.

KinectFusion uses a uniformly divided volume, and stores the data of all voxels in this volume. In a real scene, however, large amount of space is not occupied by the object's surface, therefore KinectFusion greatly wastes GPU memory, which hinders scene reconstruction in larger scale. To solve the problem, we introduce an octree structure to efficiently store the scene data. Based on the octree, we propose an algorithm to maintain the octree and integrate depth maps online. Our method sufficiently exploits the hierarchical structure of the octree and GPU parallelism. We adopt different

---

* Corresponding author.

S.-M. Hu and R.R. Martin (Eds.): CVM 2012, LNCS 7633, pp. 234–241, 2012.
© Springer-Verlag Berlin Heidelberg 2012

traversal manners in our method to update and trace the octree to achieve optimized performance. When updating the volume, we traverse the octree in a level-order manner to exploit GPU parallelism. When predicting the scene surface, we traverse the octree in a top-down way to skip large non-data spaces. Benefit from careful designs, our method performs better than KinectFusion both in memory and computational efficiency.

2 Related Work

This section introduces the related works on 3D reconstruction and octree construction on GPU. We only survey works most relevant to this paper.

3D Reconstruction. 3D reconstruction techniques capture scene information by RGB cameras or depth cameras, and then reconstruct the geometry of the scene.

Lots of researchers capture RGB images of a scene, then utilize structure from motion (SFM) and multi-view stereo (MVS) to locate cameras and recover a sparse point cloud of the scene [2,11]. This kind of method is time consuming and unable to obtain dense scene surface. Recently, some studies used RGB sequence to reconstruct the dense surface [12,13,10] of a small scene (about $1m \times 1m \times 1m$) in real time.

Depth cameras are able to capture a depth map of current scene on each frame. Leveraging this ability, we can align depth maps to form the whole scene surface. The most popular method for this task is Iterative Closest Point (ICP)[1]. It was widely used to register views of depth maps into a global coordinate. With ICP, the KinectFusion proposed by Newcombe et al. [9] and Izadi et al. [6] leverages depth camera and GPU to reconstruct a dense surface of a room-size (about $4m \times 4m \times 4m$) scene in real time. Based on the KinectFusion, Whelan et al. [15] proposed a system "Kintinuous" which supports modeling on unbounded regions by shifting volume and extracting meshes continuously. This system utilized KinectFusion as a building block, and extended the ability to support large scale scanning. In contrast to [15], our method improves the core parts of the KinectFusion, and it can be a building block of large scale scanning systems like Kintinuous.

Octree Construction on GPU. An octree adaptively splits the space of the scene according to the complexity of the scene to use memory efficiently [3]. Though the simplicity of its definition, it is hard to be maintained using parallelism feature of GPU due to the sparseness of its nodes [16]. Sun et al. [14] built an octree with only leaf nodes to store volume data and accelerated photon tracing based on the octree. Zhou et al. [16] constructed a whole octree structure on GPU to accelerate Poisson Reconstruction [7].

3 Overview

The overviews of KinectFusion and our method are shown in Figure 1 left. The Kinect-Fusion contains four main stages: Surface Measurement, Camera Pose Estimation, Reconstruction Update, and Surface Prediction (see [9,6]). In our method, we adopt the similar flowchart of KinectFusion. However, to overcome the large memory consumption due to the uniform voxel in KinectFusion, we introduce an octree structure to compactly organize the scene data in our method. Based on the octree, we design new algorithms for **Reconstruction Update** and **Surface Prediction** to utilize GPU parallelism.

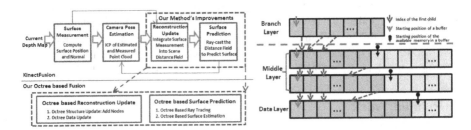

Fig. 1. Overview and Data Structure of our method. Left: overview of KinectFusion and improvements of our method. The red dash rectangle indicates the improved parts. Right: illustration of the octree structure.

In the following sections, we first introduce the octree structure in Section 4, followed by Reconstruction Update and Surface Prediction. In Section 7, we describe implementation details and experimental results, after which we give the conclusion.

4   Octree Structure

Our octree structure is stored in arrays of different layers. One array corresponds to one layer of the octree. As illustrated in Figure 1 right, there are three kinds of layers in our octree structure: Branch Layer, Middle Layer and Data Layer. All possible nodes in the branch layer are allocated, and can be randomly accessed. Nodes of other layers are not fully allocated, which can only be visited by links between adjacent layers.

- **Branch Layer:** The branch layer contains all nodes in its layer. Each node of the branch layer stores the index $idChild$ of the first child. If the node doesn't have children nodes, $idChild$ is set to -1.
- **Middle Layer:** Nodes in middle layers record both $idChild$ and **shuffled** xyz **key** [16]. The shuffled xyz key of a node at depth D is defined as a bit string: $x_1y_1z_1x_2y_2z_2...x_Dy_Dz_D$, where each 3-bit code $x_iy_iz_i$ encodes one of the eight subregions at depth i. $idChild$ can be used to traverse an octree in the depth-first manner, while shuffled xyz key can be utilized for the level-order traversal.
- **Data Layer:** Each node in this layer stores its shuffled xyz key and data of the scene [9,6]: Signed Distance Field SDF and weight w.

In the data structure, the branch layer is the starting layer, and it is not necessarily the root layer. We use a symbol $OT(T, L)$ to represent an octree with a branch layer at depth T, and data layer at depth L. Accordingly, $OF(T, L)$ represents our algorithm based on $OT(T, L)$. We also denote our algorithm with a n-depth octree as OFn. To represent the octree structure, we use following arrays to organize above data:

- $NodeBuf$ is a pre-allocated two-dimensional array to store nodes of each level. The ith node at level L is stored in $NodeBuf[L][i]$.
- $IdStart$ is a pre-allocated one-dimensional array to record the current starting index of the available buffer of each level, as black arrows shown in right of Figure 1. The current starting index of level L is recorded in $IdStart[L]$.

Algorithm 1. Add Nodes for the Octree at Level L

1: //Step1: Predict whether a node needs further split	16: //Step 2: Scan the split flag array
2: **for** Node O_i at Level L in parallel **do**	17: $(ScanOut, nNewNodeCount) \leftarrow$ **Scan**$(ScanIn, +)$
3: **if** O_i in view frustum	
4: $v_g \leftarrow$ **PosFromNode**(O_i, L)	18: //Step 3: Assign child index and compute xyz key
5: $v \leftarrow$ **WorldCoord2CamCoord**(v_g)	19: **for** O_i at level L in parallel
6: $p \leftarrow$ perspective project vertex v	20: **if** $ScanIn[i] == 1$
7: $dir \leftarrow v_g - v_{cam}$	21: $idx = IdStart[L+1] + (ScanOut[i] << 3)$
8: $sdf =\parallel v_{cam} - v_g \parallel -D(p, dir)$	22: $NodeBuf[L][i].idChild = idx$
9: **if IsSplit**(O_i, sdf) and O_i has no child	23: $key = O_i.xyzkey$
10: $ScanIn[i] = 1$	24: **for** k=0 to 7 **do**
11: **else**	25: $NodeBuf[L+1][idx + k].xyzkey = (key << 3) \mid k$
12: $ScanIn[i] = 0$	26: **end for**
13: **endif**	27: **end if**
14: **endif**	28: **end for**
15: **end for**	
	29: //Step 4: Update $IdStart$
	30: $IdStart[L+1] += 8 * nNewNodeCount$

5 Reconstruction Update Based on Octree

There are two operations in the step of reconstruction update: add nodes for new scene data, and SDF data update.

5.1 Add Nodes for Octree

To add new nodes for the octree, we adopt a top-down level-order manner to traverse the octree. We split nodes and assign children indices level by level, starting from the branch layer and moving towards the data layer, one level at a time. For level L, the pseudo code of the procedure is listed in Algorithm 1.

At the first step, we predict whether a node needs further split in parallel. For the node in the view frustum, we calculate the signed distance sdf from its center to the current depth map (Line 4 to 8). Then, given sdf, we use the function **IsSplit** (described later) to predict node splits and mark 1/0 in an auxiliary array $ScanIn$. At step 2, we take Parallel Prefix Sum (**Scan**) [5] with the add operation " $+$ " on $ScanIn$ to compute the unique id of new split nodes. At step 3, we assign index of its first child to the node to be split. At this step, we also figure out and store the shuffled xyz key of each new child node according to the shuffled xyz key of its parent node and its relative position in all eight children. Finally at step 4, we update the index of the first available node in the memory pool of the child layer.

In the function **IsSplit**, we assume the scene near the node is approximately a plane. We denote distance between center of the node and scene surface as sdf, diagonal length of the node as d, then distances from all points within the node to the surface must be in $[sdf - d/2, sdf + d/2]$. Take the further consideration that the distance field stored in scene volume is in $[-U, U]$, U is the maximal truncation value. To ensure a correct split prediction, the node split iff $[sdf - d/2, sdf + d/2]$ intersects with $[-U, U]$, i.e. $sdf \in [-U - d/2, U + d/2]$.

5.2 Update SDF for Octree

After updating the structure of the octree, the current depth map should be integrated into the scene volume to update signed distance function. We only need to update the

---

Algorithm 2 Surface Prediction

1: **for** each pixel u in imaging plane in parallel **do**	18: //estimate position and normal
2: $Ray_{dir} \leftarrow$ direction of the ray	19: **if** $l ==$ level of the finest layer **then**
3: $g \leftarrow$ first voxel along ray dir in the finest level	20: **if** zero crossing from g_{prev} to g **then**
4: $Ray_{step} \leftarrow 0$	21: $P \leftarrow$ estimate surface position
5: **while** voxel g within volume bounds **do**	22: $N \leftarrow$ estimate surface normal
6: //determine the marching step	23: **break**
7: $xyzkey \leftarrow$ **Grid2Key**(g)	24: **end if**
8: $l \leftarrow$ level of the branch layer	25: **end if**
9: $node \leftarrow$ **Key2Node**$(xyzkey, l, NodeBuf, null)$	26: **end while**
10: **while** $node$ has children **do**	27: **end for**
11: $l++$	
12: $node\leftarrow$**Key2Node**$(xyzkey, l, NodeBuf, node)$	
13: **end while**	
14: $Ray_{step} \leftarrow$ **NextStepLen**$(g, Ray_{dir}, node)$	
15: //march forward	
16: $g_{prev} \leftarrow g$	
17: $g+ = Ray_{dir} \cdot Ray_{step}$	

---

nodes at the data layer to integrate the depth map. We adopt the similar integration algorithm as the method in [6] except that we compute positions of data nodes from shuffled xyz code while [6] directly compute them from their grid indices.

6   Surface Prediction Based on Octree

After structure and data update of the octree, like [9,6], a ray tracer is taken to ray-cast the scene volume and estimate the scene surface. Algorithm 2 lists the pseudo code. Each ray marches forward until crossing the object's surface. Line 6 to 14 determine the current amount of finest steps to march forward. In Line 7, **Grid2Key** figures out the $xyzkey$. Then in Line 8 to 13, with $xyzkey$, we adopt a top-down way to find the most compact octree node holding the position g. The most compact node for g means no surface data is in the node, so the ray can "bravely" marches across this most compact node. So in Line 14, we compute the marching step according to the depth (level) of the most compact node by the function **NextStepLen**. After marching forward, if the ray crosses surface, we estimate the position and normal of the hitting points between the ray and the object's surface.

The position and normal of the intersection point are estimated in a trilinear interpolation way [9,6]. Normals of points around two sides of the zero-crossing surface can be calculated by forward/backward differences according to the relative position of the node of its siblings.

7   Implementation and Experiments

7.1   Implementation Details

We have implemented the whole pipeline of our algorithm in C++ with Nvidia CUDA, and test it on a desktop computer with an Intel Core2 Duo E7400 2.80GH CPU (use one core) and a Nvidia GeForce GTX480 graphics card. For the operator **Scan**, we used the implementation provided in the highly optimized GPU library CUDPP [4].

All data data structures are stored in the global memory. For a layer at depth D of an $OT(T, L)$, the node count N of the GPU memory buffer is as follows:

$$N = \begin{cases} 2^{3D}, & D \leq T \\ \mu \cdot 2^{3D}, & D > T \end{cases} \qquad (1)$$

where μ is proportion to all possible nodes at its depth. In our current implementation, μ is set to 0.05 for depth no deeper than 9, and 0.03 for depth 10.

7.2   Experiments

This section compares our method with KinectFusion from three aspects: memory consumption, computation time, and reconstruction for large scene.

Memory Comparison. We compare memory consumption between KinectFusion and our method on a depth map sequence "chairs" (Figure 2). For KinectFusion, we adopt the 512^3 resolution (KF512), and for our method, we test both 9-depth (OF9) and 10-depth octree (OF10). In this experiment, branch layers of both OF9 and OF10 are set at depth 7. Figure 2 middle shows the memory consumptions on each frame of "chairs" with KF512, OF9, and OF10. KF512 cost 512 MB memory constantly, while OF9 and OF10 increase the memory as the camera scans new parts of the scene. At the beginning, OF9 and OF10 pre-allocate 81.6MB and 362.6MB, respectively. Finally, OF9 uses 55.6M, and OF10 uses 227.4MB. With 512^3 resolution, memory consumption of OF9 is $81.6/512 \approx 15.9\%$ of KF512. With 1024^3 resolution, KinectFusion will consume 4GB GPU memory, which is ≥ 10 times larger than that of our method. Figure 2 right gives details of memory consumption of each layer.

Time Comparison. We show time comparisons on a test scene in Figure 3, where OF(7, 9) processes a frame in about 19ms, and OF(7, 10) processes a frame less than 25ms. They are both faster than KF512. OF(7, 9) gains about $2\times$ speed up on the improved parts than KF512. This is because KF512 needs to update its all 512^3 voxels, while our method only updates existing nodes, and it can skip large spaces on the ray-cast stage.

Large Scale Scene. Our octree based method efficiently uses memory, and OF10 can reach a maximal 1024^3 resolution, which is able to robustly track the camera in a large scale scene and reconstruct it. We scan an office in a $8m \times 8m \times 8m$ bounding box using OF10, which captures about 3800 frames of depth maps. The scene data costs 299MB in 363MB pre-allocated GPU memory, and the extracted mesh from the scene volume contains 6200K triangle faces and 3400K vertices. As shown in Figure 4, though the size of the scene is large, the reconstructed model still possesses abundant details.

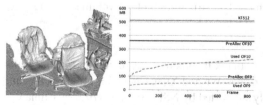

OF9	D=7	D=8	D=9	Aux	Total
PreAlloc	8.0	6.4	51.2	16.0	81.6
Used	8.0	4.0	27.6	16.0	55.6

OF10	D=7	D=8	D=9	D=10	Aux	Total
PreAlloc	8.0	6.4	51.2	245.8	51.2	362.6
Used	8.0	3.0	19.8	145.4	51.2	227.4

Fig. 2. Memory comparison of a static scene "chairs"

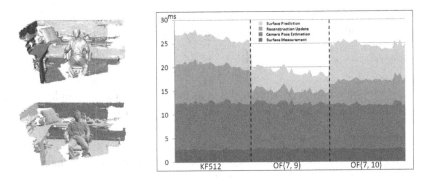

Fig. 3. Processing time for a test scene. Left are the Phong-shaded rendering and the normal map of the test scene, respectively. Right is the processing time on each stage of different methods.

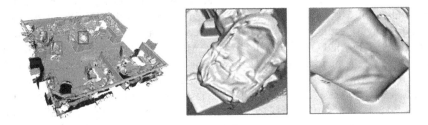

Fig. 4. Reconstruction result of a large scene and two zoom-in parts

8   Conclusion and Future Work

We propose an octree based KinectFusion. Our method represents the scene data in an octree structure, and maintains this octree by "add node" operations according to changes of the scene. We also modify KinectFusion to adapt the octree representation to highly utilize parallelism computation ability of GPU. Experiments show that our method costs only about 10% memory of original KinectFusion and runs about 2× faster than original KinectFusion on the improvement parts. Our method can reconstruct 3D scenes 8 times larger than that of KinectFusion.

The system can be extended in several ways. One is to design a more efficient memory management solution to replace current pre-allocation method. Another possible improvement may come from the combination of our method and Kintinuous [15]. A straightforward way is to use our method as a building block in Kintinuous, which may also involve some modifications both on data structures and the volume shifting algorithm of Kintinuous.

Acknowledgments. We would like to thank the anonymous reviewers for their valuable comments, and thank Bo Jiang, Zizhao Wu and Xuan Cheng for proof reading and video editing. This work was partially supported by NSFC (No. 60970074), China 973 Program (No. 2009CB320801), Fok Ying Tung Education Foundation and the Fundamental Research Funds for the Central Universities.

References

1. Chen, Y., Medioni, G.: Object modeling by registration of multiple range images. Image and Vision Computing (IVC) 10(3), 145–155 (1992)
2. Fitzgibbon, A.W., Zisserman, A.: Automatic Camera Recovery for Closed or Open Image Sequences. In: Burkhardt, H.-J., Neumann, B. (eds.) ECCV 1998. LNCS, vol. 1406, pp. 311–326. Springer, Heidelberg (1998)
3. Frisken, S.F., Perry, R.N., Rockwood, A.P., Jones, T.R.: Adaptively sampled distance fields: a general representation of shape for computer graphics. In: Proceedings of the 27th Annual Conference on Computer Graphics and Interactive Techniques, SIGGRAPH 2000, pp. 249–254. ACM Press/Addison-Wesley Publishing Co., New York (2000)
4. Harris, M., Owens, J.D., Sengupta, S., Zhang, Y., Davidson, A.: Cudpp homepage (2007), http://gpgpu.org/developer/cudpp
5. Harris, M., Sengupta, S., Owens, J.D.: Parallel prefix sum (scan) with CUDA, ch. 39. Addison Wesley (August 2007)
6. Izadi, S., Kim, D., Hilliges, O., Molyneaux, D., Newcombe, R., Kohli, P., Shotton, J., Hodges, S., Freeman, D., Davison, A., Fitzgibbon, A.: Kinectfusion: real-time 3d reconstruction and interaction using a moving depth camera. In: Proceedings of the 24th Annual ACM Symposium on user Interface Software and Technology, UIST 2011, pp. 559–568. ACM, New York (2011)
7. Michael, K., Matthew, B., Hugues, H.: Poisson surface reconstruction. In: Proceedings of the Fourth Eurographics Symposium on Geometry Processing, SGP 2006, pp. 61–70. Eurographics Association, Aire-la-Ville (2006)
8. Microsoft. Microsoft kinect project (2010), http://www.xbox.com/kinect
9. Newcombe, R.A., Izadi, S., Hilliges, O., Molyneaux, D., Kim, D., Davison, A.J., Kohli, P., Shotton, J., Hodges, S., Fitzgibbon, A.: Kinectfusion: Real-time dense surface mapping and tracking. In: Procedings of IEEE/ACM International Symposium on Mixed and Augmented Reality, pp. 127–136 (2011)
10. Newcombe, R.A., Lovegrove, S., Davison, A.J.: Dtam: Dense tracking and mapping in real-time. In: International Conference on Computer Vision, pp. 2320–2327 (2011)
11. Pollefeys, M., Gool, L.V., Vergauwen, M., Verbiest, F., Cornelis, K., Tops, J., Koch, R.: Visual modeling with a hand-held camera. International Journal of Computer Vision 59(3), 207–232 (2004)
12. Richard, A.J.D., Newcombe, A.: Live dense reconstruction with a single moving camera. In: IEEE Computer Society Conference on Computer Vision and Pattern Recognition (CVPR), pp. 1498–1505 (June 2010)
13. Stühmer, J., Gumhold, S., Cremers, D.: Real-Time Dense Geometry from a Handheld Camera. In: Goesele, M., Roth, S., Kuijper, A., Schiele, B., Schindler, K. (eds.) DAGM 2010. LNCS, vol. 6376, pp. 11–20. Springer, Heidelberg (2010)
14. Sun, X., Zhou, K., Stollnitz, E., Shi, J., Guo, B.: Interactive relighting of dynamic refractive objects. ACM Trans. Graph. 27(3), 35:1–35:9 (2008)
15. Whelan, T., McDonald, J., Kaess, M., Fallon, M., Johannsson, H., Leonard, J.J.: Kintinuous: Spatially extended kinectfusion. In: RSS Workshop on RGB-D: Advanced Reasoning with Depth Cameras (July 2012)
16. Zhou, K., Gong, M., Huang, X., Guo, B.: Data-parallel octrees for surface reconstruction. IEEE Transactions on Visualization and Computer Graphics (TVCG) 17(5), 669–681 (2011)

Vision-Based Measurement of Air Temperature Using Smoke as Medium

Zhi-Xin Zhao[1], Wen-Shu Xiang[1], Hedetomo Sakaino[2], and Yun-Cai Liu[1]

[1] School of Electronic Information and Electrical Engineer
Shanghai Jiao Tong University, Shanghai, China
{gbtysd,xiangwenshu}@gmail.com, whomliu@sjtu.edu.cn
[2] Nippon Telegraph and Telephone Corporation
s.hidetomo@lab.ntt.co.jp

Abstract. The near zone of heat diffusing machines in an equipment room is very critical for the normal functioning of the machines. Current knowledge about the near zone of heat diffusing machine is insufficient, causing an increasing need for better measuring methods and representation of the air temperature distribution.

We proposed a vision-based measuring technique for visualization of air temperatures and air flow patterns over a large area. As a medium, smoke is generated in the near zone of heat diffusing machine to make the air flow visible. A specialized capturing technique is used to record density distribution of the time-varying smoke. We place a few temperature sensors sparsely over the volume and combine the outputs of the temperature sensors and density information of the smoke to measure the temperature distribute in the space. Experiments validate the effectiveness of the proposed method.

Keywords: Computer graphics, Vision geometry, Air temperature measurement, Smoke density.

1   Introduction and Previous Works

The aim of this work is to make the air temperature visible. It is very time consuming and impractical with traditional techniques to measure air temperatures over large areas in a ventilated room and it yields insufficient information with low resolution. It takes either many sensors or transfer of single sensor to cover the temperature distribution over a large area. Measuring instruments also bring disturbance to the region.

To overcome the problems and limitation with traditional techniques, some new techniques have been developed. Wen-Yuan Tsai et al. [1] come up with an ultrasonic air temperature measurement system which can measure the average temperature of the environmental air by detecting the changes of the speed of the ultrasound in the air. A.Minamide et al. [2] proposed an acoustic computerized tomography methods based on Radon transform to measure temperature distribution in rectangular space. But these methods based on ultrasonic wave usually require precision instruments and complex installation. M.Cehlin et al. [3] developed a vision-based measurement system which needs relatively simple installation, but the system introduces considerable disturbance to the region and the measurement is limited to 2-D plane instead of 3-D volume.

S.-M. Hu and R.R. Martin (Eds.): CVM 2012, LNCS 7633, pp. 242–249, 2012.
© Springer-Verlag Berlin Heidelberg 2012

We proposed a new measuring technique based on smoke medium, making it possible to measure air temperature distribution over a large volume continuously without bringing much disturbance to the volume. Our method use smoke as medium to visualize the air flow and temperature distribution. We generate smoke near the air outlet of the heat diffusing machine. Cooling and ventilation system creates specific types of air flow which carries heat and smoke around. So the smoke will spread in the same direction as the air flow transmits which provides useful information for determining the temperature distribution. We place a few temperature sensors sparsely over the volume and combine the outputs of the temperature sensors and density information of the smoke to measure the temperature distribute in the space.

Fig. 1 gives an overview of the system which contains one color CCD camera, one smoke generator, one air heater, one 8-chanal thermograph and two arrays of laser sources, one red and the other blue.

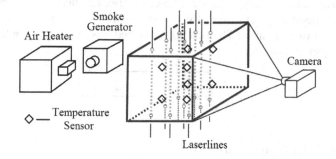

Fig. 1. The whole setup of the system. Symbol $\Diamond$ stands for temperature sensors which are fixed sparsely in the volume.

2   Basic Theory of the Method

In this section we first discuss a novel approach to capture the volumetric density of smoke proposed by Christian Fuchs et al. [4]. (In practice we applied some improvement upon it.) We then describe our assumptive model which approximates the corresponding pattern between smoke density field and temperature field and analyze the air flow field using an optical flow-based method.

2.1   Recovering Density Field from a Single Image

Christian Fuchs et al. proposed a new approach to capture the volumetric density of smoke instantaneously with a single image [4]. We adopt this method and simplify the determination of the phase function using a different method.

The phase function of smoke medium describes the angular distribution of light reflected from a body when illuminated from a specific direction. In 1941 L. C. Henyey and J. L. Greenstein introduced a function which, by the variation of one parameter, $-1 \leq g \leq 1$, ranges from backscattering through isotropic scattering to forward scattering [5]. The function is

$$p(\theta) = \frac{1}{4\pi} \frac{1-g^2}{[1+g^2-2g\cos(\theta)]^{3/2}} \tag{1}$$

where θ is the angle between the directions of incoming light and scattered light.

We use two collimated laser bundles as illumination, one red and the other blue. Then we recover separate density fields D_{red} and D_{blue} for the red and the blue laser bundle. During the capturing process, we determine the phase function by minimizing the disparity between the separate density fields recovered from the two laser bundles. We estimate the disparity between two density fields D_{red} and D_{blue} stored as voxel densities as

$$\mathrm{RMS}(D_{red}, D_{blue}) = \sqrt{\frac{\sum_{v_i \in V}(D_{red}(v_i) - D_{blue}(v_i))^2}{\|V\|}} \tag{2}$$

where V corresponding to the set of voxels defined in the measurement volume.

Due to different scattering properties of the two laser bundles, the camera's red and blue channel might respond differently. So we introduce a scale factor k to balance the response of two channels. The best approximated g is obtained by optimizing the following objective function

$$\min_{k,g} \sqrt{\frac{\sum_{v_i \in V}(D_{red}(v_i) - k \times D_{blue}(v_i))^2}{\|V\|}}. \tag{3}$$

2.2   Recovering Temperature Field

Since 3-D smoke density field can be measured with above method, the motion of air flow becomes visible. We use an oil-smoke machine to generate smoke near the air outlet of the heat diffusing machine, obviously the smoke generated will spread in the same direction as the air flow spreads, and the heat is carried away at the same time. The further the air moves, the less heat it carries.

So the corresponding pattern between the density and temperature should be positive correlation. We assume that the corresponding pattern could be roughly approximated by a polynomial type throughout the volume, and we did a lot of experiments to test and modify the assumption.

2.3   Air Flow Analysis

A number of previous works use smoke as flow visualization medium [6-8]. Generating smoke in the volume makes the air flow visible, so we proposed an optical flow-based method to recover air flow field from smoke density field.

We extend the classical 2-dimentional Horn-Schunck [9] optical flow algorithm to 3-dimention situation. The flow is formulated as a global energy functional which is then sought to be minimized:

$$E = \iiint [(I_x u + I_y v + I_z w + I_t)^2 + \alpha^2(\|\nabla_u\|^2 + \|\nabla_v\|^2 + \|\nabla_w\|^2)]dx\,dy\,dz \tag{4}$$

where I_x, I_y, I_z and I_t are the derivatives of the image intensity values along the x, y, z and time dimensions respectively and the parameter α is a regularization constant. Larger values of α lead to a smoother flow. This functional can be minimized by solving the associated Euler–Lagrange equations.

$$I_x(I_xu + I_yv + I_zw + I_t) - \alpha^2\Delta u = 0$$

$$I_y(I_xu + I_yv + I_zw + I_t) - \alpha^2\Delta v = 0$$

$$I_z(I_xu + I_yv + I_zw + I_t) - \alpha^2\Delta w = 0 \qquad (5)$$

In practice the Laplace operator ∇ is approximated numerically using finite differences, and may be written as:

$$\Delta u(x,y,z) = \bar{u}(x,y,z) - u(x,y,z) \qquad (6)$$

where $\bar{u}(x,y,z)$ is a weighted average of calculated in a neighborhood around the pixel at location (x, y, z). Since the solution depends on the neighboring values of the flow field, it must be repeated once the neighbors have been updated. The following iterative scheme is derived:

$$u^{k+1} = \bar{u}^k - \frac{I_x(I_x\bar{u}^k + I_y\bar{v}^k + I_z\bar{w}^k + I_t)}{\alpha^2 + I_x^2 + I_y^2 + I_z^2}$$

$$v^{k+1} = \bar{v}^k - \frac{I_y(I_x\bar{u}^k + I_y\bar{v}^k + I_z\bar{w}^k + I_t)}{\alpha^2 + I_x^2 + I_y^2 + I_z^2}$$

$$w^{k+1} = \bar{w}^k - \frac{I_z(I_x\bar{u}^k + I_y\bar{v}^k + I_z\bar{w}^k + I_t)}{\alpha^2 + I_x^2 + I_y^2 + I_z^2} \qquad (7)$$

where the superscript k+1 denotes the next iteration, which is to be calculated and k is the last calculated result.

3   Experiment System

We built a set of experiment system to test our ideas in practice. We place 25 5mw red laser pointers and 25 5mw blue laser pointers as a 5×5 array on two 60×60 cm^2 boards separately to constitute the laser bundles. The two laser bundles are placed roughly parallel to each other defining a 100×50×50 cm^3 measurement volume.

We use an air heater as the heat diffusing machine. An oil-smoke machine is placed near the outlet of the air heater. We select an 8-chanal thermograph which can record temperature data in terms of time and save it to computer with USB cable. We place 8 temperature sensors sparsely at several typical positions in the measurement volume, and the positions of the sensors could be calibrated in a separate step.

A 1280×960 high-quality color CCD camera is used to capture images of the measurement volume. Its placement ensures that no two rays of the same color project to the same location on the image plane. We are thus able to capture images of the smoke illuminated by the two bundles using the camera's red and blue channel separately.

4   Calibration and Capture

Recovering density field from the image data requires geometric calibration of the camera, the laser bundles, and the temperature sensors. We use a planar checkerboard pattern to calibrate the pose and intrinsic parameters of the camera using the technique of [Zhang 2000] [10].

We calibrate each of the laser pointers separately in a similar way to the work discussed in [11]. We place a checkerboard at an angle such that it is illuminated by the laser to be calibrated and also visible to the camera. We then determine the position of a given dot of laser spot in a given frame corresponding to one position of the laser line. Moving the checkerboard to another position allows the same dot of light to be observed at a different 3D position. Then we calculate the location of the laser line by connecting these dots. Here Least-squares method is used to find the best fitting. Repeating this for all the laser lines gives the locations of the laser arrays.

After fixing the temperature sensors, we calibrate the positions of the sensors similarly. We place a checkerboard behind the sensor so the sensor lies on the checkerboard. The sensors are small enough so that we can still reliably detect the corners of the checkerboard pattern.

We then generate smoke near the outlet of the air heater. A 1280×960 high-quality color CCD camera is used to capture images of the smoke illuminated by the laser bundles at and the thermograph is used to record temperature data once per second. The process continues for 30 seconds.

5   Experimental Results

We capture images of the volume for 30 seconds at 15 fps and record the temperature data at the same time. We then project the laser lines to image plane to find their corresponding location in the image and take samples along the projected lines. We extract samples I_p from the camera images by marching densely along the projections of the rays and taking a sample at each step (we take 2cm in world coordination here). As noted before, we need to ensure that the full width of the projected laser line is captured. We therefore integrate the contributions to I_p along a small line segment (we take 7 pixels here) perpendicular to the projected ray direction and recover density value [12]. Then we low-pass filter the obtained intensity samples along each ray in order to reduce noise, yielding about 150 samples per ray. Finally we interpolate the data by 3cm^3 resolution yielding about 6000 interpolated points. Captured results are shown in Fig. 2. The reconstructed density field is rendered using a Monte Carlo-based rendering method [13].

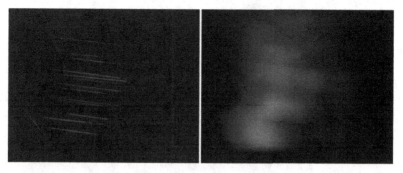

Fig. 2. Left: red channel of the captured image in which lasers are clearly visible. Right: density field reconstructed from the image.

Then we interpolate the density data at positions of the 8 temperature sensors using an approximation method [4] and find the corresponding temperature value in recorded temperature data. We put density data and temperature data together in rectangular coordinate system getting the D(density)-T(temperature) chart. The points are fit with a polynomial curve as shown in Fig. 3.

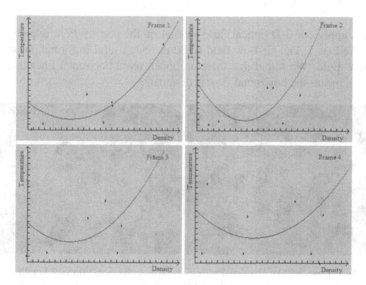

Fig. 3. D-T charts of 8 sensors in single frame. Polynomial fitting results are drawn in red lines. The curves are roughly ascending which means the corresponding pattern between the density and temperature is roughly positive correlation.

Fig. 4 shows D-T charts of single sensor in 20 frames. It's obvious that the density at positions of the sensors is almost invariant during the whole process and temperature at position of each sensor is also invariant which means the temperature distribution is nearly constant but fluctuating slightly during the 30 seconds test. From the image sequence we captured we can also see the density changes slightly.

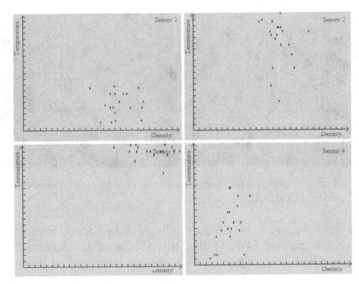

Fig. 4. D-T charts of single sensor in 20 frames. The density and temperature values are almost invariant.

We then apply our 3-D optical flow method on the density field sequence, results are shown in Fig. 5. The air flow field could provide useful imformation for infering temperature field. We found that there are much more horizontal lines than vertical lines, which means the horizontal flow is dominant.

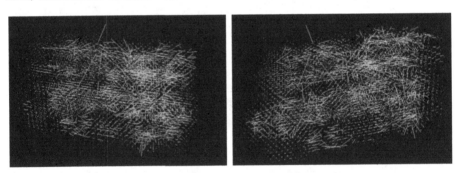

Fig. 5. Optical flow field of the density field sequence, the direction and length of the lines stand for the direction and scale of the optical flow respectively

6   Conclusions

From the experimental results, we can see that the corresponding pattern between density and temperature is roughly compatible with our assumption that the higher the density, the higher the temperature. So we could use the polynomial fitting curve to roughly determine the temperature at any position in the measurement volume. The air flow information could serve as reference or be analyzed with thermodynamics and aerodynamics theories.

But this method could only get rough temperature distribution and could introduce considerable error. The errors are caused partly by the density measurement approach itself as discussed in [4], partly by our assumption that the corresponding pattern here is a constant polynomial pattern. So our work is considered experimental rather than practicable.

References

1. Tsai, W.-Y., Chen, H.-C., Liao, T.-L.: An ultrasonic air temperaturemeasurement system with self-correction function for humidity. Meas. Sci. Technol. 13, 548–555 (2005)
2. Minamide, A., Wakatsuki, N., Mizutani, K.: Acoustic computerized tomography for temperature distribution measurement in rectangular space. Acoustics 08 Paris ·
3. Cehlin, M., Moshfegh, B., Sandberg, M.: Measurements of air temperatures close to a low-velocity diffuser in displacement ventilation using an infrared camera. Energy and Buildings 34, 687–698 (2002)
4. Fuchs, C., Chen, T., Goesele, M., Theisel, H., Seidel, H.-P.: Density estimation for dynamic volumes. Computers & Graphics 31, 205–211 (2007)
5. Henyey, L.C., Greenstein, J.L.: Diffuse radiation in thegalaxy. Astrophys. J. 93, 70–83 (1941)
6. Huang, L., El-Genk, M.S.: Heat transfer and flow visualization experiments of swirling, multi-channel, and conventional impinging jets. International Journal of Heat and Mass Transfer 41(3), 583–600 (1998)
7. Posner, J.D., Buchanan, C.R., Dunn-Rankin, D.: Measurement and prediction of indoor air flow in a model room. Energy and Buildings 35(5), 515–526 (2003)
8. Cornaro, C., Fleischer, A.S., Goldstein, R.J.: Flow visualization of a round jet impinging on cylindrical surfaces. Experimental Thermal and Fluid Science 20(2), 185–203, 66–78 (1999)
9. Horn, B.K.P., Schunck, B.G.: Determining optical flow. Artificial Intelligence 17(1-3) (August 1981)
10. Zhang, Z.Y.: A flexible new technique for camera calibration. IEEE Transactions on Pattern Analysis and Machine Intelligence (November 2000)
11. Hawkins, T., Einarsson, P., Debevec, P.: Acquisition of time-varying participating media. ACM Transactions on Graphics 24(3), 812–815 (2005)
12. Debevec, P., Malik, J.: Recovering high dynamic range radiance mapsfrom photographs. In: SIGGRAPH 1997, pp. 369–378 (1997)
13. Lafortune, E.: Mathematical models and monte carlo algorithms for physcially based rendering. Ph.D. thesis, Katholieke University, Leuven, Belgium (1995)

Intuitive Volume Eraser

Enya Shen[1], Zhi-Quan Cheng[1,*], Jiazhi Xia[2,*], and Sikun Li[1]

[1] School of Computer, National University of Defense Technology, P.R. China
cheng.zhiquan@gmail.com
[2] School of Information Science and Engineering, Central South University, P.R. China
xiajiazhi@gmail.com
http://www.computer-graphics.cn

Abstract. We present the intuitive volume eraser, an interactive volume rendering tool, to aid direct volume data visualization and Transfer Function (TF) design. Our system adopts sketch-based editing interface which enables interactive
exploring and editing operations in an intuitive and natural manner. The data features can be enlightened interactively as user desired. The editing results are saved
faithfully with the What You See Is What You Get (WYSIWYG) scheme. We also
provide a coupled transfer function editor for users who are used to the traditional
TF editing interface. The result of experiments on various data demonstrates the
effectiveness of the proposed intuitive volume eraser. The comparison of user experience also shows that our tool outperforms the state-of-the-art approaches in
friendliness and efficacy.

Keywords: volume rendering, sketch-based editing, transfer function.

1 Introduction

Direct volume rendering has been widely used to explore three-dimensional volumetric
data in different fields. In volume rendering, original volumetric data are often converted
to renderable scalar values representing the color and opacity by well-designed mapping
functions to highlight the features. Especially, the color mapping is usually performed
by transfer function (TF) design. Usually, user would like to see interested features
of the original volumetric data. Researchers proposed TF editors to change the color
mapping interactively. The desired parts can be visualized or highlighted by hiding or
erasing the unwanted parts. However, as surveyed by [1], specifying the TF is a tedious
labor work and not intuitive for human perception.

In this paper, we propose an user-friendly volume rendering tool (illustrated by Figure 1), called as intuitive volume eraser, for interactive exploration and visualization
of the interested features. With the intuitive volume eraser, users can erase/mask unimportant or uninterested parts directly. Unlike current eraser tools which are indirect and
inexact, our erasing tool affords exact cues, like position and data value, and predictive
operation. We also provide TF editor for users who are accustomed to the traditional
ways. The TF editor provides direct control of color and opacity values and some other

---

⋆ Corresponding authors.

S.-M. Hu and R.R. Martin (Eds.): CVM 2012, LNCS 7633, pp. 250–257, 2012.

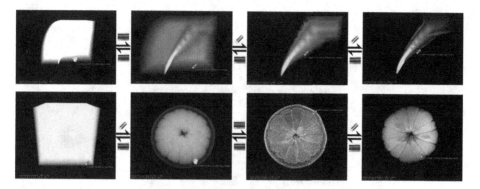

Fig. 1. From left to right: the key features of volumetric data are visualized by the volume eraser in simple way according to user's intuitive interaction. The operations are aided by useful cues with precise position, data value and color information.

useful parameters, such as density and brightness. Consequently, users can easily observe what happens in both volume data space and TF space during erasing operations. This feature is extremely useful for assisting professional TF definition and helping novice to explore and visualize their data.

2   Related Work

As the central topic in direct volume rendering, transfer function (TF) has been widely studied in the last decades [1]. According to the utilization of user-interaction, existing TF methods could be categorized into three categories, namely automatic, semiautomatic and interactive.

To realize automatic TF generation, Zhou and Takatsuka [2] utilized topological attributes derived from the contour tree of a volume. The contour tree assisted to look for global features in volumetric data by acting as the visual index of volume segments. Ruiz et al. [3] proposed an automatic approach for TF design without requiring prior knowledge or pre-segmentation information, but need the user provide a target distribution.

Selver et al. [4] proposed a semiautomatic method for initial generation of TFs, allowing users interact with integrated different features. Correa et al. [5] presented semiautomatic methods for generating visibility-driven TFs with the aim to maximize visibility of important features.

Several interactive methods have been proposed to explore volume data more freely. Wu et al. [6] presented a framework which allows users to integrate multiple features and delete features in the direct volume rendering results. Tzeng et al. [7,8] developed an interactive user interface for specifying the classification functions that consist of users painting directly on sample slices of the volume. With VolumeShop [9], Bruckner et al. proposed an interactive system for direct volume illustration. With sketching, interested features are displayed without occluding objects. Guo et al. [10] represented a volume visualization system that accepts direct manipulation through a sketch-based What You See Is What You Get (WYSIWYG) approach. In our work, we present an intuitive tool to erase volumetric data directly.

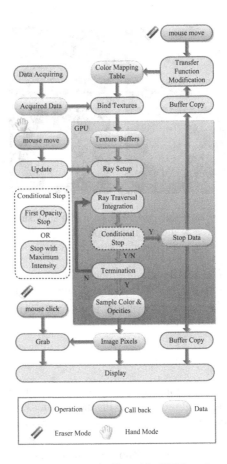

Fig. 2. The volume eraser pipeline with GPU-based ray casting

3   Volume Eraser

To implement our eraser tool, we use Graphics Processing Unit (GPU) based ray casting algorithm as shown in Figure 2. The reasons are two-folds: firstly, ray casting is the most versatile approach for direct volume rendering because of its flexibility in producing high quality images [1]. Secondly, ray casting is apt to parallel execution on GPU to obtain high frame rate, which is vital for interactive operations.

The entire GPU based ray casting process of our system includes the following four steps. Firstly, the source data and color mapping table are acquired by CPU and bound by GPU as textures [1]. Secondly, a ray is setup according to camera parameters and the respective pixel position in the screen. Thirdly, the pixel color and opacity is accumulated by stepping along the ray. Finally, the image pixels are displayed on the screen.

Besides the sampling stops required by the rendering system, we also need to collect stops for eraser. Two kinds of eraser stops are collected correspondingly to two typical erasing strategies. The first one is the first opacity sampling stops which the ray meets.

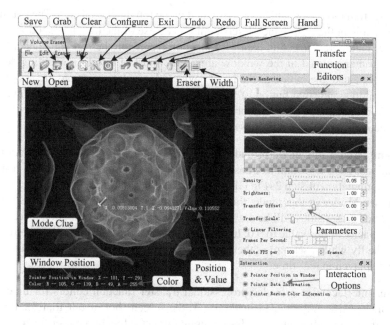

Fig. 3. Screenshot of the intuitive volume eraser tool

The second one is the stop with maximum intensity of all the stops in the ray. As a result, the voxel having the same value with the selected stop will be erased if eraser mode is enabled. If a voxel is erased, its opacity in the TF is set to be zero. It is notable that we only modify the TF without changing the source data.

Fortunately, the required stop information could be collected during the third step of the accumulation process of ray casting. Our rendering and erasing algorithm could be computed in a single pass which is crucial to efficiency. In detail, starting from the eye, the ray comes through certain pixel on the screen and then intersects with the volume. In the sampling and accumulation stage, we choose equidistant steps to benefit front to back traversal. The scalar data value is mapped to optical properties by the color mapping table [1]. The sampling and accumulation proceed along the ray until one of the following termination conditions satisfied: the accumulated alpha α_{dst} reaches a specified threshold (here we choose 0.95); the ray has come through the volume; the number of steps reaches a specified limit (here we use 500). The entire process can be expressed as following equations [1]:

$$C_{dst} = C_{dst} + (1 - \alpha_{src})C_{src} \tag{1}$$
$$\alpha_{dst} = \alpha_{dst} + (1 - \alpha_{src})\alpha_{src} \tag{2}$$

As shown above, we choose opacity-weighted colors [11]. It is worthy to note that the whole ray casting including conditional stops record is implemented by CUDA with GPU.

Figure 3 shows the interface of our tool. A set of system control functions, including setting up new canvas, opening volumetric data file(s), grabbing and saving screenshots, and interaction modes switching, are provided in the top functional area. The parameter editing area is in the right panel. Users could make use of the transfer function editors and other parameters to refine their visualization results on the fly. The data are visualized and manipulated in the window area. Like most of interface adopting desktop metaphor, we take the mouse as the input device. Manipulate functions are assigned to the left, middle and right button of the mouse. Benefited by the interactive functions, users could manipulate their data precisely and liquidly. Our GPU-based implementation effectively supports our proposed two major editing modes:

- **Hand Mode:** this mode provides a set of fundamental real-time interaction operations, such as rotation, translation and zoom. These operations will result in re-computation of step 2-4 in GPU which could be computed in real-time.
- **Eraser Mode:** in this mode, the volumetric data having the same value with the selected eraser stops will be erased by modifying the transfer function by changing the opacity of this value to 0.0. It is vital to note that the transfer function is updated on the fly while user moves their mouse to erase. The erased rendering result will be displayed in real-time.

Our user interface also provides professional transfer function editors for modifying color and opacity. As depicted in Figure 3, the screen shot of our transfer function editors, from top to bottom, includes integrated transfer function editor for modifying RGBA quadruplets at one fling and four sub-editors for changing red, green, blue and alpha channel respectively. Providing four editors for components of RGBA quadruplets has the following two advantages: Users can recognize and distinguish data values of different colors clearly; More importantly, the data of occluded region can be visible.

4   Results and Discussions

4.1   Results

We implement the intuitive volume eraser using CUDA 4.1 with Qt 4.7.4 on a PC with Intel 2.80 GHz Core i7 CPU, 12 GB RAM and GeForce GTX 580 graphics card.

As shown by Figure 1, the user could gradually operate intuitive volume eraser to produce desirable results. It provides users the functionality to visualize the features directly on volume data space, coupled with the professional transfer function editors. The main property of the eraser is that all these operations are enlightened with the real-time updating cues as discussed in the former sections. In addition, an accompany video also demonstrates the strong functionality of the interactive eraser during volume data exploration and visualization.

Benefited by the GPU-based ray casting implementation, our eraser is performed in real-time. The on-the-fly erasing interaction sequences are shown in Figure 5. The results shown in Figure 4 are achieved in 57 seconds on average for a novice after 5 minutes training. Table 1 illustrates the statistics for these experiments in Figure 4. The statistics indicate that our tool is natural to use and time-efficient. (the FPS of eraser mode is still always larger than 100.) The wide range of dataset also suggests that our tool is broadly applicable.

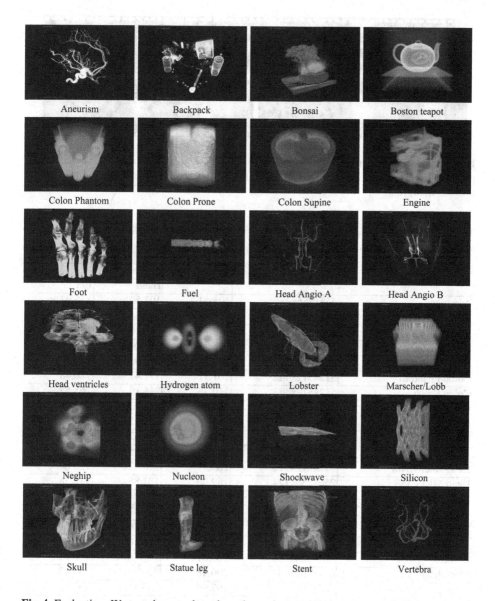

Fig. 4. Evaluation: We tested our tool on the volume datasets one by one. each is finished about 57 seconds for a novice on average.

4.2 Limitations

The visual quality of the basic ray casting algorithm suffers from the issue of interval between sampling stops. Our implementation also effected by this issue. One of our future work would be making use of the recent advances in ray casting to abate the artifacts of our rendering. The fast high-quality volume ray casting method and adaptive sampling could be hopeful candidate.

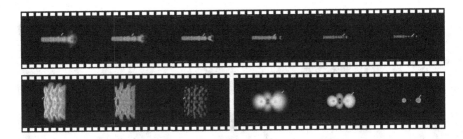

Fig. 5. Snapshots of fluent data filtering. Note that the eraser icon in every picture indicates the position that erasing operation happened. (Top: Fuel; Bottom Left: Silicon; Bottom Right: Hydrogen Atom)

Table 1. Intuitive volume eraser statistics, where frame-per-seconds (FPS) is measured on a PC with Intel 2.80 GHz Core i7 with 12 GB RAM

Dataset	Size	Idle FPS	Interaction FPS	
			Hand	Eraser
Aneurism	256x256x256	195.64	193.50	126.93
Backpack Scan	512x512x373	216.98	207.41	104.45
Bonsai	256x256x256	218.77	217.06	139.61
Boston Teapot	256x256x178	221.21	220.24	153.06
Bucky Ball	032x032x032	232.48	231.03	149.19
Colon Phantom	512x512x442	201.91	191.47	120.48
Colon Prone	512x512x463	220.73	215.19	165.57
Colon Supine	512x512x426	184.40	167.03	123.95
Engine	256x256x128	244.85	232.75	164.69
Foot	256x256x256	202.42	194.62	158.00
Fuel	064x064x064	203.51	195.05	137.71
Head Aneuyrism	512x512x512	186.31	170.42	125.64
Head MRI CISS	256x256x124	189.06	182.88	111.38
Head MRT Angiography	256x320x128	205.81	199.94	125.92
Head MRT Angiography	416x512x112	215.88	195.87	114.90
Hydrogen Atom	128x128x128	203.35	215.76	140.68
Leg of Statue	341x341x093	201.46	195.50	117.33
Lobster	301x324x056	200.07	211.76	150.63
Marschner / Lobb	041x041x041	206.48	220.72	155.47
Neghip	064x064x064	197.95	203.41	137.81
Nucleon	041x041x041	201.62	215.56	149.97
Shockwave	064x064x512	214.17	221.18	143.62
Silicon	098x034x034	212.52	226.06	151.16
Skull	256x256x256	222.23	231.32	147.19
Stented Abdominal Aorta	512x512x174	219.53	233.92	146.38

5 Conclusions

In the paper, we present an intuitive WYSIWYG volume eraser that accepts direct sketch on the volume data. Users can explore the data and change the appearance of the direct volume rendered results. The eraser gives real-time feedback to users during the interaction. The experiments on various data demonstrate the performance of our intuitive volume eraser. The comparisons of user experience show that our tool provides more effective and easier-to-use than state-of-art approach for general users.

Acknowledgement. The work was supported by NSFC grants 60970094, 61103084.

References

1. Engel, K., Hadwiger, M., Kniss, J., Rezk-Salama, C.: Real-Time Volume Graphics. A K Peters (2006) 1, 2, 3, 4
2. Zhou, J.L., Takatsuka, M.: Automatic transfer function generation using contour tree controlled residue flow model and color harmonics. IEEE Transactions on Visualization and Computer Graphics 15(6), 1481–1488 (2009) 2
3. Ruiz, M., Bardera, A., Boada, I., Viola, I., Feixas, M., Sbert, M.: Automatic transfer functions based on informational divergence. IEEE Transactions on Visualization and Computer Graphics 17(12), 1932–1941 (2011) 2
4. Selver, M.A., Guzelis, C.: Semiautomatic transfer function initialization for abdominal visualization using self-generating hierarchical radial basis function networks. IEEE Transactions on Visualization and Computer Graphics 15(3), 395–409 (2009) 2
5. Correa, C.D., Ma, K.L.: Visibility histograms and visibility-driven transfer functions. IEEE Transactions on Visualization and Computer Graphics 17(2), 192–204 (2011) 2
6. Wu, Y.C., Qu, H.M.: Interactive transfer function design based on editing direct volume rendered images. IEEE Transactions on Visualization and Computer Graphics 13(5), 1027–1040 (2007) 2
7. Tzeng, F.-Y., Lum, E.B., Ma, K.-L.: A novel interface for higher dimensional classification of volume data. In: Proceedings of IEEE Visualization, pp. 505–512 (2003) 2
8. Tzeng, F.-Y., Lum, E.B., Ma, K.-L.: An intelligent system approach to higher-dimensional classification of volume data. IEEE Transactions on Visualization and Computer Graphics 11(3), 273–284 (2005) 2
9. Bruckner, S., Groller, M.E.: Volumeshop: An interactive system for direct volume illustration. In: Proceedings of IEEE Visualization, pp. 671–678 (2005) 2
10. Guo, H.Q., Mao, N.Y., Yuan, X.R.: WYSIWYG (what you see is what you get) volume visualization. IEEE Transactions on Visualization and Computer Graphics 17(12), 2106–2114 (2011) 2
11. Wittenbrink, C.M., Malzbender, T., Goss, M.E.: Opacity-weighted color interpolation for volume sampling. In: Proceedings of IEEE Symposium on Volume Visualization, pp. 135–142 (1998) 5

Accurate Depth-of-Field Rendering
Using Adaptive Bilateral Depth Filtering

Shang Wu[1], Kai Yu[1], Bin Sheng[1,2], Feiyue Huang[3], Feng Gao[3], and Lizhuang Ma[1,*]

[1] Department of Computer Science and Engineering, Shanghai Jiao Tong University
ma-lz@cs.sjtu.edu.cn
[2] State Key Laboratory of Computer Science, Institute of Software,
Chinese Academy of Sciences
[3] Tencent Research, Gumei Road 1528, Shanghai, China, 200233

Abstract. Real-time depth of field (DoF) rendering is crucial to realistic image synthesis and VR applications. This paper presents a new method to simulate the depth-of-field effects with bilateral depth filtering. Unlike the traditional rendering methods that handle the depth-of-field with Gaussian filtering, we develop a new DoF filter, called adaptive bilateral depth filter, to adaptively postfilter the pixels according to their depth variance. Depth information is used to focus on the objects with edge-preserving property. Our approach can eliminate the artifacts of intensity leakage, which can generate adaptive high-quality DoF rendering effects dynamically, and can be fully implemented in GPU parallelization.

Keywords: Depth of field, post-processing, GPU, adaptive bilateral depth filtering, virtual reality.

1 Introduction

Depth of field (DoF) is a range of distance around the focus region where the objects look sharp, which appears in human vision system and camera. It is important to render DoF for 3D scenes in various applications, including video games and virtual reality (VR), helping to increase the users' sense of immersion and to improve users' depth perception [1]. Moreover, it can also be used to draw users' attention to a specific object in Games or VR. However, the computer graphics usually generate a "too perfect" sharp image without DoF, due to pinhole camera model.

In order to satisfy the requirement of real-time performance in 3D games and VR applications, we focus on the postfiltering method. Due to using Gaussian blur to blur each pixel, most postfiltering methods cause intensity leakage artifacts. This paper presents a new solution to simulate DoF effect in 3D scenes in real-time, based on GPU. Our method can reduce the intensity leakage by taking advantage of edge preserving feature of bilateral filtering; and reduce other artifacts by using adaptive bilateral filter.

The novelties of our approach lie in the following aspects:

- We apply the bilateral depth filtering to the DoF solution and significantly alleviate the intensity leakage by it.

---

[*] Corresponding author.

S.-M. Hu and R.R. Martin (Eds.): CVM 2012, LNCS 7633, pp. 258–265, 2012.

– We propose a complete solution to the background rendering by translating the bilateral depth filtering into adaptive bilateral depth filtering.

The rest of this paper is structured as follows. In section 2 we will introduce previous works, before discussing our method. Next, we will describe the basic DoF model (Section 3), and illustrate bilateral depth filter(Section 4). Then, we will illustrate how to apply adaptive bilateral filtering to render background(Section 5). Finally, we will show the results (Section 6), before conclusion(Section 7).

2 Previous Work

Barsky divides the different DoF algorithms into two categories: object-space and image-space [2]. Classic methods are based on object-space, which directly handle the 3D scene. The most famous one is distributed ray tracing [3]. This method can generate quite realistic result by tracing several rays per pixel, but it is very time consuming. Later the accumulation buffer[4] developed the performance, using rasterization hardware. but it also has a heavy cost, especially in complex scenes. So those are not suitable for real-time applications.

Realtime methods are all based on image-space, also called post-processing approaches. The pioneering work was conducted by Micheal PotmesilETAL. [5]. They computed the amount of each pixel's blur, namely diameter of the circle of confusion (DCoC) using the depth map, and then post-processed the original sharp image to become blur. Later a real-time postprocessing method was developed by Scheuermann and Tatarchuk [6]. Unfortunately, this approach cannot avoid depth discontinuity artifacts. In fact, most real-time DoF approaches work in the similar way, using filter to approximate CoCs at each pixel to achieve rather high performances [7,8,9,10]. Those methods almost suffer from intensity leakage or depth discontinuity in some degree, because they only use the information of single image during the post processing. However, our method uses depth as information into filter to reduce these artifacts.

Since single image is not enough, most methods split the single image into depth layers to hallucinate missing geometries [11,12,13,14]. Because plenty layers should be computed, multilayers methods are slower than gathering and cannot meet real-time requirement for very complex scenes, which are very common in video game and VR environments. Moreover, combining layer with alpha blending is still such coarse approximation that only works for separate objects. Although our method is also an approximation, we can still have the same speed as gathering Methods.

A recent method [15] combines multilayers and multi-view, to acquire high quality. Unfortunately, this method cost more and more time with the increasing of layers and views. And the large amount of layers and views are the guarantees for the high quality of complex scenes. However, our method's performance would not alter rapidly with the complexity of scenes.

Bilateral Filtering [16] is developed by Tomasi and Manduchi first in 1994, which combines the low-pass domain filter and range filter. Later, bilateral filtering has been used in amounts of applications, especially in de-noising. Zhang and Allebach [17] proposed the Adaptive bilateral filter(ABF), then De Silva et al. [18] introduced the depth filter to the ABF. They can achieve great results when used in de-noise or sharpen

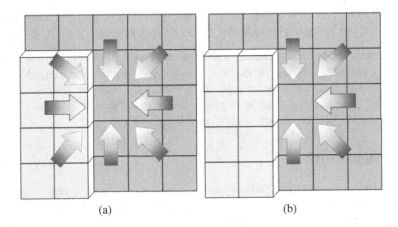

(a)   (b)

Fig. 1. A behavior comparison of (a) Gaussian filer and (b) Bilateral depth filter. Yellow rects and green rects represent pixels from focus region and background, respectively. The center pixel means the filtered pixel and arrows stand for the direction of intensity flow.

applications while they have never be used in DoF rendering.And adaptive strategy has been chosen to solve various problems, such as in [19], which apply it to a different problem edit propagation.

3   Basic Depth of Field Model

Our method is also based on the post-processing of the image rendered from scene, which is used by most real-time methods. We first get the original image by rendering the scene and get the depth map of scene using the GPU shader. Then, we compute the the diameter of CoC (DCoC)of each pixel according to the lens model, and save the DCoCs as a texture. Finally, we blur per pixel with the bilateral depth filter using the information of depth map and DCoCs.

3.1   Lens Model

We use the classic lens model proposed by Potmesil and Chakravarty[5]. In this model, the diameter of CoC (DCoC) of each pixel projected on screen is :

$$DCoC(p) = |\frac{D \times f \times (f_d - depth(p))}{f_d \times (depth(p) - f)}|, \tag{1}$$

where $DCoC(p)$ is the DCoC of pixel p, D is the diameter of lens, f is the lens focal length and f_d is the depth of focus region.

4   Bilateral Depth Filter

Many gathering methods suffer from intensity leaking because of Gaussian filter. When a point of background is near the focus region, the intensity of the focused pixels leaks

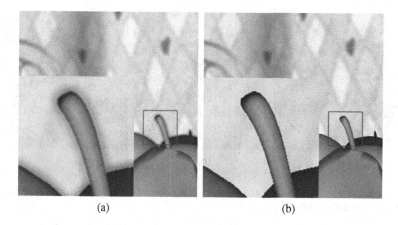

(a)   (b)

Fig. 2. A comparison of the results generated by (a) Gaussian filer and (b) Bilateral depth filter

to the background pixels by the Gaussian filter because of its isotropy (shown in figure 1(a)). So our goal is to create a filter (shown in figure 1(b)) which has anisotropy near the edge of depth map.

Bilateral filtering[16] has the edge-preserve feature by using range filtering. Actually, it is because bilateral filtering is anisotropic near the edge. Usually, bilateral filter consists of domain and range filters. However, because intensity leakage only occurs in the boundary between focus region and background, we use depth filter replacing range filter and use it when pixel's depth is less than focus distance, as shown in following formula:

$$\hat{C}(p) = \sum_{q \epsilon \Omega_p} B(p,q)C(q), Z_p > Z_f, \tag{2}$$

where $\hat{C}(p)$ is filtered color of pixel p, Ω_p is a set of pixels whose distance to pixel p is less than the radius of CoC of p, and $B(p,q)$ is defined by equation 3, where r_p^{-1} is a normalization factor, $d(p,q)$ is the distance between p and q, σ_s and σ_d are standard deviations and Z_x is the depth of pixel x.

$$B(p,q) = \begin{cases} r_p^{-1} \exp\left(-\dfrac{d^2(p,q)}{2\sigma_s^2}\right) \times \exp\left(-\dfrac{(Z_q - Z_p)^2}{2\sigma_d^2}\right), & q \epsilon \Omega_p \\ 0, & else \end{cases} \tag{3}$$

Therefore, this filter behaves like an anisotropic filter as shown in figure 1(b). Figure 2 shows the comparative results generated by Gaussian filter and our bilateral depth filter. It can be seen that our bilateral depth filter can alleviate intensity leakage artifacts significantly.

5 Adaptive Bilateral Filter

The bilateral depth filtering can cause a new artifact. In the background area, the edges are also persevered which should be blur. Figure3(b) shows the artifact. So we make the bilateral depth filter adaptive to remove this artifact.

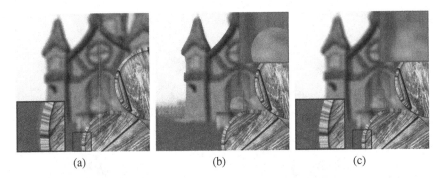

       (a)   (b)   (c)

Fig. 3. A comparison of the results generated by (a) Gaussian filter, (b) Bilateral depth filter and (c) Adaptive bilateral depth filter

The adaptive bilateral depth filter is to change the equation (3) to (4):

$$B(p,q) = \begin{cases} r_p^{-1} \exp\left(-\dfrac{d^2(p,q)}{2\sigma_s^2}\right) \times \exp\left(-\dfrac{(Z_q - Z_p - \zeta_p)^2}{2\sigma_d^2}\right), & q\epsilon\Omega_p \\ 0, & else \end{cases} \quad (4)$$

In the filter, we have three control parameters, including two standard deviations σ_s , σ_d and offset ζ_p which controls the center of depth filter. The roles of these parameters are well described in [17] and [18]. Controlling the parameters appropriately can make the filter sharpen the edge between the focus and background area while smooth others.

In our method, ζ_p is computed as

$$\zeta_p = \begin{cases} Z_p - MEAN(\Omega_p), & \Omega_p \epsilon focus \\ MEAN(\Omega_p) - Z_p, & else \end{cases} \quad (5)$$

where $MEAN(\Omega_p)$ is the mean value of pixels in Ω_p. When Ω_p has the pixels in focus area, we can sharpen the edge by shifting the depth filter away from the mean while smooth edges among backgrounds by shifting the depth filter towards the mean.

Figure 3 shows the comparison between results of traditional Gaussian filter, bilateral filter and adaptive bilateral filter.

6   Implementation Results

The proposed DoF approach is developed on 2.6GHz Intel Core(TM) CPU, together with ATI Radeon HD 5700 GPU and 2G RAM. The GPU programs described above has adopted OpenGL shader language. In the experimental results, we compare our method with other postfiltering methods in respect of rendering quality and performance.

Our implementation consists of two stages work, which can be complete in one rendering. In the first stage, we get the color image, depth map and DCoC map of scene by three GPU shaders respectively. They are all inputted to the second stage as textures. Then, we apply the adaptive bilateral filter to blur the color image with a pixel

(a)   (b)   (c)   (d)

Fig. 4. A comparison of background-blurred images. (a) the original image (b) our method (c) Scheuermann's method (d)zhou et al.method

(a)   (b)   (c)   (d)

Fig. 5. Results of our method over 4 scenes: (a)fruits,(b)booth,(c)fence,(d)barrels.

shader. And our system also allows users to change the focus region just with simple interaction.

Other methods include the work of Zhou et al.[9] and Scheuermann[6], which use separable Gaussian filtering and pre-blur the down-sampled image, respectively.

Rendering Quality. We compare the rendering quality of reducing intensity leakage. Figure 4 shows the results for "booth" scene. The intensity leakage artifact only occurs in the result of Scheuermann's approach (see figure 4(c)). In respect of background blur quality, our method generates a real natural image without intensity leakage or other artifacts. However, the result gotten by Zhou et al.'s method reveal some specific new artifacts, such as bilinear magnification artifact. Their result looks distorted and blurred strangely (see figure 4(d)),resulting from the vertical filter. Scheuermann's cannot obtain the accurate blurring degree. They did not control the blurring level over each pixel so that the result of theirs looks like a mix of the original image and a much blurred one.

Finally, figure 5 show the results of our method over 4 different scenes.

Rendering Performance. We compare our method with Zhou et al.'s and Scheuermann's in respect of frame per second (FPS). Figure 6 shows the charts. Scheuermann's is the fast because of its simplicity. And ours is also fast when in small DCoC.

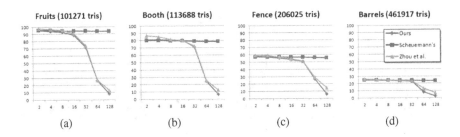

Fig. 6. Performance comparison of ours (blue),with Scheuermann's (red) and zhou et al.'s (green).The x-axis and y-axis stand for the size of DCoC and the FPS, respectively

7 Conclusion

We propose a new method for rendering DoF effects in virtual environments, which can produce high-quality rendering result and operate with tiny time and space. So our method is very suitable to the real-time graphics applications. Moreover, the function of changing focus region in our method allows the users to determine where to look at in the environment of game or VR with little interaction. Our bilateral depth filtering rendering approach generates adaptive DoF effects dynamically, and is fully implemented on GPU.

We will improve this framework to be applicable artists' use, by defining suitable parameters for interaction.

Acknowledgments. We would like to thank the anonymous reviewers for their valuable comments. This work is supported by a joint project of Tencent research and Shanghai Jiao Tong University. This work is also partially funded by the National Basic Research Project of China (No. 2011CB302203), and the National Natural Science Foundation of China (No. 61073089 and No. 61133009).This work is also partially supported by the Open Projects Program of National Laboratory of Pattern Recognition.

References

1. Mather, G.: Image blur as a pictorial depth cue. In: Proceedings of the Royal Society of London. Series B: Biological Sciences, vol. 263(1367), pp. 169–172 (1996)
2. Barsky, B.A., Kosloff, T.J.: Algorithms for rendering depth of field effects in computer graphics, pp. 999–1010 (2008)
3. Cook, R.L., Porter, T., Carpenter, L.: Distributed ray tracing, vol. 18, pp. 137–145 (1984)
4. Haeberli, P., Akeley, K.: The accumulation buffer: Hardware support for high-quality rendering, vol. 24, pp. 309–318 (1990)
5. Potmesil, M., Chakravarty, I.: A lens and aperture camera model for synthetic image generation. ACM SIGGRAPH Computer Graphics 15(3), 297–305 (1981)
6. Scheuermann, T.: Advanced depth of field. In: GDC 2004, vol. 8 (2004)
7. Hillaire, S., Lecuyer, A., Cozot, R., Casiez, G.: Depth-of-field blur effects for first-person navigation in virtual environments. IEEE Computer Graphics and Applications 28(6), 47–55 (2008)

8. Rokita, P.: Generating depth of-field effects in virtual reality applications. IEEE Computer Graphics and Applications 16(2), 18–21 (1996)

9. Zhou, T., Chen, J.X., Pullen, M.: Accurate depth of field simulation in real time, vol. 26, pp. 15–23 (2007)

10. Yu, X., Wang, R., Yu, J.: Real-time depth of field rendering via dynamic light field generation and filtering, vol. 29, pp. 2099–2107 (2010)

11. Kass, M., Lefohn, A., Owens, J.: Interactive depth of field using simulated diffusion on a gpu. Pixar Animation Studios Tech Report (2006)

12. Kraus, M., Strengert, M.: Depth-of-field rendering by pyramidal image processing, vol. 26, pp. 645–654 (2007)

13. Kosloff, T.J., Barsky, B.A.: An algorithm for rendering generalized depth of field effects based on simulated heat diffusion, pp. 1124–1140 (2007)

14. Lee, S., Eisemann, E., Seidel, H.-P.: Real-time lens blur effects and focus control. ACM Transactions on Graphics (TOG) 29(4), 65 (2010)

15. Lee, S., Eisemann, E., Seidel, H.P.: Depth-of-field rendering with multiview synthesis, vol. 28, p. 134 (2009)

16. Tomasi, C., Manduchi, R.: Bilateral filtering for gray and color images, pp. 839–846 (1998)

17. Zhang, B., Allebach, J.P.: Adaptive bilateral filter for sharpness enhancement and noise removal. IEEE Transactions on Image Processing 17(5), 664–678 (2008)

18. De Silva, D.V.S., Fernando, W.A.C., Kodikaraarachchi, H., Worrall, S.T., Kondoz, A.M.: Adaptive sharpening of depth maps for 3d-tv. Electronics Letters 46(23), 1546–1548 (2010)

19. Xu, K., Li, Y., Ju, T., Hu, S.-M., Liu, T.Q., Liu, T.-Q.: Efficient affinity-based edit propagation using kd tree, vol. 28, p. 118 (2009)

Author Index